Loving Stones

Loving Stones

Making the Impossible Possible in the
Worship of Mount Govardhan

DAVID L. HABERMAN

OXFORD
UNIVERSITY PRESS

OXFORD
UNIVERSITY PRESS

Oxford University Press is a department of the University of Oxford. It furthers the University's objective of excellence in research, scholarship, and education by publishing worldwide. Oxford is a registered trade mark of Oxford University Press in the UK and certain other countries.

Published in the United States of America by Oxford University Press
198 Madison Avenue, New York, NY 10016, United States of America.

© Oxford University Press 2020

Library of Congress Control Number: 2019034474
ISBN 978-0-19-008672-5 (pbk.)
ISBN 978-0-19-008671-8 (hbk.)

1 3 5 7 9 8 6 4 2

Paperback printed by Marquis, Canada
Hardback printed by Bridgeport National Bindery, Inc., United States of America

For Asim Krishnadas and Shyamdas,
the two who introduced me to Shri Giriraj-ji

Contents

Figures

All photographs that appear in this book were taken by the author in 2013–2015.

Acknowledgments

It is impossible to give credit to all those who contributed to this book, but I certainly owe a mountain of thanks to the following. I received a Fulbright-Nehru Senior Research Fellowship and a John Simon Guggenheim Fellowship to conduct research for this study of Mount Govardhan during the two academic years of 2013–15. I am extremely grateful to both of these sources of funding, which remain vital to the health of the humanities and social sciences these days. I feel immense appreciation to Indiana University for the wonderful support they have shown me over the years, for giving me time off teaching for the research of this book, for providing two years of supplemental support, and for the research funds to return to India for brief periods of follow-up work in 2016, 2017, and 2018. Indiana University also generously provided the subvention funds for the color photos in this book. Additionally, the Consortium for the Study of Religion, Ethics, and Society at Indiana University provided me a grant to study the relationship between anthropomorphism and anthropocentrism as related to this project.

Kristin Francoeur served as a fabulously productive research assistant at the initial stage when this study of Mount Govardhan was beginning to take shape in my mind. Vallabhadas helped me set up a residence and get my feet on the ground in the pilgrimage village of Jatipura. He also acted as a valuable research assistant during the early stages of my fieldwork. It is difficult for me to articulate the gratitude I feel for Mohan, a resident of Braj par excellence. He is not only a dear friend and a superb cook, but has taught me so much by simply living in a world in which everything is alive and conscious. Among the great joys of my life are our meandering walks through the sacred landscapes of Braj. I thank Brajesh Joshi, a resident priest in Jatipura, for his inspirational ways and informative Hindi book on Mount Govardhan.

I hold a special gratitude to Shrivatsa Goswami of the Shri Chaitanya Prema Sansthana in Vrindaban. I have recognized the immeasurable help I have received from him in the acknowledgments of every major research book I have published; and this one is no different. I have come to rely on his vast knowledge and keen insights in my studies of Braj Vaishnavism, some of which find their way into many sections of this one. He has also been a significant mentor in my understanding of and deep thinking about possible human relationships with non-human entities. One of the luckiest days of my life was the one in which I wandered into his Vrindaban ashram. He has since provided official academic sponsorship and intellectual support for the series of my research projects in India. My life would be greatly diminished had I never met him. I offer him a very grateful Radhe Radhe!

Much appreciation to Frederick Smith for making available to my wife and me his delightful place on a lovely hillside above Uttarkashi with its front-porch view of snowy Himalayan peaks while beginning the initial stage of writing this book. Pallavi and Michael Duffy supplied ample conversation and good food to make our stay extremely pleasant. I am filled with thankfulness for my *bare bhai* Jack Hawley, supportive colleague Sarah Pike, fellow scholar of Hinduism and ecology Christopher Chapple, and my wife Sandra Ducey for reading earlier drafts of this book and offering critical comments and helpful suggestions for making it better. I express a particular appreciation for Cynthia Read, Executive Editor of Religion for Oxford University Press at New York, who has kindly and professionally shepherded a number of my books through the publication process. I'm also grateful for the careful eye of Oxford copy-editor Dorothy Bauhoff. Martha Michelson graciously helped create the map of Mount Govardhan that appears on page xvii.

This book is dedicated to Shyamdas and Asim Krishnadas. To say that they introduced me to the worship of Mount Govardhan is an understatement. Their deep knowledge and fervent love of the land of Braj—especially their beloved Giriraj—inspired my interest in the sacred mountain in ways difficult to express. Both have passed on, but will always have a special place in my heart. And although I cannot mention them all by name, this book would not exist without the willingness of hundreds of worshipers of Mount Govardhan to speak with me and share their devotional love and thoughts about this remarkable mountain.

Last, but certainly not least, I come to my wife Sandy, present in this book in innumerable ways. She spent most of two years with me in India while I was conducting research for this book, providing companionship, loving support, a receptive and questioning ear for processing some of my preliminary ideas, and valuable feedback on my initial writing. This was the first time we lived in India for a lengthy research period without any children. Although we both have fond memories of our time in India with our children, it was delightful to share this time together as adventurous "empty nesters." Her enthusiastic love of India not only made my time there possible, but also enhanced it immensely. For this I am ever grateful.

David L. Haberman
Bloomington, Indiana
Holi 2019

Note on Translation and Transliteration

The translations from Sanskrit, Hindi, Braj Bhasha, and Bengali that appear in this book are mine unless otherwise attributed. In an effort to make this book more accessible to a wider readership, I have eliminated the use of diacritical marks. Combining transliterations of northern Indian languages leads to a certain amount of inconsistency. I have transliterated words from these languages in a manner that attempts to represent actual pronunciation in the Braj region of north-central India, following the standard system as closely as possible without making use of diacritics (thus "*puja*" instead of "*pooja*," although in this case the long *u* will not be differentiated from the short *u* of "*mukti*"). Consonants have been selected and medial and final vowels have been dropped when such practice more closely reflects local pronunciation (thus "Govardhan" instead of "Govardhana," "Mukharvind" instead of "Mukharavinda"). The final vowel, however, has been retained in a few words that have become familiar to English-speaking readers in such spellings (e.g., Rama, Vaishnava, Purana). Medial and final vowels have also been retained in Sanskrit technical terms (e.g., *svarupa*). I have also maintained a distinction in some cases between Sanskrit references and those in Hindi (e.g., Sanskrit Gosvamin and Hindi Goswami). A glossary of frequently used names and terms, designed as a quick reference for the general reader, can be found at the end of this book.

Map

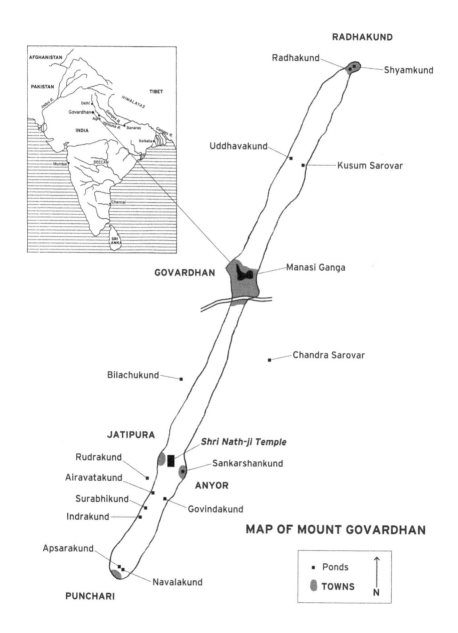

RADHAKUND

Radhakund

Shyamkund

Uddhavakund

Kusum Sarovar

GOVARDHAN

Manasi Ganga

Chandra Sarovar

Bilachukund

JATIPURA

Shri Nath-ji Temple

Rudrakund

Sankarshankund

Airavatakund

ANYOR

Surabhikund

Govindakund

Indrakund

Apsarakund

MAP OF MOUNT GOVARDHAN

Navalakund

PUNCHARI

■ Ponds

🟢 TOWNS

N

AFGHANISTAN

PAKISTAN

TIBET

Indus R.

Delhi

HIMALAYAS

Govardhan

Ganges R.

Agra

Yamuna R.

Banaras

Gunges R.

INDIA

Kolkata

Mumbai

DECCAN

Chennai

SRI
LANKA

Introduction

Seduced by a Mountain

> How is it that something like a mountain can call to us
> in the voice of a seductive lover?[1]

Sunita rises early in the morning before her husband and two children are
awake. After bathing and putting on a clean sari, she goes to the kitchen and
prepares cooked cereal, hot sweetened milk, and a bowl of fruit. She carries
these items to a small shrine recessed into a wall of the main room of the
family's home, rings a silver bell, and slides aside the cloth curtain of the
shrine while singing songs to awaken her Beloved. She reaches inside and
tenderly pulls back the covers on a little bed, revealing a dark stone about
the size of her fist. The stone is wrapped in a warm sleeping garment and is
adorned with a pair of eyes, a bright smile, red forehead mark, nose-ring, and
chin jewel. Sunita gently lifts the stone from the bed and sets it on a padded
throne. She positions a tiny turban atop its head and places the hot milk and
foods before it to enjoy. Smiling lovingly at the stone, she closes the curtain
and leaves to wake her family.

A short time later, Sunita retrieves the food from the shrine, then provides
water for rinsing and a small face towel for the stone. She takes the breakfast
she has just presented to the stone and feeds it to her family with satisfaction.
Once her husband has left for work and her children have been sent off to
school, she returns to the shrine. She removes the ornamentation from the
stone, bathes it with raw milk and warm water, and tenderly dries it with
a cloth. She talks softly to the stone as she massages scented oil onto all its
surfaces. With a dab of dark beeswax she reattaches the eyes and other facial
features onto the stone, dresses it in ornate colorful clothing, bright earrings,
and jeweled necklaces, and puts an elegant turban topped with a peacock
feather on its head. After placing a fresh jasmine garland around its neck, she

Loving Stones. David L. Haberman, Oxford University Press (2020) © Oxford University Press.
DOI: 10.1093/oso/9780190086718.001.0001

holds up a small mirror for the stone to admire its handsome appearance. After this, she presses the mirror to her heart and holds it there for a minute, absorbing her Beloved's beautiful presence.

Reverently reciting several hymns and love poems, Sunita returns to the kitchen to prepare a larger midday meal. When this feast is ready, she offers it to the stone on a small wooden table. Her family will enjoy the remnants of the blessed food when they come home for lunch. Once this meal is finished, Sunita places tiny wooden figures—two white cows, a couple of green parrots, a pair of brightly painted peacocks—and a small game board before the stone and closes the shrine for the remainder of the day. She returns to the shrine in the evening, cheerfully greeting the stone with a tasty snack and a welcoming song. After the stone consumes this meal, she removes its elaborate outfit and jewelry and readies it for bed by putting it into nightwear. She reviews the day with her cherished stone, sings more celebratory songs, and then lovingly places the stone in bed before closing the shrine for the night. She begins this ceremonial process all over again in the morning, varying the foods, scents, dress, and songs according to the seasons. The stone Sunita is worshiping is one from Mount Govardhan, a well-known sacred hill located in northern India and one of the most prominent features of Braj, a cultural region associated with the popular and playful Hindu deity Krishna. She reports that she derives great comfort and joy from her loving interaction with it.

I described these activities to an American diplomat I met at a Fulbright function during my year of research in India. "That's crazy!" he said, "Why would anyone want to do something so absurd?" This man was well traveled and culturally knowledgeable, but found such interaction with a stone preposterous, as it completely transgressed the limits of his sense of rational behavior. When I returned to the States, my neighbor asked what I had studied in India. His reaction to my accounts of the worship of Govardhan stones was much stronger; he called the behavior bizarre, ridiculous, and silly. I can imagine others I know adding the labels irrational, weird, and incomprehensible; a conservative Christian I spoke with even pronounced it an idolatrous sin. Clearly, this conduct does not sit easily with the common sense of reality most predominant in contemporary American culture. This is a case of radical difference.

I previously completed a study of the conceptions and worship of sacred trees in northern India.[2] While lecturing on this subject throughout the United States, audience members frequently approached me after the lecture to share their personal encounters and relationships with particular trees. I learned from these and other sources that although the idea that a tree is a sentient being with whom one can develop a significant relationship is quite alien to most people living in the United States, it does exist in fair measure on the periphery of our society. Trees are, after all, "alive." That one can regard a rock in a similar fashion, however, stretches the boundary of the dominant social reality to a breaking point; it is considered simply impossible. And yet within the culture that Sunita inhabits, her actions are completely normal and rational.

How are we to regard such radical difference? How do we live meaningfully in a world of perspectives characterized by such extreme disparity? What is our understanding of the gap that exists between seemingly irreconcilable and incongruous positions? Is it possible to comprehend or perhaps even appreciate something as radically different as rock worship? And what might be the benefits of doing so? These are some of the questions I take up as I explore in this book the conceptions and worship of Mount Govardhan and its many stones. While describing and examining some of the principal characteristics of the worship of Mount Govardhan, this book aims to reflect on the gap that exists between the sense of reality one experiences every day while living near the sacred hill and the dominant reality experienced in everyday life in the United States, which fosters a portrayal of such worship as absurd, or even worse. The radical difference that exists between these two views creates a fruitful space for thinking about larger, more general issues encountered in the academic study of religion.

Accordingly, I employ the subtitle of this book—"Making the Impossible Possible in the Worship of Mount Govardhan"—in two major ways. First, I use it as an entry into the conceptions and theological understandings of the divinity of Mount Govardhan, which is generally regarded as an embodied form of Krishna. It is often said in Braj that worship of Mount Govardhan "makes the impossible possible." Thus, although devotees approach the divine entity of Mount Govardhan for many reasons, most commonly it is for attaining some desired aim, frequently considered by supplicants to be largely unattainable. This investigation also includes an examination of the perplexing paradox of an infinite god embodied in finite form, wherein each particular form is non-different from the limitless. Second, I employ the subtitle to refer to theoretical pursuits in the challenge of interpreting the worship of a mountain and its stones for a culture in which this practice is quite alien. This challenge involves exploration of interpretive strategies that aspire to make the incomprehensible understandable. It leads to deep theoretical considerations of incongruity, inconceivability, and other realms of the impossible. In other words, a major aim of this book is to use the worship of Mount Govardhan as a site to explore ways in which scholars engaged in the difficult work of representing other cultures struggle to make the impossible possible.

I remain fond of Clifford Geertz's characterization of the comparative enterprise with his remark: "Anthropologists don't study villages; they study *in* villages."[3] His point is that the subject of a comparative study is something that extends beyond the boundary of the particular cultural phenomenon under investigation. Geertz explains that the foremost labor of anthropologists is to approach broad human issues from "extended acquaintances with extremely small matters."[4] In his book *Local Knowledge*, he characterizes the comparative enterprise with a sailing metaphor as "a continuous dialectical tacking between the most local of local detail and the most global of global structure in such a way as to bring them into simultaneous view."[5] Whether the local be a village, a text, a religious performance, or the conceptions of and interactions with a sacred mountain, the oscillating movement back and forth between the local and global is what, for Geertz and others, animates a successful academic study.

There is a common saying in the Hindi-speaking world of northern India: *ek panth, do kaj*; that is, "one path, two objectives." In sum, my plan is to guide the reader along the single path of reading this book, and while so doing, I strive to accomplish two different objectives. The first objective is to provide detailed information about the rich religious world associated with Mount Govardhan. The second aspires to use the worship of Mount Govardhan as a site to explore ways in which anyone occupied with the challenging task of representing other cultures might wrestle with radical difference, thereby employing this site as a springboard into theoretical reflection on the difficult and rewarding work of interpreting and translating something as strange as rock worship, often vilified in previous academic studies with the heavily pejorative religious label "idolatry" or disparaged with the psychological pronouncement "absurd." This book can therefore be read as a study of the worship of Mount Govardhan through an interpretive lens colored by a concern with radical cultural difference, or it can be read as a study of ways of addressing extreme cultural difference, with the illustrative example being the worship of Mount Govardhan.

I introduce in Chapter 1 some of the foundational stories related to Mount Govardhan and describe the physical features of the mountain, as well as the sacred terrain that surrounds it. In Chapter 2, I consider ways of thinking about the challenges of radical cultural difference posed by something like intimate interaction with a stone and explore the nature of and possibilities within anthropological cross-cultural understanding and interpretation designed to address them. Various theological conceptions of the mountain are examined in Chapter 3, much of which has never been presented in previous scholarly literature. This also helps illustrate the specific nature of the extreme cultural difference represented by Mount Govardhan. In Chapter 4, I explore ritualized ways in which the mountain is honored, specifically its circumambulation (*parikrama*) and devotional worship (*puja*). Chapter 5 is an investigation of the history of the application of the concept of idolatry as an interpretive strategy in the comparative study of religions—particularly as it has been applied to the worship of material forms such as mountains or stones—and a consideration of more productive ways of regarding religious interaction with material forms of divinity. Chapter 6 focuses attention on interaction with particular individual stones from Mount Govardhan and the anthropomorphic techniques employed to establish and develop close relationships with these divine forms. This chapter includes a re-evaluation of the nature and function of anthropomorphism in general, something that until quite recently has been regarded with much suspicion within many academic disciplines. Consideration of major philosophical tenets that circumscribe the particular Hindu worldview which supports and informs many of the conceptions and practices associated with Mount Govardhan—especially non-duality (*advaita*) and play (*lila*)—forms the subject of Chapter 7. I reflect here on some of the implications derived from the interrelated concepts of non-duality and play in the context of the worship of Mount Govardhan, particularly as they relate to the possibilities they have to offer to the larger field of religious studies. What might non-dual play contribute to the study of religion that takes difference seriously, and what might be gained from engaging in such an adventure into religious difference? This final chapter concludes with an examination of some of the environmental lessons that can be inferred from a study of the worship of Mount Govardhan.

I begin with a brief account of how I came to be introduced to the study of other religious systems and of my initial engagement with radical difference in the culture associated with the worship of Mount Govardhan. I continue to hold the strong conviction that a major purpose of higher education is to generate and nurture what I label "conscious living," and that religious studies has a great deal to offer this edifying process, which is contingent upon an expanded sense of human possibilities. There is much talk these days about freedom, yet freedom depends upon having multiple choices. There is no freedom when one is given only a single choice; genuine choice depends upon difference. Most people live their lives within the singular sense of reality they inherited through their process of socialization long before they could even think about the nature of reality. All subsequent thinking about reality is heavily shaped and influenced by this initial socialization into a particular sense of reality. Conscious living involves taking some kind of step outside this preprogrammed sense of reality and exposing oneself to wider realms of possibility. It hinges on understanding the manner in which one has involuntarily come to assume a particular worldview and to recognize the real possibility of its likely limitations as a socially fabricated reality. Conscious living would then involve systematic exploration of other ways of being and accepting worldviews other than one's own as theoretically equally valid. Only then would one be in a position to make a conscious choice about life values; short of that, freedom remains elusive. One can reside for a lifetime on a comfortable cultural couch manufactured in the unconscious process of primary socialization, so to speak, but it must be admitted that there is considerable existential narrowness in this approach to life. As unsettling as it may sometimes seem, there is much to be gained from getting up off that couch and looking out the windows of one's socially defined world, or perhaps even walking out the door to explore other ways of being human. Sincere exposure to other ways of being—including those that are radically different—expands the horizons of one's possibilities, presents real choices, and provides the opportunity to take a conscious stand on any issue.

From this perspective, singularity can seem very small, even existentially restrictive. I came to the academic study of religions through just such a troubling experience of cultural constrictiveness. My own entry into what has become a lifelong study of the various religious cultures of the world had much to do with being drawn to difference, in my case out of a somewhat desperate necessity. I began college as an electrical engineering student, the result of being the eldest son of a man who owned a successful electrical contracting and engineering company. It was assumed by all that I would one day take over this company. My freshman year in college was not a happy one; everything that excited me seemed to be happening outside of engineering school. By my sophomore year I was fairly miserable, feeling depressingly claustrophobic, that I was trapped in a world of industry in which I did not belong. But there was virtually no other world available to my imagination at that time. I presumed that if I could not fit into this singular world I could not fit into *the* world, period. I plunged into an estranged and desperate state, not knowing what to do.

It was during this time that a friend gave me a copy of a religious text. The identity of the text is relatively unimportant; rather, it was my reaction to it that became significant. In the midst of my existential crisis, I experienced this text as a window into another way of conceptualizing the world and another way of occupying it. My encounter with this text felt "salvific," for it liberated me from the claustrophobic box within which I found myself trapped. If I didn't fit into the business world of electrical engineering I didn't have to eliminate myself, for there was another world available for possible inhabitation. I could have stopped with that one text, but I didn't. I suspected that there were many more worlds of possibility to explore. I hungrily read as many religious texts as I could get my hands on, meeting each as another window into yet another way of being. My desire for difference was insatiable, and soon led me to major in religious studies, then a fledgling initiative at the University of Colorado in Boulder. During my early years of undergraduate education, religious studies was for me an exciting adventure into vast worlds of new possibility. An attraction to difference served as my initial motivation in the study of religions, and in many ways it remains so today.

But it was not always easy; feeling threatened and unraveled by difference is not unknown to me. Encountering difference in books is one thing—face to face is a more radical challenge. My first entry into the cultural region of Braj—the site of this study—did not go smoothly. Nearly four decades ago I traveled as a graduate student by train from Delhi to Mathura, the capital city of Braj, never before having spent any time in northern India. My destination was Vrindaban, a pilgrimage temple-town located about ten miles to the north. I was so ignorant of the area and the distance between Mathura and Vrindaban that I let a bicycle rickshaw driver talk me into riding with him as a passenger between the two towns. Two and a half hours later, we pulled into Loi Bazar in Vrindaban, the location of the research institute with which I was to affiliate. I was frightened by the alienness of the place, the scene before me nothing like I had expected. I had chosen to conduct my fieldwork there based on a conversation with one of my advisors back at the University of Chicago when it came time for my doctoral dissertation research. He advised me that I could either study with scholars in Calcutta, or I could conduct my work in Vrindaban, the place where the Sanskrit text I was researching had been written. Based on my aversion to big cities and a favorable impression of Vrindaban created by a former study of the pastoral and idyllic paintings of this region, I decided to work in the smaller pilgrimage-town setting of Vrindaban rather than Calcutta. Those paintings, however, turned out to be a poor representation of the town where I now found myself. The famous eighteenth-century Kangra paintings of Vrindaban, for example, portrayed it as a wonderfully lush and peaceful forest, whereas the scene before me was a crowded, rowdy, and carnivalesque bazaar lined with seemingly old weather-beaten buildings. And people stared at me as though I were an oddity. I was overcome with intense cultural shock.

I dismounted the bicycle rickshaw with uncertainty, paid the driver, and made my way up a flight of stone stairs to the research institute, then located above a dilapidated post office. I had written ahead, letting the staff know that I needed a place to live during my year of research. After brief introductions, I was shown a dark room with only one small window and a floor covered with rat droppings. I knew immediately I could not live there. Mumbling rapid thanks and something about another possible residence, I stumbled back down the stairs and out onto the street. I had no idea where to go, not even which direction to walk. At this point, what began as challenging culture shock was ratcheted up to the level of extreme discomfort, if not terror.

I am not sure what I would have done had I not heard a kind and welcoming voice. "Please come, sit and have some tea," were the words I recognized in Hindi. The voice belonged to Mahesh, a cloth merchant who was to become one of my best friends in Vrindaban. I was desperate for human contact; he later told me that I was the first foreigner he had met who treated him as a friend. I certainly needed one. As I sipped sweet milky tea with Mahesh, I felt the return of a relative calm. But this was short-lived. A man with long tangled black hair piled atop his head, carrying a wooden pot and wearing only a loincloth, approached me. He starred at me with a fiery look in his eyes and demanded five rupees. I knew from conversations during my Fulbright orientation in New Delhi that the standard rate for beggars at that time was about ten *paise*, a tenth of a rupee, a fraction of what this disturbing man was demanding. I was not going to be taken for a fool. I pulled out from my pocket a half-rupee coin, the amount I calculated would be proper for a foreigner financed by a fellowship to give, and placed it into the wild man's outstretched hand. Without breaking his fierce gaze, he barked in Hindi, "No! Give me five rupees!" Still determined to maintain some degree of pride, I offered him a two-rupee bill. His gaze became even more intense. He took the paper note in his right hand and squeezed it. A stream of water began gushing out of what had felt to me to be a dry bill. At this point the hair on the back of my neck stood on end. I reached into my pocket as quickly as possible and produced the desired five-rupee note; thus the man left with seven and a half of my rupees. Whatever calm I had achieved from Mahesh's tea and conversation vanished. I was completely unraveled. My mind began to race, seeking some kind of rational explanation to account for what had just happened, struggling to fit it into a known and familiar world. To this day, however, I remain uncertain about what took place. If it had not been for the obligations I felt to Fulbright and my own university, I might have left on the next train back to Delhi. This level of difference was just too much.

But in the end I did not leave. I spent the following year in Vrindaban being stretched, expanded, and enriched by encounters with a great variety of religious characters and practices in ways I have come to treasure. Given the choice between remaining in the known, relatively comfortable, yet restricted room of cultural certainty constructed in the process of my own socialization or encountering unknown worlds of difference that challenge and stretch me, sometimes quite uncomfortably, I have opted for the latter. A comfortable couch in a small room has its attractions, but I feel I have grown and benefited considerably from getting up and walking out the door into vast realms of possibility. Four decades of studying with openness the worlds of difference present in the religious cultures of northern India—particularly within the region of Braj—have made their apparent alienness a bit more familiar to me. The sacred land of Braj has also charmed me. Of the many different cultural phenomena I encountered there, one that now strikes me as fascinating, familiar, comprehensible, and even—shall I say—plausible is the worship of the stones of Mount Govardhan.

How is one to think about such difference? Before we consider this question, we need to know more about the sacred mountain. Having been born at the base of the mighty Mount Rainer (Tacoma) in Washington and raised on the plains just below the towering Longs Peak in Colorado, I have long been fascinated with mountains. Although no one I knew spoke of such things when I was a boy, the notion of sacred mountains appealed to me from the day I first encountered it in college. I confess, however, that having grown up with these monumental mountains, the first time I laid eyes on Mount Govardhan I found it rather disappointing. Compared to most other sacred mountains, it is quite small—a mound of stones no taller than a ten-story building; but I soon learned that the mountain makes up for its slight stature with a big and enchanting story.

1

On the Slopes of Mount Govardhan

Lay of the Land

There is nothing like this mountain in the whole world.
There are many beautiful mountains on earth,
and many much bigger than this one,
but none are like this one.
It is Purna Purushottama Bhagavan Krishna.
Although it appears to be ordinary, it is completely divine.[1]

The great secret in this special worship is that
the one who worshiped the mountain
is the same as the mountain who is worshiped.[2]

One experiences great bliss
simply being in the land lying
at the feet of Mount Govardhan.[3]

Mount Govardhan

One day the divine couple Radha and Krishna had just finished making love in a delightful but well inhabited location in the heavenly realm of Golok. In the enchantment of this moment, Radha gave Krishna a beguiling side-long glance, completely unsettling him. Now that he was vulnerable to her charms, she sensed that this was an opportune moment to make a request. She said to him, "If you are pleased with my love, then I ask that you ful-fill a desire deep within my heart." "Beloved," Krishna responded, "ask for whatever you desire and I will happily grant it." Radha revealed her heart's desire: that Krishna create a beautiful secluded place near the bank of the Yamuna River in the charming groves of the Vrindaban Forest so they might

Loving Stones. David L. Haberman, Oxford University Press (2020) © Oxford University Press.
DOI: 10.1093/oso/9780190086718.001.0001

experience the exquisite bliss of lovemaking without fear of disruption. Taking her loving desire deep within his own heart, Krishna said, "So be it!" Instantly, an intense passion (*anuraga*) gushed forth from his heart in the form of a fiery blaze accompanied with cool water (*sajalam tejo*). This combination spilled onto the ground, coagulated and grew into a mighty mountain that consisted of jewels and precious metals, and featured many caves and mountain streams. The slopes of the mountain were covered with splendid verdant trees and colorful fragrant flowers, and were inhabited by a great variety of enchanting songbirds. The mountain expanded rapidly to enormous proportions with a hundred peaks. Fearing that the mountain was getting too big, Krishna stopped its expansion with a firm touch of his hand. Radha was so pleased with this magnificent mountain that she immediately made sweet love to Krishna in their newly fashioned private accommodation.[4]

This is the story of the origin of Mount Govardhan as told in the *Garga Samhita*, a narrative widely known by worshipers of this sacred mountain and central to many theological conceptualizations of its deeper meanings.[5] Perhaps most significant for the latter initiative is that Govardhan consists of the consolidated form of supreme love that emerged out of the bliss-filled hearts of the divine couple Radha and Krishna. All this took place, according to the *Garga Samhita*, in Krishna's transcendental abode known as Golok. How, then, did Mount Govardhan end up on the plains of north-central India, where we find it today?

When the time came for Krishna to descend from Golok to relieve the sufferings of the world and bring delight to his devotees, he asked his beloved Radha to accompany him. She readily agreed, but announced that she could not be happy without the Vrindaban Forest, the Yamuna River, and the Govardhan Mountain. Krishna accordingly made arrangements to send these three entities—all made from a portion of himself—to Earth. Since the way to enter the world is through a womb, Mount Govardhan was born to the wife of the majestic Mount Drona in a distant mountainous land. All the mighty mountains of the world came to honor the birth of this marvelous son of Mount Drona. After bowing down to him, the assembly of mountains circumambulated the young Mount Govardhan in a clockwise direction and performed his worship with precious offerings while singing hymns of praise. They addressed him as *Giriraj*, "King of the Mountains," an affectionate name that stuck.

Sometime later, the powerful and intimidating sage Pulastya was on a Himalayan pilgrimage and came upon Mount Drona's exquisite son. He was so struck by the splendid beauty and peaceful environment of Mount Govardhan that he immediately desired it as a place for his own productive meditation. Pulastya approached Drona and requested the gift of his son so that he could transfer him to Kashi (Banaras/Varanasi) and establish him there as a mountainous retreat for his religious practices. Drona burst into tears knowing that he was about to lose his beloved son, as he could not deny the request of this formidable sage. He went to his son and instructed him to go with Pulastya.

Mount Govardhan turned toward the sage and asked how he intended to transport a mountain as large as himself. Pulastya explained that the young mountain was to sit on his right hand, and would be carried to Kashi by means of his yogic powers. Govardhan agreed to go with the sage under one condition: that he not be put down anywhere before they reached Kashi; if he were, he declared, that is where he would remain. Pulastya agreed. With tears in his eyes, Mount Govardhan said goodbye to his heartbroken father and hopped onto the sage's hand. Together they set off for Kashi.

Along the way they came to the land of Braj, which Govardhan recognized as the pastoral territory where the Supreme Lord Krishna was to descend and enact his youthful activities with the cowherds. Pondering this, he made himself very heavy. Pulastya became exhausted, and forgetting their prior agreement set the mountain down in the center of Braj. The sage rested for a while, took a bath, and was then ready to resume his journey. He ordered the mountain back on his hand, but Govardhan refused. The sage tried to move him with sweet words and then his powerful yogic strength, but Govardhan would not budge. Pulastya demanded to know why. The King of Mountains reminded him of their agreement and proclaimed that he would not leave this spot. Realizing that he could not move the huge mountain, the fierce sage became furious and cursed Govardhan: "Since you have frustrated my desire, you will decrease in size every day by the amount of one sesame seed." Pulastya then left in a huff for Kashi. Since that day the large mountain, now happily settled in Braj, began slowly to diminish.

An alternative narrative accounting for how Govardhan came to Braj involves Hanuman, devotional hero of the monkey warriors. The Ramayana tells of the battle between Lord Rama and the ten-headed demon Ravana, who had abducted Rama's wife, Sita, and carried her off to the island of Lanka. Rama enlisted the aid of a vast army of monkey warriors, who helped prepare for an invasion of Lanka by building a bridge to link the island with the mainland. Some of the monkeys traveled to the distant Himalayas to fetch boulders for the bridge. Eager in his devotion to Rama, the macho Hanuman picked up the entire Govardhan Mountain and flew off with it toward Lanka. Midway, however, he got a message that the bridge had been completed and he put the mountain down where he was, which happened to be in the center of Braj. Realizing that his opportunity for service to Rama had slipped away, Govardhan became disappointed and complained to Hanuman that he had made himself light so that he could easily be carried because he wanted to be of service to Rama, but now he was being deprived of the very sight and touch of Rama. Lord Rama himself then appeared and blessed him, saying: "Don't worry! In the next age I will lift you up with the finger of my own hand and make you worthy of worship." All other hills carried off to make the bridge would be touched by Rama's feet, but only Govardhan would be held high above the Lord's head. From that time on, this mountain became identified as one of the main forms of the Lord.[6]

These stories explain how Mount Govardhan came to be situated in Braj, the site of embodied encounters with Krishna. They are narrated in texts and recounted by numerous knowledgeable people residing near the sacred mountain today. Geologists, however, tell a different story. Mount Govardhan is part of the Aravalli Hills, one of the world's oldest mountain ranges. The ancient Aravalli Hills stretch for about 350 miles, primarily through the current northwest Indian state of Rajasthan, and date back to a time long before the Indian subcontinent collided with the Eurasian Plate some fifty million years ago. The Aravalli range used to consist of very tall mountains, but over time weather erosion has reduced them to the rocky hills we see today.

Mount Govardhan was formed from sediments that were laid down on a sea bottom around two billion years ago.[7] These were buried deep in the earth and transformed under pressure into large sedimentary rocks. Underground molten mineral materials invaded some of the sedimentary rocks, which heated up, metamorphosed, and then buckled under tectonic stresses. The mountain uplifted about a billion and a half years ago as tectonic forces aided in further splitting the stone. The northeast-southwest trending rocky ridge that we now see is quite fractured both horizontally and vertically, giving the impression that it is made up of a large pile of individual rocks (Figure 1.1).Indeed, it is often depicted this way in paintings (Figure 1.2) and sculpture.

The stone of Mount Govardhan consists largely of purple quartzite, which results from the metamorphism of quartz sandstone. Although quartz sandstone is often white, light gray, yellowish, or light brown, it can also be blue,

Figure 1.1. Section of Mount Govardhan showing horizontal and vertical fracturing.

Figure 1.2. Painting of cowherd Krishna holding Mount Govardhan; note the composite structure of the mountain.

green, purple, or black through the assimilation of various minerals. The stones of Mount Govardhan tend to be hard, somewhat shiny, and dark in color, with streaks of both light yellow and black. The hill is covered with *dhau* trees, age-old drought-resistant trees that are native to the Aravalli range, and is known to have several deep caves.

Whether reduced by Pulastya's curse or wind and water erosion, today Mount Govardhan stands about 100 feet tall at its highest point. The narrow ridge is seven miles long and a little over half a mile wide, aligned for the most part on a north-south axis. Although the *Garga Samhita* refers to the hundred peaks of Mount Govardhan and identifies one of its names as Shata Shringa ("Hundred Peaks"),[8] today it features only three. Regarding this difference, a contemporary Vaishnava theologian writes:

> In Vyapi Vaikuntha (Krishna's transcendental abode also known as Golok) Shri Giriraj has one hundred peaks, but the form in which it arrived on Earth features only three peaks. The first is Adi-Shikhar ("First Peak"), the second is Deva-Shikhar ("Divine Peak"), and the third is Brahma-Shikhar ("Ultimate Peak"). Each of the three peaks differs according to the divine play (*lilas*) manifest there during different time periods. The initial grace-filled play (*pushti-lila*) occurred on the First Peak during the Sarasvat period of Krishna's descent. Then another grace-filled play occurred on the Divine Peak during the founding Svetavaraha period of Shri Vallabhacharya and Shri Vitthalnath's descent. In the future the grace-filled play will occur on the Ultimate Peak near the tail (*punchari*) of Govardhan.[9]

While quite aware that many mountains in the world are much higher and more majestic than Govardhan, many of the latter's devotees still agree with Rupa Gosvamin, who wrote in his Sanskrit poem the *Hansaduta*: "We believe that the Govardhan Hill is the greatest of all the mountains on the earth."[10] We will see why.

Mount Govardhan is the most distinguishing feature of the sacred landscape of Braj, the cultural region in northern India long associated in literature, religious imagination, temple festivities, and pilgrimage with Krishna and his playful activities.[11] The historian Alan Entwistle maintains that the current rocky ridge identified as Mount Govardhan has been "universally recognized as the mythical Govardhan" referred to in early authoritative texts, and is "almost certainly the oldest sacred object in Braj."[12] A common perspective today also has it that "Shri Giriraj Govardhan is the very heart (*hridaya*) of the sacred land of Braj."[13] Thus, Govardhan is often regarded as the vital center of Braj, a region that has been crucially involved in many cultural developments in northern India. The area of Braj defined by pilgrimage activity is conceived of as a circle (*mandal*), and indeed is somewhat circular, with a diameter of about sixty miles, although its cultural and linguistic influences stretch far beyond this boundary. The governmental and commercial capital of Braj is Mathura, the largest city in the area, located about one hundred miles south of Delhi. Positioned on both sides of the Yamuna River (the sacred land's other major natural defining feature), Braj is situated in the cultivated river valley of the western Mathura district of Uttar Pradesh and extends into the desert terrain of the Bharatpur district of eastern Rajasthan. This region witnessed an explosion of cultural developments during a Krishnaite renaissance that occurred here at the dawn of the sixteenth century and produced many of the physical structures, religious philosophies, ritual practices, and arts that are still found in Braj today. The religion associated with Braj is known generally as Braj Vaishnavism; this is a form of *bhakti*, a term often translated as "devotionalism," but perhaps more accurately translated as "conscious participation." Diana Eck, a scholar of Hinduism, writes: "*Bhakti* comes from a Sanskrit verb which means 'to share,' and *bhakti* is relational love, shared by both God and the devotee."[14] Although people came from all parts of India to participate in this dynamic creation, two of the greatest contributing factors were the creative activities of the followers of two influential saints, Vallabhacharya and Chaitanya, who respectively founded what are commonly known as the Pushti Marg and Gaudiya Vaishnavism, the most prominent forms of Vaishnavism in Braj today.

The Pushti Marg, or "Path of Grace," is a form of Vaishnavism that focuses on the playful Krishna of Braj, depicted in the *Bhagavata Purana* as the highest and complete reality. This group is also referred to as the Vallabha Sampraday, since it was initiated by Vallabhacharya (1479–1530). Vallabha was born in central India into a Tailang brahman family from what is now the southern Indian state of Andhra Pradesh, although he spent the great majority of his life in northern India. (Much of the Krishnaite Vaishnavism of Braj is the result of a blending of the devotionalism of northern and southern India.)[15] According to sectarian sources, Vallabha first came to wander Braj in 1492.[16] Significant among his recorded activities in Braj were the performance of the circumambulation (*parikrama*) and worship (*puja*) of Mount Govardhan. Vallabha produced many Sanskrit treatises that established the philosophical foundation for the Pushti Marg, and was also crucially involved in the initial worship of the widely celebrated form of Krishna at Mount Govardhan known as Shri Nath-ji. Vallabha's second son and subsequent leader of the Pushti Marg, Vitthalnath (1516–86), did much to further Pushti Margiya teachings and to enhance the elaborate worship conducted in the Shri Nath-ji temple. Householders maintain a position of leadership in this sect of Vaishnavism, which gives great importance to the loving worship (*seva*) of an embodied form (*svarupa*) of Krishna in one's own home. There are numerous Pushti Margis living throughout India today, many of whom reside in the northwestern states of Rajasthan and Gujarat.

Gaudiya Vaishnavism is another denomination of Vaishnavism that focuses on the playful Krishna of Braj. It is so called because many of its major leaders came from the province of Gauda in what is now the northeastern Indian state of West Bengal. This sect of Vaishnavism is alternatively called the Chaitanya Sampraday, since it was introduced by Chaitanya (1486–1533), who was born in the northeastern state of Bengal in the scholastic center of Nabadwip. *Sannyasis* who have renounced ordinary domestic life occupy places of prominence in this sect, which places major emphasis on singing the names of Krishna (*sankirtan*). The worship of embodied forms of Krishna, however, also occupies a place of importance in this sect of Vaishnavism. Gaudiya sources recount that Chaitanya came to Braj in 1514; during his visit he too circumambulated Mount Govardhan and performed its worship. Although he received a traditional Sanskrit education in Nabadwip, he soon left his studies to take up a life of ecstatic devotional practice. He did not produce written treatises himself, but inspired a talented group of theologians to move to Braj and take up this work. These became known as the Six Gosvamins of Vrindaban; most important among them was Rupa Gosvamin, who articulated a new approach to devotionalism, expressed in terms of classical aesthetics and dramatic theory.[17] Although Gaudiya Vaishnavas are found throughout India today, most reside in northeastern region of India in and around the state of West Bengal.

Many of the major political developments that took place in northern India around the sixteenth century also involved the region of Braj. The great Mughal emperor Akbar ascended the throne in 1556 and was able to extend and stabilize the nominally Muslim Mughal empire by forming alliances with powerful Hindu Rajput kings who ruled the desert regions to the west of Delhi and were known for their valor and military skills. Chief among these was the family of Raja Bharmal Kacchhwaha of Amber, a town located on a fortified hill just north of what is now Jaipur. Bharmal's eldest daughter Heer Kunwari was married to Akbar, and became his most beloved wife and mother of his successor, Jahangir. Bharmal's eldest son and grandson, Bhagwant Das and his son Man Singh, were the first Rajputs to enter into the service of Akbar. Man Singh and Akbar were to become fast friends, and the Hindu Rajput eventually became one of the most powerful political figures in Akbar's empire. This alliance between Akbar and powerful Hindu kings in the sixteenth century led to a political compromise which supported the birth of a wide-reaching cultural renaissance in the region of Braj that attracted the creative services of Krishna devotees from many parts of India. The results of these developments were many, but included Man Singh's patronage of the Gaudiya Vaishnavas in Braj, particularly in the construction of the famous Govindadev temple of Vrindaban (later shifted to Jaipur), which was the largest Hindu building erected during the reign of Akbar, and also Akbar's renowned Hindu counselor Birbal's patronage of the followers of Vallabhacharya, who were developing the Shri Nath-ji temple on top of Mount Govardhan. There is documentary evidence that in 1583 Akbar produced a *farman* that granted to Vallabha's son Vitthalnath the village of Jatipura tax free for the maintenance of the Shri Govardhan Nath-ji temple.[18]

King Jai Singh II, successor of Bharmal and builder of the new capital "Pink City" of Jaipur, continued his family's patronage of the Vrindaban-based Gaudiya Vaishnavas, giving special attention to Vrindaban's crown-jewel temple of Govindadev.[19] The decline of Mughal support for Hindu temples in Braj initiated by the emperor Aurangzeb raised a concern that the Vrindaban temple was under threat. Consequently, in 1735 Jai Singh had Govindadev shifted to a temple built at the very center of his royal palace in Jaipur. Jai Singh assumed a protective role in watching over the affairs of Braj, and struck up an alliance with Badan Singh, head of a powerful family of Jat kings in this region who inhabited the magnificent palace town of Dig, located just ten miles west of Mount Govardhan (now in the state of Rajasthan), and the nearby fortress town of Bharatpur. Jats are closely related to the Rajputs and consider themselves to be the descendants of Krishna's own clan, the Yadavas. These early devotees of Krishna tend to be non-sectarian. Jats are primarily farmers who make up a large segment of the Braj population and are known for their courageous competence in fighting. Jai Singh put Badan Singh in charge of patrolling the royal highways between Delhi, Agra, and Jaipur and awarded him the title of Braj Raja, the "king of Braj."[20] With the aid of a talented group of artisans and craftsmen recently unemployed because of the declining Mughal empire, Badan Singh began work in 1725 on his glorious palace in Dig, which soon rivaled the Mughal courts of Delhi and Agra.

As his eyesight began to fail, Badan turned his title of king of Braj and the responsibility of ruling the Jat kingdom over to his favorite son, Suraj Mal Singh, an ardent devotee of Mount Govardhan, now considered the family deity. After an elaborate worship of Mount Govardhan, Suraj Mal began work in his new capital town of Bharatpur, which later came to be known as the only fort to have withstood the British cannon fire of Lord Lake.[21] Soon after the death of Jai Singh in 1743, Suraj Mal was recognized by Mughal authorities as the legitimate protector of the land of Krishna. He was an important patron of Braj culture, and his family was responsible for building many of the ornate buildings that still stand in the town of Govardhan today. Suraj Mal's personal "chosen deity" (ishta-devata) was the embodied form of Krishna as Mount Govardhan, which he raised to the status of state deity. His power grew to such an extent that he eventually sacked the courts of both Delhi and Agra and became the wealthiest king in northern India. Before long, however, this drew the attention of powerful Afghani invaders, who attacked the forces of Suraj Mal and killed him in the fierce battle that ensued. His ornate sandstone memorial now stands on the edge of Mount Govardhan above the shore of a tranquil pond named Kusum Sarovar. Saints, such as Vallabha and Chaitanya, as well as powerful rulers like Man Singh, Jai Singh, and Suraj Mal Singh, were all drawn to the divine presence and stories of Mount Govardhan.

The most important and widely known narrative associated with Mount Govardhan is found in the defining text of Braj religious culture, the *Bhagavata Purana*.[22] This is the story of Krishna's lifting Mount Govardhan, an incident that has been celebrated for centuries in paintings (Figure 1.2) and sculpture throughout the entire Indian subcontinent.[23] Moreover, this text is essential for understanding central conceptions of Mount Govardhan.

The *Bhagavata Purana* narrates that Nanda, Krishna's father and chief of his clan, annually directed the inhabitants of Braj to assemble a huge mound of food at the end of the monsoon season in preparation for the customary grand sacrificial offering to Indra, the god of rain and storms. One year, however, Krishna went to his father and questioned the efficacy of the gods headed by Indra, arguing that as cowherds who live in the forest their lives depended not on Indra but on the Govardhan Hill, which supplies them with fresh water, abundant sustenance, safe shelter, and nourishing grass for their cows. Accordingly, Krishna suggested that they offer the heap of sacrificial food intended for Indra to Mount Govardhan instead. Nanda and the other elders agreed; following Krishna's lead, they conducted a worship (*puja*) of the mountain, fed it Indra's offerings, and circumambulated (*pradakshina/parikrama*) it with reverence. Most significantly, Krishna assumed the form of Mount Govardhan, proclaiming: "I am the mountain,"[24] and devoured the abundant offerings with his huge body. The text states that Krishna performed the worship by means of himself (*atmana*) to himself (*atmane*).[25] The *Bhagavata Purana* makes clear in this episode that Krishna assumed two forms simultaneously: one the cowherd youth who directed the worship of the mountain, and the other the mountain who received the worshipful offerings.

Proud Indra became extremely angry at the loss of his tribute and unleashed a horrific rain, hail, and wind storm on the residents of Braj to punish them. The villagers ran to Krishna for protection from the onslaught of this lethal storm. Krishna responded to Indra's attack by "playfully" (*lilaya*) lifting the entire Govardhan Hill with his left arm, using it as an enormous umbrella to shelter the inhabitants of Braj. The storm raged for seven days, after which Indra finally realized the true nature of the supreme divinity holding the mountain; with his pride subdued, he surrendered to Krishna. Apologizing profusely, he begged forgiveness for his arrogance and showered Krishna with exalted praise. With the aid of his elephant mount Airavata and the celestial cow Surabhi, Indra honored Krishna by giving him a grand ceremonial bath with milk and water. Like the story of Krishna's first worship of Govardhan, the lifting of Mount Govardhan also reveals the double identity of Krishna, as he is both the cowherd boy lifting the mountain as well as the protective mountain that is lifted.

The Tareti

Reside at the base (*tareti*) of Blessed Govardhan.
Fix your mind constantly on the lotus-feet of the
Enchanting Cowherd Lad.
Your body will become ecstatic rolling in the dust of Braj
and bathing in the Govinda Pond.
Reveal the highest love in your heart to the
Sensitive Beloved, who assumes the
form of the Blessed Mountain.[26]

Alternatively spelled *tarahati* and *talahati*, the dictionary meaning of the Braj Bhasha word *tareti* is "the low land beneath a mountain,"[27] in this case the flat plain surrounding Mount Govardhan and extending out from it for about a mile. Although this is its general geographical meaning, the Govardhan *tareti* is most importantly a sacred space around the mountain that is considered highly beneficial for religious practice and divine knowledge. For the many devotees who out of devotional respect would never climb or even set foot on Mount Govardhan, the *tareti* is the special space in which they make close contact with the mountain. As the well-known poem in the preceding indicates, it is a place where Krishna's presence is felt to be particularly strong. The poem also refers to the sacredness of certain physical features of the *tareti*, such as ponds and the grounds encircling the mountain. The ponds and other natural features comprise an enhanced setting for the sacred stone mountain at the center, like a ring of ornaments holding the precious jewel at the core of a circular brooch. I take readers on an introductory journey around the circular pathway of the *tareti* to give a sense of the geographical, historical, and mythological setting of Mount Govardhan.

The *tareti* is most commonly experienced while walking around the mountain in a clockwise direction, a manner of honoring the body of a divinity or person known as *parikrama*. One can begin a circumambulation or *parikrama* within the *tareti* of Mount Govardhan anywhere, as long as one completes the circle by returning to the spot where one started. The most popular worshipful walk around Mount Govardhan is called the *sat-kos parikrama*, the "seven-*kos* circumambulation," since the most commonly traversed pathway around the mountain, known as the *parikrama marg*, follows a route that is seven *kos* in length. A *kos* is a measure of distance that is approximately three miles, thus the circuit around Mount Govardhan is about fourteen miles, or twenty-three kilometers, in length. The entire circuit takes around six to eight hours to complete, not including significant rests or stops at temples, sacred ponds, and other inviting sites.

The *parikrama* is commonly performed barefoot; this shows reverence for the mountain, as well as giving one intimate connection to its sacred land. A *baba* living in Radhakund who does the seven-kos *parikrama* every day told me: "We do *parikrama* barefoot not only to honor Govardhan, but also by being in direct contact with this sacred (*pavitra*) ground we get spiritual power (*shakti*)—specifically the *shakti* of love (*prem*) that is *bhakti*. So we gain *bhakti* by doing the *parikrama* barefoot." *Parikrama* is a bodily experience that engages all the senses when the body of the devotee meets the body of the God at the base of the mountain. The ground is felt with the feet while walking or with the whole body while prostrating in the dust; calls of peacocks and parrots, chants and hymns (and these days motorcycle horns and loud devotional music) fill the ears; scents of flowers, incense, and sour milk infuse the nose; sweets from the temples and even grains of sand from the earth (some people take a pinch of dirt from the *tareti* and pop it into their mouths when they begin their *parikrama*) are tasted with the tongue; and the ever-changing vistas of the mountain, clad with a variety of flora and fauna, provide delight to the eyes. Visual communion—known as *darshan*— is typically singled out for special emphasis in divine encounters. The *Garga Samhita*, for example, asserts: "The blessed Giriraj Govardhan Mountain is a physical form (*rupa*) of Shri Hari (Krishna). By merely seeing (*darshan*) it a human being achieves the highest goal."[28]

Potent worshipful interactions that engage all the senses obviously require interaction with an embodied form of divinity. In his *Bhaktirasamritasindhu*, Rupa Gosvamin cites a definition of bhakti as worship "with the senses to the Lord of Senses."[29] From this Vaishnava perspective, the senses can lead to trouble when directed egotistically to the wrong things, but are spiritually beneficial when directed to the ultimate "object," Krishna. Mental aspects of worship are recognized as important in this tradition, but effective connections with divinity would be greatly diminished if the senses were left out, and for this to occur a physical divine "object" that engages the senses is essential. Vallabhacharya concurs, stating in his *Nirodhalakshana* that for their benefit the senses, which have become disturbed and jaded in their ordinary involvements, should be connected to Krishna. He further explains that when people develop a painfully intense longing for him, Krishna, who resides in the heart of all beings, is moved by compassion and comes out of their hearts to appear directly before them in physical form so that they can interact with him with their whole being.[30] Hence sensual worship and embodied forms of divinity are intimately interconnected.

Although starting points vary depending on a particular person's tradition or choosing, I begin the following description of the circumambulatory pathway (*parikrama marg*) around the mountain at the Dandavati Shila in the temple town of Jatipura. This is one of the five towns that are located in the *tareti* of Mount Govardhan. It is a picturesque pilgrimage village with a permanent population of about four thousand, swelling to tens—or even hundreds—of thousands more on a special *parikrama* day. Jatipura dates

Figure 1.3. Morning worship of Jatipura Mukharvind stone.

back to the sixteenth century, when founding leaders of the Pushti Marg were active here. *Baithak*s ("seats") honoring both Vallabhacharya and his son Vitthalnath are located near the mountain in Jatipura, and this remains a major center of the Pushti Marg in Braj today. It is a common place to begin the *parikrama* for this particular group of Vaishnavas. It was an obvious location for me to begin, since I spent most of my year of research in India living in Jatipura atop a sixteenth-century temple overlooking the Dandavati Shila with the mountain rising up immediately behind it.

Jatipura is best known today for two Govardhan shrines that house renowned stones from the mountain. One of these is the Mukharvind, or "Lotus Mouth" (Figure 1.3). The late anthropologist Paul Toomey writes of it: "The pride of Jatipura village is unquestionably the *mukharvind* shrine, also known as '*bhog shila*' (the 'food rock') because this is the spot where Pushtimargis offer Govardhan *puja* and other food offerings."[31] I will describe this site of worship in more detail as we come back around the mountain to re-enter Jatipura on its southern side and close the *parikrama* circle.

The other famous stone in Jatipura is the Dandavati Shila, the "Prostration Stone," located at the base of the mountain on the northern edge of Jatipura

Figure 1.4. Women circumambulating unadorned Dandavati Shila stone in Jatipura.

(Figure 1.4). This shrine features a dark Govardhan stone that measures about two feet long, a foot and a half wide, and a foot tall. Some say that this stone was as tall as a man several centuries ago, but has shrunk to its present height due to Pulastya's curse.[32] A sign posted here proclaims that by circumambulating this stone seven times[33] one obtains the same results as doing the entire seven-*kos parikrama*. It is recognized in early Pushti Margiya literature as a favorable place for beneficial religious practice,[34] and is identified as the place where Vallabhacharya worshiped the mountain and at the end of his life entered it in a blaze of fire. A black marble memorial column behind the Dandavati Shila marks the spot of his radiant entrance. One of the shrine's attendant priests told me: "Although there are so many stones worshiped around Mount Govardhan, this one is most special. Why is it called Dandavati Shila? Because Vallabhacharya Mahaprabhu-ji himself prostrated (*dandavat*) before it and worshiped Mount Govardhan through this stone (*shila*)." He directed my attention to a painting hanging above the shrine depicting this event. After bowing to the Dandavati Shila and asking

forgiveness from Mount Govardhan for any offenses they might inadvertently commit during their visit, many pilgrims begin their *parikrama* of the
sacred mountain at this place. The hill is at its tallest here, arising steeply behind the Dandavati Shila with progressive layers of fractured rocks divided
by low verdant plants, creating the impression of a stairway to the heavenly
top of the mountain. The original renowned Shri Nath-ji temple is located in
this lofty location.

Moving north out of Jatipura, one has the choice of walking a soft dirt
inner path or an asphalt road. The road was built in the past few decades
to handle the growing vehicular traffic and accommodate those pilgrims
who do not want to traverse the fourteen-mile circuit around the mountain
on foot, but instead encircle it by bicycle, motor rickshaw, car, or even bus.
Many people living near Mount Govardhan frown on vehicular *parikrama*.
A temple priest residing in Jatipura wrote in his recent book on Govardhan,
for example, that healthy people who think they are achieving good results
from a vehicular circumambulation are deceiving themselves.[35] He reiter-
ated this contention to me during several conversations. The notion seems
to be that riding in a motorized vehicle on an asphalt road cuts one off from
the more intimate experiences of walking the dirt path. The inner pathway
maintains a distance from the business of the asphalt road, and provides a
closer view of the mountain's rocky slopes and large boulders spread among
aged *dhau* trees. The dirt path provides a more natural experience, for here
one enters into a regenerating forest with a remarkable variety of verdant
trees. It is said that Krishna's cowherd girl friends, the *gopi*s, spoke with these
marvelous trees while searching for him.[36]

I regularly passed through this forest on my way around the mountain.
On several occasions I encountered a bulky black *nilgai* bull with a group of
lighter brown females and young calves. The impressive "blue cows" are the
largest of the Asian antelope, and are frequently seen on the ridges and slopes
of Mount Govardhan. On another walk through these woods, an excited
group of pilgrims directed me to a large white and black python. This forest is
also home to a number of peacocks that strut among the boulders, displaying
their shimmery blue necks and surprisingly long tails, and a great diversity
of song birds which flit through the trees, filling the air with their chatter
and songs: bright green rose-ringed parakeets, red-vented bulbuls, grey
hornbills, crested hoopoes, and others. And, of course, ubiquitous troops
of rhesus monkeys scamper mischievously about these abundant woods.
The asphalt road provides a very different experience. Sounds of wildlife

are replaced with motorcycle and car horns, and the outer side of the route is lined with small temples, ashrams, shops, and tea stalls. Signs of the new globalized economic development are here, too. A luxurious and exclusive residency boasting a future golf course has recently come under construction along this section of the road.

The Govardhan *tareti* is a storied landscape that is "read" by performing *parikrama*. Underground springs and runoff from the mountain feed over two dozen ponds located within the *tareti*. One located to the west of the regenerating forest north of Jatipura well illustrates the storied nature of this sacred land. The name of this pond is Bilachukund, the "Toe-Ring Pond," for one afternoon Radha came here to play in this tree-lined pond with her *sakhi*s, or girlfriends, and lost a toe-ring.[37] Disguised as a *sakhi*, Krishna secretly joined the group. After much searching, which failed to find the toe-ring, Radha became despondent. Still masquerading as one of her girlfriends, Krishna found the lost toe-ring. Radha was so delighted that she asked her girlfriend what she might give as an expression of her appreciation. When the girlfriend requested they spend the night together, Radha recognized her beloved Krishna beneath the disguise. The two passed the night in blissful pleasure in a bower on the shore of this pond. Bilachukund is also considered one of eight doorways into Mount Govardhan.[38] Today pilgrims sit on the edge of this pond contemplating its story while appreciating the reflection of a circle of large verdant trees on the rippling surface of the water.

About two miles from Jatipura, the inner pathway ends and spills out of the forest into the town of Govardhan. The soft dirt path gives way to cement and asphalt roads, which tear at the bare feet of tender-footed walkers. The rocky mountain is progressively obscured by an increasing number of buildings strung along the road. Govardhan is the largest of the five towns located in the *tareti*, with a population approaching twenty thousand. Many of the buildings within the town were built by the descendants of the Jat kings of Dig and Bharatpur, who were patrons of the town from the eighteenth to mid-twentieth century. Buses loaded with pilgrims rumble through the town on a regular basis.

A road running east and west cuts through the middle of Govardhan town and is the only road that crosses over the mountain. This road was built during the British period; during its construction it generated much controversy among local residents who thought the road would harm Mount Govardhan. A compromise was reached. Truckloads of dirt were laid down as a thick cushion on top of the tender stone mountain before the road was completed. The road was placed in this particular location because of a naturally occurring passageway through the hill called Dan Ghati. A "ghati" is a narrow mountain pass, and "dan" means a tribute or toll tax, since this is said to be the place where Krishna would position himself with his buddies to stop Radha and her girlfriends to demand payment for safe passage with their milk and yogurt. This, of course, was a ploy for a playful interaction with Radha and her friends.

Dan Ghati is the site of the very popular Daniray temple. Within this temple complex is a large and imposing Govardhan stone that is considered to be a major Mukharvind, or "Lotus-Mouth," of the mountain. During the daytime this stone is accessible for direct worship by devotees, including caressing and making offerings of milk and flowers, but in the evening the attendant priests take over and with ornate clothing and jewelry transform the stone into the cowherd Krishna. This is likely the most visited of all the public Govardhan stones, since buses frequently stop immediately outside the entrance of the Daniray temple at Dan Ghati some steps below the surface of the road to unload pilgrims. If the temple is too crowded or their time is too short, pilgrims can also peek at this impressive Govardhan stone through large openings in the arched wall of the temple that lines the road above.

The *parikrama* pathway continues through Bara Bazar, the main market of Govardhan. Those performing the circumambulation of the mountain have to push their way through crowds of busy shoppers and dodge loud-horned motorcycles whizzing along this main thoroughfare. On their right they pass the Lakshmi-Narayana temple, another popular place to start the *parikrama* of Mount Govardhan. Inside this temple are embodied forms of two divine couples, the majestic goddess Lakshmi and the lordly Narayana, as well as the more intimate forms of the lovers Radha and Krishna. The embodied forms of all four deities consist of ornately adorned Govardhan stones.

Before leaving the town of Govardhan, those circumnavigating the sacred hill usually visit the important site of Manasi Ganga (Figure 1.5), which is situated in the center of the mountain and is the largest of the many ponds found within the *tareti*. A crop of Govardhan rocks poke out from the middle of this pond, which is ringed with many temples and filled with water said to have been brought by Krishna from the Ganges River. One day he was grazing his cows at the base of Mount Govardhan when a demon named Vatsasur ("Calf Demon") disguised itself as one of Krishna's calves. Krishna recognized the demon and killed it before it could do any damage, but in so doing he incurred the sin of killing a cow.[39] In order to wash away this

Figure 1.5. Manasi Ganga pond in center of Govardhan town; the Mukut Mukharvind temple is featured prominently.

burden without leaving Braj, Krishna mentally transported water from the Ganges River into a hollow in the center of the Mount Govardhan and bathed in it, thus creating Manasi Ganga, the "Mental Ganges," and making its holy water available at the mountain. Sometime later, Krishna's father, Nanda, was preparing the cowherds for a journey to the Ganges for a sacred bath. Not wanting them to leave Braj, Krishna announced: "The Ganges is right here!" He further astonished the cowherds by causing the goddess of the Ganges to appear out of the pond. The cowherds honored Ganga Devi by bathing in the pond and placing a ring of lamps around its shore. The custom of encircling this pond with a ring of oil lamps continues to be practiced today on the dark night of Diwali, the new moon of the fall lunar month of Kartik.

Based on early textual itineraries, some people believe that the best way to begin the *parikrama* of Mount Govardhan is by first bathing in Manasi Ganga. The *Varaha Purana*, for example, instructs pilgrims to begin this way and then to visit Haridev, an early temple on the pond's shore that houses a form of Krishna in his mountain-lifting pose.[40] According to Pushti Margiya and Gaudiya Vaishnava sources, both Vallabhacharya and Chaitanya established a precedent for their respective denominations of Vaishnavas by beginning their circumambulation of Mount Govardhan with a bath at Manasi Ganga, although today the majority of Pushti Margis initiate their *parikrama* from Jatipura, and most Gaudiya Vaishnavas start at Radhakund.[41] Following the older tradition, the Gaudiya leader Rupa Gosvamin in his Sanskrit *Mathura Mahatmya* recommends taking a bath in Manasi Ganga, having *darshan* of Haridev, and then beginning the circumambulation of Mount Govardhan.[42]

Situated on the southern bank of Manasi Ganga, the Haridev temple was in all probability the most important Krishna temple in the Govardhan complex prior to the sixteenth century. The *murti*, or embodied form of divinity accommodated in this temple, is Govardhan Dhara, Krishna holding Mount Govardhan aloft on the tip of the little finger of his left hand. This is one of the oldest temples in Braj, and is said to be one of four major Krishna temples established by Krishna's great-grandson Vajranabh. The current Gosvami priests of the Haridev temple narrate a rediscovery of Haridev in the sixteenth century that involves the temple's founder saint, Keshavacharya. They say this saint had a dream that told him to go to the nearby pond of Bilachukund and retrieve from its waters the *murti* of Haridev. The present temple housing this *murti* is a long-standing structure, built in 1580 out of red sandstone by Raja Bhagawant Das of Amber, Rajasthan, just after he joined the service of the Mughal emperor Akbar. It later came under the patronage of the Bharatpur-based Vaishnava Jat kings, who managed the temple until India's independence in 1947.

The other temple at Manasi Ganga mentioned in early literature is Chakreshwar, or "Lord of the Circle." This temple is located on the northern side of the pond and is said to be one of the four Shiva shrines established by Vajranabh in Braj shortly after Krishna's departure. The Shankara priests who maintain this temple, which houses five Shiva lingams, report that it honors Chakreshwar, Shiva as a protector of the sphere of Braj, who drank up all the water from the violent seven-day storm unleashed by Indra. Nearby stands a meditation hut that was used by the early Gaudiya Vaishnava leader Sanatana Gosvamin, who lived here during the years he was daily circumambulating Mount Govardhan. It is said that mosquitoes were once so thick that Sanatana decided to leave the pond. But Chakreshwar appeared before him and promised to ensure the mosquitoes would leave him alone. Local inhabitants attest that this place still remains mosquito free. There is also a *baithak* on this spot where Vallabhacharya performed a seven-day reading of the *Bhagavata*

Purana. The *Chaurasi Baithak Charitra* records that Chakreshwar appeared on each of the seven days to listen to his readings.[43]

Although it was not mentioned in the older texts, today the most visited temple at Manasi Ganga is the Shri Giriraj Mukut Mukharvind ("Crown Lotus-Mouth of Shri Giriraj") temple, located on the east side of the pond. Many people claim that this temple, built under patronage of the eighteenth-century Jat king Suraj Mal Singh, is the most important place in Braj for worshiping Mount Govardhan. Devakinandan Kumheriya, a local poet and scholar of the sacred mountain living in Govardhan town, writes: "Among all the major temples within the area of Govardhan this temple is the one where hundreds of devotees daily bathe and worship the supreme 'crown-stone' (*mukut-shila*) of Shri Giriraj Maharaj."[44] The crest-stone of the Mukut Mukharvind rests on the tip of a rocky outcrop from the hill that is pro-truding above the surface of Manasi Ganga and is now surrounded by the large temple described in some detail in Chapter 3. The Mukut Mukharvind consists of a pair of Govardhan stones that are elaborately dressed every eve-ning and give strong indication of the dual identity of Mount Govardhan as both divinity and supreme devotee.

The mountain progressively disappears as one leaves the town of Govardhan and travels north along the west side of the mountain, passing numerous temples, ashrams, and tea stalls lining the outer rim of the road, with farm fields and wetlands behind. There is no inner path on this section of the *parikrama* circuit, but those who do not care to walk on the asphalt road can take a dirt path that follows the inner side of the motorway. About two miles north of Govardhan town, one comes to another pond on the inner side of the pathway called Uddhavakund, the "Pond of Uddhava."

Uddhava was one of Krishna's close advisers. After Krishna departed Braj for Mathura, he sent Uddhava back to Braj to counsel and comfort the love-torn *gopi*s, the female lovers of Krishna, and teach them the renuncia-tory path of yoga. Krishna's real intention in doing this, however, was to give Uddhava exposure to the exemplary love of the Braj *gopi*s. Once he witnessed their supreme love, Uddhava abandoned his arrogant knowledge and ascetic yoga and became immersed in devotional love. Arriving at the place of this pond, he prayed to be reborn in Braj as a humble creeper so that he could be immersed in dust from the feet of the *gopi*s. He is believed to still reside near this pond in vegetative form. Pilgrims come here to honor the *gopi*s as the exemplars of devotional love and to ask Uddhava to grant them the same devotional abilities, so that they too can sink more deeply into the loving world of Mount Govardhan.[45]

After Uddhavakund, the *parikrama* path crosses the Yamuna canal via an arched bridge and enters the complex of Radhakund, "Radha's Pond," a town in the *tareti* with a population of about eight thousand. There is no discernible sign of the mountain above ground at this northernmost tip of the *parikrama*; local word has it that the mountain has already disappeared here due to Pulastya's curse. There are a great many temples in Radhakund—most containing Govardhan stones—but Radhakund pond is the dominant feature and major focus of this sacred site. The *parikrama* pathway loops around the pond, which is actually two interconnected ponds: Radhakund and Shyamkund. These two ponds are considered by many to be the eyes of Mount Govardhan, as this northern-most section of the mountain is regarded as its head. The story of these ponds tells how they came into being.

A fierce demon named Arishta once took the form of a bull and planned to attack Krishna's encampment of cowherds. Krishna went out to meet Arishta and killed him before he could hurt anyone. That night Krishna rendez-voused with his favorite lover Radha in the forest. He reached out with great eagerness to take her into his arms. But Radha stopped him, saying, "Hey Shyamsundar, you killed a bull today which made you unclean. Don't touch me!" Taken aback, Krishna asked Radha how he could cleanse himself of this polluting sin. She informed him that he could purify himself only by bathing in the waters of all pilgrimage sites, and declared that only after so doing would she allow him to embrace her. Krishna was too impatient to make love to Radha to leave for a few moments, let alone the amount of time re-quired to visit every pilgrimage site in the world. He immediately shoved the heel of his foot into the ground, forming a large crater, and then summoned the sacred waters of all pilgrimage sites to fill the depression and create the enchanting pond that came to be known as Shyamkund, "Krishna's Pond." When it was full, Krishna quickly bathed and readied himself for Radha's em-brace. Radha was very impressed, but Krishna's boastful attitude presented a challenge, which she and her girlfriends met by using their bracelets to dig another pond. Not a drop of water, however, came into the hole they exca-vated. To remedy this situation, Radha and her girlfriends formed a line to Manasi Ganga and with the aid of clay pots began transferring water to the new pond. This proved to be an impossible task. Seeing Radha in a humil-iating situation, Krishna gave her a wink and began filling her pond with the holy water from his own. Thus the pair of sacred ponds came into being.

Today the entire complex of the two interconnected ponds and the village that sprang up around them is referred to as Radhakund.

The pair of ponds are sacred not only because of their divine origins, but also because they are the site of the midday lovemaking of the affectionate couple, who are especially fond of sporting in the water of Radha's pond near Mount Govardhan. Since the ponds are now believed to contain the love juice that flows between Radha and Krishna, the very water is regarded as a concrete form of the love of Radha and Krishna. Moreover, the two ponds are considered natural embodied forms of the divine couple; Radhakund is non-different from Radha, and Shyamkund non-different from Krishna.[46]

A passageway exists beneath the causeway that separates the two ponds, allowing the sacred liquid that fills them to flow back and forth and inter-mingle. Radhakund and Shyamkund, then, are two bodies of water that share the same fluid. The two ponds aptly serve as concrete forms for the theological contemplation of the relationship between Radha and Krishna. They are aquatic forms of the divine couple that can be compared to an illustration found on the walls of many homes, shops, and temples throughout Braj. Entitled *ek pran do deha* ("one life essence, two bodies"), this picture shows Radha and Krishna's limbs so entwined that it is difficult to discern where one body begins and the other ends (Figure 1.6).

Thus, the real deity of much Braj Vaishnavism is not simply Krishna, or Radha, but the non-dual–dual divinity Radha-Krishna. Two bodies, one life essence; two ponds, one liquid—multiplicity in non-duality. These images tell us much about the conception of ultimate reality or divinity in Braj Vaishnavism.[47]

Many Gaudiya Vaishnavas consider the Radhakund pond to be the most sacred place of all "because it overflows with the nectar of Krishna's love."[48] According to Gaudiya sources, Chaitanya specifically sought out Radhakund when he visited Govardhan, but no one could show him its exact location. Through meditative insight he identified a small pond northeast of Mount Govardhan as Radhakund and bathed in it ecstatically. He left the work of excavating the pond and developing the site to his followers. On his travels around Bengal, Chaitanya met the son of a wealthy landowner. This man, later known as Raghunath Das, had a childhood characterized by profound religious feelings; after meeting the charismatic saint Chaitanya, he firmly resolved to lead a religious life. Escaping the ambitious plans of his father, Raghunath joined Chaitanya and his band of Krishna devotees. The saint gave him a stone from Mount Govardhan, which he devoutly worshiped

Figure 1.6. Radha and Krishna in "one life essence, two bodies" pose.

throughout his life as a special form of Krishna. Raghunath stayed with Chaitanya in Bengal until the saint's death in 1533, and then traveled to Braj to take up residency in Radhakund at the edge of his beloved mountain. Here he spent the remainder of his life worshiping the Lord of the Mountain and composing amorous poems about the love affair of Radha and Krishna. As the first *mahant*, or head priest of Radhakund, Raghunath was responsible for enlarging the ponds in the mid-sixteenth century. As the excavation of Shyamkund began, Raghunath had a dream in which King Yudhisthira revealed to him that the five Pandavas, the heroes of the Mahabharata, now resided on the banks of this pond in the form of trees. The pond was thus constructed so as not to disturb these trees, giving it an irregular shape.

Raghunath did not want to use water from the sacred ponds to wash his cooking pots, so he ordered a well to be excavated on the eastern side of the ponds. Workers stopped digging when blood filled the bottom of the well.[49] That night Mount Govardhan appeared to Raghunath in a dream and explained that the workers had cut off the tip of his tongue. The next morning the workers returned to the well and found a stone from the mountain covered with blood. Raghunatha gave instructions to remove the stone, give it a healing bath with milk, and set it up for worship in a temple. The reddish stone, called Giriraj ki Jibhya, the "Tongue of Govardhan," is now housed in a small temple just north of Shyamkund, where it is bathed daily with milk (Figure 1.7). Such stories attest to the animate fashion in which the mountain is regarded.

After walking around the Radhakund ponds, those performing the *parikrama* of Mount Govardhan turn south and begin the journey down the eastern side of the mountain. There is no inner pathway here, only a dirt trail along the inner side of the asphalt road. The Radhakund complex is left behind once the Yamuna canal is crossed. Although the rocky ridge of the mountain begins to reappear here, it is still quite low. After about a mile, one comes to a spectacular pond named Kusum Sarovar, the "Flower Lake." Each side of this square pond is lined with sandstone steps that lead down to the water. On all four sides, octagonal pavilions feature arched windows facing

Figure 1.7. The tongue of Mount Govardhan in its Radhakund temple.

the water; these catch cool breezes coming off the surface of the pond and afford a view of the huge turtles that inhabit its waters. In a garden of flowers near the mountain on the pond's western shore stand impressively ornate cenotaphs built in memory of the famous Jat king Suraj Mal Singh, the great patron of the Braj region and ardent devotee of Mount Govardhan. This is a favorite stop for many of the pilgrims who wander Braj; tour buses are also a frequent sight at the main entrance gate. The pond is said to have been a favorite haunt of Krishna's, too; he would come to this once lush forest and gather flowers to braid into the hair of his beloved Radha. Nearby is another pond, Naradakund, where pilgrims are told the celestial sage Narada bathed to obtain the body of a female *gopi*, allowing him to participate in the intimate love play of Krishna, afterward transforming himself back into a male.

Soon after Kusum Sarovar, continuing south, rock walls of the mountain reappear. The *parikrama* path returns to the bustling town of Govardhan, and the pilgrims once again pass along congested roads through a dense assortment of temples and shops. Less than a mile out of the town, pilgrims are again faced with the choice of taking an inner path that winds through forested terrain or remaining on the road. A mile or two down the inner path, nestled against the eastern slope of Mount Govardhan, is Anyor, another of the five towns in the Govardhan *tareti*, with a population of around five thousand permanent residents. A foot trail over the mountain connects Anyor to Jatipura, situated directly on the other side of the hill. Many associate Anyor with the story of Krishna who, in the form of Mount Govardhan, consumed huge quantities of the food offered by the Braj cowherds before Indra's jealous attack. A popular derivation of the name Anyor is *an or*, which means "Bring more!"—words spoken by Krishna as the hungry mountain when he wanted another helping of food. This is also the location of the house of Saddu Pande, who, according to Pushti Margi sources, at the end of the fifteenth century played a major role in the discovery of Shri Nath-ji, the form of Krishna that emerged from the heart of the Govardhan hill.

After the narrow lanes of Anyor, one comes to Govindkund. This pond is located next to the mountain just below one of its highest points. Surrounded on all four sides with sandstone steps, crowned with a number of large green shade trees, it is remarkably serene. Govindkund is identified with the story of Indra's humble surrender to Krishna after his stormy attack on Braj. Indra respectfully bathed Krishna with abundant water from the celestial Ganges carried in the trunk of his mount, the elephant Airavat, and gave Krishna the name Govind, or "Guardian of the Cows."[50] The sacred water from this honorific bathing produced the Govindkund pond.

Two miles south of Anyor, the inner *parikrama* path, now a continuous stretch of forested land, passes into the state of Rajasthan. This section offers rewarding views of the mountain: steep slopes of stone and imposing boulders, *nilgai* walking along the top of the ridge, and peacocks prancing on its large rocks. This southernmost tip of the mountain is considered to be the tail or foot of Mount Govardhan, hence it is called Punchari, the "Tail." A small temple has recently been built at this site to mark the tip of the mountain; but more importantly, behind the temple is a prominent stone protruding from the mountain that is considered to be the mountain's foot. Pilgrims touch their heads to it with reverence, making direct bodily contact with the mountain god.

Punchari is also the name of a small town of around two thousand people located at the southern end of the mountain. Among the temples of this town, the most famous is Punchari ka Lautha, Lautha being the name of a cowherd friend of Krishna. When Krishna left Braj for Dwarka, Lautha—whose name means "Return"—took a vow not to eat or drink anything until Krishna returned, determined to give up his life here if necessary.[51] However, out of his immense grace for his devotee, Krishna blessed Lautha with the ability to thrive without eating or drinking.[52] The *sindur*-smeared form of Lautha that sits in the temple is quite chubby.[53] In more edible form, pilgrims too have the chance for a taste of Krishna's grace. Across the street from the temple are many outdoor cafes serving a variety of snacks and drinks.

Two interconnected ponds surrounded by sandstone ghats are located near Punchari: Apsarakund ("Pond of the Beautiful Woman") and Navalakund ("Pond of the Youthful Man"). Like Radhakund and Shyamkund, the water is shared by both ponds through an underground passageway; hence they are considered another aquatic version of Radha and Krishna as *ek pran do deha* ("one essence, two bodies). Thus Mount Govardhan is sandwiched between two such pairs of ponds, one at its head in Radhakund and the other at its tail in Punchari.

The *parikrama* path takes a sharp turn here and heads back north. The inner path of deep soft dirt on this part of the mountain is comforting to the feet and quite enjoyable as it passes through another regenerating forest with a large population of monkeys. Vendors frequent these woods with wooden carts loaded with carrots, chickpeas, and bananas for purchase by pilgrims to feed the monkeys, who are considered blessed to be living on the slopes of the sacred mountain. Mount Govardhan appears in rocky splendor as the highest peak on the hill looms above the path. About a mile from Punchari, one comes to Indra Puja, identified as the place where Indra offered a massive amount of food in his repentant worship of Krishna in the form of the mountain. A large Govardhan stone sits beneath a sheltered roof located about twenty meters up the hillside. Today this is a popular site for festive *chappan bhog* offerings, where fifty-six different kinds of food are placed inside a large colorful tent that shelters the elaborate treats. I was told that the figure of fifty-six is calculated by multiplying the quantity of food offerings typically given in a day (eight) by the number of days (seven) Krishna went without food while holding the mountain. During the time of the *chappan bhog* offering, this particular Govardhan stone is elaborately adorned as Krishna in his mountain-holding pose.

In the vicinity of Indra Puja are three ponds also associated with Indra's story. Indrakund is a small, undeveloped pond where Indra is said to have prayed to Krishna for forgiveness for his arrogant attack. A short distance from it is an intricate square pond, surrounded on all four sides with ornate sandstone steps and named Surabhikund after Surabhi, the celestial cow of plenty who supplied the copious amount of milk used by Indra to perform Krishna's worshipful bath (*abhishek*). Close by is Airavatakund, named after Indra's divine elephant mount Airavata, who filled this pond with Ganges water when Indra performed an honorific *abhishek* bath for Krishna. As one returns to the town of Jatipura, there is yet another pond called Rudrakund, "Shiva's Pond." It is said that here Shiva, who in Braj is considered to be a great devotee of Radha and Krishna, shed tears of love while meditating on the divine couple. A temple dedicated to Shiva stands on the shore of this tear-filled pond.

The *parikrama* path has now brought us full circle back to Jatipura. As one approaches the center of Jatipura, thick crowds of enthusiastic Mount Govardhan worshipers fill the narrow lanes approaching the most important religious site in Jatipura these days, Shri Giriraj Mukharvind, "The Lotus-Mouth of the Blessed King of Mountains." One can enter this site from the asphalt road through a bustling market that sells bountiful sweets and copious amounts of milk for worshiping the mountain, or by way of the inner path that hugs the mountain. The major focus of devotional activity here is the Mukharvind *shila*, a very popular place for worshiping the mountain (Figure 1.8).

Figure 1.8. Crowd of pilgrims worshiping the Mukharvind stone in Jatipura.

A large Govardhan stone is attached to the top of a much bigger stone pro-truding from the mountain, forming a sizable body with a head. Two smaller stones have been added to the base of this figure as feet, with the collective effect being an imposing stone body. Throughout most of the day and night the Mukharvind is accessible to anyone who desires to worship here, com-monly by pouring milk over the stone and offering flowers and sweets. But in the evening, attendant priests take charge of the worship. This is much more elaborate worship, involving an ornate dressing of the stone that makes its identification with Krishna apparent.

Considerable developments have taken place here since I first visited this site in the early 1980s, a sign of its steady growth in popularity over re-cent decades. The human-sized stone body now sits under a metal roof that measures approximately one hundred by forty feet. The metal pillars and roof trusses holding up the roof are painted a bright pink, as is a metal fence enclosing the entire structure. The floor within the enclosure is dirt; on a number of occasions I observed people taking a pinch of this sacred substance and popping it into their mouths. Directly in front of the Mukharvind is an opening in the fence that gives access to a *baithak* ("seat") of Vallabhacharya, and just behind this is a *baithak* of his eminent son Vitthalnath, honoring the places where these founder saints once sat. When the nightly honorific waving of the *arati* flame before the Mukharvind takes place, the gathered crowd parts, leaving an open passage so that the two saints can have *darshan* of the adorned stone. The complex worship that is conducted here by the attending priests every evening is described in detail in Chapter 4. To the right of the Mukharvind is a black marble memorial column marking the place where Vallabha's son Vitthalnath is believed to have entered the sacred hill. A large painting of Krishna holding up Mount Govardhan has been placed above the Mukharvind stone. Cowherds gather beneath the shelter of the huge mountain, comprised of a conglomeration of stones, as Krishna smiles alluringly. A short distance from the Mukharvind site is the Dandavati Shila, the place where this description of the *parikrama* circuit began. The circle is now complete. To the left of the Dandavati Shila a natural stone stairway leads to the top of the mountain, to a highly significant temple for many who come to worship Mount Govardhan, especially Pushti Margis, but other groups of Braj Vaishnavas as well.

Shri Govardhan Nath-ji

Situated on one of the tallest spots of the mountain, the Shri Govardhan Nath-ji temple has for centuries been another major center for the worship of Mount Govardhan in yet another of its many intriguing forms. The temple once housed a form of this deity, which is believed to have emerged directly from the heart of the sacred mountain and is therefore considered non-different from it. This appearance of Govardhan, commonly referred to by the shorter name Shri Nath-ji, is perhaps the most prominent of the temple forms of Krishna established in Braj. The cowherd Krishna is depicted in a mountain cave with his left hand holding up Mount Govardhan. Some give a more esoteric explanation, that the gesture of the raised left hand is beckoning his lovers to him. There is something playfully circular about the relationship between Mount Govardhan and the embodied form of Krishna as Shri Nath-ji: the *Garga Samhita* narrates how Mount Govardhan emerged from Krishna's heart, and the stories related to Shri Nath-ji tell how he emerged from the heart of Mount Govardhan. Although Pushti Margi and Gaudiya sources both recount the emergence of Shri Nath-ji, there are significant differences in the versions they tell.

The Pushti Margi account of the emergence of Shri Nath-ji is most fully told in the *Shri Nathji Prakatya Varta*, a text attributed to Hariray, a descendant of Vallabhacharya and influential Pushti Margi writer from the seventeenth century. According to this text, the emerging form of Krishna as Shri Nath-ji was discovered by an Anyor villager named Saddu Pande.[54] One day his cow went missing. While searching for this cow on Mount Govardhan, Saddu Pade discovered an arm sticking out of the ground. A strange voice informed him that the arm belonged to Krishna, who lifted Mount Govardhan and was now standing in a rock cave beneath the mountain. Saddu Pande and nearby residents began worshiping the arm with showers of milk. On the day of Vallabhacharya's birth, the mouth of Shri Nath-ji appeared and Saddu Pande was instructed to daily serve it milk. About this time a saint by the name of Madhavendra Puri arrived at Saddu Pande's house and asked to see the form of Krishna that had emerged out of the hill. Madhevendra tried to offer the deity solid foods, but the deity informed him that he would accept his first food only from the hands of Vallabhacharya.

When Vallabha arrived at Govardhan, he installed the now fully emerged Shri Nath-ji on a pedestal and offered him solid food. Soon after, a wealthy merchant named Purnamal had a dream in which Shri Nath-ji asked him to finance the construction of a temple on Mount Govardhan. A renowned architect from the royal city of Agra had a similar dream and designed the temple. The foundation was laid in 1499 and the temple was finished in 1519.[55] Vallabha initiated the elaborate temple service that has come to characterize the worship of Shri Nath-ji. Because Madhevendra Puri had knowledge of temple worship, Vallabha appointed him, along with some of his Bengali followers from Radhakund, to conduct the necessary rituals.

Madhavendra Puri was most likely a member of a Vedantic school that followed the monistic teachings of the great eighth-century Shaivite ascetic Shankara, but he also drew devotional inspiration from the *Bhagavata Purana*. It is unclear whether he came from Bengal or from southern India, but regardless, he brought with him a form of Vaishnavism linked to passionate bhakti movements that can be traced back to the ninth-century south Indian mysticism of the Alvars, which emphasized an intimate relationship with the Lord.[56] His influence on Gaudiya Vaishnavism is particularly significant, since he was the guru of Chaitanya's guru, Ishwara Puri, the man who initiated Chaitanya into the ecstatic love of Krishna.

Madhavendra Puri's role in establishing the worship of Krishna at Govardhan from a Gaudiya Vaishnava perspective is told in the *Chaitanya*

Charitamrita, composed late in the sixteenth century by Krishnadas Kaviraj.[57] Shortly after arriving in Braj, Madhavendra was drawn to Mount Govardhan. Intoxicated with love, he circumambulated the mountain with great reverence. He took a bath in the Govindkund pond and sat on its bank to fast and meditate. (A small shrine standing on the west side of Govindkund commemorates this event.) While meditating, Madhavendra was approached by a beautiful cowherd boy who offered him some milk, informing him that no one fasts in Braj, a land of pleasurable enjoyment. When Madhavendra asked him where he was from, the boy told him that he lived nearby. That night the beautiful boy returned to Madhavendra in a dream and took him to a nearby grove of trees on Mount Govardhan. He explained that this is where he resided and complained that he was suffering from the cold rains and scorching heat. The boy revealed himself to be Krishna-Gopal, the one who lifted Mount Govardhan, and then instructed Madhavendra to take him out of the grove, bathe him with water from Govindkund, and install him in a sheltered temple on top of the mountain. The next morning Madhavendra went to the grove of trees and uncovered an astonishing life-size form of Krishna, his left arm raised in the mountain-holding posture. With the aid of nearby villagers he performed the requested tasks. He organized a huge feast and offered it to the divine form that had emerged from the mountain, and that came to be known as Shri Nath-ji. After overseeing the services in the temple for a period of two years, Madhavendra had another dream in which he was instructed to travel to southern India to secure sandalwood paste for cooling Shri Nath-ji. He turned the service of the temple over to some Bengali priests and set off on his journey. He never retuned.

Although Gaudiya sources attribute an even greater role to Madhavendra Puri in the discovery of Shri Nath-ji and the initiation of his worship, both Pushti Margi and Gaudiya Vaishnava accounts agree that the early services in the Shri Nath-ji temple were in the hands of Bengali Brahmin priests. This arrangement lasted for fourteen years until the temple manager assigned by Vallabhacharya, a fiery poet named Krishnadas with ambitions to control the temple's worship, expelled the Bengalis. The expulsion of the Bengalis from the Shri Nath-ji temple atop Mount Govardhan is one of the earliest signs of a developing competition between the Pushti Margis and Gaudiya Vaishnavas in Braj. According to Pushti Margiya sources, the dispute eventually came before the Mughal court in Agra, where Krishnadas was supported by Todar Mal and Birbal, two powerful Hindu officers serving in Akbar's court.[58] The resulting royal ruling put Pushti Margis in sole possession of the Shri Nath-ji temple.

Because of growing concerns caused by some anti-Hindu activities of the Mughal emperor Aurangzeb, Shri Nath-ji was removed from the top of Mount Govardhan in 1669. After a two-year sojourn, Shri Nath-ji arrived in the Rajasthani desert just north of Udaipur, and according to Pushti Margiya sources, refused to move from this location. A new temple was constructed and a pilgrimage town that came to be known as Nathdwara gradually sprang up. The Shri Nath-ji temple of Nathdwara is now one of the most popular Krishna temples in the world.

Vallabha's son, Vitthalnath, bears responsibility for the elaborate style of worship associated with Shri Nath-ji. The embellishment includes the use of seasonally varied perfumes, weather-dependent clothing, bright jewels, fragrant flowers, ornate paintings, and abundant food offerings. Vitthalnath also emphasized the role of temple music; Pushti Margi sources credit him with appointing eight poets to sing before Shri Nath-ji, who came to be known as the Ashtachap, or "Eight Seals." This group was comprised of four disciples of Vallabhacharya—the famous blind poet Surdas, Paramanandadas, Kumbhandas, and Krishnadas—and four disciples of Vitthalnath—Chaturbhujdas, Nandadas, Chhitaswami, and Govindaswami.

Ties between Mount Govardhan in Braj and the Shri Nath-ji temple in Nathdwara remain strong. A temple priest at the Shri Nath-ji temple atop Mount Govardhan took me to the divine couple's bedroom at the back of the temple. On one wall of this large and beautifully decorated room is a doorway. The priest opened the door with a knowing smile, revealing an entrance to a cave. He explained that an underground passageway connects this temple with the temple of Shri Nath-ji some 350 miles away in Rajasthan. Each night Shri Nath-ji returns to this bedchamber via the tunnel to make love with his beloved Radha.

Both story and ritual performance illustrate the notion that there is no difference between Mount Govardhan and Krishna as Shri Govardhan Nath-ji. In fact, Shri Nath-ji is considered by many to be the divine personified form (*adhidaivik svarupa*) of Mount Govardhan. Again, this is an account of mutual emergence: Mount Govardhan emerged from the heart of the cowherd Krishna, and Krishna in the form of Shri Nath-ji emerged from the heart of Mount Govardhan. The divine figure currently housed in the Mathuradhish temple in Jatipura aptly demonstrates this emerging dual identity of Mount Govardhan and Shri Nath-ji.[59] Unlike the relief form of

Shri Nath-ji in Nathdwara, the form of Shri Nath-ji worshiped in the Jatipura temple has been carved out of—or as one of the head priests of this temple told me, emerged out of—a large stone from Mount Govardhan. Although the Nathdwara deity is a free-standing sculptural form, the Jatipura deity is still connected to an uncarved portion of the mountain stone. Both the stone and Shri Nath-ji are simultaneously visible.

The dual forms give clear expression to the identification between Krishna and Mount Govardhan. The deity that holds the mountain and the mountain itself are one and the same. Krishna as Shri Govardhan Nath-ji, the glorious Lord of Govardhan, is a god of stone.

2

Between a Rock and a Hard Place

The Challenges of Difference

Our challenge is to find a meaningful way to hold together at once
two or more irreconcilable positions and to do so without forced or
too easy difference-denying solutions.[1]

Between a rock and a hard place
You'd better stop, put on a kind face.[2]

Worship of a god of stone. What are we to do with that? As one who works to
interpret, translate, and explain aspects of Hindu religious culture primarily
for an American readership, I stand between a rock—Mount Govardhan—
and a hard place—American society. For most Americans the worship of
stones exemplified by Sunita at the beginning of the Introduction is hard to
understand. This practice is alien, weird, absurd, unreasonable, or silly and
childish, perhaps even sinful. Comprehending it in any acceptable manner
seems extremely difficult, maybe impossible. The object of worship is
strange, and the method of worship is strange. Ultimate divinity appearing
in a natural form like a mountain, a singular shape-shifting deity assuming
countless forms, and the infinite taking the finite form of a physical stone that
graciously presents itself for bathing, dressing, feeding, and other kinds of
intimate interaction are very foreign to the dominant religious perspective of
the United States, largely shaped by the post-Reformational interpretations
of an Abrahamic religion. This is a case of radical difference.

Loving Stones. David L. Haberman, Oxford University Press (2020) © Oxford University Press.
DOI: 10.1093/oso/9780190086718.001.0001

Why Cultural Difference?

How is it some people take for granted that God can take the form of a mountain or stone while others regard this notion as absurd—or even worse, as an egregious religious error? Why is there such extreme difference among human beings? Although answers based on ethnic and racial variances were popular during much of the period of colonial expansion, these have long since been discredited as categorically problematic and have been left behind for explanations that take into account the dissimilar circumstances and histories experienced by different groups of humans. The latter approach assumes a universal human nature that varies considerably in dissimilar environments—both physical and cultural. But how do we account for the specific cause of cultural differences?

I made a point of asking worshipers of Mount Govardhan how they would explain the difference between the way they regard sacred mountains and stone worship and the way these are typically viewed in the United States. While observing activities in the Dan Ghati temple in the town of Govardhan one morning, I met a businessman from Agra who, after finishing the honorific circumambulation of Mount Govardhan, had come to this temple to worship the mountain through the Mukharvind stone housed here. I asked him why he thinks most Americans and Indians generally view mountain and stone worship differently. He said, "Customs (*riti*) and traditions (*parampara*) in India have taught us that God can appear as a mountain or stone. In American people are taught something different." He, of course, believed his particular cultural way of viewing the mountain to be correct. The first term he used—*riti*, which I translate as "custom"—refers to the specific habits of behavior accompanied by shared understandings that develop within a particular society. It can also be rendered as "way," for, in a sense, this man was saying the worship of stones and mountains "is our way," while Americans have different ways. The second term he used is worthy of further consideration. The dictionary meaning of the Sanskritic-Hindi word *parampara* is "tradition," "succession," or "proceeding from one to another (as from father to son);" but *parampara* literally means "one following the other"—or even more literally, "an other following an other," since *para* by itself means "an other."[3] It also may be translated to mean "family line,"[4] for the other that one typically follows is what sociologists of knowledge refer to as a "significant other," usually understood to be the parent or elder responsible for raising a child. Here in a very different language is expressed an insight shared by sociologists of knowledge: people conceptualize reality the way they do because they were socialized into a certain reality while growing up within a particular family in a specific time and place.[5] Change the birth family or social setting and the sense of reality is altered.

Most would agree that the world of everyday life generally taken for granted by people varies from group to group. One has only to survey the wide-ranging diversity of cultures around the globe and throughout history to be struck by the enormous multiplicity in human conceptions of reality and related behavior. Neither fixed nor singular, reality is remarkably fluid and variable for human beings. The immense plasticity of human beings and the vast creative variety in ways of being human seem to be rooted in a biological condition that lacks the instincts that provide programmed, stable direction in the conduct of other animals. Some social scientists have labeled this characteristic of human beings as "world-openness" (*Weltoffenheit*).[6] This enables humans to occupy a plurality of possible realities. Any degree of meaningful directional stability that we are to achieve, then, must be provided by non-biological means—that is, by culture. To a large degree, we must make our own world of meaning; conceptual reality for humans is therefore not given, but rather socioculturally constructed. As the anthropologist Michael Taussig writes, "most of what seems important in life is made up and is neither more (nor less) than, as a certain turn of phrase would have it, 'a social construction.'"[7] Socialization is the process by which individuals are inducted into a particular framework of perception, meaning, and behavior; before we are even able to engage in reflection on the nature of reality, we have already come to regard our particular social reality as the really real.

Human beings are remarkably successful at this task, for when we examine the many cultures of the world we do not find people in a state of constant and unstable flux; rather, they occupy a taken-for-granted everyday reality, complete with conceptual commitments and established patterns of conduct.[8] Since human conceptions and corresponding behavior are constructed in different ways in different places and times, they are by nature bound to be different. Although the reality of the everyday into which one is first socialized seems to have an unshakable hold on one for life, it may be possible through conscious effort to glimpse the world in another fashion. Though there is much debate about the degree to which this is achievable, it is nevertheless the aim of cross-cultural understanding. What might the world be like from another cultural perspective? What is our relationship to other conceptual worlds of meaning? At the very least, this all suggests that something as simple as a mountain is not so simple after all.

When I asked a man I met in the town of Govardhan who was circum-ambulating the sacred mountain with a group of friends what he would say to Americans who do not believe that God takes the form of a mountain or stone, he barked with a disdainful wave of his hand: "There's no need to ex-plain this to anyone who does not understand. Let the fools be! We will carry on honoring Giriraj-ji." Reality seemed to be firmly set for this man, who assumed that anyone who did not share his outlook was an idiot—not an uncommon human response. The French statesman Montaigne had already noted in the sixteenth century that "each man calls barbarism whatever is not his own practice . . . for we have no other criterion of reason than the example and idea of the opinions and customs of the country we live in."[9] Most people simply assume that the way they see the world is the correct way of seeing it. Recognition of this appears to have occurred since humans began reflecting on cultural differences. Back in the fifth century BCE, the Greek historian Herodotus stated: "If anyone, no matter who, were given the opportunity of choosing from amongst all the nations in the world the set of beliefs which he thought best, he would inevitably—after careful considerations of their relative merits—choose that of his own country. Everyone without exception believes his own native customs, and the religion he was brought up in, to be the best."[10] All this is due to the manner in which the reality one is socialized into becomes taken for granted and is experienced subjectively as the way things unquestionably are.

With an increasing awareness of today's pluralistic world, a number of worshipers of Mount Govardhan I spoke with seemed to have given thoughtful consideration to the existence of different viewpoints and were able to recognize the cultural source of their own views about sacred stones and mountains. One man acknowledged that he himself believes God can assume the form of a mountain because the great majority of people in India believe this, venturing, "ninety percent of the Hindus in this country accept this."[11] He attributed the ease with which people in India accept this to the widespread belief that "though one, Krishna has thousands of forms." Some explained the differing conceptions of stone-worshiping Indians and their non-stone-worshiping American counterparts implicitly in terms of social-ization or enculturation. A man I came to know in Jatipura told me: "We see Giriraj this way because our fathers see him this way, and our grandfathers saw him this way too. We follow in their footsteps." Some even employed the concept of culture explicitly, using either the Hindi word *sanskriti* or occasionally the English word "culture" in their explanations. "This is our 'culture,'" a Hindi-speaking woman from Bombay said to me near the Mukharvind stone in Jatipura while explaining why she regards Mount Govardhan as an embodied form of divinity (*Bhagavan svarupa*); "Americans have a different culture." Others explained the differences in terms of history. A woman from Pune visiting the Jatipura Mukharvind maintained, "You see, we have particular feelings and experiences because of our history (*itihas*, a Sanskritic-Hindi word that can also be translated as 'tradition'). We see Giriraj-ji through this history. Those with a different history will not see it this way." During a conversation about Mount Govardhan with a young priest living in Vrindaban, I remarked that it might seem strange to some people that a mountain is worshiped as God. He responded, "This isn't really strange because Hinduism has a long and unbroken history of nature worship (*prakriti pujan*). We worship not just mountains, but also trees and rivers. Europeans used to do this too, but their history changed. Worship of Giriraj-ji is just a continuation of Hindu nature worship."

A number of people accounted for the different American views in terms of a lack of right knowledge. "You have to have the right knowledge to see God in this stone, and many Americans don't have this kind of knowledge," a couple from Gujarat told me. A resident of Jatipura expressed this in a more judgmental fashion:

> They do not have the right knowledge. There are two kinds of souls: bright and dimwitted. The ones that do not regard Giriraj as God (*Bhagavan*) are ignorant. They just look at Giriraj and only see an ordinary physical mountain. They have a veil of delusion over their eyes and cannot see deeply. But just as Bhagavan gave Arjuna a divine eye so that he could see his divine form, so too with the grace of Bhagavan the veil can be pulled back and the divine form of Giriraj can be revealed to anyone.

I asked an English-speaking computer programmer from Bangalore who had just finished worshiping and circumambulating Mount Govardhan with his wife and young daughter what he would say to those who believed that God could not possibly manifest as a mountain or stone. He put the matter in terms of story, a major carrier of Vaishnava views: "They would need to know the stories. We see the mountain through the eyes of certain stories, they don't. I would tell them to learn the stories about Giriraj-ji, then they would see the mountain differently." My good friend Mohan, a close companion from a Braj village with whom I lived while staying in Jatipura, expressed a similar notion when I asked him what he would say to those in America who don't believe that God can take the form of a mountain or stone. He first reaction was: "I would just tell them that it is a form of God (*Bhagavan svarupa*). That's all." But after a few moments of reflection he added, "They don't have the knowledge. If they came to India and spent time here like you have then they would understand how this mountain is a form of God."

Shrivatsa Goswami, an eminent scholar-priest who lives in Vrindaban, offered his view on this issue with more specificity. He told me that the difference has to do with those raised within the "Abrahamic religious traditions" and those raised within non-dual religious traditions such as Hinduism.

> Americans are still greatly influenced by certain elements of the Abrahamic traditions. They see God as very abstract and distant. But here God is before our eyes. For us, everything is God. That tree, that river, that stone, and so forth. We think of God as *sat-chid-ananda* ("being-consciousness-bliss"). The *sat*—being or existence—element means that everything that exists is God. So for us regarding a mountain or stone as a form of God is not difficult or problematic. One's perception is determined by one's knowledge. So those in the West would have to become open to the idea that a mountain can be divine to see Mount Govardhan as God. I think that consideration of the environmental crisis and ecological developments within Christian theology are beginning to make this more possible.

One of the implications of this non-dual perspective, then, is a comfortable acceptance of the immanent presence of divinity in the world of natural entities such as mountains or stones. A Western-educated, English-speaking professional woman who has lived her entire life in northern India said to me during a conversation about cultural difference: "For me the idea that God can take the form of a mountain or a stone is completely normal. That's how we see it. That is how we were brought up. I don't think that I could see the world otherwise." In effect, she was acknowledging that the reality one is socialized into is assumed to be singularly authentic.

Possibilities of Understanding Cultural Difference

But can any of us really ever "see the world otherwise?" Can we actually understand the worlds of meaning within other cultures? Can a person raised outside of Hindu culture come to see Mount Govardhan in a manner anywhere near the way it is viewed by its worshipers in Braj, or from—in the famous words of the founder of the ethnographic method, Bronislaw Malinowski—"the native's point of view?"[12] Most simply, can we understand a cultural other? This question has animated a great deal of renewed debate within the field of anthropology in recent decades, much of it sparked by the publication of Edward Said's book *Orientalism* (1978),[13] widely recognized as an initial cornerstone of postcolonial studies; and given prominent voice in *Writing Culture* (1986),[14] a volume of essays edited by James Clifford and George Marcus said to be "perhaps the single most influential anthropological book in recent decades."[15] The former demonstrated how the Oriental "other" turns out to be a construction of the West employed to assert a "civilized" self-identity; the latter raised deep suspicions about the validity of ethnography in general. Much of the current debate regarding the possibility of cross-cultural understanding hinges on the nature of anthropological knowledge and the impasse of relativism generated by some of the insights of postmodernism. The anthropologist Maurice Godelier renders the crucial question this way: "How can we come to understand and explain the existence of facts, attitudes and representations that have never been part of our own ways of living and thinking?"[16] Attuned to our current challenge, how can we come to understand and explain the religious world associated with the worship of Mount Govardhan?

The academic study of other cultures yields what is typically called "anthropological knowledge." What is anthropological knowledge, and what kind of understanding does it offer? As might be expected, there is no single answer to this question. Furthermore, there is much disagreement regarding the very possibility of even understanding other cultures. Horns of another dilemma appear between the proverbial rock and a hard place, for the task of understanding the "other" in a world of cultural difference is a complicated affair. Two opposite prospects materialize to bookend the wide gamut of perspectives on the possibility of cross-cultural understanding. The first assumes that understanding others is fairly easy and straightforward, while the second has serious doubts that it is even possible. Differing conceptions of the "other" inform both of these positions. Furthermore, the former is itself composed of at least two dissimilar views: We know them because they are essentially us, and we know them because they are the opposite of us. This last view is sometimes accompanied by the assertion that we know them perhaps better than they know themselves, and frequently, that they are wrong and in need of radical change. This was a common mode of operation in the construction of knowledge about the other within colonial scholarship.

Consideration of specific cultural differences found within the great variety of religious perspectives and practices worldwide is a major enterprise of the comparative study of religions. Assertions that all religions are the same have not been uncommon, and continue to be expressed, especially in the context of today's "new-age" culture. Although laudable irenic aspirations often prompt this claim, such an interpretive approach is questionable, as it ends up eliminating or doing what some call "violence" to difference and otherness.[17] The assertion of the unity of all religions—which tends to focus on the "essence" of religion rather than on practice—is by no means a new idea. At the beginning of the last century, for example, the prominent US Episcopal priest and writer Heber Newton explains, in an article titled "Religion and Religions": "My aim is to suggest hints of the essential unity of religion even now underlying all religions, and the ultimate oneness toward which all religions are forth-reaching."[18] More as declaration than demonstration, he asserts: "All religions are at one in the ideals before them, in the goal towards which they strive. . . . The ethical and spiritual life of all these varieties of Paganism is one and the same ethical and spiritual life which tides the soul of the Christian. . . . One inner essence, therefore, within all the bewildering variant forms which religion assumes."[19] If this is so, there is really no need for "the Christian" to study other religious traditions, for their "bewildering variance" or otherness disappears in an assumption of sameness, and the quest for understanding difference is finished before it begins. In many ways, the popular belief in the essential unity of all religions parallels more serious academic theories about religion formulated in the nineteenth and twentieth centuries by a variety of scholars who sought to identify the universal essence of religion.[20]

The other position that has tended to presume ease in knowing the other involves the assertion of a positive self in opposition to a negative other; that is, rather than avowing the unity of all cultures, here extreme difference is asserted as the self is defined in sharp contrast to the "known" other. Understood through "expert" knowledge, the other is exposed as debased and primitive in comparison to a self whose identity is virtuous and modern.

This is a key insight set forth in Said's *Orientalism*. According to Said, Orientalism is the source of distorted and erroneous cultural representations that depict the (Oriental) other as irrational and psychologically weak, in opposition to the (Western) self, which is rational and psychologically strong. An unbridgeable gap appears between the two. In this case, too, the other is reduced to an "essence" that is assumed to be readily recognizable; the binary opposition of Orientalist knowledge professed the cultural inequality of the exotic other as it privileged the reliable self and justified colonialism in the construction of a superior self-image. Western intervention was thus needed to rescue other cultures from themselves. Violence is done to the other in this binary form of absolute knowledge claimed by Oriental scholars that asserts that "we" know the other better than "they" know themselves. Here, too, however, the other disappears, as it functions as "a sort of surrogate and even underground self."[21]

A foreign cultural practice as unfamiliar as the worship of sacred stones is "known" with assumed confidence through the Western category of "idolatry" without ever engaging the practitioner in conversation, and serves to define the contrasting non-idolatrous "highly civilized" self. The renowned colonial anthropologist Edward B. Tylor's "progressive theory of civilization" is a classic expression of the imperial hierarchical approach of colonialism. "The educated world of Europe and America practically settles a standard by simply placing its own notions at one end of the social series and savage tribes at the other." [22] Tylor identified the most "primitive stage of thought" as that "in which personality and life are ascribed not to men and beasts only, but to *things*. It has been shown how what we call inanimate objects—rivers, *stones,* trees, and so forth—are treated as living intelligent beings."[23] Regarding Hindu stone worship, he writes: "This stone-worship among the Hindus seems a survival of a rite belonging originally to a low civilization." It can be "no doubt dated from remote barbaric antiquity" and is still practiced by Hindus, who are "the greatest idolaters of the world."[24] (The common interpretive strategy that depends on the concept of idolatry will be examined in fair detail in Chapter 5.) Without leaving the comfort of his study, Tylor "knows" the worship of a mountain to be a clear indication of misguided primitive thought. These idolaters are stuck hopelessly in a world of false values, which must be abandoned in the march toward modern civilization as defined by the European self. Difference is erased when sameness is stressed, but in the case where difference is exaggerated yet somehow assumed to be known, it becomes a non-negotiable partition rendering any equitable interaction with the other impossible. The inaccuracies in the representations of other cultures in such approaches have been so great that Said raises serious doubt about the very possibility of understanding cultural differences. True understanding is impossible where the cultural other is obscured by a projection of (non)self.

Many attitudes toward cultural difference have included intentional efforts to expunge it, an approach that is commonly found, for example, in the hegemonic discourse of past missionaries and colonial administrators. Obvious examples of this approach would include the "extirpation of idolatries" and forced conversion of the indigenous populations of the Americas by the Spanish alliance between the conquistadors and Catholic religious orders; the compulsory placement of Native American children in distant East Coast boarding schools where they were forced to give up their name, language, religion, and even haircut; and military warfare, such as the use of Chinese troops to destroy Buddhist institutions in Tibet, and the employment of the US Calvary to end the ghost dance among the Lakota Sioux. More subtle approaches also exist, however, which are sometimes just as effective and insidious. These would include the cooperation between colonial administrators and Oriental scholars in the colonial centers of Calcutta and Bombay that, through historical claims and scholarly discrediting, produced a powerful psychological weapon aimed at undermining the legitimacy of traditional Hindu culture.[25] Ridicule has also served as an effective cultural weapon. The nineteenth-century missionary scholar Abbe Dubois writes, for example, that the worship of sacred stones demonstrates that within Hinduism "there are absolutely no limits to the follies of idolatry."[26] What all these interpretive approaches share is the elimination of difference— which for one reason or another is regarded as threatening. In part, this is because the existence of the other and other ways of being make one's own way less than inevitable and undermines the certainty of one's own reality. Why is there, for example, such tremendous energy expended and anxiety exuded in trying to divorce relationships with inanimate things or objects from the realm of human rationality? The possibility of being challenged and expanded by the other becomes impossible within this kind of approach.

The problematic history of failed bids to understand other cultures has led some scholars to hold grave suspicions about the very possibility of cross-cultural understanding. These sometimes push the radical alterity of another culture to the extreme, typically motivated by strong recognition of cultural relativism. As Hans Penner writes: "Pressed to its logical conclusion, relativism asserts that world-views are incommensurable, that is to say, not translatable, since there is no universal truth, or grammar that provides a bridge between them. . . . It is not religions that are ineffable, inscrutable, incapable of interpretation or translation but languages and cultures themselves. Notice, the logic of relativism does not claim that we have good or bad translations; rather, it claims that translations are impossible because cultures or languages are incommensurable."[27] Is it then possible to make the impossible possible? Penner's own affirmative answer involves recognition that there are some things universally shared by all human beings. He notes that we share

> an indefinite number of beliefs that we agree upon as true. . . . That is to say, we must first of all be in a linguistic context of massive agreement before we can disagree. Thus to assert that people live in different worlds, or that they hold incommensurable world views, or that something can be true in one culture but false in another, is incomprehensible. This conclusion should not be taken to imply that therefore all cultures or religions are the same. It should be clear that "translatability" or "interpretation" entails different languages, cultures, religions.[28]

Penner's position seems to fall in line with the old adage, "nothing human is completely alien to me."[29] But note the middle ground Penner stakes out: other cultures and religion are indeed different, and yet translatable—although this process is never fully complete.

Characterizing the other as too radically different can foster a dangerous denial of any common humanity that can lead to a form of hostility some have labeled "othering." The Croatian writer Slavenka Drakulic, for example, states: "I understand now that nothing but 'otherness' killed the Jews, and it began with naming them, by reducing them to the other."[30] Othering Native Americans allowed Europeans to kill them and take their land; othering Africans allowed Europeans to enslave them and consider them commercial property. Othering the enemy with some non-human label is one of the first moves of warfare. Too great an emphasis on alterity can contribute to the justification and enactment of violence.[31]

What will be our response to the otherness of the religious culture associated with Mount Govardhan? Condemn it, regard it as too radically other to understand, tolerate it with an amused distance, or give it serious consideration as a plausible possibility? In sum, we are presented with two possible oppositional positions with regard to the kind of otherness asserted by the worship of Mount Govardhan. One tends to dismiss its difference in a dark night of sameness, while the other emphasizes radical alterity to such a degree that its understanding is deemed impossible. Regarding the magnitude of understanding, one problematic horn of our dilemma comprises simple realism, the totalizing objectivity of absolute knowledge in which the whole is assumed to be completely representable. The other unfavorable horn maintains a position of radical relativism and incommensurability that in its extreme leads to the solipsistic claim that nothing in the end can be known of a cultural other. In different ways, both do violence to the "other." Might there be a productive middle ground between these two oppositional positions? Between everything and nothing there seems to be something; and this something is better than nothing.

Some years ago, James Clifford declared in his introductory essay for the influential book *Writing Culture*: "Ethnographic truths are thus inherently *partial*—committed and incomplete."[32] Ethnographers work with chance fragments of other cultures, and put them together in their own unique way in a manner determined by their own historical moment and personal concerns. While conducting ethnographic research on Mount Govardhan, for example, I sometimes sought out particular individuals for interviews, but much of the information recorded in this book comes from portions of conversations with people I encountered randomly on my daily excursions to various sites of Mount Govardhan worship, and was determined by my own idiosyncratic set of questions. The partiality of knowledge, then, has to do with both the limited access one has to another culture and the specific interpretive lens through which that culture is viewed. I am aware that much of my own perspective is shaped by a historical moment defined in many ways by an ever-growing environmental crisis and increasing recognition that our relationship with the non-human world has become seriously flawed. The readings of other cultures are always subjective and anthropologists are more present in their ethnographic texts than previously acknowledged. Nevertheless, there remains a significant distinction between ethnography and a novel.[33]

Although the boundary between subjectivity and objectivity, and between imaginative creation and the recording of observable data, is never sharp, there is a difference between explicitly recognized partial knowledge and claims of either complete subjectivity (no knowledge of the other is possible) or complete objectivity (full knowledge of the other is possible). The anthropologist is undoubtedly present in every ethnographic text, and all texts are produced with a particular agenda and set of questions, but this does not rule out the possibility of productive partial knowledge. The mountain and its worshipers really do exist, as can be corroborated by a visit to the mountain, though again my portrayal of them is taken from a particular angle and time, and is thus characteristically partial. How I tell the story of the worship of Mount Govardhan and moreover how readers read this story are influenced by individual interests and proclivities. It is difficult to deny Clifford's assertion that "[i]t has become clear that every version of an 'other,' wherever found, is also the construction of a 'self,' and the making of ethnographic texts . . . has always involved a process of 'self-fashioning.' "[34] The partial truths I pass along in my writing are largely shaped by a longtime search for variety in possible ways of conceptualizing the "natural" world.

Playful Approaches to Understanding Otherness

What does the understanding of something like the worship of Mount Govardhan look like from a middle ground in which certainty is surrendered and absolute knowledge declared unattainable? Many anthropologists have responded to the claims of partial knowledge articulated in *Writing Culture* with a desire to formulate better ways of doing anthropology. David Zeitlyn, for example, asks: "What if the point of anthropology is not to produce a synoptic view of everything. . . . what if we accept our limitations and start thinking seriously and positively about partial views, and about incompleteness."[35] Earnest anthropological knowledge today, then, is more explicitly modest in its claims, but that does not mean that the desire for conveying truthful knowledge has been abandoned. Zeitlyn gives expression to a productive attitude for a middle ground: "In short, without the impulse or desire for accurate description there's no point in continuing, there is nothing to debate. That said, it is not straightforward, which is both the problem and what makes it so interesting."[36] A more humble approach ends the quest for absolute knowledge (historically tied to the politics of control) and accepts that all understanding is incomplete. What makes partial knowledge so interesting? The "something" (as opposed to the everything or nothing) of partial knowledge is a kind of knowledge in which difference remains. And this ever-remaining difference is key to an interpretive approach associated with the concept of playfulness.

The phrase "between a rock and a hard place," like its related companion "being on the horns of a dilemma," conveys a sense of being situated uncomfortably between two problematic choices. The two positions just reviewed concerning the possibility of cross-cultural understanding pose two such extremes: easily available complete knowledge versus no possible knowledge. The question is, how are we to approach the alien other in a productive manner that avoids these two extremes? Might there be fertile ground between a rock and a hard place? Intriguingly, this is the space occupied by Krishna as he lifted the sacred mountain above his head in the most well-known story about Mount Govardhan. And how does he occupy the space between the huge rock of Mount Govardhan and the hard ground beneath him? All the major texts that narrate this story state that Krishna holds the mountain *lilaya*, that is, "playfully."[37] Krishna's mountain-lifting pose is a very popular subject in Hindu art, in which he is almost always portrayed with a teasingly kind smile. Might Krishna's playful stance between a rock and a hard place suggest a more favorable occupation of an in-between territory in the consideration of extreme difference? It is into this playground—situated between the seemingly alien rock of Mount Govardhan worship and the seemingly firm ground of the taken-for-granted reality of primary socialization—that I invite the reader for an appreciative and expansive encounter with the worship of Mount Govardhan. This middle ground provides space for the appearance of an anomalous "third" perspective sandwiched between two opposing and problematic extremes. What might a playful occupation of the middle ground between facile understanding and the impossibility of understanding look like? What kind of interpretation emerges on the borderline between the simultaneously "both/and" or "neither/nor"? Interestingly, the conceptual characteristic of holding together contradictory ideas is at the very heart of the non-dual Vaishnava philosophical traditions of Braj: expressed as *viruddha-dharma-ashraya* (the abode of contradictory views) in Pushti Margiya philosophy and as *achintya-bheda-abheda* (inconceivable simultaneity of difference and non-difference) in Gaudiya Vaishnava thought. Both signal the simultaneity of contradictory opposites within the reality of Krishna's being and actions.

The anomalous characteristic of play has been examined by a number of scholars in the humanities and social sciences. Notably among them is the anthropologist Gregory Bateson, whose notions of play may be useful for further consideration of the in-between position of Krishna's graceful play. Bateson evokes the playful bite of a monkey—an apt example, since monkeys can readily be observed playing on and around Mount Govardhan—and explores the paradoxical nature of play in the context of this playful nip, noting that it is simultaneously a bite and not a bite. Articulating his definition of play, Bateson writes: "These actions, in which we now engage, do not denote what would be denoted by those actions which these actions denote. The playful nip denotes the bite, but it does not denote what would be denoted by the bite."[38] Monkeys are certainly capable of violent bites whose aim is to do great harm to the other for some kind of controlling gain. They are also capable of remaining distant from others, ignoring or refusing to engage in any significant way. The playful nip is a type of genuine engagement, but it has no purpose other than enjoyable interaction. It is at the same time a bite and not a bite, an anomaly appearing between the two. The monkey's playful nip has neither the profit of an actual bite nor the aloofness of a non-bite, and as such has much to offer the consideration of possibilities between controlling the other through absolute knowledge and dismissing the other with no knowledgeable connection. Bateson's conception of play as occupying the in-between space of "not this, not that" opens up an intermediate zone of playfully productive interpretation. In another work he writes: "Play is not the name of an act or action; it is the name of a *frame* for action."[39] In perhaps more pertinent terms, play is a fruitful "approach" to an understanding that requires two seemingly irreconcilable positions be held simultaneously.

Paul Armstrong's representation of the search for fair and fruitful interpretive approaches in transcultural understanding is worthy of serious consideration in our encounter with the conceptions and worship of Mount Govardhan. He begins an essay titled "Play and Cultural Differences" by recognizing the apt critique of the cross-cultural scholarship examined in Said's *Orientalism*, but then proceeds to tease out an implicit ideal for better methods of understanding in Said's analysis. He too places emphasis on striving rather than fully arriving. "If only as an ethical ideal—that is, as a goal to orient our actions as interpreters without necessarily hoping to attain it—contemporary criticism needs a model of transcultural understanding which respects alterity without rendering it inaccessible and which would allow worlds to communicate without sacrificing their integrity, their defining difference."[40] The middle ground between disparaging alterity and rendering it inaccessible is a playful one for Armstrong, as he turns to ponder notions of play in the productive processes of understanding, interpretation, and translation. "The goal of the play between cultures should not be the eradication of differences, a move which would stop the game just as surely as the insistence on the primacy of a single opposition would. . . . the aim of cross-cultural play should be to acknowledge the otherness of different ways of seeing and being in a manner which keeps the encounter between them open to ever new developments."[41] Cross-cultural understanding, then, is a process that keeps moving forward in a world of difference in which novelty, astonishment, and the unknown are ever present. Consideration of the cultural world of Mount Govardhan certainly provides rich occasion for this.

An additional pair of oppositional horns appear while deliberating the place of existing suppositions in understanding the other, for successful understanding in the play of difference has much to do with the way we regard presuppositions. Whether conscious of their source or not, we all hold prior assumptions about something like rock worship, but the manner in which we work with these assumptions is of great importance. One side holds too rigidly to presuppositions, while the other discounts the value of presuppositions altogether. Occupation of the playful middle ground involves working with presuppositions in a conscious and vulnerable manner. All understanding must begin with what one presumes, but one's suppositions must be surrendered as the process of understanding another cultural phenomenon proceeds. Armstrong maintains: "Simply doing without presuppositions in order to make one's mind a more faithful mirror of its objects is not epistemologically possible. Holding oneself open to the challenge of bewilderment is an ethical imperative if one would avoid being captive to one's beliefs."[42] Humility, looseness, and vulnerability with regard to presuppositions are vital to experiencing the potentially enlightening disorientation that leads to an expansion of one's sense of possibilities. Openness to change is an essential element in the distinction between mutable prejudgment and blinding prejudice. Presuppositions are the starting point of all understanding, but must be worked with consciously and left behind when their point no longer fits the case.

While paving the way toward an interstitial perspective on cross-cultural understanding, Godelier insists that the anthropologist "must maintain a state of critical vigilance against the ever-possible intrusion of the judgments that the anthropologist's own society has already formulated about other societies. To decentre oneself is also to suspend one's own judgment, to push back to the very horizon of consciousness the presuppositions of one's own culture and society, including those of one's own life story."[43] I mentioned in the Introduction my encounter with cultural assessments of the worship of Govardhan stones in the United States as absurd, childish, and even sinful.

My own illustrative struggle with the decentering that Godelier promotes began the first time I came to India for the purpose of academic research. I had already made a brief visit to southeastern India several years before this, during which I went to the Aurobindo Ashram in Pondicherry, Tamil Nadu. While on a tour of the area around the ashram, our group passed an active Hindu temple that housed the elephant-headed god Ganesh. I curiously peaked inside the massive, inviting stone doorway. "We don't really pay any attention to what goes on in there," our American-born guide dismissively announced while hurrying me along. "This is what the common uneducated people do." Later that year I re-entered the university and took up what I thought to be a serious study of Hinduism. I developed an understanding of Hinduism that was the result of an educational approach which focused on philosophical systems, an interpretation of the Upanishads based on Shankara's Advaita Vedanta, and conceptions of the divine as impersonal and formless. This was all before the pioneering publications of Diana Eck's book *Darshan* (1981) and the collection of essays titled *Gods of Flesh, Gods of Stone* (1985), both of which introduced the worship of embodied forms of divinity as a central feature of Hindu religious practice.[44]

I returned to India in 1981 to conduct textual research for my doctoral dissertation in the temple town of Vrindaban. Through a series of haphazard events that occurred after the disorientating encounters I described in the Introduction, I met Shrivatsa Goswami, a knowledgeable scholar and temple priest with previous ties to American academics, who arranged for me to stay for the year in his family home within the compound of the Radharaman temple, one of the earliest and most important of the Vrindaban temples. I had come to Vrindaban to study a medieval Sanskrit text,[45] not to observe temple worship, but out of respect for those I was now living with I decided to visit the temple. Nothing had prepared me for the living religious practices I witnessed in this temple: people worshiping and prostrating before a statue-like form of Krishna fashioned from stone. A weak but ever-present voice of my own Protestant religious background resounded within my head. "These people are bowing down before an idol. This is idolatry. I'm in the midst of a bunch of idolaters," I thought as I held my head high above the bowing crowd.

Inadvertently, I found myself face to face with the cultural concept of idolatry embedded within my mind through the particular course of my own socialization. The rather long and complicated process of opening myself to a more productive understanding of what was going on in this temple— initially motivated by the awkward experience of being the only one whose head was not bowed—included developing an awareness of this internalized concept and deconstructing its presence in my thoughts as an appropriate way of looking at Hindu *murti-puja*, the worship of embodied forms of divinity.[46] Perhaps, for me, the most disorienting and challenging of all embodied forms of divinity was the worship of aniconic inanimate objects, particularly stones. It was during my first year of residence in Vrindaban that I encountered the worship of stones from Mount Govardhan, which included dressing and feeding the stones. "Cute, but silly," I believe was my first response. "What kind of religion is this?"

It did not take me long to recognize the limitations and misconceptions in my own interpretive approach to the worship of embodied forms of divinity within temple Hinduism (I include in this designation worship in home shrines and at the pilgrimage sites of natural entities). I realized that my understanding was restricted and distorted by biased cultural presuppositions determined by a particular understanding of the biblical concept of idolatry. Yet it was the very confrontation with my cultural presuppositions, occasioned by time spent in Hindu temples, that precipitated my learning experience. Although disoriented by my initial encounters with *murti-puja*, I remained open to different ways of viewing this unfamiliar cultural phenomenon. In Armstrong's words, I was willing to keep playing: "Interpretation must be playful to move beyond simple self-replication of the assumptions with which one begins . . . a playful attitude includes a willingness to let one's presuppositions and hypotheses be challenged and changed by the encounter."[47] Initially, this is perhaps somewhat akin to the willingness to suspend judgment as one enters into an aesthetic experience; real tears are often shed while reading a novel or watching a film known to be fiction. The "as if" feature of imagination may function as a doorway into another cultural reality, reinforced eventually by the recognition that millions of people are actually living it.

The process of moving beyond one's presuppositions has an intellectual component as well as a situational one. Godelier contends that the process of understanding another culture involves the construction of a "cognitive ego," which he defines as "an intellectual ego that is put together before leaving for the field from mental components—concepts, theories, discussions, controversies—acquired at the university or elsewhere and bearing the mark of their time."[48] My subsequent work at attempting to better understand worshipful interaction with embodied forms of divinity within Hindu religious culture in India, such as Mount Govardhan and its stones, involved a great deal of research into the extensive and sophisticated philosophical conceptions that inform this religious practice, some of them presented in later sections of this book. But this is not enough. Godelier insists that the identity of a productive anthropologist "is not made up of ideas alone. The anthropologist must engage in a practice called participant observation, in the course of which he immerses himself in another society or social milieu so as to study and understand them."[49] The ways of others become more familiar and understandable as one lives among them. The attitude of absurdity toward worshiping stones itself begins to appear questionable—sometimes even absurd—after being immersed in a cultural context where this practice is being performed by hundreds of thousands of people every day—some of whom become good friends.

What attitude toward the other, then, is most conducive to cross-cultural understanding in the academic efforts of a post-colonial world? An attitude of equality and mutual respect of others and their ways of being is crucial to this process. (Equality is not identical to sameness.) Striving to avoid the power differentials and concomitant sense of condescending superiority found within the relationship the missionizing colonizer had toward the colonized other is important. One of the greatest problems with most of the early Oriental scholars, according to Said, is that they did not listen to cultural others and refused to afford them the right to speak for themselves. The professional scholars assumed they already had the keys to truth. Said's Orientalist stood on high judgmental ground, certain about the superiority of his scholarly perspectives and knowledge while holding tightly to his presuppositions. There was no reason in this case to listen to the cultural other, certainly not as an equal. Much is missed in the process of understanding under such circumstances. Said contends that "the principle of inequality" between knower and known in Oriental scholarship rendered understanding impossible. Armstrong counters this tendency by insisting, "The principle of equality between knower and known is hermeneutically necessary."[50] A playful, open interpretive approach implies this equality. Stone worship is no more or less absurd than any other kind of religious practice. Humility with regard to knowledge and one's own ways opens one to the recognition of the equality of the other. If we admit that reality is socially constructed—as I think we must—then we have to recognize that other ways of seeing and being are just as valid (or invalid) as our own. There is no solid place to stand for condescending judgment. An attitude of equality does not mean that difference disappears, but it does involve recognition of a shared humanity. "In Said's view, Orientalism could not see similarity because it was blinded by difference. Its insistence on cultural opposition prevented a recognition of common humanity."[51] In the encounter with the other, Emmanuel Levinas emphasizes honoring the "face of the other," and has argued that "seeing the other as one like me" engenders respect and ethical responsibility.[52] The other is like me, but also other than me; not my self, nor my not-self—different but equal. Krishna smiles upon all with a "kind face"—to use the words of the Rolling Stones—as he stands between a rock and a hard place.

Straddling

If equality and mutual respect characterize playful interpretive relationships in cross-cultural encounters, the situation is one of difference without hierarchy. From this perspective, the worship of Mount Govardhan is viewed as another plausible way of being human, rather than as something enacted by foolish, childish, or deluded people. Fruitful cross-cultural understanding is not conducted from the viewpoint of a high hilltop where the superior looks down on an inferior, but rather on an even *playing* field situated between two different cultures, with a foot partially in each while standing firmly nowhere. The anthropologist Vincent Crapanzano calls this position "straddling." Anthropologists "straddle not just two or more cultures but two or more artifactual realities—call them social constructions if you prefer—that proclaim their reality as their contingent juxtaposition (brought about by the anthropologist's presence) disclaims that reality."[53] The middle ground between a rock and a hard place that is neither fully here nor there is the *place* of straddling; the outlook that operates within this in-between is the *perspective* of straddling; the ethnographic text or translation is the *product* of straddling; and the anthropologist who inhabits the interstices between cultures is the *person* of straddling.

The playful encounter that straddles two cultures, however, does not mean some synthesis that eradicates the unique nature of each culture. The interpretive work and translation of straddling is the result of a meeting of cultures that always leaves a remainder of difference. Alexis Nouss calls the resulting translation "métissage," a combination in which both parts remain fully present. "But métissage should not be confused with mixture, which implies fusion, or with hybridity, which produces a new unit. In the process of interweaving, unforeseeable and unstable, never finished and never final, the different parts retain their identity and their history."[54] The advantage to approaching interpretation through playful straddling is that it does not seek resolution of incongruity, nor involve a flattening of difference, but rather a holding at once of mutually exclusive positions. The marginal translator situated between two cultures has a unique position that gives rise to potentially insightful perspectives on both cultures. Occupying the borderland between cultures, playful anthropologists take the otherness of others seriously and also gain an expanded sense of human possibilities for themselves and their readers, thus broadening their understanding of the nature of human reality. This book aims to accomplish this via a playful encounter with the culture associated with the worship of Mount Govardhan.

Benefits of Cross-Cultural Understanding

In their book titled *Anthropology as Cultural Critique*, Marcus and Fischer write:

> Twentieth-century social and cultural anthropology has promised its still largely Western readership enlightenment on two fronts. The one has been the salvaging of distinct cultural forms of life from a process of apparent global Westernization. . . . The other promise of anthropology, one less fully distinguished and attended to than the first, has been to serve as a form of cultural critique for ourselves. In using portraits of other cultural patterns to reflect self-critically on our own ways, anthropology disrupts common sense and makes us reexamine our taken-for-granted assumptions.[55]

The first promise addresses the value of otherness and diversity, and resists monoculturalism. Respectful knowledge of other cultures is highly beneficial, for it can nurture an attitude of openness and appreciation for cultural difference—and sometimes even a commitment to work to protect it. This has obvious benefits for the other, as well as oneself: respectful and open exposure to another culture can enlarge one's sense of human reality and expand one's existential possibilities in life. To be stretched by an encounter with otherness has long been a major agenda of the humanities. Serious ("playful") study of another culture leads to perspectival enrichment: breaking out of the assumed, seeing from new angles, and thereby perceiving more.

Recognition of the expansive possibilities in cross-cultural encounters leads into the second important promise, that of cultural critique. Anthropology is an approach to knowledge that provides understandings of difference as it critiques the limitations of one's own culture. The anthropological perspective can serve to dislodge and bring into question assumed ways of being in the home society; as it provides consideration of other ways, it pulls the authoritative rug out from underneath the taken-for-granted nature of reality. Margaret Mead is often recognized as the pioneer of this approach, questioning premarital sexual expectations and the psychological well-being of teenagers in the United States in comparison to her study of Samoan sexual attitudes and behavior.[56] Crapanzano maintains: "The field situation, especially in foreign cultures or unfamiliar settings, lays bare dimensions of ordinary social encounters that, in their ordinariness, are usually ignored." The anthropological straddler experiences a unique kind of distance that leads "to a break from the way the world usually presents itself."[57] This close encounter with another culture and the ensuing distance from their own are what allow anthropologists a new perspective that makes them effective cultural critics.[58] This disorientation engenders fresh perspectives on vital, and often unexamined, issues in one's own culture.

What might the benefits of an encounter with other cultural conceptions and interactions with natural entities such as Mount Govardhan have to offer? Many insist that the key to getting out of our environmentally destructive ways has to do with establishing new conceptions of the natural world. The environmental historian Neil Evernden maintains that we not only need to treat "things" differently, but also *see* them differently: "The so-called environmental crisis demands not inventing of solutions, but the re-creation of *the things themselves*."[59] The psychologist Ralph Metzner argues: "Recognizing and respecting worldviews and spiritual practices different from our own is probably the best antidote to the West's fixation in the life-destroying dissociation between spirit and nature."[60] The different conceptions of a mountain presented in the next chapter certainly pose an alternative view and challenge the taken-for-granted nature of the dominant American view of mountains and stones—and by extension the entire other-than-human world, especially what we call "inanimate objects." The anthropocentric worldview dominant in the United States that regards humans as vastly more valuable than non-humans takes its most extreme form in the way the so-called inanimate world is regarded. Appalachian mountains, for example, are now routinely blasted into oblivion to fuel human endeavors.[61]

Although there are subaltern or alternative views to be found throughout its history, inanimate objects such as mountains and stones have long been regarded in modern European thought as the lowest of all entities. They are found, for example, on the very bottom of the great chain of being shared by Aristotle and Plato, and are positioned last on the General Animacy Scale.[62] However, within the non-dual (*advaita*) context of the Vaishnava Vedanta outlook that informs much of the religious culture associated with Mount Govardhan, there is no absolute ontological boundary between a stone and a human, as everything has its origins in the same unified ulti-mate reality referred to as Brahman. A consideration of reverential attitudes toward stones and mountains opens up new possibilities in conceptions of and relationships with the more-than-human world. A process that acknow-ledges the sentience of animals is already well under way in American so-ciety;[63] this is also beginning to occur with plants, particularly trees.[64] But a study of a different cultural view of stones potentially pushes these increas-ingly inclusive perspectives further beyond established cultural boundaries, past the animate to include even the so-called "inanimate" world. As such, consideration of the perspectives, relationships, and interactions with Mount Govardhan of millions of stone worshipers—whose ranks include doctors, lawyers, academics, engineers, and those working in the globalized informa-tion technology (IT) sector—holds even greater disruptive possibilities for expansion into wider realms of conceptualizing the non-human.

Porous Sites in Cultural Boundaries

Like many societies, American society is highly complex, especially during this pluralistic era of the twenty-first century. The people of the United States today comprise many ethnic groups, including Indian Hindus, a small minority of whom worship Govardhan stones in their homes. But theirs is a peripheral view. My general comparative remarks about the boundary that exists between the worshipers of Mount Govardhan and Americans who would consider this practice absurd are aimed at a socially dominant outlook, which has been shaped largely by post-Reformational Christianity. I emphasize "dominant" because there are conceptual soft spots in hard places, sites of porousness within this boundary that might help render the worship of Mount Govardhan more understandable.

Though extreme difference certainly remains between the two cultures, new considerations of inanimate entities such as stones are now beginning to appear as rays of light through emerging chinks in the wall that separates the prevailing outlook of many Western societies from those such as stone-worshiping Hindus, and that has cordoned off humans from the rest of the world. Contributions to an approach to understanding another cultural phenomenon would therefore include examination of places of resonance within one's home culture. Although these places are most often on the edge of prevailing social views, they represent potential resources that may be highlighted as useful aides in the labor of cross-cultural understanding. Such sites may help soften the ground between the rock and a hard place in a manner that makes it more possible to comprehend the worship of Mount Govardhan and accompanying perceptions. This approach need proceed with caution, however, for resonances should not be taken for sameness; rather, they are places within one's own culture that are more permeable to obstinate cultural boundaries. They offer hints of affinity, not complete knowledge. Current examples of such places of resonance might include the following.

I begin a brief and somewhat random exploration of porous openings to regarding stones as sentient beings, or even to an understanding of God in the corporeal form of a stone, with a look at an assertion resulting from changes in biblical reading habits. Developments in postmodern literary criticism have brought new ways of reading texts, including the Bible. An example relevant to this study is an article published by the scholar of Ancient Israelite religion Ithamar Gruenwald. He begins with the observation that God is frequently referred to in the Hebrew Bible with the names "rock" or "stone" (e.g., "The Rock, his work is perfect; for all his ways are justice" [Deut. 32:4]), but notes that "a literal understanding of these names, according to which God really is a 'rock' or 'stone,' is viewed as running counter to customarily maintained theological beliefs and assumptions."[65] Gruenwald is quite aware that any other reading goes against well-established reading habits that assume such names are metaphorical. Nonetheless, he asks the provocative question: "Since the borderlines of hermeneutical decoding are not set by the text itself, the question arises, What are the limits of such a decoding, and in whose hands should their setting be entrusted?"[66] Allegory has so dominated biblical interpretation throughout the history of Jewish and Christian exegesis that it is nearly impossible for other interpretive possibilities to be taken seriously. Gruenwald maintains, "a similar problem exists with regard to those utterances in Scripture in which God is spoken of in terms of 'stone' and 'rock.' People would indeed find it difficult to read these words in terms differently from their usually accepted metaphorical meaning. . . . all utterances implying cultic fetishism and corporeal anthropomorphism are explained away as similes and metaphors."[67] Philosophical ends justify interpretive means; interpretation has to fall in line with dominant theological positions. Gruenwald shows how the influential twelfth-century Jewish theologian Maimonides contributed considerably to the dominant hermeneutical scene of biblical interpretation by eliminating materiality from the conception of God. But what happens when this foundational text is read in a more literal manner? Gruenwald claims that this opens new interpretive options that lead to a better understanding of early biblical religion. He finds many biblical passages that refer to worship of God in the form of a stone, and concludes:

> Initially, then, rocks and stones could be worshipped or serve as cultic places. It made sense to worship such a rock only when it was believed actually to contain an aspect of divine essence or representation. . . . Sacred profanation was always a real threat, even in the case of the God of the Israelites. God's aloofness protected him from physical damage. However, in a considerable number of cases, different things happened: God was either seen or envisioned in some aspect of corporeality or physicality. One such form of corporeality was the rock or stone.[68]

Gruenwald sharpens his point in a footnote in which he compares his view to that of the religious studies scholar Mircea Eliade: "I go one step further than Eliade. For Eliade speaks about a sacred manifestation *in* the material object, whereas I refer to the identification of deities with stones."[69] Gruenwald thereby presents the possibility of seeing conceptions of God in biblical religion as including the material form of a stone. What would serious consideration of this possibility mean for those who base their religious outlook on biblical texts?

Acknowledging that Gruenwald's article would have limited effect on popular religious culture in the United States, I turn to areas that, although they do not occupy the dominant center of American society, have a more solid place on its creative edge. A precise definition of life has long been an open question in scientific inquiry, and uncertainty with regard to the boundary between the living and non-living, or between the biological and physical, is becoming increasingly common in a number of scientific disciplines today.[70] In many ways, this signals a return to the position articulated by Aristotle, who wrote that "Nature proceeds little by little from inanimate things to living creatures in such a way that we are unable, in the continuous sequence, to determine the boundary line between them."[71] The semiotic scientist Thomas Sebeok explains that there "may not be an absolutely rigorous distinction between inanimate matter and matter in a living state."[72] Such scientific positions have led to deeper reflection on the nature of the relationship between human and other life forms, and between animate and inanimate entities.

Environmental thinkers, for example, are reflecting more and more on ecological insights into the interrelated nature of all elements in ecosystems; among those involved in serious contemplation of the implications of these scientific positions are deep ecologists. Deep ecologists aim to replace what they perceive to be the arrogance of anthropocentrism with the recognition that all Earth entities have value. The first of the eight deep ecological principles articulated by Arne Naess, the recognized founder of the philosophical movement of deep ecology, reads: "The well-being and flourishing of human and nonhuman Life on Earth have value in themselves (synonyms: intrinsic value, inherent value). These values are independent of the usefulness of the nonhuman world for human purposes."[73] To check current anthropocentric tendencies and stress the all-inclusive nature of this ecocentric statement, he adds: "The term 'life' is used here in a more comprehensive nontechnical way to refer also to what biologists classify as 'nonliving': rivers, landscapes, ecosystems."[74] Appreciating Earth developments and the permeable nature of the boundary between organic and inorganic entities, the deep ecologist John Seed celebrates the connection between human beings and rocks:

> As the implications of evolution and ecology are internalized and replace the outmoded anthropocentric structures in your mind, there is an identification with all life. Then follows the realization that the distinction between "life" and "lifeless" is a human construct. Every atom in this body existed before organic life emerged 4000 million years ago. Rocks contain the potentiality to weave themselves into such stuff as this. We are rocks dancing.[75]

The scholar David Skrbina includes a consideration of rocks in his rethinking of materiality in terms of panpsychism, the philosophical position that regards consciousness, mind, or soul to be all-pervasive. He asserts that "[f]or most of humanity, for most of history, panpsychism has been an accepted and respected view of the world."[76] For him, panpsychism has important ethical consequences that "can serve as a source for more compassionate and ecological values, and therefore new ways of acting in the world."[77] The greatest challenge for an all-inclusive panpsychism that regards everything as sentient is, of course, inanimate entities such as stones.

> Upon laying out a panpsychist position, one is immediately faced with the charge that he believes that "rocks are conscious"—a statement taken as so obviously ludicrous that panpsychism can be dismissed out of hand. . . . We may see no such analogies to plants or inanimate objects, and so to attribute consciousness to them seems ridiculous. This is our human bias. To overcome this anthropocentric perspective, the panpsychist asks us to see the "mentality" of other objects not in terms of *human* consciousness but as a subset of a certain *universal quality* of physical things, in which both inanimate mentality and human consciousness are taken as particular manifestations.[78]

The majority of Skrbina's book traces the presence and history of panpsychism, wherein viewing something like a stone as sentient has been taken seriously in Western philosophy, from ancient times to the present. He regards a revival of panpsychist thinking that generates a reverence for all life as a potential remedy for healing the ecological damage caused by modern industrial society. This reverential respect for all life includes rocks. He endorses the environmental historian Roderick Nash, who in an article titled "Do Rocks Have Rights?"[79] argues that "rocks, rightly seen, *are* alive, hence deserving of the full measure of ethical respect, accorded to all life."[80]

Eco-theologians have also deliberated on the boundary issues of the sentience or sacrality of rocks in their examination of the environmental crisis. While pondering what he called the problematic "man-nature dualism," the seminal figure Lynn White, Jr., wrote, for example:

> The problem grows if we ask "Do people have ethical obligations toward rocks?" To an ancient Greek, to an American Indian, or perhaps to certain kinds of Buddhists, the question would have meaning. For quite different reasons they would probably reply "Yes," and the replies would reflect not prudential ethics but their ideas about the nature of reality. But today to

almost all Americans, still saturated with ideas historically dominant in Christianity (although perhaps not necessarily so), the question makes no sense at all. If the time comes when to any considerable group of us such a question is no longer ridiculous, we may be on the verge of a change of value structures that will make possible measures to cope with the growing ecologic crisis.[81]

I might add that I hope this book demonstrates that Hindus, too, should be included in White's list of those who affirm his question. The biblical scholar and Christian eco-theologian Sallie McFague continues this line of thought when she includes rocks and mountains in her theological understanding of God's all-inclusive body, of which all parts are deserving of ethical concern.[82]

Yet another arena in which rethinking our conception of and attitude and behavior toward stones can be found is the emerging sub-culture of "neo-paganism" or "new animism" in popular American and European society. In general, this is a spiritual movement that regards everything on Earth as alive. Graham Harvey gives voice to this perspective in his book *Animism: Respecting the Living World*. For him, the new animism has much to do with a reconsideration of personhood that claims allegiance to a much more inclusive view of persons. Harvey relies on the work of Irving Hallowell, writing: "Consideration of the 'new animism' necessarily begins with what Irving Hallowell learnt from dialog with Ojibwe hosts in southern Canada in the early mid-twentieth century." [83] Rocks are grammatically animate in the Ojibwe language and are often regarded as persons. "Persons is the wider category, beneath which there may be listed sub-groups such as 'human persons,' 'rock persons,' bear persons,' and others."[84] The inclusion of the inanimate object of a stone is important for Harvey's notion of "other-than-human persons." "These stones, at least, are not treated merely *as if* they are persons, they are treated *as* persons."[85] Here personhood is an all-encompassing category: there are many kinds of persons, only some of whom are human.

Native American religious traditions provide another area of influence on the periphery of dominant American society that gives voice to alternative views of mountains and stones. Sacred mountains are found throughout the Native American religious landscape. The better known among them include Mount Shasta (called Úytaahkoo by the Karuk) in California, Mount Rainer (the indigenous designation is Tacoma; some say this name means "mountain god") in Washington, Devils Tower (the preferred name for many Native Americans is Bear's Lodge) in Wyoming, and Harney Peak (known by the Lakota as Hinhan Kaga) in South Dakota. This lithic reverence extends to certain stones. Since the Lakota Sioux have held a prominent place in contemporary understandings of Native American worldviews, I cite as an exemplary illustration the figure of the Lakota elder and teacher John Fire Lame Deer. Sacred stones figure significantly in traditional Lakota religion, including the special red stone used to make prayer pipes and the stones used in the Inipi sweat lodge ceremonies. Sacred stones are also said to speak to people in visions, especially during the *Yuwipi* ceremony. Lame Deer explicates these stones:

> *Yuwipi* is our word for the tiny, glistening rocks we pick up from the anthills. They are sacred. They have power. *Yuwipi wasicun*—that is the power of the sacred rocks. It is also another name for Tunkan, our oldest god, who is like a rock, old beyond imagination, ageless, eternal. The ancient ones worshiped this god in the form of a huge stone painted red. The old word for god and the old word for stone are the same—*tunkashila*, grandfather—but it is also a name for the Great Spirit. . . . In the *yuwipi* ceremony the spirits and the lights dwell in the stones. The bright spark which you see in the dark, that light is *iyan*—the round pebble. It has the power; a soul goes into that rock and starts talking to you.[86]

Lame Deer augments this with an account of the more general view of stones in Lakota tradition:

> *Inyan*—the rocks—are holy. Every man needs a stone to help him. . . . In the old days we used to have many boulders which we painted and covered with feathers, or sage, praying to them. . . . Nothing is so small and unimportant but it has a spirit given to it by Waken Tanka. Tunkan is what you might call a stone god, but he is also part of the Great Spirit. . . . Tunkan—the stone god—is the oldest spirit.[87]

Such Native American views have influenced both popular American culture and environmental thinkers. Writing about Lame Deer's outlook, the environmental philosopher Baird Callicott declares: "The Indian attitude, as represented by Lame Deer, apparently was based upon the consideration that since human beings have a physical body *and* an associated consciousness (conceptually hypostatized or reified as 'spirit'), all other bodily things, animals, plants, and, yes, *even stones*, were also similar in this respect. Indeed, this strikes me as an eminently reasonable assumption."[88]

Finally, I give consideration to alternative views of stones that appear in novels. *The Hummingbird's Daughter*, for instance, is a beautifully written Mexican-American novel that takes place on the borderlands of northern Mexico and southern Texas. The novel contains a conversation between a sensitive young woman named Teresita and Huila, an elderly woman with healing abilities. Teresita overhears Huila talking to some plants and questions her about this:

> "Everything," Huila said, "talks."
> "I never heard it."
> "You never listened."
> Huila pointed around herself with her pipe. "Life. Life. Life," she said. She was pointing at everything: tree, hill, rock.
> "Life in rocks?" Teresita said.
> "Every rock comes from God, and God is in every rock if you look for Him."[89]

Granted, this is a novel, yet it has a historical basis and provides the reader imaginative access to another cultural approach on the edge of dominant American society. And there is certainly a significant role for the imagination to play in efforts to regard reality in some other way. When it comes to the playful interpretive work of understanding the reality of other cultures, however, we need to keep in mind that this is the "really real" for millions of people. This is indeed the case in the conceptions of God in the form of a stone mountain in the Hindu culture associated with the worship of Mount Govardhan.

3

A God of Stone

Divine Conceptions

Mount Govardhan itself is a direct and visible
form of Shri Krishna.[1]

Each and every stone of Mount Govardhan is an essential
embodied form of Shri Krishna.[2]

Sacred Mountains

Sacred mountains and religious interactions with them are a worldwide phenomenon. To name but a few, the snow-ringed volcanic cone of Kilimanjaro
has been regarded as an exalted personality by the Chagga people of
Tanzania, who make offerings to the mountain; Mount Fuji has been celebrated as a mysterious presence for centuries in Japan and is now climbed
by millions for religious benefits; the massive sandstone monolith of Uluru
(also known as Ayers Rock) has long been a ritual site for the Aborigines
of Australia; Mount Olympus is where the early Greeks encountered their
gods; Mount Sinai was a site of great revelation for the ancient Israelites; the
rugged San Francisco Peaks are regarded as the *kiva*-like residence of the divine *katsina*s by the Hopis; Bear Lodge (also known as Devils Tower) has
served the Lakota Sioux and other plains tribes as a holy butte for vision
quests; Mount Kailash has been conceived as the abode of a powerful meditative god at the spiritual center of the world and circumambulated for spiritual
gains by countless Buddhists living in the Tibetan Himalayas; and Mount
Ausangate is only one of a number of tall peaks in Peru to be considered an
apu, an exalted form of Quechua embodied divinity.

Mountains have been conceived in many ways within the great variety of
human cultures. For many they are objects of aesthetic beauty, challenging

Loving Stones. David L. Haberman, Oxford University Press (2020) © Oxford University Press.
DOI: 10.1093/oso/9780190086718.001.0001

climbs, geological wonders, and tourist destinations. But they have also been regarded as the abode or even body of some divinity. In his *Sacred Mountains of the World*, Edwin Bernbaum has written: "Like the sacred values they express, the mountains revered by cultures around the world appear infinite in number and kind. They range from the highest peaks on earth to hills that barely rise above the surrounding landscape."[3] He quotes Lama Anagarika Govinda, a Tibetan Buddhist, on sacred mountains: "The power of such a mountain is so great and yet so subtle that, without compulsion, people are drawn to it from near and far, as if by the force of some invisible magnet; and they will undergo untold hardships and privations in their inexplicable urge to approach and to worship the center of this sacred power."[4] Such a power may be an inherent draw, but most people's view of the sacredness of a mountain is strongly influenced by the particular cultural stories and practices associated with a specific mountain.

Among the great diversity in sacred mountains, Bernbaum identifies several basic themes in conceptualizing these famous mountains of the world. Sacred mountains have been regarded as a "center, heaven, source of water, place of the dead, and so forth."[5] He places much emphasis on the first, evoking Mircea Eliade's assertion that sacred mountains are often considered the center of the world. For Eliade a sacred mountain is an "*axis mundi*," specifically a world center that connects heaven and earth and functions as a passageway between the two. It is a sacred place that "constitutes a break in the homogeneity of space; this break is symbolized by an opening by which passage from one cosmic region to another is possible."[6] Diana Eck affirms this point: "As the center of the world, linking heaven and earth and anchoring the cardinal directions, the mountain often functions as an *axis mundi*—the centerpost of the world."[7] A mountain is sacred, according to Eliade, "*because it is the place nearest to heaven*";[8] it is the site of a *hierophany*, a revelation of the sacred that comes from somewhere else. "Its sacred value is always due to that something or that somewhere, never to its own actual existence."[9] Note the implied devaluation of embodiment in this dualistic account. But what if the physicality of the mountain isn't conceived of as a doorway into another world, but as a divine presence in this one?

Bernbaum continues Eliade's themes: "As heavens on high, often situated at the center of the world, mountains serve as abodes of gods and goddesses."[10] Although the residential view of sacred mountains is dominant among those recorded by Bernbaum, he does acknowledge that some mountains are treated "as living embodiments of the deities." That is, in addition to the view of mountains as the habitat of a god or goddess, he recognizes that sometimes they are conceptualized as the "body" of a god or goddess. This is an important distinction. The latter view is the one most frequently applied to Mount Govardhan.

Although the conception of a mountain as the residence of a divinity is more common worldwide, the conception of a mountain as the body of a divinity is found in a number of religious traditions.[11] As is true in other places, most of the sacred mountains in India are identified as the abodes of divinities: Mount Kailas, for example, is considered a meditative residence of Shiva, Nanda Devi as the snowy abode of the goddess by that name, and the mountainous area of Badrinath as the Himalayan home of Vishnu. In pan-Indian Hinduism, the only other sacred mountain besides Mount Govardhan that Puranic literature recognizes as the body of a divinity is Mount Arunachala, located in the southeastern state of Tamil Nadu. Mount Arunachala is larger than Mount Govardhan; at an elevation of 2,668 feet, it rises over 2,000 feet above the surrounding plains. It is considered to be a body of the supreme god Shiva and has a fascinating story associated with it.

The gods Brahma and Vishnu were once arguing over who was the most powerful when a huge luminous column of fire rose up before them. They decided to investigate its dimensions. Brahma took the form of a swan and flew upward to find the top, and Vishnu took the form of a boar and plunged downward to locate the bottom. After covering enormous distances, both returned to where they began, exhausted and unsuccessful in finding the ends of the boundless fiery column. An opening suddenly appeared in the side of the column and Shiva appeared, revealing that he had manifested himself in the form of this infinite column, designated a *linga*.[12] As an act of divine grace, the column of fire reduced itself and coagulated into the "red mountain," Mount Arunachala. The *Shiva Purana* proclaims: "For the benefit of the world the Shiva *linga* appeared as a mountain of fire that became the reddish Aruna Mountain."[13] A devotee scholar writes: "The Mountain Linga can be seen, touched, and meditated upon, and is available to everyone. Since Shiva grew so enormous as the Column-of-Fire, and because He is the Cause of the whole universe which was generated out of Himself, which has no beginning and has no end, it is out of His Divine-Love that the Mighty One reduced the vision of Himself in size."[14] The Arunachala *linga*, then, is the embodied form of Shiva's infinite firey *linga*. The Supreme God assumed the form of this mountain to become graciously approachable for all. Ramana Maharishi, a twentieth-century south Indian saint who spent most of his life in devotional meditation on the mountain, stated: "The formless Supreme Being, out of compassion, took this holy form of Arunachala Hill."[15] So while some mountains in India are considered the residence of divinities, Mount Arunachala is considered the embodied form of Shiva. The saint continues: "Mount Kailas is Shiva's abode, but this hill has been declared by Shiva to be Shiva Himself."[16] Shiva is recorded in the *Skanda Purana* as saying: "While mountains like Kailasa and Meru are my places of abode, this Arunagiri is my true form and here I abide eternally as this Hill."[17]

The following story is told about Ramana Maharishi (referred to here as Bhagavan) that illustrates the belief that the mountain is a material form of Shiva. "When an earnest devotee took the liberty of challenging Bhagavan and asked: 'Bhagavan! I do not want any metaphysical argument. Give me some tangible evidence. Is there a God? Can you show me God?' Sri Bhagavan gave a broad smile and said: 'What else do you think it is?' and pointed his hand to the Holy Hill, Arunachala!"[18] This also applies not only to the mountain, but to every stone on Mount Arunachala, which is considered to be a natural *linga*, an embodied form of Shiva. Another story about the mountain devotee Ramana Maharishi makes this evident: "Once when he (Ramana) was walking on the Hill he said to Dr. T. N. Krishnaswami who was with him: 'Some devotee from a far off land has asked for a stone to be taken from the most holy part of the Hill and sent to him. He thinks that some part of the Hill alone is holy; does he not know that Arunachala Himself is the Hill.' And picking up a small stone, he added, 'I sent him a stone like this.'"[19] The most common conception of Mount Arunachala is that it is a condensed form of Shiva's blaze of fiery light that cuts through ignorance and gracefully supports self-realization and the deep knowledge that leads to liberation (*mukti*). Whereas Mount Govardhan is associated with the Krishna devotional traditions that emphasize the love (*prema*) of intimate relationality, Mount Arunachala tends to be connected with the Shiva ascetic traditions that emphasize the liberation (*moksha*) brought about by identification with Shiva.

A recent case that gained recent international attention provides a more localized example of embodied notions of sacred mountains in India. In 2003 Vedanta Resources, a mining company based in London, announced plans to open a large pit mine for bauxite, an ore used to make aluminum, on one of the Niyamgiri hills located in the northeast state of Orissa. The hill is sacred to the Dongria Kondh, a tribal people who live in this mountainous region and consider the Niyamgiri Hill the body of their god Niyam Raja.

With much effort and global support from the non-governmental organization (NGO) Survival, the tribe asserted its religious views of the mountain. A young Dongria woman gives voice to these beliefs: "We can only live because of our mountain. He is our God. We worship Him. He gives us everything, which is why we worship Him."[20] In 2013 the Indian Supreme Court recognized the Dongria Kondh's right to worship their sacred mountain and in January 2014 the Ministry of Environment and Forests rejected the mining project. The Court decreed: "If the project affects their religious rights, especially their right to worship their deity, known as Niyam Raja, in the hills top of the Niyamgiri range of hills, that right has to be preserved and protected."[21] The religious regard for the physical mountain itself seems to be have been a key factor in the Court's decision. The mountain is considered an embodied form of a divinity. The most widely known and celebrated instance of a mountain in India being regarded as an embodied form of God, however, is Mount Govardhan.

General Theological Features of Mount Govardhan

The most common theological identification of Mount Govardhan found within Braj Vaishnava culture is that the entire hill is an important—even unique—form of Krishna. Ram Lakhan Sharma, for example, writes: "Shri Giriraj Govardhan and Shri Krishna are not different from one another. Shri Krishna can never be separated from Shri Govardhan and Shri Govardhan can never be separated from Shri Krishna. Shri Krishna is Shri Govardhan and Shri Govardhan is Shri Krishna."[22] When asked who Mount Govardhan is, the overwhelming majority of the people I interviewed answered simply, "He is Krishna." A slightly more complex response was, "Giriraj-ji is a *svarupa* of Shri Krishna," or "Govardhan is *sakshat* Bhagavan Krishna." Use of the word *svarupa* indicates that Giriraj is an "essential form" of Krishna; the term *sakshat* denotes that Giriraj is a physically available and visible form of Krishna. Brajesh Joshi declares in his Hindi book on Govardhan: "Mount Govardhan, the king of mountains, is no ordinary mountain. Mount Govardhan is a direct and visible form (*sakshat*) of Shri Krishna."[23]

I would frequently sit on a quiet platform beside the *parikrama* path about a kilometer south of Jatipura in the shade of a small tree often inhabited by a flock of bright green rose-ringed parakeets to observe and interview people circumambulating Mount Govardhan. His attention focused on the open

notebook on my lap, an elderly man from Jatipura who knew something of
my project from a previous conversation approached me one sunny winter
day with these instructive words, chosen carefully to ensure that I understood a crucial point: "God is not *in* Giriraj, Giriraj himself *is* God." Rather
than being the abode of Krishna, then, the mountain itself *is* Krishna. Many
others confirmed this perspective.[24] A Gaudiya Vaishnava I spoke with in the
Dan Ghati temple told me: "Giriraj-ji is Shri Krishna. Mount Govardhan is
the body (*sharir*) of Shri Krishna." A local scholar wrote: "Shri Giriraj is the
embodied form (*vigrah*) of Shri Krishna."[25] A man from Vrindaban who regularly circumambulates the mountain informed me: "When I look at Mount
Govardhan I see Krishna." These statements drive home the point that the
physical mountain is considered a corporal form of God. This is also true of
the many stones on the mountain, for numerous people informed me: "Each
and every stone of Mount Govardhan is an embodied form of Shri Krishna."
This perspective, which fully embraces the materiality of God, is the one
I wish to highlight, as it not only is the most commonly held view, but also
marks the greatest difference with regard to perspectives dominant in the
contemporary West. This viewpoint expressed frequently in conversation,
ritual action, poetry, and story poses the greatest interpretive challenge.

I asked one of the attendant priests at the Mukharvind stone in Jatipura
about the identity of Mount Govardhan. "He is God," the priest remarked,
using the English word God. He pointed to a large picture of Krishna as a
young cowherd holding up Mount Govardhan with his left arm. I inquired
whether "God" was the one holding the mountain or the mountain itself.
"Both," he retorted, and then quoted a partial verse from the *Bhagavata
Purana*: "He performed the worship by himself to himself."[26] Indeed, the
Bhagavata Purana provides the most authoritative scriptural basis for
the identification of Mount Govardhan and Krishna. When Krishna per-
suaded the residents of Braj to offer their mound of sacrificial food to
Mount Govardhan instead of to the storm god Indra, he assumed the form
of the mountain, saying, "I am the mountain," and devoured the abundant
offerings. During this paradigmatic worship of the mountain, Krishna
assumed two forms simultaneously: one the cowherd boy who directed the
worship of the mountain, and the other the mountain who received the worshipful offerings.

The point is often made that Krishna demonstrates in this performance
that Govardhan Giriraj is his chosen deity, or *ishta-dev*.[27] Many people
I spoke with referred to this story explicitly while discussing their views on

the theological character of the mountain. Significantly, in his Hindi book on Mount Govardhan, Joshi alters the *Bhagavata Purana* statement from "I am the mountain" to "I am Giriraj."[28] As both the worshiper of the mountain and the mountain that is worshiped, the lifter of the mountain as well as the mountain that is lifted, Krishna assumes an important dual identity in Braj Vaishnavism.

Common names for Krishna include Govardhan-dhara, Giri-dhari, and Giriraj-dharan. The Sanskrit/Hindi words *dhara, dhari,* or *dharan* all are formed from the same root (*dhṛ*) and have an expedient double meaning: they can mean either "holding" or "assuming the shape of."[29] That is, Krishna is concurrently the "holder" of the mountain and the one who "assumes the form of" the mountain. Joshi labels this double identity of Krishna the "mysterious secret" in the worship of Mount Govardhan: "Krishna, the Supreme Reality (*Parabrahma*) and Highest Lord (*Parameshwar*), performed the first worship (*puja*) of Shri Govardhan-ji; in this greatest of all forms of worship there is a mysterious secret (*rahsya*): with one form he performs the worship, with another form he himself is worshiped."[30] This profound secret is celebrated in Braj poetry and is ritually enacted in many of the temples around Mount Govardhan.

The following eight-lined poem, composed in Braj Bhasha and attributed to the famous poet Surdas, is included in many Pushti Margiya songbooks. It gives poetic voice to the dual identity of Krishna as both cowherd boy, who directs the worship, and Mount Govardhan, who receives the worship. Radha's close girlfriend Lalita is often the one in Braj narratives who is able to discern the truth within Krishna's playful activities (*lilas*) and disclose their secret.

> Nanda experienced great joy watching the offering being consumed
> 　　after Krishna manifested himself as the deity (Mount Govardhan). [1]
> Observing the mountain consume the food offering,
> 　　the residents of Braj considered their lives to be successful. [2]
> Lalita informed Radha: "The one eating is Krishna, who is the same as
> 　　the boy holding Nanda's hand. [3]
> I recognize Krishna's cleverness; he himself (as the mountain)
> 　　is devouring Indra's sacrifice. [4]
> Over there he is eating and here he is beginning to speak,
> 　　saying to the feasting mountain:
> 　　　'What I said has come to be!' [5]

> Assuming a form with a thousand arms
>> he gobbled up the food offering. [6]
> Other gods take his refuge, for here he is talking and
>> over there he is eating." [7]
> Such is the divine play (*lila*) of Surdas's lord, the darling of Nanda and
>> the handsome dandy of Braj. [8][31]

The identity of Mount Govardhan as Krishna is expressed ritually in virtually every Giriraj temple in Braj or wherever a Govardhan stone is dressed up as the cowherd Krishna. This is nowhere truer than in the Mukut Mukharvind temple, on the eastern shore of the Manasi Ganga pond in the middle of the town of Govardhan (see Figure 1.5 in Chapter 1). This large compound features a number of shrines that house several Govardhan stones adorned as Krishna. One enters the temple complex from the east by way of an open corridor that borders the lake. Over the main entrance to this corridor is an enormous painting of the cowherd Krishna holding up Mount Govardhan, with a crowd of cowherds huddling under the protective shelter of the mountain. Colorful paintings on the inside wall depict Krishna performing several *lila*s in pastoral settings. Just before the passageway opens into the central courtyard, a fountain in the shape of a white cow stands near the shore of the pond, four streams of water gushing forth from her udder.

The heart of the complex is a temple constructed from light pink sandstone that rises up to culminate in a tall ornate spire. At its center is an octagonal grey and white marble chamber about thirty feet in diameter, encircled by an inner pathway. Directly below the temple's peak sit two Govardhan stones (Figure 3.1), which are the main attraction of this Mukharvind temple.

Both sit in a black marble throne that is framed with a low wall of smooth sandstone. One of the stones has four flat sides like a miniature skyscraper, standing approximately three feet high with a foot wide square base; the face of this dark purple stone features a distinctive large yellowish-red oval ring. The second stone is low, about a foot high; it is roundish and spreads to a diameter of two feet. One of the attendant priests told me that the tall stone is Krishna the cowherd boy who worshiped the mountain, and the low one is Mount Govardhan whom he worships, but that both were Giriraj stones and essential forms of Krishna. This identity was made evident in the elaborate ritual conducted by temple priests every evening when the stones are ornately adorned as Krishna (Figure 3.2).

Figure 3.1. Unadorned Govardhan stones in the Mukut Mukharvind temple of Govardhan town.

Figure 3.2. Ornately adorned Govardhan stones in the Mukut Mukharvind temple of Govardhan town.

This priest directed my attention to a Hindi inscription carved into the stone lintel over the archway leading into the central sanctum. It reads: "With one form he conducts the worship, with another form he is worshiped. Stretching out his thousand arms he asks for more and more food, then devours it."[32] Again, the two forms of the worshiper and the worshiped are really one and the same. In this temple ritual the mountain becomes Krishna who makes the offering to the mountain, and then takes the form of the mountain to consume the offering. In the story found within the *Bhagavata Purana*, Krishna assumes a human form that takes the form of a mountain, whereas here the mountain assumes the form of the cowherd Krishna through the transformative ritual enacted by the priests. There is something wonderfully circular in all this. As the ever-playful shape-shifting form of the ultimate unified reality, Krishna is both the enjoyer and the enjoyed.

Identification with the general theology of supreme Krishna makes Govardhan Giriraj by definition non-different from the totality of reality. Stated more simply, he is *everything*. A number of people I spoke with referred to Giriraj with terms such as Para-Brahman, Parama-Atma, or Purna-Purushottama, indicating that they consider Govardhan to be an aspect of the Ultimate Reality, Supreme Soul, or Complete and Highest Personality. A man from Jaipur who had come to circumambulate and worship the mountain told me how he thinks of Mount Govardhan using a quote from the *Bhagavad Gita*: "Krishna is everything" (*Vasudevah sarvam,* 7.19). He explained that Giriraj is Bhagavan or God (he used both terms interchangeably), and that all living beings and entities are simply parts of this greater reality. He compared this to the relationship between a drop of rain and the ocean, the source of all drops of water. "Giriraj is God, and God is infinite. He is everything. God is like the ocean and we are the small parts (*amshas*)—like drops of rain." From this perspective, the mountain divinity Giriraj, as the totality of reality, is the source of our being and sustenance, and the very substance and foundation of all that is. "For me Giriraj is Bhagavan Krishna," a woman from Gwalior told me. "He is the source of all life. For this reason I come here to honor (*manti*) him." The supremacy of Govardhan elevates him to the preeminent position of the Lord of the Lords. The *Garga Samhita* places the Lord of Mount Govardhan (Govardhannath) at the very center of the central realm of India (Bharata), situated in the middle of the four Naths or "Lords" of Jagannath in the east, Ranganath in the south, Dvarakanath in the west, and Badrinath in the north.[33]

In addition to such cosmic conceptions of the divinity that is Mount Govardhan are more personal and specific conceptions at the heart of people's thoughts. A Braj poem composed by the famous poet Paramanandadas identifies Govardhan as the Cow of Plenty and the Wishing Tree, who provide whatever one is personally seeking. Perhaps more importantly, however, Paramanandadas identifies Govardhan as "mother, father, and guru."[34] As mother and father, Giriraj is not only the source of one's life, but also one's protector. Several people I spoke with reinforced this view. While walking around the mountain I met a man from Mumbai who told me, "Giriraj is my protector; I feel his presence here very strongly." Pointing to the mountain, he added: "This is my God. I come here each year to walk around Him. I then feel his presence more in my life back in Mumbai." Many residents of Braj consider Giriraj to be their clan deity (*kula-devata*) who once protected the residents of Braj from Indra's storm, and still protects them from harm today.

In Hindu culture the ultimate protective elder is the guru. A temple worker in the Dan Ghati Mukharvind temple related:

> Giriraj is my guru. I don't have any other guru besides him. Giriraj is my true guru. But he is also like a family member. He lives in my house as our guru. Because of this we are happy and there is no tension in our lives.

This man was not alone in identifying Giriraj as the guru. The most popular day to circumambulate Mount Govardhan is Guru Purnima, the full moon in the month of Ashadh (June–July) on which many Hindus honor their gurus with a reverential visit. A resident of Gokul explained to me: "The residents of Braj consider Giriraj as their guru. So they honor him by doing *parikrama* on Guru Purnima." Indeed, the number of people who come to revere Govardhan on this day can be quite large. Crowds circling Mount Govardhan on Guru Purnima of 2015 (July 31st) were estimated to be between eight and ten million people.[35]

In addition to being regarded as an esteemed elder such as one's mother, father, or guru, Giriraj is considered to be an intimate friend. A young man who lives in the town of Govardhan told me while talking on the shore of Manasi Ganga: "I think of Giriraj as a friend (*sakha*), not the almighty Lord (*Ishvara*). In this way I feel very close to him." A devotee of Giriraj living in Gokul shared his consideration of Giriraj:

"He is very special to me because he is easy to please, so very kind, and gives blessings immediately. Whatever you want he gives quickly. You just have to keep your love (*bhav*) pure and remember him. You don't have to ask for anything. He already knows your desires and fulfills them quickly. We residents of Braj say Giriraj is our friend. We worship him in the mood of friendship (*sakha-bhav*), so we can do anything with him. Some even offer tea [which is traditionally prohibited in Vaishnava food offerings]. We drink tea, so he too drinks tea with us. No other form of God is like Giriraj. He is available to anyone at any time in any situation. No other form is equal to him."

The close relational familiarity with Giriraj is perhaps even more obvious in the words of a young woman who worships a Govardhan stone in her home in Jatipura. "We love Giriraj and Giriraj loves us. We cannot live without him and he cannot live without us." With a bright smile she proudly added, "So when *we* offer him *rotis* (flat breads) he gobbles them up immediately!"

In even greater realms of intimacy, Giriraj is considered an exquisite lover, as well as the very source of all love. The entire region of Braj is identified with the divine body of Krishna, and many regard Mount Govardhan as its very heart (*hriday*).[36] As both the physical center of the world as well as the source of all love that exists in it, the notion of Govardhan as the heart of Braj has both spatial and emotional connotation. "Govardhan is the center and source of all love (*prem*)," exclaimed a man I met in the forest just north of Jatipura who visits a Giriraj shrine in these woods every morning. A resident of Jatipura told me, "Shri Giriraj-ji is the form of Bhagavan that inspires love and gives love (*prem*) quickly. Just one good look at Giriraj-ji and love comes to a person." As an essential form of the divine lover Krishna, each and every stone from Mount Govardhan radiates love and is available to devotees for a divine love affair. These stones of love are considered the devotee's most cherished beloved, the ultimate source and object of love. Joshi writes: "Giriraj just gives and gives love (*prem*), and in return he wants only love."[37] Accordingly, the most suitable response to these stones of love is to love them in return, through worshipful acts of love. Here is the double meaning of "loving stones."

Although Mount Govardhan is considered an essential form of supreme Krishna, from the worshiper's perspective the mountain is often said to have certain advantages over the cowherd form of Krishna. One morning at the Jatipura Mukharvind, a woman from Pune spoke with me about the mountain: "You see, Krishna left Braj, but before he left he said that he would remain here in the form of this mountain. He departed us in his human form, but always remains here in this form. So we come to see him here. This mountain will always be here for us." A priest at the Manasi Ganga Mukharvind told me something similar as we stood before the two Govardhan stones enshrined there. "God (Bhagavan) has taken human forms as Ram and Krishna. But they went away. This form (the mountain with its many stones), however, remains here. It is still here for us now to see (*darshan*) and touch (*sparshan*)." That is, Mount Govardhan is not only a concrete form of God, but a form that is ever present and available at all times for interaction. Joshi concurs: "Even in this decadent age (*kali-yug*) it is possible to have direct sight (*sakshat darshan*) of Krishna in the form of Mount Govardhan."[38] Joshi's proclamation stands out sharply for those who know the familiar narrative that the corrupt age of *kali-yug* began with the "death" or disappearance of the cowherd Krishna when he was accidently shot in the foot by a hunter's arrow.[39]

Many believe that Krishna the cowherd is concealed at the present time. The terms *avirbhut* (manifest or visible) and *tirobhut* (unmanifest or concealed) are commonly used to express this in Braj Vaishnava thought, particularly within the Pushti Marg. "The manifestation (*avirbhav*) of Lord Krishna occurred during the time of incarnation (*avatar-kal*); but during non-incarnational time (*anavatar-kal*) his concealment (*tirobhav*) ensues."[40] But Krishna remains manifestly present in his embodied forms (*svarupas*). Embodied forms shaped by human artisans (*murtis*) have to be "enlivened" through a ritual process called *prana-pratistha* (or *pushta karana*) before they are considered to be legitimate forms for worship. But this is not necessary in the case of Govardhan stones; they are regarded as stable natural forms of God in which divinity is always manifestly present. For this reason, many worshipers of Mount Govardhan stones privilege these self-manifest forms of Krishna over the handcrafted images also found in temples and home shrines around the mountain. A well-informed priest living near the mountain explained:

> Giriraj stones are "self-manifest" (*svayambhu*), whereas a handmade *murti* must be "established" (*pushta karana*). Without being established, the divine force will not be present in it. But Giriraj is a natural self-manifest form of Krishna. Until its power is ritually established, a handmade *murti* is just like an ordinary piece of stone or metal. But Giriraj stones are naturally

Bhagavan Shri Krishna himself. For this reason Giriraj stones are very special.

I asked a *baba* who maintains a Giriraj shrine in his home if a Govardhan stone is superior to a handmade *murti*. "Yes," he insisted, "it is the highest form of *svarupa*. The most supreme form of Krishna." My friend Mohan put it this way:

> There is a great difference between a Giriraj *shila* and a *murti* made by hand. The *murti* has to be installed (*pratistha*) and is not so stable, but a Giriraj *shila* is a natural form (*prakriti-rupa*), so it is solid. It can never be uninstalled or defiled like a crafted *murti*. Therefore a Giriraj *shila* is very superior to a *murti*; it is the highest form of Krishna.

In short, Mount Govardhan is considered a constantly present and readily available form of God, which is further indication of the stone god's ever-compassionate nature (*kripa*).

The concreteness of God as stone is expressed through another oppositional pair of conceptual terms that are frequently employed in Hindu theological discussions relating to worship: *sakar* ("with form") and *nirakar* ("formless"). Before going into the field, I spent two weeks at the Landour Language School in preparation for interviewing people in Hindi about beliefs and practices related to Mount Govardhan. During a discussion of these issues, one of the instructors there explained to me how she regards something like the worship of Govardhan stones. "There is no problem with this for us. Some people think of God as having form (*sakar*), and others think of God as having no form (*nirakar*). Both are fine. They are just different ways of thinking of God. But God is one! (*Bhagavan ek hi hai.*)" Although people I spoke with in Braj agreed that Bhagavan is both multi-formed and formless, they were often less willing to give equal weight to these two perspectives, especially with regard to Mount Govardhan. They claim there are advantages to the *sakar* dimension. In response to my question about how he conceives of Giriraj, a man from Madhya Pradesh said, "He is *sakshat* Bhagavan Krishna. Bhagavan is both *nirakar* and *sakar*. But Giriraj is the *sakar* form of Bhagavan Krishna who we can see (*darshan*) and touch (*sparshan*), and thereby make contact with in close relationship (*sambandha*)." The favorability of *sakar* is an important point, as divine relationship is at the very heart of devotional Hinduism. Several people I spoke with connected this notion with the verse in the *Bhagavad Gita* that states that the manifest form of Krishna is preferred since it is difficult for embodied beings to connect with the unmanifest (12.5).

I had an opportunity to discuss the concepts of *sakar* and *nirakar* with Shrivatsa Goswami, a Vaishnava theologian whose thinking is especially grounded in the *Bhagavata Purana*. He began with the declaration: "It's painful to worship the *nirakar*." A bit taken aback by his use of the word "painful," I pressed him for further explanation. "Devotional connection is about relationship, and that requires the *sakar* form," he said.

> It is painful to worship the *nirakar* because the devotees need something tangible. They need *sakar*, Krishna's form. *Nirakar* frustrates attempts to establish relationship. This is the lesson that the yogi Uddhava learned from the gopis.[41] Uddhava was sent to the gopis to teach them about yoga and meditation on the all-pervasive *nirakar*, but instead they converted him to the devotional way of intimate connection that requires form—*sakar*. Form (*akar*) is the source and foundation of the divine loving relationship (*sambandha*). Thus Uddhava learned the pain of *nirakar*.

The pain of Uddhava that Shrivatsa referred to was a result of his realization of how much he was missing out on—the *nirakar* cannot lead to the intimate and joyful connection with the Ultimate; this requires *sakar* for embodied beings. "This is why people are so attracted to Giriraj," Shrivatsa said. "He is a *sakar* form of Krishna that readily establishes and makes possible loving relationships."

The terms *sakar* and *nirakar* are related to a series of paired oppositional terms found within Vedantic scriptures such as the Upanishads and the *Bhagavad Gita*: *saguna* (with qualities) and *nirguna* (without qualities), *murta* (form) and *amurta* (formless), *vyakta* (manifest) and *avyakta* (unmanifest), *vyaya* (finite) and *avyaya* (infinite), and *kshara* (changing) and *akshara* (unchanging). The Vedantic schools of Braj Vaishnavism all agree that Krishna encompasses both aspects of the oppositional pairs. This is expressed with the notion of *viruddha-dharma-ashraya* (simultaneity of the mutually exclusive or coincidence of the seemingly contradictory) within the Suddhadvaita system of the Pushti Marg and with the core concept of *achintya-bheda-abheda* (inconceivable concurrence of difference and non-difference) in Gaudiya Vaishnavism. A major feature of Krishna's grace according to Braj Vaishnavism, however, is that he makes himself visibly available in concrete, material forms for the beneficial purpose of establishing relationships. This means that the first term in each of the conceptual pairs is favored in Braj Vaishnava theology, with the understanding that this does not exclude the second of the paired terms. It is in this manner that the concrete mountain of Govardhan as a material form of God is regarded. The stone mountain is a finite form of the Infinite, made graciously available to worshipers.

Considerations of the divine nature of Mount Govardhan relate also to the predominant Braj Vaishnava view of the world. A contemporary scholar of Vallabhacharya's philosophical system of Suddhadvaita ("Pure Non-dualism"), for example, defines this philosophical position as meaning "that there does not exist any ultimate distinction between the world (jagat) and Brahman."[42] This is consistent with the Bhagavad Gita's teaching that the world is an aspect of Krishna. Many also see the worship of Mount Govardhan as the continuation of nature worship that has long been prevalent in Hinduism. Natural entities such as the sun, rivers, ponds, and trees, as well as mountains, have been regarded on the South Asian subcontinent as aspects of divine presence for thousands of years.

Not only is Giriraj Govardhan a concrete form of God that is approachable at all times; it is also a form that is available to anyone and everyone. Joshi puts it this way: "'One for all, all for One.' Shri Giriraj-ji belongs to everyone, and everyone belongs to Shri Govardhan Giriraj-ji."[43] Because of priestly concerns about ritual purity, ordinary worshipers are kept at a distance from the embodied forms of Krishna housed in the famous temples of Braj and elsewhere, but Giriraj is directly accessible to anyone at any time. The postmaster of Jatipura told me, "You could never touch Banke Bihari in Vrindaban (one of the most popular forms of Krishna in the temples of Vrindaban), but here Giriraj-ji lets everyone touch him and worship him anytime with their own hands." Again, Govardhan is a readily accessible, approachable, and concrete form of divinity. Although many embodied forms of God housed in the Hindu temples of India cannot be worshiped by lower castes or even directly by ordinary people, Joshi emphasizes the universal availability of Giriraj by highlighting the fact that people from all castes (and religions) can worship Mount Govardhan directly with their own hands. This, for him, is one of the things that make the worship of Giriraj the greatest and most powerful of all in the world. "In most temples, mosques, churches, and gurudvaras there is some kind of priest who has been appointed to mediate the interaction between God and the devotee. But the devotee himself worships Shri Giriraj Maharaj directly with his own hands. After touching (*sparshan*) this divine body of the Lord, the devotee becomes immersed in God."[44] The ever-present and inclusive nature of Giriraj Govardhan is one of the major reasons he is called Kripa-Nath, the "Compassionate Lord." He is available to all people at all times, under all circumstances. For this reason many people come to Mount Govardhan seeking blessings of all kinds— including those that are considered to be very difficult, or even impossible, to achieve.

Three *Svarupas* of Mount Govardhan

Besides these general views on the identity of Mount Govardhan, there exist within Braj Vaishnava literature sophisticated theological discussions about the nature of the sacred mountain. These provide more complex expressions of ideas commonly held by many serious worshipers of Mount Govardhan. This is particularly true within Pushti Margiya accounts, since nearly all Pushti Margiya Vaishnavas are ardent devotees of Giriraj.[45] The Pushti Margiya scholar Omprakash Yadav, for example, writes: "Shri Giriraj-ji is not only a physical mountain or material form of God (*bhautik parvat svarupa*), but also has a spiritual form (*adhyatmik svarupa*) and a divine form (*adhidaivik svarupa*)."[46] Yadav draws on tripartite terminology from the *Bhagavad Gita*, which serves as a foundational scripture for many of the teachings of the founder of the Pushti Marg, Vallabhacharya.[47] The three terms *adhibhuta*, *adhyatma*, and *adhidaiva* are delineated in the beginning of the eighth chapter of the *Bhagavad Gita*. *Adhibhuta* is defined as the ever-changing manifest world (*kshara*), *adhyatma* is identified with all-pervasive *brahman* and defined as the unmanifest and unchanging dimension of reality (*akshara*), and *adhidaiva* is defined as the Supreme Person (*purusha*). It is clear from these verses and others that all three dimensions of reality are aspects of Krishna, and that the *adhidaiva* dimension—identified as Purushottama, the "Highest Person"—encompasses and surpasses the other two dimensions.[48]

These three concepts are given added specificity in the *Siddhanta-muktavali*, a Sanskrit text written by Vallabhacharya.[49] Pushti Margiya biographical accounts record that this short text was composed as a teaching for a dedicated devotee of Mount Govardhan to assist him in better understanding the nature of Krishna.[50] In this text Vallabhacharya defines the tripartite nature of ultimate reality, using as an example the Ganges River.

One dimension of the Ganges is her physical stream of water; the second dimension is her all-pervasive spiritual greatness that draws worshipers to her and yields worldly enjoyment (*bhukti*) as well as liberation (*mukti*); and the third is the divine or goddess form (*devata-murti*) that is perceived and engaged as a personality through devotion (*bhakti*). The latter dimension is said to be non-different (*abheda*) yet distinct from her physical water. Vallabhacharya then declares that in this analogy the water of the Ganges is extended to mean the entire visible world (*jagat*), the spiritual power of the Ganges represents the all-pervasive *brahman*, and the Goddess Ganges is to be understood as the Supreme Person, Krishna. Although the terms *adhibhuta*, *adhyatma*, and *adhidaiva* are not specifically mentioned in these verses, all commentaries and later writings presume that the three dimensions of reality referred to here are coterminous with the three conceptual terms used in the *Bhagavad Gita*. The three terms of the *Bhagavad Gita* and *Siddhantamuktavali* are also utilized to develop and express the theology of the Yamuna River, an important Vaishnava riverine goddess;[51] likewise, they are employed to expound the theology of Mount Govardhan. Yadav writes: "Just like with Shri Yamuna-ji, Shri Giriraj-ji also has three *svarupa*s: *adhibhautika*, *adhyatmika*, and *adhidaivika*."[52]

A thorough and erudite theological discussion of Mount Govardhan appears in a remarkable work entitled *Giriyaga*, a recent book written in Sanskritic Hindi by Goswami Shyammanohar, a major Pushti Margiya leader who is head of the Shri Mukundaray-ji temple in Varanasi.[53] The second half of the book is dedicated to an examination of the esoteric meaning of the sacred mountain from the perspective of affectual insight (*bhavatmak*). Shyammanohar's claims are grounded in a close reading of the Giriraj section of the *Garga Samhita*, a text that appears critical to all deep theological reflection on the nature of Mount Govardhan. Shyammanohar's thinking on the complex nature of Mount Govardhan also relies on the concept of the three *svarupa*s as key to accessing a deeper perspective. "In order to fully understand the *bhavatmak* perspective of the Shri Govardhan *lila*, we should first of all come to understand the three *svarupa*s of Mount Govardhan. . . . The authoritative scriptures of India firmly establish that there are three forms of everything: *adhibhautika*, *adhyatmika*, and *adhidaivika*."[54]

Shyammanohar begins his exposition of the three dimensions of Mount Govardhan with an explanation of the *adhibhautika* form:

Adhibhuta is defined as that level of existence that comprises the world of living creatures and inanimate objects. The meaning is that the *adhibhuta* is the physical mountain comprised of the five main elements: earth, water, fires, air, and ether. It is the ever-changing (*kshara*) state that involves a body (*deha*). As it says in the *Bhagavad Gita* (8.4): "*Adhibhuta* is the ever-changing dimension of existence."[55]

The *adhibhautika* form of Mount Govardhan, then, is the material form, the physical mountain that is shrinking the size of a sesame seed every day. Although it is recognized as ever changing (*kshara*), Shyammanohar turns to the *Bhagavad Gita* to establish that the *adhibhautika* dimension of reality is an essential aspect of Krishna.[56] As such, the natural tangible mountain *qua* mountain is fully divine. Yadav concurs: "The form that is the mountain on Earth is his *adhibhautika svarupa*. In this divine play (*lila*) the stone of Shri Giriraj consists of quartzite and precious minerals."[57] A *Bhagavata Purana* scholar who lives in Gokul also declared: "The *adhibhautika svarupa* of Mount Govardhan is the visible mountain." This dimension of Govardhan, then, is the material entity that is the mountain of a heap of physical stones. Although multidimensional, Mount Govardhan is a god of stone.

The physical dimension of the mountain, however, should not be regarded in overly simple terms. Extraordinariness appears in the ordinary when seen through the eyes of story. When I first sat down many years ago to view the film *To Find Our Life: The Peyote Hunt of the Huichols of Mexico*, I had read Barbara Myerhoff's book *The Peyote Hunt: The Sacred Journey of the Huichol Indians*[58] and was very excited to see the footage of the destination of Huichol pilgrimage, Wirikuta, a mountainous site sacred to the Huichol that is identified as the center of creation and inhabited by many colorful divinities. I confess, however, that I was woefully disappointed with how ordinary this area looked to my outsider eyes. Yet I realized that those people in the film crying as they gazed upon Wirikuta were seeing something quite different from what I saw. Likewise, Mount Govardhan from the outside may indeed look like an "ordinary" hill (whatever that may be, as we realize that the ordinary too is socially constructed). But many worshipers told me that in order to perceive even the true physical mountain, one has to see it with eyes prepared by story, knowledge, and belief. It is this perspective that allows some kind of access to the viewpoint of another culture, or perhaps, the "native point of view."

This idea was driven home for me in a conversation I had with a resident of Mathura I met in the Mukut Mukharvind temple at Mansi Ganga in the town of Govardhan. He asked me if I knew what my great-grandfather looked like; I confessed that I did not. He said if he showed me a photo of my great-grandfather without telling me who it was, I would most likely feel nothing and just look at the man in the picture as an "ordinary man." But if he were to inform me that the man in the picture was my great-grandfather I would look at the photo very differently, feeling something toward the man in the photo and most likely honoring him with keen interest. "It is like this with Giriraj," he said. "Those who do not know him see only an ordinary mountain, but when those who know who Giriraj is look at him they feel something deeply and honor him accordingly. We have been listening to stories about Giriraj since we were very young. Therefore, we see the specialness of this mountain in a way outsiders cannot." While not the complete theological perspective, the material dimension remains an important one.

The next dimension of reality is designated the *adhyatmika svarupa*. Yadav offers a fairly standard explanation of this form of Mount Govardhan that associates it with the spiritual aspect of divinity encountered by pilgrims when they come to perform worshipful activities such as circumambulating (*parikrama*) the sacred mountain. "Shri Giriraj-ji removes the sufferings and sorrow (*dukha*) of his devotees with his marvelous grace and kindness (*kripa*), and fulfills their heart's desire (*mano-kamana*). Because of this a large number of devotees perform his *parikrama* with loving faith."[59] Shyammanohar has much more to say about this dimension of Mount Govardhan.[60] He begins with the foundational understanding of the term *adhyatma* as defined by the *Bhagavad Gita* (8.3), as "that level of reality related to the *atma* (the radically interconnected reality or Self)." He expands on this, quoting another verse from the Gita (11.1): "You have shown me kindness by revealing the highest 'secret' (*guhya*) about *adhyatma*." Shyammanohar asserts that use of the term *guhya* means that the *adhyatmik svarupa* is not known by everyone. That is, while everyone may be able to see the physical mountain, the *adhyatmika* dimension cannot be seen, as it is not available to visual perception. The *adhyatmika svarupa* is that unified all-pervasive dimension of reality that is unmanifest, the nothingness that is non-different from everything. Shyammanohar connects the word *atma* with that other important Vedantic term, *brahman* (the radically unified reality), and asserts that the *adhyatmika* perspective establishes the "*brahman*-ness" of everything. Following the *Siddhantamuktavali*, he maintains that this is the aspect of the mountain approached by pilgrims (*tirtha-rupa*) following the scriptural path (*maryada marg*) to gain both worldly enjoyments (*bhoga*) and spiritual liberation (*moksha*). Although the *adhyatmika* dimension of reality is all-pervasive, it is most concentrated and available at special places like Mount Govardhan. As such, it is the imperceptible spiritual energy (*shakti*) of the mountain that attracts pilgrims, who strive to access this power.

Shyammanohar introduces the preeminent *adhidaivika svarupa* by asserting that it is the divine form (*devata-rupa*) of Krishna, which is different from—though not unrelated to—both the *adhibhautika* form and the *adhyatmika* form. He identifies it with the "divinely embodied form" (*murti-rupa*), and defines it in terms of the *Bhagavad Gita*'s assertion that "the *adhidaiva* is the Supreme Person (*Purusha*)" (8.4). According to Pushti Margiya teachings, the *adhidaivika svarupa* is the "foundational" divinity (*adhisthata devata*) upon which all else depends. Most importantly, however, the *adhidaivika svarupa* is the supreme personality of Krishna that is encountered in the intimate realms of divine relationship. The *adhidaivika svarupa* is linked with the concept of Purushottama, a complex term that is somewhat difficult to grasp since it is situated conceptually in the interstitial space that both encompasses and surpasses the polar opposites of changing (*kshara*) form and unchanging (*akshara*) formlessness, or of the *adhibhautika* and *adhyatamika*.[61] Some refer to it as *arupa-rupa-rupa*, the "form that is simultaneously form and formlessness."[62] But what is this?

The eleventh chapter of the *Bhagavad Gita* gives narrative illustration of the traits of Purushottama. At this point in the text, Arjuna has realized that his assumption that Krishna could be fully accounted for by the particular physical form of his friend the chariot driver was misleadingly incomplete; he was previously unaware of the immense, unmanifest, and all-pervasive dimension of Krishna. Much of Krishna's teaching to Arjuna up to this point in the text is aimed at opening him up to an awareness of the *adhyatmika* dimension of reality through the ultimate knowledge (*jnana*) that leads to a deep cognizance of its radical interconnectedness and unmanifest formlessness (*akshara brahman*). Arjuna consequently asks Krishna to disclose his imperishable essence (*avyaya atma*). Krishna obliges him by in effect removing his mask of particular form to expose his majestic *aishvara rupa*—his limitless, imperishable, unmanifest awesome form; he reveals this "universal form" (*vishva-rupa*) as the infinity of all forms situated in a single place (*eka-stha*). From the perspective of human perception, however, there is no difference between everything and nothing (consider colorless white light [nothing] in which all colors [everything] are simultaneously present, but become visible only when differentiated via something like a prism), and indeed this "form" of Krishna is identified as *akshara Brahman* (11.18), the all-pervasive, formless, unchanging dimension of divinity.

Arjuna gains an important kind of knowledge from this revelation, but expresses increasing alarm as he is now bewildered and finds no orientation, no peace, no approach, and no intimacy or loving connection with his former friend. The universal form is too vast and too amorphous; it's also frighteningly disorienting. Arjuna begs Krishna to replace his mask of particularity and resume a familiar form that allows personal relationship—as a Father to a son, a Friend to a friend, or a Beloved to a lover (11.44). Specifically, Arjuna asks Krishna to once again return to the friendly form that had been the basis of their affectionate connection. Importantly, the form that produces the most intimate relationship for humans is identified as a "familiar human form" (*saumya manusha rupa*).[63] This form is now recognized as being non-different from both form and formlessness (and yet offers more than either), but the former is privileged in the devotional relationship. The favorable form that allows a peaceful approach is also called the *sva-rupa*, literally "own form" (11.50). This term has an expedient double meaning: it means both an essential form of Krishna, as well as the devotee's own form; that is, the particular form in which Krishna comes to the devotee is the form most attractive to the devotee. This form, which enables an intimate relationship with Krishna, will, of course, vary from individual to individual. This is Purushottama, the "Supreme Personality"—perhaps best understood poetically as the face of the most exquisite Beloved imaginable to the devotee floating on the Infinite Void. Within the conceptual context of the three dimensions of Mount Govardhan, this is the supreme personality of the mountain that allows for deep connective relationship.

In summary, Shyammanohar states: "From the position of the scriptures, we know that blessed Mount Govardhan's *adhibhautika svarupa* is the physical mountain (*parvat*), the *adhyatmika svarupa* is its all-pervasive and unchanging essence (*aksharatmak*), and the *adhidaivika svarupa* is its supreme divinity (*adhisthata devata*)."[64] He finishes his general introduction of Mount Govardhan's three *svarupas* by relating them to the three aspects of Brahman as defined in the Vedantic scriptures. He begins by maintaining that Govardhan is a form of the ultimate reality Brahman, most specifically a form of *sac-chid-ananda Parabrahman*; that is, as *sac-chid-ananda Brahman*, Mount Govardhan is ultimate reality that consists of "existence" (*sat*), "consciousness" (*chid*), and "bliss" (*ananda*). Shyammanohar relates these three aspects of ultimate reality to the three *svarupa*s, claiming that the *adhibhautika* form of Govardhan is a portion of Brahman's physical existence (*sad-amsha*), the *adhyatmika* dimension is a portion of the highest consciousness (*chid-amsha*), and the *adhidaivika* aspect is a portion of supreme bliss (*ananda-amsha*).

Yadav's writing on the *adhidaivika svarupa* reveals something further about the complex nature of the highest divinity. "Shri Giriraj-ji has two *adhidaivika svarupa*s: *Bhagavat* (Lord) *svarupa* and the *Haridasavarya* ("Best Devotee of Hari") *svarupa*."[65] Here Yadav discloses an important feature of the *adhidaivika svarupa*: it has a double identity, the form of Krishna and the form of Krishna's highest devotee. This theological perspective is widespread. As a well-known *swami* in Braj informed me: "Shri Giriraj-ji is *sakshat* Krishna. He is both Hari (another name for Krishna) and Hari-dasa (devotee of Krishna). To worship and enjoy himself he became both worshiper and worshiped." These dual identities of the *adhidaivika svarupa* are revealed in two narratives found in the *Bhagavata Purana*; they are based, respectively, on the story told about Krishna's initial worship of Mount Govardhan and on what is called the Venu Gita, or "Song of the Flute."

In addition to these two personalities of the *adhidaivika svarupa*, Shyammanohar identifies in his *Giriyaga* yet a third: this is the *Svamini svarupa*, the feminine personality of Mount Govardhan that is identified with Radha, the preeminent lover of Krishna. His theological articulation of this esoteric identity is based on a close reading of the narrative of the origin of Mount Govardhan found in the *Garga Samhita*. Although I was to discover that the *Svamini svarupa* identity of Govardhan is not an uncommon feature of Braj Vaishnava culture, among all I learned while conducting research on Mount Govardhan, this was the most novel. I had never encountered this conception of the mountain in any English literature on Govardhan. Once I discovered the female *Svamini* identity of the mountain, however, I encountered it everywhere around the mountain in embodied forms, temple and home shrine rituals, theological conversations, artwork, and stories.

Besides the general understanding of Mount Govardhan already examined, then, a more esoteric conception of Mount Govardhan exists that is grounded in what is called the *bhavatmak* perspective, meaning a perspective based on affectual insight into the true nature of reality. A reading of the *Garga Samhita* is crucial for the *bhavatmak* perspective, for the story told in this text about the origin of the sacred mountain is not found in other important scriptural texts, such as the *Bhagavata Purana*. In his book *Giriyaga*, Shyammanohar draws a distinction between the more general view and esoteric *bhavatmak* one. He first reminds us of the conventional scriptural perspective of the three kinds of *svarupas*: "The *adhibhautika svarupa* is stone (*pashan*). The *adhyatmika svarupa* is the innermost and highest essence of reality (*tattvatmak sadantantargata*), and the *adhidaivika svarupa* is the supreme divinity of Mount Govardhan (*Govardhan parvat adhisthata devata*)." The esoteric *bhavatmak* perspective, however, reveals something more: "But when we consider them from a *bhavatmak* perspective the *adhibhautika svarupa* is the Lord's pleasurable playground (*vihar-sthali*) in the form of a mountain, the *adhyatmika svarupa* is a condensed form of the nectar of divine love (*ghani-bhuta rasa*), and the *adhidaivika svarupa* is the blissful female Svamini form of Haridasavarya."[66] The implication of this is that the multifaceted and comprehensive theological perspective of Mount Govardhan affirms three forms or *svarupas* of the sacred mountain—the *adhibhautika* (physical), *adhyatmika* (spiritual), and the *adhidaivika* (divine). Significantly, the latter *adhidaivika svarupa* itself has three subtypes or personalities, the three major identities of Mount Govardhan: Sakshat Bhagavan Krishna, Haridasavarya, and Svamini-ji (Radha).

Sakshat Bhagavan Krishna

As indicated earlier in this chapter, the most prevalent theological conception of Govardhan is that the mountain is a tangible form of Krishna, or in other words, the most common identity of its *adhidaivika svarupa* is *sakshat* Bhagavan Krishna. There is no need to repeat these features here, only to add that this notion is further supported by a more esoteric and sophisticated understanding based on an interpretation of the *Garga Samhita*. According to the story of Mount Govardhan's birth told in this text, the mountain came from a fiery mass of love gushing forth from Krishna's own heart; hence, it is a concrete manifestation issuing from his own body in the form of an intense passion, and in this sense is non-different from Krishna himself. Thus the mountain is *sakshat* Krishna, a direct, tangible, and exceptional form of God. Working with the disclosures of the *Garga Samhita*, Shyammanohar explicates a fuller identification of the sacred mountain with Krishna that leads to a more complex theological conception of the divinity of Mount Govardhan. He maintains that since the sacred mountain manifested directly from Krishna, it consists of all pilgrimage sites (*sarva-tirtha-maya*), is the beloved of the gods (*devatao ka priya*), and is the color of a dark cloud (*megha-shyam*), the same color of Krishna as Ghanashyam Bhagavan, the Dark Lord.[67] Most importantly for him and many others, Mount Govardhan is considered an essential concrete form of the highest reality Purna Purushottam, the complete and ever blissful Supreme Being that is Krishna.[68] Mount Govardhan is regarded as a vibrant form of Krishna's own heart (*hriday svarupa*) and a manifestation of his infinite passionate love (*anurag*), or more specifically, a condensed form of the very essence of ultimate love itself (*ghani-bhuta-rasa*). We will see in the following section on the *Svamini svarupa*, however, that Mount Govardhan consists of far more than Krishna's love alone.

Haridasavarya: Best of Krishna's Devotees

The twenty-first chapter in the tenth book of the *Bhagavata Purana* is known as the Venu Gita, or "Song of the Flute." The chapter opens with Krishna entering the Vrindaban forest accompanied by his cows and cowherd buddies. The season is autumn; the forest is lush and fragrant with blossoming flowers. Krishna lifts his flute to his lips and plays an alluring tune that creates a surge of ecstatic desire in all beings who hear it, including the deer, birds, cows, and rivers, but especially the *gopi*s, Krishna's cowherd girlfriends. The women begin to praise Krishna and sing a song that expresses their longing. In the eighteenth verse of the song inspired by Krishna's flute, the gopis sing about Mount Govardhan, and praise it as Hari-dasa-varya, the "Best of Krishna's Devotees," because the mountain has intimate contact with Krishna and serves him and his cows with abundant grass and flowers, cool water, secret caves, and fruits and roots. Vallabhacharya explicates this verse in his *Subodhini* commentary on the *Bhagavata Purana*. Although lacking monetary wealth, the mountain offers Krishna the four traditional gifts of a hospitable host: a grass seat, refreshing water, a place on the earth to entertain, and sweet speech. Mount Govardhan has plenty of grass on its slopes to provide a comfortable seat for Krishna as well as nourishment for his cows; the mountain's springs dispense pure cool water; the level ground at its base provides ample space for entertainment and other activities; and since it cannot speak, it offers sweet roots for the palate.[69] Shyammanohar points out that the mountain still offers all these things today. Others add to this list of services. A Gaudiya Vaishnava *baba* living in an ashram near the mountain, for example, claimed, "the hard stones become yielding when Krishna walks on them and soft as a bed when he chooses to rest. And when Krishna wants to climb the mountain the stones become like a stairway."

Perhaps most important among the gifts Govardhan offers Krishna are secret caves for his love play with his beloved Radha.[70] Some people say the love caves number eight, but whatever their quantity, they are a vital feature of Mount Govardhan.[71] The Ashta Chap poet Chaturbhujadas is said to have had a vision of Radha and Krishna emerging from such a cave in Govardhan and expressed it in a well-known poem.[72] I met a man who told me that he circumambulates the mountain primarily to contemplate the amorous activities of the divine couple within these love caves. What is recognized as the greatest feature of the mountain's loving service (*seva*), however, is that Mount Govardhan serves Krishna with his entire body. Loving service with the entire body is the mark of the highest service of the supreme romantic mood of devotion (*madhurya bhava*).[73] Because of his many devotional services, Mount Govardhan is known as Haridasavarya and is rewarded with the bliss of both the sight (*darshan*) and touch (*sparshan*) of Krishna. As such, he is an inspirational model for devotional worship who himself is worshiped by devotees seeking his blessings for ever-intensified levels of devotion.

One of the meanings of Go-vardhan is the "Nurturer of the Senses"; in the context of Krishna *bhakti*, Govardhan is considered specifically to be the "Increaser of Love."[74] The following poem by the seventeenth-century Pushti Margiya writer Hariray gives expanded expression of the good fortune of Haridasavarya:

> Fortunate Haridasavarya is full of the nectar of bliss.
> He is the supreme abode for Krishna's love play,
> And is the intensifier of the devotees' love.
> He brought about the great blessing of the forest women,
> And is the residence of all inexpressible qualities and stories.
> The Beloved and his Lover play here eternally,
> And the connoisseurs of devotion thirst to see it.[75]

This poem underscores the special quality of Govardhan as a nurturer of the devotees' love. The special features of Mount Govardhan's service that are highlighted here culminate in the provision of a wonderful playground for Krishna to make love with his foremost beloved, Radha. This harkens back to the story of Govardhan's origin in Radha's desire for a secluded place for her romantic dalliances with Krishna. The identification of Govardhan as Haridasavarya, however, seems to make an apparent distinction between Krishna and the mountain as Krishna's highest devotee.

The overwhelming majority of people I interviewed regard Mount Govardhan as *sakhat* Bhagavan Krishna, a direct form of Krishna; yet many of these acknowledge that he is also Haridasavarya. Although it is rare for someone to identify Govardhan exclusively as Haridasavarya, a contemporary Gaudiya Vaishnava teacher, Swami Gour Govinda, claims: "This mountain, Giriraja Govardhana is known *as hari-dasa-varya....* We accept Giriraja Govardhana as a devotee of Lord Hari, not as Bhagavan. Some devotees have a misconception and worship Giriraja Govardhana as Bhagavan Krishna, placing a peacock feather or a flute on him." He insists that this is wrong, emphasizing: "He (Govardhan) is not Krishna."[76] This is very much a minority position. I found it expressed in no other literature about Mount Govardhan, nor did I hear it articulated in any of my conversations with worshipers of the mountain. Indeed, without exception, everyone to whom I presented this view disagreed strongly. Shrivatsa Goswami of Vrindaban, for example, told me that any insistence that Mount Govardhan is only a devotee of Krishna and not Krishna himself is a "limited and dualistic view. It does not represent the dominant viewpoint of Gaudiya Vaishnavism. The *Bhagavata Purana* makes it clear that Govardhan is both *sakshat* Krishna and a devotee of Krishna, in fact, the very best of devotees."

How are the two seemingly contradictory conceptions of Mount Govardhan as an essential form of Krishna and as a devotee of Krishna reconciled? One Gaudiya Vaishnava *swami* explained: "Govardhan is defined as Haridasavarya in *Bhagavata Purana* 10.21.18 and is identified with Krishna in 10.24.35. How are these two views to be connected? Govardhan as Haridasavarya is the manifestation Krishna assumed to have the experience of tasting his own sweet form as a devotee. So from a certain perspective, Krishna and his chief devotee Haridasavarya are the same." Shrivatsa Goswami had much more to say about this:

Krishna did something very revolutionary. He elevated a devotee to the position of God. He touched the feet of Govardhan when Indra's distress came upon the residents of Braj, and I think that Govardhan just jumped into the air out of surprise; this is how Krishna was able to lift the mountain.

But where do we find the definition of Govardhan as Haridasavarya? In the Venu Gita of the *gopis*. Everyone acknowledges the *gopis* as the highest gurus on the path of *prem-bhakti* (devotional love), but the *gopis* themselves acknowledge Govardhan as the highest devotee. This means that Govardhan is even higher than the *gopis*.

Giriraj Govardhan is Haridasavarya, the devotee par excellence. But who is this devotee? Krishna becomes the very best devotee Haridasavarya to experience the joy of worshiping himself. So Krishna is both worshiper and worshiped. This is *bheda-abheda*, "difference in non-difference." There is no difference between God and the devotee or worshiper, and yet to experience love there has to be a difference between the lover and the Beloved. Krishna comes to experience all *rasas* (emotional moods), so he assumes the form of both the lover and the beloved. This is the dialectic of love.

To experience the bliss of the amorous *rasa* (*madhurya*) he becomes the beloved and lover; to experience the parental *rasa* (*vatsalya*) he becomes child and father; to experience the friendship *rasa* (*sakhya*) he becomes mutual friends; and to experience the devotional *rasa* (*dasya*) he becomes lord and devotee. And this is Giriraj as Haridasavarya.

All this happens because it is all a question of relationship. And relationship always requires *two*: the *ashraya* ("vessel") and the *vishaya* ("object"). There has to be a taster and a tasted for blissful taste to occur. This is because of *rasa*; there has to be two and one. The one becomes the two to experience itself. This is the relationship between Krishna and Haridasavarya. They are the two that are really one.

This response is informed by the complex non-dual Gaudiya Vaishnava Vedantic philosophy articulated by the Vrindaban Gosvamins, most particularly the sophisticated *rasa* theory articulated by Rupa Gosvamin in his sixteenth-century Sanskrit treatise the *Bhaktirasamritasindhu*.[77] In many ways the perspective Shrivatsa Goswami expressed is grounded in the Upanishadic notion that the creative process involves a differentiation of the original One. *Brihadaranyaka Upanishad* 1.4, for example, describes the primordial One (termed alternatively *atma*, *purusha*, and *brahman*) as lonely, bored, and without joy in its singularity. For the purposes of pleasure, the One divided itself into two—male and female—and proceeded to make love with itself as a joyful act of creative play. The pleasurable feature of this original division and productive process was emphasized in later renderings of this account of creation, especially by those interested in the dynamics of divine love and its resulting bliss (*ananda*), which is considered to be the highest aspect of divinity within the Braj Vaishnava traditions.[78] The dynamics of love require twoness, a split between the lover and beloved, as love is found in the relationship *between* the two. Two can experience each other as lovers, but what can one do? The theoreticians of Braj *bhakti* are fond of saying that they don't want to become sugar, rather they want to taste sugar. Here taste is the blissful experience of love, and sugar is Krishna as Parabrahman, the supreme reality that is the foundation of everything. Tasting requires a differentiation between the tasting tongue and tasted sugar, but of course, in the non-dual context of Vaishnava Vedanta, there is no ultimate difference between the tasting tongue ("vessel"/*ashraya*) and the sugar ("object"/*vishaya*). Both are essentially sugar. This is what is referred to as *bheda-abheda*, the simultaneity of difference and non-difference.

In his *Bhaktirasamritasindhu*, Rupa Gosvamin expresses the dynamics of love in terms of the classical Sanskrit aesthetic theory that originated in dramatics. His primary concern in this work is to articulate the intricacies of the highest devotional emotion of supreme love, called *bhakti-rasa* or Krishna-*prema*. He recognizes three components of emotional experience: the emotion itself (*bhava*),[79] the "object" of the emotion (*vishaya*), and the "vessel" of the emotion (*ashraya*). Using the dramatic example of Shakespeare's *Romeo and Juliet*, Romeo is the object of Juliet's love, Juliet is the vessel of that love, and their romantic love itself (*bhava*) arises out of the relationship between them. This viewpoint can, of course, be reversed, with Juliet as the object of Romeo's love and Romeo as the vessel of this love; here we see the non-dual circular nature of dynamic love that is replicated in the Govardhan story. Supreme Krishna, the One, becomes two; he assumes the form of both the lover or worshiper of the mountain as well as the worshiped or beloved mountain itself.[80] Krishna the cowherd performs an exemplary act of love by worshiping the beloved mountain, and the mountain takes the form of Haridasavarya to become the devoted lover of Krishna, the beloved object of the mountain's devotion. This is what Shrivatsa Goswami meant by "[t]hey are the two that are really one."

Shrivatsa did not develop his comments in this direction, but according to the devotional aesthetic (*rasa*) theory that underlies Braj Vaishnavism, one could say that although in the mood of servitude (*dasya bhava*) Govardhan as Haridasavarya becomes the "vessel" as a devoted servant, in the elevated amorous mood (*madhurya bhava*) Govardhan as Haridasavarya becomes the devotional vessel as a passionate lover. This is precisely the direction in which Shyammanohar moves. Relying on Pushti Margiya philosophical sources and a close reading of the *Garga Samhita*, he too articulates a view of Haridasavarya as the highest devotee, but takes it to a remarkable conclusion. Building on the notion that Haridasavarya is non-different from Krishna, is the best of his devotee lovers, and performs loving service (*seva*) with the entire body, he reveals that Mount Govardhan operates within the *madhurya bhava* as a female form that is identified with Krishna's highest lover, Radha. "Considering the essential form of Shri Govardhan from the perspective of *rasa*, she is Haridasavarya as the female lover form (*nayika ka svarupa*) that increases love (*rati*)."[81] This female form of Mount Govardhan identified with Radha is called the *Svamini svarupa*.

Svamini Svarupa (Radha)

In addition to conceptualizing Mount Govardhan as a female (*svamini*) form through a connection with the Haridasavarya identity, Shyammanohar makes a case for the *Svamini svarupa* in a number of other ways, all of which find their basis in the story told in the *Garga Samhita* about the original manifestation of the mountain. He focuses on the detail that although the mountain manifested as a form of passion (*anuraga*) from Krishna's heart, it was instigated by Radha's loving desire (*manorath*). Drawing out the implicit meaning of this narrative, he writes: "Shri Govardhan manifest from a sprout of loving passion (*anurag*). Having taken in Shri Radha's request that was full of her passion, Bhagavan Shri Krishna himself became full of passion and manifest Shri Govardhan as a material form (*murti*) of this composite passion that was overflowing from his own heart."[82] That is, Radha's love was injected, through her loving glance, into Krishna's heart, where it became commingled with his love, and then manifested as the combined form of their love as Mount Govardhan. Shyammanohar's leading point is that Mount Govardhan is a congealed form of the united love of both Radha and Krishna.

Shyammanohar extends his exposition on the feminine nature of Mount Govardhan by underscoring the fact that the *Garga Samhita* characterizes the jet of passion that gushes from Krishna's heart as a stream of fire and water (*sajalam tejo*).[83] According to his understanding, the fiery brilliance (*tejas*) is Krishna's intense love and the cool water (*jala*) is Radha's soothing love, and Govardhan is the resulting mixture of both. "Since the manifestation of

Govardhan was born from the heart's desire (*manorath*) of Svamini (Radha), the *svarupa* of Govardhan is Svamini's heart (*hridaya*). The very glance of Svamini's heart was absorbed into the heart of Bhagavan (Krishna), then Bhagavan, whose own heart became filled with love through his lotus-eyes that took in her love-filled glance and allowed him to see the heart of his Svamini, manifest Govardhan in the form of a stream of brilliant fire mixed with water."[84] The mountain, accordingly, is an amalgamation of Radha and Krishna's passionate love.

Shyammanohar adds another point regarding Mount Govardhan's identity with Radha. A verse in the *Garga Samhita* states that Govardhan consists of jewels (*ratna*) and precious metals (*dhatu*).[85] After acknowledging the ordinary meaning of these terms, he moves on to explore their "deeper meaning" (*gambhirya-purvak*). Dictionary definitions, as well as poetic usages, demonstrate that *ratna* is a feminine noun associated with "Shri" and the *gopis*, or female lovers of Krishna.[86] Shyammanohar quotes Vedantic texts to illustrate that *dhatu* is a masculine noun that can mean Paramatma, another name for Krishna. "From all this we can conclude after considering the words *dhatu* and *ratna* that *dhatu* is a term for Bhagavan and *ratna* is a term for a special *gopi*. The statement that Shri Govardhan consists of *ratna-dhatu*, then, means that it consists of Bhagavan Para-Brahman Shri Krishna and his Beloved Shri Radha."[87] From this perspective, too, the true identity of Govardhan is a condensed form of the combined love of the divine couple that streamed out of Krishna's heart.

Shyammanohar further supports his contention that Mount Govardhan is also a form of Radha by interpreting the word "Shri" that usually proceeds Govardhan as an indication of the presence of the goddess, in this case Krishna's beloved, Radha.[88] This is in line with the theological assertion that Radha and Krishna, though two, are essentially one. This is often expressed in Braj with the Hindi phrase *ek pran do deha* ("one essence, two bodies")—though the two are of one essence, for the dynamics of love they assume two bodies. In essence, Radha and Krishna share the same heart: "It can be said that the creation of Govardhan in the Lord's heart corresponded to Shri Radha's desire. Actually, Shri Radha is an essential form of Lord Krishna. Therefore, Shri Radha's heart itself is Lord Krishna's heart, which manifest outwardly in the form of Govardhan."[89] The true and most profound identity of Govardhan, then, is a condensed form of the combined love of the divine couple that streamed out of their shared heart. The most mysterious form of Mount Govardhan for Shyammanohar, however, is revealed to be an essential form of Radha's heart. Although the identity of Mount Govardhan's *adhidaivik svarupa* includes both Krishna and Radha, here Radha as the origin of the passion that created the mountain is privileged. "Bhagavan manifest Shri Govardhan from his heart, which is the essential form of Shri Radha-ji's heart; therefore, Govardhan is the heart form (*hridaya svarupa*) of Radha-ji."[90]

If Shyammanohar's contention that the major identities of the *adhidaivika svarupa* of Mount Govardhan include Radha had no expression in actual religious practice, then it would remain solely in the realm of theological speculation. This, however, is not the case. Although the identification of Mount Govardhan as a form of Radha is not commonly voiced, it is nonetheless fairly widespread. One of the main priests at the Manasi Ganga Mukharvind temple told me regarding the dual Govardhan stones there: "This Giriraj *svarupa* is really Radha and Krishna, for nothing happens without Radha. This single unit is both Krishna and Radha. They are the two that are really one, just like *ek pran do deha*." The attending priest of a Govardhan temple in Vrindaban that houses an adorned Giriraj stone explained: "Giriraj-ji is Krishna himself, but as the name of this temple indicates (Shri Radha Giridhari-ji Maharaj Mandir.), it can also be seen as a form of Radha." An attendant priest at the Jatipura Mukharvind informed for me, "You should know that this mountain is also a form (*svarupa*) of Radha."

Once I became aware of the concept of the *svamini svarupa*, or simply the idea that the esoteric identity of Mount Govardhan involves Radha, I began to hear and see indications of this everywhere. I attended a lecture at a Pushti Margiya pilgrimage camp near Surabhi Kund with a Pushti Margiya man from Jatipura. During the lecture I thought that I heard the preacher make the point that Mount Govardhan has a female (*svamini*) form and shout "Shri Giridharan Maharani ki Jaya!" (All Glory be to the Queen who Held/Assumed the Form of the Mountain). I turned to my friend and asked him if I had heard correctly. He affirmed that I had. Later, when we were sitting together at my house in Jatipura, I asked him again if this is what the preacher had said. With an elated shout of "Shri Giridharan Maharani ki Jaya!" he assured me that this was so, and from that day on whenever he saw me he greeted me with this exclamation. He supported and elaborated this point with a story.

After Krishna had held Mount Govardhan with his left hand for seven full days he appeared somewhat tired, so his mother and some of the other cowherd women began to massage his left arm. At this point Radha's close girlfriend Lalita arrived and asked Krishna why they were massaging his arm. He informed her, and she retorted that it was not he who held up the mountain. When Krishna expressed surprise at this remark and asked her what she meant, she went on to explain that "your left half is my Svamini Shri Radha, and so it was she who held up the mountain, not you." My friend then evoked the *ek pran do deha* statement and explained that Govardhan was both Krishna and Radha. "Thus," he concluded, "one can praise the mountain either as Krishna by saying 'Shri Giriraj Maharaj ki Jaya!' or as Radha by saying 'Shri Giridharan Maharani ki Jaya!' " Paintings exist in the Braj region that confirm this perspective. They portray the divinity of Mount Govardhan (Shri Nath-ji) as half Radha and half Krishna, and indeed Radha is depicted as the left half of this composite divinity with her left arm extended upward in the mountain-holding pose.

Stories circulate in Braj that tell how Krishna was a bit shaky while he was holding the mountain until he had eye contact with Radha; only then did full strength come to him. Poems also exist that tell how Krishna was only able to hold the mountain because of the graceful glance of Radha. A few lines from a well-known poem delivered to me by a Radhakund-dwelling Gaudiya Vaishanva *baba* describe this:

> I get strength from my mother by eating butter.
> I get fresh yogurt from the cowherd women.
> But from the grace of Radha I was able to support Mount Govardhan.[91]

Rock-solid evidence of this perspective also exists in the form of numerous temples around the mountain that feature a pair of Govardhan stones, one decorated and dressed as Krishna and the other as Radha (Figures 3.3, 3.4, and 3.5). These include temples open to public viewing as well as private home shrines; some are generic Braj Vaishnava shrines, whereas others are maintained by either Gaudiya or Pushti Margiya Vaishnava practitioners. My encounter with pairs of Govardhan stones decorated and dressed as Radha and Krishna included a shrine with the divine couple resting on a raised platform in a forest on the west side of the mountain, a small temple in the ashram of a group of Bengali *babas* living near the tail of the mountain, a couple of roadside temples on the circumambulatory path, two side shrines in the famous Lakshmi-Narayana temple within the town of Govardhan, as well as many home shrines.

Figure 3.3. Radha and Krishna Govardhan stones in forest north of Jatipura.

Among the latter was a home shrine of a Gaudiya Vaishnava *baba* residing at Radhakund who explained: "I worship Govardhan as a couple (*yugal*). That is why there are two stones. There is really no success unless you worship God as *yugal*. There has to be the feminine; there has to be the feminine along with the masculine. This is what is meant by *yugal*—the 'pair.' Therefore, I worship Govardhan as both Radha and Krishna." Although it is very rare, I did encounter a forest shrine site featuring a single stone dressed and decorated as Radha alone (Figure 3.6).

One of the highest conceptions of Mount Govardhan, then, is as a congealed form of Supreme Love that streamed forth from the bliss-filled hearts of the divine couple. One day a priest at the Mathuradish Mandir in Jatipura took me over to a large Govardhan stone that had been set up on a shelf for worship in the corner of the temple courtyard (Figure 3.7).

He instructed me to look closely at it and tell him what I saw. Not sure what he wanted me to focus on, I asked him what he saw. "Look," he said, "you see these yellow streaks in the stone?" I looked and reported that I did indeed see them. "Radha is golden in color, and these streaks are from her heart. And look here at these streaks of black. They are from Krishna's heart, since

Figure 3.4. Stones dressed as Radha and Krishna in ashram of Bengali babas near Punchari.

Figure 3.5. Radha and Krishna stones in Radhakund home shrine.

Figure 3.6. Govardhan stone decorated as Radha in forest north of Jatipura.

Figure 3.7. Govardhan stone set up in Mathuradish temple courtyard in Jatipura.

he is dark in color. You can see that the two are mixed together in the form of this Govardhan stone. It is a condensed form of the combined love of the divine pair Radha and Krishna." As he finished this explanation, he touched the base of the stone reverently with his right hand and then placed it to his forehead, eyes, and heart exclaiming, "Shri Giriraj Dharan ki Jaya!"

In sum, Mount Govardhan is a mountain of embodied love, and being non-different from supreme divinity Parabrahman Purna-Purushottama Bhagavan Krishna, is identified with the very source of all love. Govardhan is a mountainous form of divinity that is said to give love quickly and is readily available for a loving relationship with those devotees who approach it. This goes for every stone on the mountain, for as the head priest at the Manasi Ganga Mukharvind temple explained: "Each and every Giriraj *shila* is non-different from the whole mountain." In this sense, Govardhan is a mountain of "loving stones." In return, what the mountain asks for is love. And indeed, Mount Govardhan and its stones are honored and loved intensely through a great variety of forms of worship. The devotional responses, then, are the means of "loving stones." Public worship of the whole mountain is generally expressed through circumambulation (*parikrama*) and ritual veneration (*puja*) in large temples, while the private worship of smaller stones takes place in the more intimate setting of home shrines. Consideration of the former follows, while detailed examination of the latter will be taken up in Chapter 6.

4

Honoring the King of Mountains

Embodied Worship

Just one look at this mountain and love comes to a person.[1]

You too can have your heart's desire fulfilled by coming into
the presence of Shri Govardhan Giriraj just once.[2]

Encircling the Mountain with a Wish in Their Hearts

A steady march of bare-footed devotees advances around Mount Govardhan
with reverence and desire, their hearts tied to the mountain by an emotional
connection like a cord holding an object swinging around a central pivot.
One of the chief ways of honoring a sacred entity within Hindu devotional
practice is circumambulating it clockwise. Called in the Sanskritic north
Indian languages *pradakshina*, or more commonly *parikrama*, ritual circumambulation is an ancient way of revering some special figure in South Asian
religious cultures. Many people told me that *parikrama* is one of the most
important ways of venerating Mount Govardhan; it is a form of worshiping
the entire mountain with the whole body. Specifically, it involves walking the
entire fourteen-mile *parikrama* pathway around Mount Govardhan, keeping
the right side of the body toward the mountain while holding it in one's heart
and holding certain attitudes in one's mind.

I spoke to a young man who is a member of the family in charge of the
worship in one of the major temples in Jatipura just after he had completed a
parikrama of Mount Govardhan. I asked him why he and others perform this
parikrama. He answered: "Nanda Baba (Krishna's father) did this *parikrama*
and took the residents of Braj with him. And our fathers too do *parikrama*
and so we follow (*anusaran*) them and do it. For generations and generations
our ancestors have been doing the Giriraj *parikrama*, so we do too." Another

Loving Stones. David L. Haberman, Oxford University Press (2020) © Oxford University Press.
DOI: 10.1093/oso/9780190086718.001.0001

man I spoke with put it this way: "Krishna himself worshiped this mountain. He was the first to perform its *parikrama*, and by doing so taught us how to honor (*manana*) Giriraj-ji in this way." Both of these men were referring to a well-known narrative recounted in the *Bhagavata Purana*. When Krishna appropriated the huge offering that was to have gone to Indra and offered it to Mount Govardhan, he conducted an elaborate worship of the mountain and led the residents of Braj around the mountain in an honorific circumambulation.[3] In the role of a foundational teacher, Krishna established a ritual paradigm for later worshipers of Mount Govardhan.

Although not mentioned in the *Bhagavata Purana*, and less well known than that of Krishna's first worship, an account of a previous paradigm for circumambulating Mount Govardhan is narrated within the *Garga Samhita*. At the time of Mount Govardhan's descent and birth into the family of Mount Drona, all of the sacred mountains came and glorified the magnificent new mountain as Giriraj, the "King of Mountains." They worshiped him with lavish offerings and circumambulated him with reverence. Aware of this double paradigm, the Jatipura priest and author Brajesh Joshi writes: "At the time of Mount Govardhan's birth, the gods rained flowers upon him. After worshiping him, the kings of the Himalayan Mountains performed the first *parikrama*. At the end of the Dvapara age, Lord Krishna worshiped Govardhan and performed his *parikrama*, and since then the *parikrama* of Shri Govardhan Giriraj-ji has continued without interruption right up to the present day."[4] In addition to the paradigmatic circumambulation of the mountain performed by Krishna, many of the founding saints of Braj Vaishnavism, such as Vallabhacharya and Chaitanya, established additional models for their followers by performing the *parikrama* of Mount Govardhan themselves.[5]

Regardless of which paradigm is followed, pious pilgrims have been circumambulating Mount Govardhan for centuries, and today their number seems to be increasing steadily. No official statistical information is available, but residents of the five towns around the mountain report swelling crowds of visitors coming to circumambulate the sacred mountain. The routine *parikrama* draws thousands of pilgrims daily, and these numbers surge considerably on special days. Newspaper articles from the mid-1980s, for example, report that a half million people came to perform the Govardhan *parikrama* on the occasion of Guru Purnima (also called Muriya Purnima and Vyas Purnima), the full moon of the lunar month of Ashadh.[6] As mentioned in the previous chapter, more than eight million were recorded to have come to do the same during Guru Purnima of 2015.[7] Every month, hundreds of thousands now come to Govardhan for *parikrama* during the four days leading up to the full moon, between the eleventh day of the bright half of the lunar month (*ekadashi*) and the full moon (*purnima*). There is a saying in this area: *puran masi, puran kam* ("full moon, fulfilled desire"), which indicates that one's desires are best achieved during the full moon period. The time between the eleventh day of the dark half of the lunar month and the new moon (*amavasya*) also draws large numbers of pilgrims to the mountain.

Due to an increasingly standardized schedule for the contemporary workweek, weekends are also the occasion for large numbers of worshipers to circumambulate Mount Govardhan, particularly from New Delhi. Government offices in New Delhi are closed on the weekends, and the distance between this megacity and Mount Govardhan (about 100 miles) is such that it allows for an enjoyable weekend outing with the added incentive of meritorious benefits derived from the performance of this *parikrama*. When I asked people living around the mountain why they thought the numbers were increasing so dramatically, they cited such factors as the greater ease and availability of modern transportation and the recent growth of a religious view that involves the pursuit of the fulfillment of certain desires. Specific reasons for why people perform the *parikrama* of Mount Govardhan will be addressed toward the end of this chapter, but in brief, besides being a way to revere the mountain, people generally report, "it is a way to fulfill one's heart's desire" (*mano-kamana puri hoti hai*). Based on conversations with hundreds of people who performed this *parikrama*, it seems the most convincing reason for the increase in numbers is what one man called the "herd effect." That is, people report to friends and neighbors in their village, town, or city that they had great success in obtaining their "heart's desire" by completing the Govardhan *parikrama*. These friends and neighbors perform the *parikrama* with similar hopes, and if successful consequently tell more people, and the numbers multiply exponentially.

In addition to the National Capital Territory of Delhi, today large numbers of pilgrims come to do the *parikrama* of Mount Govardhan from all over India, mainly from the nearby states of Rajasthan, Uttar Pradesh, Haryana, and Madhya Pradesh, but also many from Bengal and Gujarat; I even met a large group from the distant southern state of Tamil Nadu. These days, they even come from abroad. I encountered Indians now residents or citizens of the United States, Great Britain, and Kenya performing the *parikrama*; the numbers of nationalities represented would increase significantly by including members of the International Society for Krishna Consciousness who perform the *parikrama* with regularity.

While the most common and well-marked *parikrama* path around Mount Govardhan is the seven-*kos* (roughly 14 miles or 23 kilometers) route described in Chapter 1, there are several routes for performing the *parikrama* of the sacred mountain. Those pressed for time or with an interest focused on a particular section of the mountain sometimes opt for a three-*kos parikrama*, which encircles the northern portion of the mountain dominated by the Gaudiya Vaishnava site of Radhakund, or a four-*kos parikrama* that encircles the southern portion of the mountain, which features the tallest peaks of the hill and is dominated by the Pushti Margiya site of Jatipura. Those choosing to visit the important pond of Chandra Sarovar, a noteworthy site identified with the great Braj poet Surdas, opt for a nine-*kos parikrama* track that includes circumambulation of this sacred pond.[8] The overwhelming majority of those performing the *parikrama*, however, follow the seven-*kos* route. Although some pilgrims complete the *parikrama* of Mount Govardhan only once in a lifetime, many people told me that they perform it every month, usually around the full moon. I spoke with a group of five men from Jaipur, Rajasthan, who follow the practice of monthly circumambulation: "Because we have much affection (*sneha*) for Giriraj-ji we do this every month, and so everyone in our families is well."

The customary way of performing the circumambulation of Mount Govardhan consists of walking around the hill reverentially in a clockwise direction. All are to fix their hearts and minds on this mountain form of Krishna and commune with it visually through sight (*darshan*) and physically with touch (*sparshan*). The great majority of pilgrims do the *parikrama* barefoot. Some carry burning sticks of incense as they go around, and some sing devotional songs. Others transport clay pots full of milk swinging from the end of a cord with a small hole punched in the bottom, thereby dripping a milk offering to the entire mountain while encircling it. Some do the *parikrama* alone, but most do it with a friend or two, or even in groups of various sizes. I met a group of a fifteen men from Jhansi, Uttar Pradesh, doing the *parikrama* together, all wearing bright pink Hawaiian-looking shirts and colorful belts with a line of small bells hanging from them. They were a cheerful crew; one of them informed me they were doing the *parikrama* together as an act of "thanks to Bhagavan in the form of this mountain who gives us everything." Whole villages sometimes do the *parikrama* together, often carrying a colorful flag to plant on top of one of the big temples upon finishing. Although many strongly disapprove of this, some rely on vehicles to circumambulate the mountain, including buses, cars, motorcycles, and bicycle rickshaws. I met a woman from Kota, Rajasthan, who had hired a three-wheeled motorcycle with an attached truck bed to carry her around Mount Govardhan. She sat in the rear with a blue 10-gallon plastic tank filled with milk to dispense as a devotional offering from her clay pot.

These days more and more people can be seen performing what is called the *dandavat parikrama*. The Hindi term *dandavat* literally means "stick-like" and has come to denote a prostration where the entire body is laid flat on the ground. The *dandavat parikrama* refers to a method of encircling Mount Govardhan by performing a continuous series of such prostrations. After making a full prostration on the ground, those completing the *parikrama* in this fashion mark the span of their body by placing a stone with their outstretched right hand, and then stand up to move forward one body length to the stone before repeating the process. Estimating an average body length (including the outstretched arm) to be about 2.25 meters, over 10,000 prostrations are required to cover the 23 kilometers of the circumambulatory pathway by the *dandavat* method. It generally takes about ten days to complete the circuit. A man who had just finished a *dandavat parikrama* told me that in using the whole body in this manner, laying it in the dirt again and again, one becomes completely absorbed in contemplation of the mountain god. This is important since many understand Vaishnava *bhakti* as a way of using all the senses to concentrate on and connect with Krishna.[9]

While some people complete the *dandavat parikrama* alone, most do it in groups. I observed an inspiring group of twenty-two men from Jaipur, Rajasthan, engaged in the *dandavat parikrama*, but this number was later dwarfed by a group of nearly 600 people I observed performing the *dandavat parikrama* together under the guidance of a Pushti Margiya leader from Mumbai. People living in Jatipura reported that they had never before seen such a large number of people performing the *dandavat parikrama* together. Included in this group was a married couple marking the length of their prostrations with rocks wrapped with red and yellow string. When I asked them about this, they explained: "Before beginning this *dandavat parikrama* we took a vow (*sankalp*) to finish it. The rocks were wrapped at this time to bless our efforts to complete the entire round as loving service (*seva*) for Him (gesturing toward to the mountain)." This couple accomplished the *dandavat parikrama* by measuring out the distance with their own individual bodies, but I encountered husband-wife pairs executing it relay style where each started the next prostration where the partner's last prostration ended.

The most difficult and time-consuming method for worshipfully circumambulating the sacred mountain, however, is what is called the 108-*dandavat parikrama*. This rare method involves performing 108 full prostrations before moving forward one body length, typically keeping track of the number of prostrations by means of a pile of 108 stones. The pile is moved forward one stone at a time as the practitioner does each prostration. When the last of the stones has been pushed forward, the person advances one body length and begins the procedure all over again. This method requires over one million prostrations to complete the circuit and takes several years to complete. It is typically performed by *sadhus* who have renounced the duties of ordinary domestic life, or at least by those that have no immediate social responsibilities. I met one *sadhu*, doing the 108-*dandavat parikrama* "for the benefit of all people," who advanced around the mountain with a small altar that featured a picture of Krishna lifting Mount Govardhan placed just ahead of his prostrations. He informed me that it would take him about four years to complete the circumambulation of the mountain by this method. I spoke with another elderly *sadhu* who was performing a 108-*dandavat parikrama* of the mountain who told me that it would take him about five years to complete his slow orbit around the mountain. I asked him what he planned to do after he had finished the circuit. "Start all over again," he replied. He had no goal other than to remain deeply immersed in this embodied meditation on Mount Govardhan as he honored the mountainous form of Krishna.

Hindu religious practices are typically governed by a set of restrictions (*yamas*) and prescriptions (*niyamas*); this is true for the *parikrama* of Mount Govardhan. Lists of these regulations can be found in guidebooks for conducting the *parikrama*, as well as on boards posted along the *parikrama* pathway. Pilgrims, of course, follow these guidelines with different degrees of observation. I translate two lists to give a sense of the nature and range of the regulations: the first is from a readily available guidebook written by a local scholar;[10] the second I copied from a large board mounted on the wall of a small restaurant and tea shop located on the *parikrama* path in the town of Jatipura that was complied by the owner's son, a *Bhagavata Purana* preacher.

"The Rules for the Shri Giriraj Parikrama":

1) Before the *parikrama* take a bath and make the body pure.
2) Do not wear shoes or sandals during the *parikrama*.[11]

3) Finish the *parikrama* wherever you begin it. The *parikrama* can be started anywhere on the seven-kos pathway.

4) Don't go to the toilet on the right side of the pathway.

5) Sleep on the ground the night of the day you do *parikrama*.

6) Take a ritual sip of the water (*achaman*) from the ponds and lakes, and have *darshan* at the temples.

7) It is very necessary to perform the worship (*puja*) of Giriraj. Any Giriraj stone on the seven-kos pathway can be worshiped.

8) Keep the mind pure during *parikrama*; keep singing praises or chanting the name of God and complete bliss will be obtained.

9) Speak no harsh words to anyone, and be generous to all.

"The Minimal Rules Necessary to Observe in the Parikrama of Shri Giriraj-ji":

1) First of all bow to and honor Shri Giriraj-ji, and then begin the *parikrama*.

2) Bow to whatever temples you come to on the path.

3) Don't talk in willy-nilly ways while doing the *parikrama*, but praise the name of Hari (Krishna).

4) Don't make the pathway dirty, rather give special attention to keeping it clean.

5) Don't go to the toilet near Giriraj-ji.

6) Don't drink alcohol or smoke cigarettes while doing the *parikrama*.

7) Don't harm trees on the pathway, but give special attention to protecting the environment.

8) Take the gift of power from doing loving service to saints and cows and share the merit.

These rules set the proper reverential attitude for honoring the mountain through circumambulation, for *parikrama* is a bodily form of making contact with and worshiping this embodied form of divinity. As one moves around the base of the mountain, the whole body with all its senses is engaged in interacting with an aspect of divinity that is assumed to be abundantly present in this readily available tangible form. Besides *parikrama*, however, there is an additional way of worshiping Mount Govardhan—this is called *puja*.

Buckets of Milk and Baskets of Sweets

Normally translated as "worship," *puja* is a ritualized means of honoring and revering a particular divinity through praises, hymns, and offerings of special substances. Most *puja* is highly sensual, meaning that it involves all five senses and bodily interaction with some embodied form of divinity. The adorned body of the deity is seen; songs and sacred music are heard; incense, scented oils, and flower fragrances are smelled; the embodied form is touched; offered foods returned as *prasad* (grace in edible form) are relished; and the body is engaged in a variety of actions as offerings are made and service is rendered to the body of the deity. As in the case of *parikrama*, Krishna is understood to have established the sacred paradigm for this form of worship to Mount Govardhan: "The first *puja* of Shri Govardhan-ji was performed by Lord Krishna himself, who is the Highest Reality (Parabrahma) and Supreme Divinity (Parameshvara)."[12] A priest who conducts worship at a popular Govardhan shrine informed me: "We do this because Krishna was the first to perform this *puja* and he taught us that we should do it too." This of course refers to the renowned incident in which Krishna directed praises and offered Indra's mound of food to the mountain. Although in theory *puja* can be done to the entire mountain, in actual practice it is almost always directed to a particular *shila* or stone from Mount Govardhan. As the seventh rule in the first of the two preceding lists indicates, one can effectively worship the entire mountain through any one of its numerous stones. Joshi agrees: "Shri Krishna, who assumes innumerable forms, appears as each and every particle of Shri Giriraj Mountain. Every particular form (*svarupa*) of Shri Giriraj-ji is Shri Giriraj-ji himself. There is no difference among these particular forms. Some people make distinctions between a particular Giriraj *svarupa* and others, but this is wrong. Giriraj-ji is simply Giriraj-ji."[13]

Priests employed in a popular temple that houses a famous Govardhan stone, however, have much at stake economically in promoting their site as the best of all places to worship the mountain, and indeed a relatively few sites draw the great majority of the pilgrims who come from the outside to worship the mountain. This is particularly true for the three major competing Mukharvinds ("Lotus Mouths") at Manasi Ganga, Dan Ghati, and Jatipura. I describe in this section the performance of the common form of public and spectacular worship of Mount Govardhan that takes place at the Mukharvind sites, focusing particular attention on the Mukharvind in Jatipura, while leaving examination of the private worship in the much more intimate environment of the home shrine for Chapter 6. The public shrines are typically sites of occasional visits; although some do visit them quite frequently, a pilgrim might come to worship at one of them only once in a lifetime. The Giriraj *shila*s in the home shrines, however, are worshiped daily over long periods of time, during which worshipers develop very close and personal relationships with them.

The Mukharvind of Jatipura, alternatively called Sundar Shila ("Beautiful Stone"), is in many ways the hub of activities in the town.[14] It is a very active site and is frequently bustling with large crowds of pilgrims who come here to worship the Mukharvind stone themselves, or have *darshan* of the much more elaborate *puja* conducted by the priests every morning and evening. In most Hindu temples dedicated to Krishna, ordinary worshipers do not have direct access to the *svarupa*, or embodied form of the divinity. Not so here at the Mukharvind of Jatipura, or most every other site around Mount Govardhan; pilgrims coming to Mount Govardhan have the opportunity to worship the sacred mountain with their own hands. Indeed, many maintain that the greatest benefits are to be gained from the direct worship of the sacred mountain: "Those devotees who come to Govardhan to perform the *puja* of Shri Govardhan Giriraj, experience the highest bliss by performing this supreme and sacred *puja* themselves with their own hands."[15]

I arrive at the Jatipura Mukharvind site at six o'clock in the morning.[16] The site is already busy with activity; since Giriraj is a very compassionate form of God who is always accessible, the temple never closes. This is true of all the Mukharvind sites. Everyone seems excited, even a little pushy, as they are eager to encounter God in this mountainous form. An elderly couple at the front of the crowd is pouring milk from a container they hold jointly over the body-like Mukharvind stone. The recipient of the offering is the head-sized stone protruding from the mountain four feet high off the platform floor. Many other pilgrims carry cups or buckets of milk and wait in line to empty them on the Mukharvind stone. The acts of worship here are quite varied, but almost all worshipers bathe the Mukharvind stone with milk. Joshi reports that "the milk bath (*dugdh abhishek*) is the most important element in the worship of Govardhan."[17] He also remarks: "One's life becomes blessed by performing the *parikrama* and milk bath of Shri Giriraj-ji."[18] The effectiveness of worshiping a Govardhan stone with milk is found in one of the hagiographies of the Pushti Marg tradition, which defines cow milk as a bright and pure form of devotional nectar (*ujjvala bhakti-rasa*) that is greatly loved by God in the form of Mount Govardhan.[19] Numerous shops in the nearby bazar sell large quantities of milk for the pilgrims to offer, and a covered drain has been constructed to carry the gallons of milk and water away from the Mukharvind stone to a distant field.

A woman dressed in a bright red sari, her head covered with the end piece, is next in line behind the elderly couple. Standing directly before the Mukharvind stone, she pours a small clay pot full of milk onto it with her left hand and rubs it in with her right. She places two bright yellow marigold blossoms on top of the stone, kneels to bow her head to the pair of feet at its base, and then stands and yields the space to the next enthusiastic worshiper. A man wearing a white shirt and dark green slacks makes his way noisily through the crowd, holding a metal bucket of milk on his head. He empties the contents onto the Mukharvind stone, working it in with his right hand while shouting "Shri Giriraj Dharan ki Jaya!" A young couple moves in to make a more extensive offering. They bathe the stone with milk, rub scented oil on its body, and apply a *tilak* mark to its forehead with red *kumkum* powder. With the aid of one of the attending priests, they wrap an orange *dhoti* on the lower portion of the stone, drape a marigold garland around its neck, and place some sweets in an open cardboard box at its feet. After a few minutes they remove the sweets and pay the attendant priest, who has been holding back the crowd. Two teenage boys dressed in blue jeans and white t-shirts push their way up to the stone, each holding a plastic glass of milk with a red rose floating on the surface and a small leaf basket of orange *jalebi* sweets. They make their offerings, and one of the boys takes a photo of the milk-drenched Mukharvind with his cell phone. A family of four is next. The mother and two children place their hands on the back of the father to participate in the offering as he pours a pot of milk over the stone. Afterward the mother and children arrange flowers at the foot of the Mukharvind stone, and the woman applies a V-shaped *tilak* mark to its forehead with red *kumkum* powder. They bow their heads to the feet of the stone in unison; when they turn around, all are smiling. Another person approaches the Mukharvind stone and the *pujas* continue. Occasionally someone makes arrangements for a special dressing, such as the one in Figure 4.1.

This is a typical early morning scene at the Jatipura Mukharvind stone—ceaseless worshipful actions in the constant din of pilgrimage crowds. Many mornings I observed hundreds of people perform their *puja* to the famous stone bulging from the mountain, each doing so in their own way. Some would simply pour a glass of milk over the stone and quickly turn away, whereas others would perform their *puja* more slowly and with much

Figure 4.1. Special dressing of Jatipura Mukharvind stone.

pageantry, offering clothing, flowers, and sweets. All would make some kind of respectful contact with the stone, many bowing their head to its base, and when space allowed, some would perform a full prostration. Around seven o'clock, the attending priests stop the flow of outside worshipers and begin their own more complex morning *puja*. Another sizable Govardhan stone has been set up in a small shrine thirty feet away from the Mukharvind for general worshipers to continue performing their own direct *puja* at this site when access to the Mukharvind is restricted for the priest's *puja* (Figure 4.2).

This public spectacle is typically attended by a large assembly of people, including many who live in Jatipura and begin their day with *darshan* of the priests' daily *puja*. The ritual worship begins with a morning bath. A priest dressed in a white *dhoti* and *bandhi* pours gallons of milk over the Mukharvind stone from the spout of a large silver pitcher (Figure 4.3). The milk cascades down the face of the dark stone, creating a wavering white veil.

Throughout the celebratory ceremony, a priest who stands to the side of the stone sings morning hymns in a strong voice. Gallons of water are used to wash the stone clean, the attendant priest carefully rubbing the stone to ensure that all milk is removed from every nook and cranny. He dries the large

Figure 4.2. Individual worship of Govardhan stone set up near Jatipura Mukharvind stone.

stone completely with a red-and-white checkered towel, and then massages scented oil onto all its surfaces. The glistening body of the Mukharvind stone is now ready for dressing (Figure 4.4). Compared to that of the evening, the morning attire is fairly simple, beginning with a V-shaped *tilak* forehead decoration applied to the head stone with red *kumkum* powder. A brightly colored shawl (*uparna*) is placed around the shoulders of the stone, and a lower garment (*dhoti*) is attached to the waist and draped down to its two feet. Finally, a colorful turban is sometimes placed atop the head stone and a large garland made with roses and other bright flowers is looped around the neck.

Figure 4.3. Bathing the Jatipura Mukharvind stone with milk in the morning.

When the dressing is complete, the priests place a handful of fresh *tulsi* leaves and several baskets of sweets before the Mukharvind stone. Two attendants hold up a curtain to provide privacy while the breakfast offering is consumed. Once the meal is finished, the curtain is removed and the remaining food taken away to be distributed as *prasad*, grace in edible form. Water is then poured into a silver bowl to allow the stone deity to wash his hands and rinse his mouth, and a clean white cloth is offered for drying. The Mukharvind stone is now ready for the final act of the morning *puja*; using a silver candelabra, a priest waves the honorific *arati* flame before the adorned stone as the assembled crowd enthusiastically sings songs of praise. This ritual gesture finished, the priests remove the decorative clothing from the

Figure 4.4. Morning ornamentation of Jatipura Mukharvind stone.

stone and the eager spectators rush in to resume their own direct worship, which continues unbroken throughout the day.

In the evening the attending priests once again stop the flow of public worship and prepare for another *puja*.[20] The evening *puja* is more elaborate than the one in the morning, as the identification of Mount Govardhan as Krishna becomes even more evident. The participating priests arrive around five o'clock with a metal trunk full of items to be used in the *puja*, and guards cordon off access to the Mukharvind stone with the aid of portable stainless steel railings. The public can continue their direct worship at the alternative site nearby. Many people sit on the ground before the Mukharvind to watch the priests' performance. One priest bathes the Mukharvind stone with milk and water from a stainless steel bucket, washing away residues from the day's ritual activities. He vigorously rubs yogurt and sugar over the stone, making sure to scrub every part of its body. This mixture is then washed off with more buckets of water, and the stone is again thoroughly dried with a red-and-white checkered towel. After fragrant oil is massaged into the stone, an elderly priest who walks over the mountain from Anyor every evening takes over the worship. From this point on, photography is strictly prohibited.

The head priest from Anyor wraps a large bright cloth around the stone, leaving only the face exposed; the cloth colors vary from day to day, with more ornate cloth used during special festivals. From the trunk he takes a pair of legs made from stuffed black felt and dressed with cloth that matches the main wrap, fastening these to the lower portion of the stone so that the dark feet are exposed and resting on the ground. He covers the legs with a matching skirt. A chest piece with two arms attached—fabricated and dressed similarly to the legs—is added to the upper portion of the stone, and secured just below the head. The right arm is tucked close to the waist, but the left arm is raised, so that the body begins to take the human form of the cowherd Krishna in the mountain-lifting pose. The Mukharvind stone is now completely covered, with only the head exposed.

The identification with the cowherd Krishna becomes increasingly apparent as the head priest decorates the famous "lotus-face." He first attaches a pair of prominent eyes with beeswax adhesive. Next he adds a red-jeweled *tilak* to the forehead, a diamond chin jewel, and a red-jeweled nose-ring dangling a white pearl. A necklace is fastened just below the chin, and earrings are attached at ear level. A line of pearls is strung along the hairline, and an ornate crown with a side ornament is affixed atop the head. Multiple strings of necklaces are hung across the breast so that the whole chest glistens. A head-scarf is draped over the head and behind the crown, then tucked behind the ears. Only the face of the stone is now visible. Colorful flower garlands are looped around the neck, and a silver staff and flute are placed in the arms. The opulently adorned stone divinity is now shown his image in a mirror. The end result is stunning. In the midst of the pandemonium of pilgrim chatter and screeching monkeys in the eaves, the once-bare Mukharvind stone has been transformed into Shri Govardhan Nath-ji, the cowherd form of Krishna holding the mountain aloft. Or perhaps the ritual only makes apparent what always is. The worship culminates in a huge offering of baskets of sweets, sometimes requiring two bullock carts to deliver, and the honorific waving of the *arati* lamps, accompanied by the ringing of gongs and bells. When this is finished, the priests' ornamentation is taken off and individual worshipers are again welcome to approach the Mukharvind to perform personal worship all night long, when many pilgrims choose to perform their *puja*, as at that time the crowds are not as thick or rowdy.

The other two major Mukharvind temples are also busy with Govardhan *puja*s throughout the day and night. The Dan Ghati Mukharvind temple is located in the town of Govardhan, directly on top of the hill just to the north of the road that passes over the mountain. During the British period the roadbed was built up with dirt to protect the mountain, so that the temple is now located below road level, entered via a flight of stairs that descend into it. The large space within contains the main Mukharvind stone, as well as a number of other shrines, including three more Govardhan stones. Two of these are always adorned in the Shri Nath-ji style, featuring prominent eyes, jewelry ornamentation, and colorful clothing. The third is left bare; this is where pilgrims perform the milk bath and *puja* of Giriraj with their own hands when access to the main Mukharvind stone is restricted during the priests' elaborate *puja*.

However, the main Mukharvind *shila* is the center of worship in the Dan Ghati temple. The stone housed here is very striking, with streaks of dark grey and yellowish brown running through the large ruddy rock. During much of the day public worshipers file past the imposing stone, bathing it with milk and offering sweets and flowers. All make sure to touch the *shila* with their right hand and bow before it. In the evening the attendant priests take over the worship, as they do at the Jatipura Mukharvind, bathing the stone with buckets of milk and water, then dressing and adorning it in the Shri Nath-ji style with the left arm raised. On one of my visits, a large backdrop had been added that depicted Mount Govardhan hovering in the air. Monkeys, trees, and peacocks had been painted on the many boulders of the mountain, and cowherds were huddled below. The center of this scene, however, had been left blank. The painting was positioned so that the adorned Mukharvind stone with its raised left arm assumed the form of Krishna holding the mountain. Once again, we see the circularity of the dual form. The mountain assumes the form of the cowherd holding the mountain, who himself has assumed the form of the mountain: the two that are really one. The intricate *puja* that follows the bathing and adornment of the Mukharvind stone is similar to that which takes place at the Jatipura Mukharvind. The same is true for the *puja* at the Mukharvind temple that is located on the edge of the Manasi Ganga Lake in the town of Govardhan.

Figure 4.5. Full body ornamentation of Govardhan stone in small temple on the road around the mountain.

Besides these large public temples, there are hundreds of smaller temples and shrines situated around Mount Govardhan that feature a Giriraj stone available for worship. Some of the sacred stones are located in temples on the *parikrama* pathway; some are tucked in nearby ashrams; while others are set up in simple outdoor shrines open to the elements. What distinguishes these stones from the multitude of others on the edge of the mountain is that they have some kind of ornamentation and are worshiped routinely. The ornamentation and worship in many of the more prominent mid-sized temples located on the *parikrama* road tend to follow a pattern of worship similar to that which takes place in the larger Mukharvind sites wherein the stone is given an entire body (Figure 4.5).

Some of the smaller temples and shrines are attended by priests, others by the residents of an ashram or the owner of an attached tea stall, whereas others have no assigned attendants at all and are simply available for whomever desires to worship there (Figure 4.6). Several shrines also feature

Figure 4.6. Example of small Govardhan temple located on the road around the mountain.

Govardhan Baba, the large bodily form of the mountain that consumed the food offering first intended for Indra (Figure 4.7).

Worship at outdoor shrines featuring particular Govardhan stones is conducted by individuals in a manner that is determined by a combination of cultural convention (*riti*) and individual desire (*manorath*). Again, any stone will do, as the widespread belief is that the mountain can be worshiped through any of its stones, though people tend to frequent stone shrines for which they feel a special attraction. The adornment and worship of a particular Govardhan stone, then, varies according to the family customs, training,

Figure 4.7. Govardhan Baba shrine on the road around the mountain.

ideas, and desires of the worshiper, resulting in decorated stones with an astonishing range of personalities.

The inner dirt pathway of the *parikrama* track between Jatipura and the
town of Govardhan runs through a peaceful regenerating forest that contains
two shrines which exemplify the outdoor style. Both are on government
property controlled by the Department of Forestry, and as such are a type of
Giriraj shrine that is not "owned" or controlled by anyone in particular, but
is visited regularly by specific individuals and more occasionally by random
pilgrims who pass by while doing the Govardhan *parikrama*. One features
a Govardhan stone that has been set up on a cement platform under a large
dhau tree tucked up against the base of the mountain, quiet and secluded.
The fairly flat stone, measuring about three feet high, a foot and a half wide,
and eight inches thick, has been mounted so that its rounded top stands tall
(Figure 4.8). Attached eyes with bright blue irises surrounding black pupils
dancing at the center of the white sclera draw the viewer into intimate engagement. Other than these large enameled eyes and a sizable red *tilak* made
with *kumkum* powder, little adorns this stone, except on special occasions
when an individual devotee decides to make a special offering. I visited this

Figure 4.8. Govardhan stone set up for worship under a tree in the forest north of Jatipura.

shrine a year later to find that the eyes had been replaced and a skirt and a flower garland had been added (Figure 4.9).

As this forest was one of my favorite places for taking walks, I often met a man who visits this shrine every morning and evening. Just after sunrise he bathes the stone with milk and water, and offers flowers and sweets. He comes again at sunset to offer incense and an oil lamp in a small clay dish. "I come here to worship every day. I have a special relationship with this Giriraj stone. There are many stones along the mountain, but this is the one I'm drawn to worship," he told me. One day I met a Gaudiya Vaishnava swami who taught me a mantra he uses when worshiping this Mount Govardhan stone: "All glory be to Shri Govardhan, King of All Mountains, who is the destroyer of all misfortunes and the giver of supreme bliss (*paramananda*)."[21] My friend Mohan visited this site with me one evening and remarked: "When people worship a Giriraj stone its *svarupa* ("essential form" or "presence") comes out. Look, there are so many *shila*s here, but this one is really showing itself

Figure 4.9. Special ornamentation of Govardhan stone in forest north of Jatipura.

because people have worshiped it with milk, ornamentation, and special offerings."

The other shrine located in this same forest is composed of two stones that sit atop a white tile platform built around a tree with a circumambulatory pathway encircling it. The platform measures six by six feet and is about three feet high. One stone is taller than the other, but both are painted with large blue eyes, bright red lips, golden *tilak*, and floral facial decorations (Figure 4.10; see also Figure 3.3 in Chapter 3). I encountered a young man who came to this shrine every day for a while, painting the stones afresh.

The ornamentation clearly marks the shorter stone as Radha and the taller one to her right as Krishna. I have seen pilgrims performing the *parikrama* stop long enough to bow their heads to this pair of stones, often taking the time to circumambulate the deities numerous times. Here, too, however, several local residents come every evening to offer oil lamps for *arati*. I observed one man place a lit oil lamp before the divine couple, and circumambulate

Figure 4.10. Painted embellishment of Radha and Krishna stones in the forest north of Jatipura.

them while singing songs of praise. This was an evening in late December when the nights were getting quite chilly. When he had finished worshiping the pair of Govardhan stones, he brought out a bright yellow quilt from a bag he was carrying and wrapped the divine couple with it for protection against the cold. He returned in the morning, removed the winter garment, offered another lamp, and hung a fresh marigold flower garland around the neck of each. These caring gestures make evident that this man regards these Govardhan stones as sentient presences. He is not alone. This assumption lies at the very heart of the attentive acts that comprise the worship of Mount Govardhan.

Mountain on the Move

Hundreds of thousands of pilgrims come every month from many regions of India to worship Mount Govardhan. Moreover, Govardhan stones are taken from the sacred mountain to other places in India. Stones are not simply taken arbitrarily from the sacred mountain, however, but must be "received" through some special means. Stories circulate about what misfortunes happen to those who take a stone away from the mountain on their own initiative. A stone could be acquired through a guru, an advanced devotee of Govardhan, or perhaps inherited from a family member; a person might also be directed to a particular stone in a dream. Govardhan stones are commonly installed in temples throughout other parts of Braj. Stones from the mountain, for example, are present in all the temples dedicated to the river goddess Yamuna at the famous Vishram Ghat in the city of Mathura. The love affair between Yamuna Devi (closely associated with Radha) and Krishna is celebrated in the shrines here with the physical presence of the aquatic form of the goddess as River Yamuna and the mountainous form of the god as Mount Govardhan.[22]

Another rather common arrangement is the one located in the Shri Radharaman Temple in the town of Vrindaban. Inside the temple are two stout hexagonal stone pillars, about five feet tall and covered with decorative tile. They were built to contain and honor *tulsi*, a plant sacred to Vaishnavas throughout India. Near the *tulsi* plant, atop one of them stands a small ornate throne made out of white marble. A Govardhan stone sits on this throne and is the recipient of worshipful offerings (Figure 4.11). Unlike the interaction with the major focus of this temple, the famous Radharaman *murti* of Krishna as the beautiful cowherd lover of Radha that is served by the priests alone, the Govardhan stone is worshiped directly by anyone who chooses to do so. This arrangement allows for intimate contact with the divine form of a Giriraj *shila* on a regular basis. Eyes have not been added to this particular stone, yet it is often dressed with a simple scarf and garlanded with roses and marigolds. A peacock feather adorns its head, a clear indication that this stone is regarded as an embodied form of Krishna.

The stone is occasionally bathed with milk, and every night during the chilly winter months it is covered with a small quilt. Many stop here to offer a stick of incense or an honorific oil lamp in a clay dish; some circumambulate the Govardhan stone upon the pillar, and others simply touch its base with their right hand, place this hand to the top of their heads, and then bow before moving on.

Another context in which worshipers can encounter Mount Govardhan in Vrindaban is in a temple dedicated solely to this purpose, the Shri Radha Giridhari-ji Maharaj Temple located near Vrindaban's forested Seva Kunj.

Figure 4.11. Govardhan stone inside Radharaman temple in Vrindaban.

This ornate sandstone temple houses a Govardhan stone that receives daily worship in the central sanctum by a paid priest. As elsewhere, the foot-tall stone is bathed every morning with milk and water, and scented oil is applied to its body. The priest attaches eyes to the stone and decorates it with facial designs and a sandalwood-paste *tilak*. He then dresses it with attractive clothing, fresh flower garlands, and a crown, before beginning a daily round of food offerings and waving of the honorific *arati* lamp. This historic temple is owned by a family of successful cloth merchants and is open daily to the general public so that they can have *darshan* of Giriraj while here in Vrindaban.

The most famous Govardhan stone in Vrindaban, however, is the one now housed in the Shri Radhadamodar Temple. It is said that this is the stone that was worshiped by Sanatana Gosvamin, the most senior of the sixteenth-century founding Gaudiya Vaishnava Gosvamins of Vrindaban. There is a well-known story attached to this Govardhan stone, called the "Shri Giriraj Charan ('Foot') Shila." The story is posted in Hindi on a wall within the courtyard of the temple and also included in a booklet sold there:

Shrila Sanatana Gosvami-ji used to travel every day from Vrindaban to do the *parikrama* of Shri Giriraj-ji, and only after completing the *parikrama* would he take water. Seeing his resolve to continue this practice even in old age, Shri Krishna appeared directly before him and gave him a Giriraj stone imprinted with His own foot, flute and staff, and with the foot of a cow, saying: "Sanatana, now place this stone in the Shri Radhadamodar Temple and circumambulate it four times and your daily practice will be fulfilled as you will easily obtain the fruit of performing the entire seven-*kos parikrama*." Since then this Shri Giriraj stone has been enthroned on a lion-seat (*sinhasana*), and according to the directive from Shri Krishna's own mouth, the fruit of doing the entire seven-*kos parikrama* of Govardhan is obtained by doing *parikrama* of the Shri Radhadamodar Temple four times. Still today, devotees who have *darshan* of this Giriraj "Footprint" stone in the Shri Radhadamodar Temple and circumambulate it are given unlimited results.[23]

Many people come to the Radhadamodar temple to have *darshan* of the Giriraj stone worshiped by Sanatana Gosvamin and reverently circumambulate it four times. This is especially true during the auspicious lunar month of Kartik, which falls within October and November. In 2013 I visited the Radhadamodar temple three times during this month to view the special Govardhan stone and speak with those performing its *parikrama*. During this month the stone on its silver lion-throne is brought out before the temple deities in the front of the central sanctum, giving a close view for those who come to receive its *darshan*. It is usually encircled with a garland of flowers and *tulsi*, and covered with an ornate cloth (Figure 4.12).

From time to time an attending priest pulls back the cover to give viewers a good look at the entire stone. A sign posted to the right of the inner sanctum identifies the four marks imprinted in the stone. As this is a formal temple controlled by official priests, there is no chance for visitors to touch the stone or worship it directly with their own hands.

Pilgrims do interact with this special stone, however, by circumambulating it four times, with the hope that this honorific action will yield the same results as the performance of the entire seven-*kos parikrama* of Mount Govardhan. A marble-paved walkway delineates the *parikrama* path, snaking through the *samadhi* gardens that contain memorials to many great saints associated with the Gaudiya Vaishnava Sampradaya and around the central shrine that houses the famous deities of this temple. Most people

Figure 4.12. Govardhan stone of Sanatana Gosvamin inside Radhadamodar temple in Vrindaban.

I spoke with repeated the words of one woman, "Yes, four times around this Giriraj stone is equivalent to doing the full seven-*kos parikrama* of Mount Govardhan." I asked a man who had just completed the *parikrama* here if he thought that it produced the same results as the complete *parikrama* of Mount Govardhan. "That is what they say," he responded. I pressed him further for his own thoughts. "Who knows what results are to come from this? Only God knows," he said with a laugh and walked off.

Govardhan stones are also found in temple environments in other sacred towns and sites in Braj. I visited three public shrines containing Giriraj stones in the town of Gokul. About an hour drive from Mount Govardhan, this important early Pushti Margiya settlement is associated with the childhood stories of Krishna. One was a freestanding temple dedicated solely to the worship of an adorned stone from Mount Govardhan. The style of ornamentation here follows the fairly standard Pushti Margiya style of eyes, jewelry, decorative clothing, a red-and-white *gunja*-bead necklace, and a peacock-feathered crown. Full food and *puja* offerings are made throughout the day, and everyone is welcome to enter the temple for *darshan* and worshipful interaction with a Giriraj stone without making the drive to Mount Govardhan. I also visited the Dwarakadhish Mandir, a large Pushti Margiya Krishna temple in Gokul that has a freestanding white-marble shrine in the courtyard that features two Giriraj stones. They are housed a short distance from the presiding form of Krishna served by priests in this temple, but visitors to this side shrine have direct access to these stone forms of Krishna to make food and flower offerings and worship them in whatever way they desire.

Another Giriraj stone in Gokul is located in a *baithak* of Vallabhacharya. One of the principal *baithak*s in this town, it is entered via a courtyard that is dominated by a large gnarly *chokar* tree. Underneath this tree is a small raised shrine that contains a Giriraj stone available for direct worship. Posted above the opening to the shrine is the refrain from the "Shri Girirajadharyashtakam," a Sanskrit hymn written by Vallabhacharya in celebration of the one who holds or assumes the form of Mount Govardhan.[24] Giriraj stones are found in practically every Pushti Margiya *baithak* in Braj, including one at Madhuban, a sacred forest site across the Yamuna River from Gokul. Within the complex of this well-known *baithak* is a Giriraj stone that is bathed, adorned and worshiped every day in the Pushti Margiya style. Just outside its shrine is a stunning painting that is similar to a Rubin's vase in that it portrays two distinct interpretive perspectives. One view depicts an image of Shri Govardhan Nath-ji emerging from a cave of Mount Govardhan, but from another perspective the image is of Radha and Krishna, their bodies merged, with her on the left and him on the right. Significantly, the left arm that holds up the mountain belongs to Radha. This not only indicates that the divinity of Govardhan is both Radha and Krishna, but also that Radha plays a crucial role in the lifting of Mount Govardhan.

The migration of Mount Govardhan, however, does not stop at the border of Braj. The most prominent Krishna temple in the important pan-Indian pilgrimage center of Varanasi (Banaras) is the Shri Mukundaray-ji Mandir, known affectionately as Gopal-ji. This is one of the major seats of the Pushti Marg, and a very popular temple for worshiping Krishna. In addition to revering the *murti* of Mukundaray-ji, an embodied form of child Krishna, many who come to worship here visit a wooded courtyard within the temple's compound. In the center of this beautiful garden is a reconstruction of Mount Govardhan surrounded by a horizontal relief map of Braj. Before it is a collection of five Govardhan stones, the focus of much devotional worship. During my hour-long visit to this Govardhan shrine, I observed the interactions of dozens of people at this shrine, almost always including a circumambulatory *parikrama* on the walkway circling this shrine. A group of six people I met told me that they do this every day. They informed me that for them this is just like doing the *parikrama* of Mount Govardhan. "Braj is far from us, but by the grace of Shri Krishna, Giriraj-ji is with us here."

I watched one man circumambulate the whole shrine, then stop before the Govardhan stones to bathe them with milk and water, and offer them several red roses. When he finished, he bowed to the stones and left. A family of four came next to perform a Govardhan *puja*. The man in the family bathed the central stone with milk and water, and then applied a *tilak* to each of the five stones with red *kumkum* powder. His wife placed a white flower garland around the central stone and produced an apple and a bowl of *jelebi* sweets for a food offering. While this was taking place, onlookers shouted repeatedly: "Shri Giriraj Dharan ki Jaya!" After several minutes, the apple and sweets were retrieved. All members of the family touched the central stone reverently with their right hand, placing it to their heart before touching their heads to the foot of the stone. An elderly woman showed up next, pouring milk over the main stone and offering red rose petals. A man and two women then approached the shrine and circumambulated it; they stopped to touch the Govardhan stones with their right hands and then transferred the blessing to their eyes and heart. Unlike the embodied form of Krishna worshiped inside the Shri Gopal-ji temple, the Govardhan stones are continuously available for direct and intimate contact.

Mount Govardhan shrines exist in a number of other cities in India. Among the many Pushti Margiya temples in the megacity of Mumbai, for example, is one called Shri Madan Mohan. A replica of Mount Govardhan has been constructed in a courtyard of this temple that is protected by a metal roof and has a well-defined pathway around it for performing *parikrama*. On one side of the mountain, a stone that has been brought from Mount Govardhan sits on a silver throne inside a miniature temple. It is fully adorned with facial ornamentation, clothing, a peacock feather crown, and flower garlands, and is worshiped daily in the Pushti Margiya style. Many people living in Mumbai come here to circumambulate this mountain form of Krishna and have *darshan* of a portion of Mount Govardhan without ever having to leave their city. This same setup is found in other Pushti Margiya temples in Mumbai that also feature a *parikrama* pathway encircling a reproduction of Mount Govardhan and a place to make offerings to an actual Govardhan stone. Even more impressive is the reconstruction of Mount Govardhan at the Govardhan Ecovillage in a hilly forested area 60 miles north of Mumbai.

The replica of the mountain takes about fifteen minutes to circumambulate and features not only the major sites around Mount Govardhan, but also a shrine accommodating a stone brought from the sacred mountain in Braj (Figure 4.13).

A Pushti Margiya woman who lives in Kolkata told me she frequently visits a temple there that is solely dedicated to the worship of a large Govardhan stone. Just like the Mukharvind in Jatipura, the stone is available for the direct worship of the public most of the day, but in the evening the attending priests take over and bathe, adorn, and worship the stone in the same fashion as that performed to the Mukharvind stone in Jatipura. She described a temple with similar arrangements in Hyderabad. Undoubtedly, the worship of Mount Govardhan and its stones is widely accepted and prevalent throughout much of India. Visitors to Jatipura even told me of Govardhan stones being worshiped in Krishna temples in England, Australia, and the United States. A large rock reproduction of Mount Govardhan that I estimated to be about

Figure 4.13. Govardhan stone worshiped near a reconstruction of Mount Govardhan in Govardhan Ecovillage north of Mumbai.

275 feet long, 50 feet wide, and 30 feet high has been constructed at a Pushti Margiya site in Vraj, Pennsylvania, which features a replica of the Jatipura Mukharvind stone located within a cave temple in one side of the mountain. Wherever there is a Krishna temple, one is liable to encounter some form of Mount Govardhan. Although the mountain in Braj remains central, distance does not seem to reduce the efficacy of Giriraj. This seems to reinforce the notion that the part (stone) represents the whole (mountain) in the world-view of Braj Vaishnavism.

An Abundance of Fruits

Why do people perform the *parikrama* and *puja* of Mount Govardhan? What do they hope to accomplish through these embodied acts of worship? By far the most common response I received when I asked people why they worshiped Mount Govardhan—honoring it either by circumambulation or the presentation of offerings—was *mano-kamana puri hoti hai*; that is, "one's heart's desire is fulfilled" by the worship of Mount Govardhan. In addition to hearing this from scores of people I interviewed, this claim is affirmed in virtually all of the local writings about Mount Govardhan. "You too can surely have your heart's desire (*mano-kamana*) fulfilled by coming into the presence of Shri Govardhan Giriraj-ji just once. That's enough, just one time."[25] The minimal phrase "fulfilling one's heart's desire" can be deceptive, however, for it masks a vast diversity of fruits or objectives, those that aim for specific outcomes as well as those that are expressly without expectation of explicit gain.

Early one November morning I rode my bicycle from Jatipura to the Dan Ghati Mukharvind temple to speak with people who came to participate in the *puja* performed to the magnificent Govardhan *shila* housed in this temple. While there, I asked a man from Delhi why people worship Govardhan. He replied simply: "To get our wishes fulfilled." He explained to me that he and his wife were married for several years and very much wanted a child. Having difficulty getting pregnant, they consulted a doctor who told them they most likely would never be able to conceive a child. When all seemed hopeless, he and his wife decided to perform the *parikrama* of Mount Govardhan and conduct a *puja* of the mountain here in the Dan Ghati temple. They had already done this and had now returned to repeat the process, this time as a way of giving thanks for a blessing from Giriraj-ji. The man called to his wife and she joined us, holding a smiling baby girl. "She is the blessing (*ashirbad*) of Giriraj-ji," the man declared as he took his adorable daughter into his hands and held her up with much pride and delight. "You see how kind Giriraj is. Through his blessing we got her. So we are here to honor and give thanks to Giriraj-ji."

During another morning visit to this same temple, I asked a man who was part of a small group of pilgrims from Jaipur what benefits might be gained from worshiping Mount Govardhan. "You can ask Giriraj-ji for money, a child, a job, or whatever," he replied, "but we ask only for devotion (*bhakti*). We do *parikrama* as an act of *bhakti*, and only ask for more *bhakti*." Here deeper relationship is sought through the intimacy of embodied interaction with the mountain. I spoke with a young married couple from among the 600 people from Mumbai performing a *dandavat parikrama* together, and asked them why they were doing it. The man answered first: "We do this for faith (*shraddha*). It is also a way of doing *seva*, "loving service," to him (pointing to Mount Govardhan)." I pressed them further, inquiring if they were doing it to fulfill a heart's desire (*mano-kamana*) for something. This time the woman responded:

> Perhaps others are doing it to fulfill a heart's desire to gain something, but we are doing it only for faith. In our religion (they were Pushti Margiya Vaishnavas) we don't do *seva* for any desire (*kamana*), we do it as an expression of love (*prem*). We are doing this as an act of love. We do *nishkam seva* (loving service with no expectation of gain). We have faith in this land of Braj at the base of Giriraj and press our bodies to the ground with love.

These responses represent essentially two different kinds of reasons people give for conducting the worship of Mount Govardhan—the first involving pursuit of some concrete gain (such as the child), whether material or situational; the second as an expression of love with no desire for gain other than an increase of loving devotion. This difference is recognized in common discourse regarding the benefits of worshiping the mountain: the Hindi term *sakam* refers to an action performed "with a specific desire;" the term *nishkam* means it is done "without a specific desire." Considerations of what is to be gained from *parikrama* and *puja* are a substantial part of discussions about the worship of Mount Govardhan. Words used to express this are *phayda* ("benefit "or "advantage"), *labh* ("profit" or "gain"), and *phal* ("result," literally "fruit"). The great variety of "fruits" sought range from material blessings for a successful life of abundance to more sublime spiritual goals, although the two are not firmly distinct and often overlap during reflection on this subject.

A great many of the people who perform the worship of Mount Govardhan do so with the intention of pursuing a particular outcome. Their heart's desires frequently take the shape of a variety of personal life-blessings, such as procuring a good marriage, birth of a healthy child, landing a good job, an increase in wealth, entrance into a good school, acquisition of a house, and the well-being of one's self and family. The young couple I met in the Dan Ghati temple was certainly not the only one to approach the sacred mountain for a child; a number of people I encountered doing *parikrama* were pursuing this particular heart's desire. I came across a young couple on the forested dirt pathway between the towns of Jatipura and Govardhan who were conducting the *dandavat parikrama* together. The husband stretched out his body on the ground in full prostration, and then the wife performed a prostration by placing her feet where his reach had ended. The husband began his next prostration at the end of his wife's reach, and the two went on around the mountain repeating this procedure in relay fashion. I asked them why they were doing this. Shyly, the man answered, "To be blessed with a child."

Healing and well-being are often sought in the worship Mount Govardhan. Every month a group of villagers from a settlement near Jaipur, Rajasthan, make the journey to Govardhan, usually by bus. The morning I encountered them in the Dan Ghati temple, one of the men informed me that this time they had walked the entire distance barefoot while carrying a colorful orange flag. The journey took nine days. Upon arriving in Govardhan they bathed in the Manasi Ganga pond and then performed the *parikrama* of the mountain. After this they worshiped the two Mukharvind *shilas* at Dan Ghati and Manasi Ganga, and planted their flag on top of the Manasi Ganga temple. Why? "We get deep peace from this. We have much affection (*sneha*) for Giriraj-ji. By doing this every month everyone in our families stays healthy and well. If there are even small problems, they disappear by our coming to Giriraj-ji for *puja* and *parikrama*." This group of Rajasthani villagers sought the general welfare of their family members; more serious problems, however, are also brought to Giriraj. I met two Gujarati brothers now living in New Jersey who had come to Jatipura from Mumbai for a day to do the *parikrama* of the mountain. "Our mother was in a terrible car accident. We came to thank Giriraj-ji for allowing her to survive the accident, and to seek his blessing for further healing." (She is paralyzed from the waist down from the accident.) Why come to Mount Govardhan for this purpose instead of somewhere else? "Because as a mountain of love Giriraj-ji is the most compassionate form (*svarupa*) of Lord Krishna, so we are here to seek his blessings."

I also heard accounts of successful healing related to the worship of the mountain. One day while sipping tea at one of the shops in the Jatipura market, I fell into a conversation with a man from a town in Haryana who had just finished the *parikrama*. He told me that he regards Mount Govardhan as "a direct form of God (Bhagavan *svarupa*) where one can readily experience the results of compassionate grace." To illustrate his point he narrated this story:

> There is a man who lives in my town. He had a big problem with his foot and couldn't walk. Since he had lots of money he went to several different doctors over five years, but they were unable to heal him. He then started coming to Giriraj-ji and began to heal. In the beginning he could only take a couple of steps, but now by the grace (*kripa*) of Giriraj-ji he is able to walk the entire *parikrama*.

His voice quivered with emotion uttering this last sentence and tears flowed down his cheeks as he finished, "Giriraj-ji is so compassionate." A man from Anyor stopped to talk with me while he was walking around the mountain. In response to my query about the benefits of the *parikrama* he simply said: "Life becomes good!"

One of the more energetic characters I met during my year of research near Mount Govardhan was a *baba* with a graying beard and long black hair named Devakipran Baba. (*Baba* is an honorific term for a man who has renounced ordinary domestic life for religious purposes.) I first met Devakipran Baba in his ashram room in Radhakund where he had been living for the past seventeen years. He is well known in the area for his great affection for Govardhan, expressing his *seva* by cleaning the Radhakund pond and picking up trash scattered around the mountain by careless pilgrims. After our initial meeting, I often encountered Devakipran Baba on the *parikrama* pathway. He was not always a *baba*; previously he had been a successful accountant (CPA) in Mumbai. His current residence in Radhakund, he told me, is the result of his pursuit of a particular *mano-kamana*, or "heart's desire." He once visited Mount Govardhan from Mumbai with a few of his friends and learned that people stack stones at the foot of the mountain to represent small houses in order to acquire homes of their own. He fell in love with Giriraj on this visit, and wished his reward would be a residence near Mount Govardhan. With this in mind, while doing the *parikrama* he stacked stones near the pathway to replicate a dwelling near Giriraj. Soon he left Mumbai to take up residence in his current home at Radhakund. He considers himself to be living proof of the effectiveness of this practice.

There surely have been failed attempts at obtaining a home by this method, but I met others with similar stories, most of whom had acquired a house in their own town. Devakipran Baba, however, was not the only one I met whose heart's desire was to live in Braj. I know a man who lives in Vrindaban and frequently comes to Mount Govardhan to perform its *parikrama* and *puja*. He explained:

> In addition to increasing love, you get your heart's desire fulfilled by worshiping this mountain. This happened to me. When I was eight years old my parents brought me to Braj and we did the Giriraj *parikrama*. My feet did not hurt at all; in fact, I ran around Giriraj-ji with great happiness. My heart's desire was to live in Vrindaban, and that came true. Today I live in Vrindaban.

Most devotees would not tolerate any suggestions of doubt regarding the achievement of a heart's desire through the circumambulation of the mountain. A talented singer who tends a shrine near the mountain in Jatipura told me that it was "one thousand percent certain" that those who perform the *parikrama* will get their heart's desire fulfilled. To prove his point, he said, "Look, I'll show you." He randomly called over a woman who was standing among a group of Gujarati pilgrims. "Did you get your *mano-kamana* fulfilled by doing the Giriraj *parikrama*?" When she replied yes, he snapped at me, "There's your proof!"

Some people come to Mount Govardhan with doubt and perform the *parikrama* to test the effectiveness of worshiping the mountain. I assume that a number of them leave with their doubt still intact, but I heard a few stories with different outcomes. One evening I had another conversation with Devakipran Baba about belief in Mount Govardhan. "Not all Indians believe that this mountain is God," he told me. He related a recent experience.

> I met a young woman about twenty years old who had come here with her father. She said: "I don't accept that this mountain is God. I don't believe it.

I just came to accompany my father." Later she confessed to me that she was performing the *parikrama* to see if by doing it she would get admission into one of the prestigious IIT universities to get a good job and find a good husband. "If this happens," she said, "I will believe that this mountain is God. Otherwise not." I told her to put some dust from the *parikrama* pathway on her forehead and do the *parikrama*. Then for sure this will come to be.

I never heard the results of this young woman's test, but a civil engineer from Jhansi whom I met in the Dan Ghati temple related his successful examination of Giriraj.

> I had terrible back pains. I saw many doctors but they could not help me, so I decided to do the *parikrama*. At that time I was in great danger of losing my job because the company was running out of work for me. While doing the *parikrama* I said to Giriraj: "Okay if you are real then take care of my business problem." Immediately my cell phone rang. It was my boss telling me that they had new work for me. After I hung up the phone I realized who the real boss is. Shri Giriraj Maharaj ki Jaya! I love all people, but there is only one boss (pointing to the mountain). After completing the *parikrama*, I went to see a specialist in Delhi about my back problems. But the doctor told me that I was completely cured and sent me home. I know that this too was due to the grace of Giriraj-ji. After this, I developed a loving relationship with Giriraj-ji. Now all I want is more love and to see Krishna clearly before my very eyes.

This man now comes to Mount Govardhan every month to honor the mountain with *parikrama*. He is an example of a person who begins by testing Giriraj, seeking something very specific. Once it is received, a more devotional relationship with the mountain ensues.

Many of the views regarding the effectiveness of the worship of Mount Govardhan or Giriraj *shilas* are circulated in the form of stories. The largest genera consist of stories about how a particular *mano-kamana* was fulfilled by performing the *parikrama* and *puja* of Giriraj. Someone tells a neighbor about a miraculous healing, another has a story about a child born to an infertile couple, another narrates a sudden increase in wealth, and someone else reports the achievement of great peace of mind. These stories spread and add to the great popularity of Mount Govardhan. In addition to these oral accounts, stories are transmitted through easily available literature. Perhaps the best known of these stories comes from the tenth chapter of the third section of the *Garga Samhita*.[26]

A Brahmin named Vijay residing on the bank of the Gautami (Godavari) River in southern India had to travel to Mathura to pay his debt to his ancestors. Returning home after completing his obligations, he passed by Mount Govardhan and randomly picked up one of its stones. He took the stone with him as he continued on his way. As he left the vicinity of Braj he saw a terrifying demon with three heads, six arms and legs, a body covered with thorny bristles, and bloodshot eyes. He had a long darting tongue and alarming fangs. The demon attacked this Brahmin with the intention of devouring him. Instinctively, Vijay threw the Govardhan stone he was carrying at the menacing demon, who immediately fell to the ground dead. The body of the demon suddenly arose, now transformed into a divine form resembling Krishna. The transformed demon bowed again and again before the Brahmin, thanking him profusely for liberating him from his demonic state with the touch of the stone. The astonished Brahmin confessed that he did not know how this had happened. The former demon explained. "Shri Govardhan, King of the Mountains, is a form of Hari (Krishna); by merely seeing (*darshan*) it, a person accomplishes the highest aim." He went on to extoll the supreme results one achieves through some kind of contact with Mount Govardhan, declaring that no other sacred place in the entire world can compare to it. After retelling this story in his popular booklet on Mount Govardhan, Kumheriya underscores its lesson: "From the mere touch of a small stone from the blessed Mount Govardhan this divine liberation occurred. What kind of fruits (*phal*) might be obtained by a person who intentionally worships Shri Giriraj Govardhan?"[27]

Keshavdev Sharma, the author of an article in a local scholarly publication on Mount Govardhan, recounts a number of stories he recorded regarding the results of worshiping Mount Govardhan.[28] I translate and retell three of them to give a sense of their nature. The first is about an old woman who was disabled and walked with crutches. She left her family in Bengal and somehow managed to reach the town of Govardhan with the intention of spending the remainder of her life in the sacred land of Braj. Here she survived by begging. One day she had a great desire to perform a *dandavat parikrama* of Mount Govardhan. She fell asleep that night in great sorrow because her crippled condition would not allow this. When she awoke in the morning her body had been transformed; she stood without the use of her crutches and began to walk, filled with the power of her determination to

perform the seven-kos *dandavat parikrama*. Soon after, she performed the
entire *parikrama* without the aid of her crutches or any person, realizing that
"Shri Giriraj Maharaj-ji is my true crutch." Her deep faith in Giriraj was such
that when her family came to take her back home to Bengal she refused to
leave the sacred ground around Mount Govardhan, recognizing that all her
happiness came from Giriraj rather than her family. From this time on she
acquired a profound love for Giriraj, and Sharma concludes, "today she is
thriving in body, mind, and wealth."

The second of Sharma's stories features the worship of Mount Govardhan
as a means of healing and obtaining a child. He prefaces this story by saying
that Shri Giriraj Maharaj is able to remove those misfortunes that even
doctors cannot cure. The story has an added aura of factuality, as the author knows and names the person involved. Babulal, the son of Chiddilal
who lives in Bara Bazar in the town of Govardhan, was married for fifteen
years but had no children. He finally went to a doctor for examination, but
no treatments were successful. Babulal became greatly disturbed. He began
performing the worship of Giriraj with great faith, surrendering his life
completely. Discerning the faith and desire in his worship, Giriraj rewarded
Babulal with a "darling" son.

Perhaps the most astonishing of the accounts Sharma relates is one
that begins with the question: "What is Lord Giriraj willing to do for his
devotees?" He presents the following story as an answer. There was a barber
living in the town of Alawar who one day got into a fight and killed a man.
The police arrested the barber and put him in jail. After he was arraigned and
a court date was set, he was temporarily released. Thinking that he would
receive either life in prison or the death penalty, the barber decided that he
would do the *parikrama* of Giriraj before either occurred. He arrived at Dan
Ghati to begin his *parikrama* and observed a nearby group of people doing
the *dandavat parikrama*. He asked a shopkeeper what benefit (*phal*) came
from performing the *parikrama* in this fashion. The shopkeeper informed
him that by this worshipful action the sins of a million lifetimes are wiped
out and one receives one's heart's desire. The barber resolved to perform a
dandavat parikrama of Mount Govardhan.

He proceeded to the Lakshmi-Narayan temple in the main bazar of
Govardhan and began his *dandavat parikrama* with firm faith there. He had
gotten all the way around the northern end of the mountain at Radhakund
and was nearing Punchari when his wife visited him. This made him remember his day in court was nearing. But his wife said to him: "Turn

everything over to Shri Giriraj Maharaj and finish your *parikrama*, then Shri Giriraj Maharaj will make everything okay." Trusting her outlook, he continued his *parikrama* with renewed faith. Meanwhile, the day of his judgment arrived and the court convened to consider his case. The "body of a barber" showed up as scheduled and the hearing proceeded. After receiving a surprisingly light sentence, this barber paid a fifty-rupee fine, gave his lawyer the required fee, and provided a mandatory signature before leaving the courtroom. After finishing his *parikrama*, the barber went to his lawyer to deal with the case. He was dumbfounded to learn from his lawyer that the case had already taken place with satisfying results. Puzzled, his lawyer explained to him that a few days back he had come to court as scheduled, and after receiving his judgment and paying a fifty-rupee fine, he was now a free man. Astonished, the barber immediately understood what had happened. As a result of the *dandavat parikrama* that he had performed with total faith, Shri Giriraj Maharaj had taken on a form that looked like him and had gone to the courtroom to arrange for his sin of killing to be exonerated for a mere fifty-rupee fine. Sharma informs the reader that every month now the barber travels to Mount Govardhan to worship and perform the *parikrama* of the sacred mountain.

Much is conveyed in these kinds of stories. Irrespective of their veracity, they both express and spread belief in the effectiveness of the worship of Mount Govardhan. Sharma ends his list of stories with a concluding statement about the benefits of performing the *parikrama*: "Why do people perform the seven-kos *parikrama*? Shri Giriraj Maharaj fulfills each and every heart's desire (*mano-kamana*). Shri Giriraj Maharaj is the most powerfully generous form of God in the present time period."[29] Expressed in these stories and other testimonials is the idea that the worship of Mount Govardhan can make possible the impossible.

In addition to concerns with material abundance and physical healing, many pilgrims worship Mount Govardhan for psychological and spiritual well-being. I was told that worshiping Giriraj "removes all troubles," "destroys all sins and misfortunes," "makes one's karma good," "eliminates all tension," "brings great happiness," and "causes peace of mind." A man who comes to Govardhan every month for the *parikrama* and *puja* of Mount Govardhan told me that he does this "to fulfill my heart's desire, and also because it gives much peace (*shanti*) and satisfaction (*santosh*) to my mind." He tapped his heart. "All tension (this English word is now used widely by Hindi speakers in northern India) goes away and I experience deep satisfaction. I know that everything is fine." Many other people I spoke with related the deep peace they felt in their souls (*atma-shanti*) as a result of worshiping Giriraj. A man from Jaipur who was doing the *dandavat parikrama* explained that it would take him ten days to complete his revolution of the mountain. His clothing was very dirty, but his face beamed with a bright smile as he explained: "We meet God by doing this. This gives us peace. We get our desires fulfilled by doing this *parikrama*, but the main thing is to get the peace that comes from meeting God in this form. We become very close to him by doing this kind of *parikrama*."

Loving devotion (*bhakti*) too may be considered to be a desired fruit, for numerous people told me that they were worshiping Mount Govardhan "for *bhakti*." A woman from Agra, for example, informed me: "Many people worship Giriraj-ji for things like a good marriage or for children, but I worship Giriraj-ji from my deepest heart's desire for intense *bhakti*." Joshi concurs: "By performing informed *puja* to Shri Govardhan a Vaishnava devotee gets the wish of *bhakti*."[30] Omprakash Yadav identifies *bhakti* with the highest of fruits: "Shri Giriraj-ji, the Treasure of Compassion, fulfills the heart's desires and gives *bhakti*, the best gift of all."[31] While walking together in the forest north of Jatipura one evening, I fell into a discussion with my friend Mohan about the reasons people worship Giriraj. I asked him what percentage of the people were doing it for *bhakti*. "One hundred percent," he answered. Surprised by this response, I pressed him for further explanation. "They are all affected by *bhakti* in some way by doing Giriraj-ji's *parikrama* or *puja*, but sure, only about half of them are inspired enough to make *bhakti* part of their daily life, such as starting a new *puja* practice in their homes." But aren't many worshiping Giriraj to fulfill a desire such as getting a child, a good marriage, a secure job, or a new house? "Yes, of course. Around fifty percent are doing it for this reason, but even they are influenced by the *bhakti* in this practice. The other fifty percent are doing it to encounter Krishna in this form and to increase their loving relationship with him." Mohan's contention was that although people might be pursuing some particular material aim, such as acquiring a new house, the physical acts of *parikrama* and other forms of worship have a positive effect on them regardless of their intentions.

Devakipran Baba expressed a similar notion in a more graphic fashion as we talked during the night of an October full moon.

> Most of the 500,000 people doing the *parikrama* tonight are doing it to get something like a good job, a happy marriage, a healthy child, or a house

of their own to live in. But doing the *parikrama* has an effect on them that is very positive. *Bhakti* too will come to them from this. It doesn't matter how you put food into your mouth. Some do it like this (he mimicked putting food into his mouth with his hand in a straightforward manner), while others do it in a very roundabout way like this (he mimed getting food into his mouth by wrapping his arm all the way around his head). But still the food gets into the mouth.

His point was that irrespective of the desire that motives the performance of a Govardhan *parikrama* or *puja*, it yields beneficial spiritual results. His experience has led him to believe that such embodied action itself has a transformative effect; the bodily performance of the *parikrama* or *puja* of Mount Govardhan *for any reason* tends to lead the performer into a deeper involvement in a devotional relationship with Giriraj. This is in line with a common understanding of the transformative power of ritual action over intentionality prevalent not only within Braj Vaishnavism, but within much Hinduism in general.[32] During our conversation, Devakipran Baba made reference to the well-known story of Ajamila.

In a story found at the beginning of the sixth chapter of the *Bhagavata Purana*, Ajamila is introduced as an upright brahmin who was corrupted by his lust for a beautiful servant woman. Ajamila's attraction to this young woman caused him to abandon his legal wife and virtuous ways. He supported the children he had with the servant woman by gambling, theft, and kidnapping for ransom. He even resorted to murder. Ajamila was very fond of the children in his new family, especially his youngest son Narayana (one of the chief names of Vishnu), whom he assiduously cared for. One day he fell gravely ill. At his moment of death, he saw the attendants of Yama (Death) rapidly approaching and became frightened. He began shouting repeatedly for his son Narayana. Hearing the name of their master, the attendants of Vishnu rushed to the scene to stop the attendants of Yama from dragging Ajamila away for punishment. When Yama's servants demanded justification for this intervention, the servants of Vishnu explained that the very act of uttering the name "Narayana" freed Ajamila from all sins, even though his intention was only to call to his son for help. Indeed, after calling out to Narayana at his moment of death, Ajamila was so transformed that he was restored to life and returned to his former virtuous ways; he spent the remainder of his years in devoted religious practice and upon death became an attendant of Vishnu. This story concludes with an appraisal of the lesson learned: the text asserts that the wise know that recitation of Vishnu's name destroys sins whatever its intention, whether it is directed to someone else, uttered inadvertently, said in jest, or even out of disrespect. The effects of the act are positive regardless of the knowledge of the actor, just as when one lights a fire it consumes the wood whether one knows it will do this or not, or when one takes medicine it will have an effect whether it was taken accidently or on purpose.[33] The point is that the key agent of ritual transformation is the physical action itself. Regardless of intentionality, the performance of the ritual act produces results. Devakipran Baba and others use this story to affirm that whatever one's intention, the bodily worship of Mount Govardhan results in some attainment or increase of *bhakti*.

One morning I watched a woman perform a moving *puja* of the Dan Ghati Mukharvind *shila*. When she had finished, I approached her and asked why she worshiped Giriraj. She explained to me that she did it "for the love (*bhava*) that is *bhakti*." This discussion with her, along with many others, makes it clear that *bhakti-bhava*, or the "love that is *bhakti*," is considered to be both a means (a physical practice) and an end (a wonderful state); that is, love is both an action expressed as worship for Giriraj as well as a joyful emotional state that is experienced as a result of worshiping Giriraj. In a sense, then, love is a "goalless goal." Rather than a controlling means to obtain something, true love according to the Braj Vaishnava traditions is its own reward. There is a saying in Braj: the highest Love is found through love itself.[34] There is nothing to achieve other than the very taste of supreme love itself; the practice is the goal. For many, the worship of Mount Govardhan is done as an expression of love, and the only reward desired in this worship is increased love. This is the way of supreme selfless love, that highest form of love called *prema*.

I had a conversation with one of the attendants at the Jatipura Mukharvind site in which I asked him what benefit (*phayda*) is derived from performing the worship of Giriraj. He responded immediately: "That is not the right question. We perform this worship because Krishna first did it and taught us that we too should do it. He showed us the way to experience the highest loving joy in life. We don't worship Giriraj for some benefit, we just do it out of our love for Krishna." A man I talked with at the Jatipura Mukharvind expressed a similar notion: "I do this for *bhakti*. I do this as loving service for Giriraj-ji. It is a way to show our love to the very source of love, and in the process we experience more love." For many, this means that the worship of Giriraj is done as an expression of sheer appreciation alone. A woman I spoke with who lives near the mountain explained: "I worship Giriraj-ji because he takes care of me. He gives me everything without even asking, so I just honor him." Some worshipers of Mount Govardhan even tie this into a kind of appreciative nature worship. A man from Gwalior worshiping at the Jatipura Mukharvind site said:

> This mountain is worthy of worship because it is a part of nature (*prakriti*). We should worship nature because we come from nature, and nature supports us completely. It supports our very life. If we respect (*adhar*) nature the realization comes that it gives us so much. This feeling spills out in appreciation as *puja*. This is why we worship Giriraj-ji.

Another common way people express their reason for worshiping Giriraj is with the word *seva*, best translated in this context as "loving service." A Gaudiya Vaishnava who was doing the *dandavat parikrama* together with five friends told me: "I am doing this as *seva* for Giriraj-ji. I have been a devotee of Giriraj-ji for a long time and this is my way of honoring him in a special way. Giriraj-ji can fulfill any wish you have, and many people do it for this reason, but I am doing it only for *seva*. I just want to connect with and be closer to God (Bhagavan) in the form of this mountain." Here *parikrama* is a form of worship that is done not with some expectation of material gain, but simply to honor God in the form of Mount Govardhan. One morning I watched a man do a simple but heartfelt *puja* to a Giriraj *shila* in the forest north of Jatipura. He told me that he does this every morning because "Giriraj is Bhagavan Krishna. He is the source of everything for me, so I come here with gratitude and honor him with *seva* in this way." This is not an uncommon position. A young man from Madhya Pradesh who comes to Mount Govardhan every month with a group of his friends informed me: "Giriraj is a powerful form of Bhagavan." What benefit (*phayda*) do you get from performing this *parikrama* and *puja*? "Benefit? What to speak of benefit? We love Giriraj-ji! We just do this to honor (*mante*) this form of Bhagavan. We worship Giriraj-ji to express and experience our love. This is our *seva*." A man who makes offerings every morning and evening to a Giriraj *shila* set up near the mountain explained: "We worship Giriraj-ji to show our love, and we get more love by doing it. Through our *seva* we become more connected to Bhagavan as Giriraj-ji." What these people have in common is an understanding that their worship of Giriraj is not an action that aims to get some expected return, but rather is simply a gracious expression of love.

In the more technical language of Braj Vaishnavism, this is said to be *nishkam seva*, that is, "loving service rendered without desire." A Pushti Margiya Vaishnava from Jatipura told me that he "worships Giriraj *nishkam*. I don't do it for any desire (*kamana*). The action itself is the reward (*phal*)." Some of this has to do with the notion that one gets more by trusting the ultimate giver of all gifts than relying on one's own desire. "He (Giriraj) fulfills the wishes of those who ask, and gives even more to those who ask for nothing."[35] But more importantly, this has to do with an understanding that the highest kind of love is egoless or selfless. Ordinary love is typically controlling, often motivated by self-referential desires. Truth be told, most gifts are given with the expectation of some kind of personal gain. A gift is given to a boss with the hope of getting a raise; a gift is presented to a friend with the expectation that this will somehow be reciprocated. It is conceivable, however, that a gift can be given as an expression of pure love, without any anticipation other than the experience of love itself. In the case of *nishkam seva*, actions are performed and offerings made as an expression of such love. This is opposed to what is called *sakam seva*, an act of worship that has the expectation of a desired gain. Much of this is based on the teaching of *karma-yoga* as described in the *Bhagavad Gita*. Most action is done with the intention of getting a particular result, but *karma-yoga* is surrendered action, defined as the performance of an action (*karma*) without being attached to the result or fruit (*phal*) of that action. For the *Bhagavad Gita*, *karma-yoga* is a means of freeing oneself from karmic bondage, but in the later discourse about love within Braj Vaishnavism it becomes *nishkam seva*, the basis of the highest expression of love and a means to experience the greatest connection to God.

Most of the goals sought in the worship of Mount Govardhan—including a child, a happy marriage, a miraculous healing, a secure job, or a house of one's own—are considered extremely difficult or even impossible to attain. That is why people approach Giriraj, a loving form of God who is known to be extremely compassionate and eager to fulfill one's heart's desire. The aim regarded as the highest of all, the one considered to be most difficult (*prapta karna kathin*) or impossible (*asambhav*) to achieve, however, is supreme egoless, non-controlling love (*parama-prem*).[36] A priest who attends a small Giriraj temple explained to me: "Giriraj-ji is very compassionate, so he readily gives the best of all. He gives love (*prem*)—the most difficult of anything to obtain—very quickly." The knowledgeable Pushti Margiya theologian, Shyammanohar Goswami, writes: "the highest fruit (*phal*) of worshiping Shri Govardhan is to be drenched in *prema-rasa*, the nectar of supreme love."[37] Perhaps the *Padma Purana* sums it most succinctly: "by doing the *puja* and *parikrama* of Govardhan one can achieve supreme bliss (*paramananda*)."[38]

The worship of Mount Govardhan and Giriraj *shilas*, then, involves loving interaction with the mountain and its many stones, and the function of the ritual acts of *parikrama* and *puja* is to establish a deep connection with Krishna in and as these tangible forms. While observing the adornment and dramatic transformation of the Jatipura Mukharvind stone, for example, I was stuck by the fact that the procedural transformation of the stone into the cowherd Krishna is done completely in full view of the public gathered to watch this daily ritual. No effort is made to hide the fact that the resulting elaborate form of Krishna that is worshiped by the priests is a rock that is attached to the mountain. Quite the contrary; all is in the open. The stone is Krishna; Krishna is the stone. How has the worship of physical objects such as stones or mountains, with its concomitant conception of the visible materiality of God, been represented in the comparative study of religions, and what are the available interpretive options—past and present—for understanding this practice?

5

A Tale of Two Mountains

Idolatry Applied

Idolatry and iconoclasm have much to do with the understanding of religion as a historical phenomenon, because this ideological pairing has played a major role in the history of cultural conflicts along religious lines.[1]

Mount Govardhan is a direct form of Krishna, the very source of my life.[2]

The Hindoo system . . . is the most puerile, impure, and bloody, of any system of idolatry that was ever established on earth.[3]

Applying Idolatry

Devotees of Mount Govardhan agree that the mountain and all its stones are eminently worthy of worship, and that Mount Govardhan is a graciously approachable and concrete form of God. Such claims, however, have been quite challenging for many encountering such a phenomenon from the viewpoint of other cultural perspectives, particularly from those shaped by European Reformational Christianity. For centuries, the concept of idolatry has played a major role in interpretations of religious otherness. The American travel writer John Stoddard, for example, wrote at the close of the nineteenth century that the Hindu worship of embodied forms ("idols") involves "the most repulsive exhibition of idolatry, fanaticism, and filth that one can well imagine."[4] Hindu worship did not fair much better in nineteenth-century European scholarly representations—especially the portrayal of interactions with sacred stones. Two of the most influential books at this time, William Ward's *History, Literature, and Mythology of the Hindoos*

Loving Stones. David L. Haberman, Oxford University Press (2020) © Oxford University Press.
DOI: 10.1093/oso/9780190086718.001.0001

and Abbe Dubois's *Hindu Manners, Customs and Ceremonies* provide ample evidence.[5] Although earlier Oriental scholars outrightly disregarded Hindu worship of embodied forms as contemporary corruptions of true Hinduism, Ward and Dubois spent considerable effort describing and interpreting this widespread form of religious practice. Both were missionary scholars who shared with countless other nineteenth-century Christian missionaries and European scholars of Hinduism the assumption that this was a form of idolatry—in fact, the grossest or most abhorrent form of all idolatry. Ward assigned so much culpability to idolatry that he blamed what he understood as its Hindu version for all evils in Indian society. In a section of his book titled "Inanimate Objects of Worship," Dubois introduces the worst of Hindu idolatrous foolishness, stating, "in matters of superstition truth is sometimes stranger than fiction. What I have already said and what I am now about to say respecting the Hindus will show incontestably that there are absolutely no limits to the follies of idolatry."[6] He goes on to discuss and condemn what he calls "inanimate objects of worship," with a particular emphasis on the worship of stones.

The standard assumption in early European accounts of the Hindu practice of stone worship was that it is one of the lowliest and most egregious forms of idolatry in the world. In his nineteenth-century study of popular religion in India, W. Crooke includes a consideration of stones from Mount Govardhan in a section titled "Fetish Stones." According to Crooke, fetish stones epitomize the very lowest form of idolatry since they illustrate a case wherein gods are "supposed to be embodied."[7] Max Müller, considered by many to have been the greatest authority in nineteenth-century Europe on India and comparative religion, also judged stone worship as fetishism, which he regarded as the crudest form of religious idolatry.[8] What is idolatry, and how did it become routine for most scholars of religion to employ it as a common interpretive strategy for something like stone worship? The question is important since this interpretive legacy in many ways remains with us today.[9]

A brief look into the history of the application of idolatry as an interpretive approach is germane to a study of the worship of Mount Govardhan and its many stones, since it was the interpretive tool automatically employed in past Western representations of Hindu stone worship. More generally, the concept of idolatry helped shape modern attitudes about reverent interaction with religious objects and was a defining feature of the early comparative study of religion. The concept of idolatry used by missionary and colonial scholars as an interpretive tool is derived from Greek terminology that became

intertwined with later Christian concerns.[10] The concept of idolatry, however, has deeper roots, based on early Jewish theological notions stretching
back to the Hebrew Bible. I now shift attention from Mount Govardhan to
a paradigmatic story associated with another religiously significant mountain, with particular interest in the resulting (mis)understandings that arise
when the two mountain traditions clash—if only indirectly through interpretive endeavors. The definitive site for early Jewish notions about idolatry is Mount Sinai, and the interpretive roots of the concept of idolatry are
grounded in two fundamental narratives associated with it. This mountain
was the location of the revelation that prohibited what came to be regarded
as idolatry, as well as the scene of a justified response to an exemplary act of
idolatry. In a general sense, idolatry is understood as the worship of an *idol*,
a material object venerated as an embodied form of a deity. The biblical book
of Exodus was the key text for establishing the meaning of idolatry, particularly in terms of the weighty Second Commandment and the story of the
worship of the golden calf, the very epitome of idolatry for biblical traditions.

Having successfully led the people of Israel out of Egypt and into the desert of Sinai, Moses ascended Mount Sinai and in a fiery encounter with God
was given two tablets inscribed with the Ten Commandments. The second of
the ten reads:

> You shall not make for yourself an image in the form of anything in heaven
> above or on the earth beneath or in the waters below. You shall not bow
> down to them or worship them; for I, the Lord your God, am a jealous God,
> punishing the children for the sin of the parents to the third and fourth gen-
> eration of those who hate me, but showing love to a thousand generations
> of those who love me and keep my commandments. (NIV Exodus 20:4–6)

The possible meanings of this passage are many, but it has clear implications
for the status of the physical world that is experienced with the senses. The
sacrality of the visible world of material entities was rejected as the nature-
centered religions of the Near East of that time were contested. Reflecting on
the second commandment, Egyptologist and biblical scholar Jan Assmann
writes: "God is invisible. Therefore, he cannot be worshipped in anything
visible—be it an image or a heavenly body."[11] Including—we might add—
a mountain or stone.[12] Mount Sinai is the *place* where Moses encountered
God, not the *form* in which he encountered God. The second commandment
gives expression to a highly transcendent conception of God, ontologically

distant from the domain of all visible forms. Any attempt to communicate with or worship God through visible forms is not only a ludicrous mistake, but also an atrocious sin. Later texts in the Hebrew Bible openly ridicule the worship of visible forms.[13] The "idols" of those who sacralize the physical world are worthless matter, dumb stuff without any power to help anyone—including themselves. Since God is utterly other than visible matter, any attempt to interact with the divine through physical forms is not only fruitless, but leads one astray from true transcendent divinity. "To prohibit the production of images, therefore, means to prohibit the adoration of the visible world."[14] The result is a disenchantment of the world.

By contrast, traditions that regard the domain of material entities as sacred—such as those associated with the worship of Mount Govardhan—presuppose theological immanence and inhabit a physical world of divine presence. At stake between these two worldviews is the very value of the world. Assmann articulates the iconoclastic position of the second commandment: "According to the aniconists, images idolize the world and blind the eyes from being able to look beyond the world and focus on the creator. . . . Idolatry, they declare, is *Weltverstickung*—entanglement within the world, addiction to the visible and material."[15] This is the central problem with divinizing material objects; they seduce one's attention and obscure a transcendent God. From the perspective of the iconoclast, being on friendly terms with the world is a major problem. "Instead of making humans feel at home in the world, it strives at estranging them from the world."[16]

But those who regard the sphere of material entities as divine have a very different outlook. For them, tangible objects provide direct contact and interaction with an immanent God. Since the deeply enchanted world is understood to be fully divine and appreciated as such, involvement with it is not problematic. On the contrary, everything becomes a potential object of worship. Those invested in the religion of visible forms take issue with the iconoclast's worldview: "Iconoclasm would deprive the world of this divine animation and would turn it into mere inanimate matter, doomed to pollution and decomposition."[17] Assmann quotes the *Asclepius*, a third-century Egyptian text written in resistance to the rising tide of Christian iconoclasm, to showcase the consequences of iconoclasm's success: "In their weariness the people of that time will find the world nothing to wonder at or to worship. . . . They will not cherish this entire world, a glorious construction, a bounty composed of images in multiform variety, a multiform accumulation taken as a single thing. . . . Every divine voice will grow mute in enforced silence."[18] At the heart of this matter is the question: What is the relationship between God and the physical world?[19] Particular answers significantly influence human attitudes toward and behavior in the natural world. The second commandment has tended to strongly discourage any sacralization of the tangible world.

The other major narrative associated with Mount Sinai is the story of the golden calf.[20] While Moses was on the mountain for a period of forty days, the Israelites grew restless, worried that he would not return and they would lose their connection with God. They approached the high priest Aaron and demanded that he make an image for them, at the time not an unusual request. He collected the peoples' gold jewelry, fashioned a golden calf with it, and organized a special worship the following day. Meanwhile, God informed Moses that the Israelites were committing a grave sin and that he planned to destroy them for their idolatrous act. Moses convinced God to spare the people and descended the mountain with two tablets inscribed with the Ten Commandments. When he arrived back at camp in time to witness the worship of the golden calf, Moses became outraged. He hurled the tablets to the ground and destroyed the offensive calf. He then called the sons of Levi to his side and ordered them to slaughter three thousand people as punishment for their idolatry.

This act of violence is legitimized as defense of the second commandment. Assmann contends that "[t]he prohibition of images divides the world into two parties: the idolaters and the iconoclasts, the first being the enemies of and the second being the friends of God."[21] Considering the fundamental roots of the concept of idolatry in the second of the Ten Commandments, W. J. T. Mitchell points out that idolatry is regarded as the "ultimate evil," and that its prohibition "is clearly the most important commandment of them all, occupying the central place in defining sins against God."[22] Indeed, we will see that idolatry came to mean all manner of grievous sins, and became the very hallmark of religious error. Idolatry is not just a sin, but *the* sin par excellence. Its condemnation, moreover, has much to do with the very nature of worship.

In their extensive study of the foundations of Jewish notions about idolatry, Moshe Halbertal and Avishai Margalit assert that the biblical word translated as "idolatry" really means "strange worship." "The adjective in 'strange worship' has two senses. One is the strangeness of the object toward which the worship is directed, not the 'proper' God but other gods. The other refers to the method of worship." [23] These two notions of strangeness—the strangeness of the ritual and the strangeness of the ritual object—constitute the two major apprehensions regarding idolatry. The embodied worship of a lithic god would certainly fit the definition. What is the proper treatment of those who are worshiping the wrong object in the wrong way? The story of the golden calf gives voice to an approach to difference that strives to eliminate it through forceful and violent means. I do not aim to judge the concept of idolatry as a component of a particular religious tradition; rather, my interest in the concept of idolatry has to do with the way it has been used as an interpretive strategy in the encounter with other religions, especially with regard to considerations of the worshipful practices of Hinduism.

It is important to realize that in many ways idolatry is the invention of the iconoclast. There is no idolatry without an iconoclasm to define it. Mitchell claims that "*idolatry* is a word that mainly appears in the discourse of iconoclasm, a militant monotheism obsessed with its own claims to universality."[24] That is, it is one way of dealing with difference that aims to exterminate it in the assertion of singularity. Halbertal and Margalit maintain: "The ban on idolatry is an attempt to dictate exclusivity, to map the unique territory of the one God. . . . Monotheism, in its war against polytheism, is an attempt to impose unity of opinions and beliefs by force, as a result of an uncompromising attitude toward the unity of God."[25] In other words, the monotheism that is associated with the concept of idolatry does not tend to promote pluralism, but rather works to undermine it. Employed as an interpretive lens, idolatry becomes part of an intentional strategy for eradicating difference.

Halbertal and Margalit's excellent book examines the nature of idolatry in great detail. In many ways, idolatry presupposes—indeed, it is the very root of—the concept of symbolic representation. These two authors write, for example: "The prophets describe idol worship as the worship of wood and stone. When the idolater bows down to the idol, according to Isaiah, he worships the image itself and not what the image represents. In their polemics the prophets taunt the idol worshipers with the idiocy of worshiping wood and stone."[26] Recognizing that in many religious traditions the embodied form or "idol" is a manifestation of God, Halbertal and Margalit contend that the biblical fear of this kind of idolatry "is the possibility of a substitutive error, in which the idol ceases to be the representation or symbol of God and comes to be seen as God himself or part of him. In such a case, the idol is regarded as a fetish."[27] This leads them to assert a crucial difference between the correctness of symbolic representation and the mistake of idolatrous "fetishism": "This error occurs when a representation acquires the features of the thing represented." In other words, idolatrous fetishism for these authors is symbolic representation gone awry.

Although the very concept of the fetish has been seriously questioned by many academics, the perspective presented by Halbertal and Margalit is suitable for the prevailing viewpoint of the dualistic and highly transcendent Abrahamic traditions. The issue I wish to stress, however, is whether this is a neutral or fair lens through which to view other religious traditions. We have seen, for example, that within the non-dual Vedantic worldview of Braj Vaishnavism, God is identified with both the visible material realm (*adhibhuta*) as well as the invisible transcendent (*adhyatma*). In this context, there is no strict ontological divide between the thing representing the divine (the signifier or symbol) and the divine represented (the signified or symbolized); thus, the concept of symbolic representation does not apply. While being identified with the infinite beyond all representation, Krishna also becomes present in the finite material realm in such forms as Mount Govardhan.

One way of expressing the central problem so common in idolatry according to much Jewish thought, then, is the "blurring of the distinction between the symbol and the thing symbolized."[28] There is perhaps no figure more influential on this issue in Jewish thought than the twelfth-century philosopher Maimonides, whose views continued to have significant influence over such sixteenth-century Protestant thinkers as John Calvin. [29] The error of substitution, according to Maimonides, eventually caused the "ordinary folk, including women and children," to stray from true transcendent monotheism and take up the worship of "the images of wood and stone."[30] The only perceived solution to this threat was to outlaw idolatry. "Since it is the error of substitution that is the cause of idolatry, according to Maimonides the purpose of the prohibitions against idolatry is to ensure that such errors will not be made."[31] Another problem with idolatrous embodiment for Maimonides is that it supports the "false belief" of multiplicity, as "the strict demand on unity implies a rejection of corporeality."[32] Maimonides rejected any notion of a complex unity; for him, multiple embodied manifestations of a unified divinity completely undermine the transcendent nature of God. This, of course, is precisely the kind of philosophical system that informs the Braj Vaishnavism associated with the worship of Mount Govardhan, often expressed with the Sanskrit compound *bheda-abheda*, "difference in non-difference."

Ultimate judgment of these positions is impossible; from the outside, both viewpoints have equal validity. But when one system is used to judge another, the other by definition comes up short. Regarding the notion of transcendent unity as the only position that protects the perfection of God, Maimonides saw the war against idolatry as the very heart of the Torah. "Corporeality," he dismissively argues, foreshadowing later Enlightenment thinkers such as David Hume, "is a gross error in being the vulgar notion of the common people."[33] According to Halbertal and Margalit, the attack on idolatry is a major feature of "the intolerant nature of the monotheistic tradition" that leads to "the orthodox insistence on one form of worship, to one object and in one way."[34] What would be the utility and consequences of employing such an interpretive lens to understand and translate the religious practices of others?

Sixteenth-Century Developments

Although the roots of the concept of idolatry can be traced back to the times of the Hebrew Bible and theological reflections of Jewish thinkers like Maimonides, sixteenth-century Europe witnessed enormous changes wherein this concept came to overshadow much thought and action.[35] This is not to suggest that idolatry had not been a matter of concern for earlier Christians; based on their reading of biblical texts, the early church fathers condemned the worship of both fashioned images and natural objects.[36] Maintaining a distinction between worshiping anything in the created world and worshiping the Creator has been fundamental to much Christian theology. The influential works of Augustine in the fourth century give classic expression to the importance of maintaining the boundary between Creator and creation; for Augustine, this is one of the defining features that set the Jewish and Christian traditions apart from all other religious options.[37] During the sixteenth century, however, application of the concept of idolatry became the crucial concern, and was employed in a much stricter and extensive manner.[38] For an understanding of the role the concept of idolatry played in European interpretations of Hinduism, as well as many other religious traditions throughout the world, consideration of sixteenth-century developments is crucial.

At the beginning of the sixteenth century, Western Christianity participated in a religion of immanence in which the sacred was still present in the material. The historian of European religion Carlos Eire explains: "In 1509, when John Calvin was born, Western Christendom still shared a common religion of immanence. Heaven was never too far from earth. The sacred was diffused in the profane, the spiritual in the material. Divine power, embodied in the Church and its sacraments, reached down through innumerable points of contact to make itself felt."[39] But as the century progressed, the validity of this kind religion came to be abolished. In short, "[t]he religion of immanence was replaced by the religion of transcendence."[40] Much of this was due to the religious revolution known as the Protestant Reformation, particularly under the influence of John Calvin. Eire maintains that idolatry was *the central issue* of the Reformation, and the main thesis of his book *War against the Idols* is that "John Calvin, in defending the heritage of the Reformed attitude toward idolatry, forged a new, spiritually based, theological metaphysics in which the boundaries between the spiritual and the material were more clearly drawn than ever before."[41] The fundamental focus of Reformed Protestantism was a strong concern for correct worship, which involved a preoccupation with the relationship between the spiritual and the material. The Platonic tradition of maintaining a dualism of spirit and matter fed into this development through such influential figures as Erasmus, who wrote: "You can only establish perfect piety when you turn away from visible things."[42] From this perspective, the aim of human existence becomes the emancipation of spirit from the "prison" of the material world.[43]

According to Calvin, true religion involves the spiritual worship of a highly transcendent God. Its opposite—the material worship of an immanent God—is "idolatry," a sin warranting severe punishment. The historian Jonathan Sheehan reminds us: "If any biblical book was indispensable to the Calvinist project, however, it was Exodus."[44] Calvin inherited the older view of idolatry drawn from the Hebrew Bible, but augmented it with Paul's notions expressed in his Letter to the Romans: "They exchanged the truth about God for a lie, and worshiped and served created things rather than the Creator" (NIV 1:25). This led to an expanded understanding of idolatry beyond images made by human hand to now include the "lie" that attributes any "bodily shape" to God or associates God with any "created thing." This expanded conception of idolatry as worship of anything in the world was the one commonly taken up by later Christian writers.

During Calvin's time, idolatry became a fighting word and the ideological foundations of iconoclasm were greatly reinforced. He insisted that there is nothing whatsoever visible or earthly about God; for him, worship of God in any physical form is the very antithesis of true religion. His views on idolatry are well represented in the eleventh chapter of his major work, *Institutes of the Christian Religion*, entitled "Impiety of Attributing a Visible Form to God."[45] Calvin begins by noting that in their "brutish stupidity" humans long for "visible forms of God." This is highly problematic, since "as any form is assigned to God, his glory is corrupted by an impious lie." He interprets the second commandment as a prohibition from associating God with any "visible shape." For Calvin, "the majesty of God is defiled by an absurd and indecorous fiction, when he who is incorporeal is assimilated to corporeal matter; he who is invisible to a visible image; he who is a spirit to an inanimate object; and he who fills all space to a bit of paltry wood, or stone, or gold." Although Calvin marshals a skillful and gallant effort at preserving the unlimited nature of God, from a non-dual theological perspective he limits God by cordoning off the divine from the realm of matter. Concomitantly, Calvin's theology greatly undermines the cogency of the senses in cultivating a relationship with the divine.

Calvin learned from Augustine that "idolaters" might have a sophisticated understanding of the visible object, writing: "The vulgar, when accused, replied that they did not worship the visible object, but the Deity which dwelt in it invisibly. Those, again, who had what he calls a more refined religion, said, that they neither worshipped the image, nor any inhabiting Deity, but by means of the corporeal image beheld a symbol of that which it was duty to worship." Nonetheless, for Calvin, there remains a grave danger in worshiping material forms, for one risks becoming fixated on them, thereby limiting the infinity of God. The seductive quality of idols is especially dangerous. Accordingly, Calvin warns that one should "beware, not only of the worship of idols, but also of idols themselves." He acknowledges that idolatry comes from the deep-seated desire to connect with divinity in the "created" world. Yet this is precisely what is condemned by the enhanced concept of idolatry that arose in sixteenth-century Europe, which was informed by a strict dualism that maintains a sharp boundary between the Creator and created, and fosters a highly transcendent conception of worship. Any confusion concerning this dualism leads to idolatry, an egregious sin punishable by extreme violence.

Calvin's teachings were used to support aggression; indeed, for some it became a devout duty to destroy any form of worship deemed idolatrous. Prior to Calvin, the Protestant Andreas Karlstadt had written a tract titled "On the Abolition of Images" to justify iconoclasm and violence, for he insisted that it was an individual's obligation to obliterate "false worship."[46] The chief target of Protestant judgmental vigilance regarding correct worship was, of course, Roman Catholicism with its various forms of physical worship. Over the course of time, however, vigilant concerns over idolatry were extended far beyond European Catholicism, and such Hindu practices as stone worship became one of the many targets in the sights of iconoclasts.

Early Modern Europe and the Birth of the Comparative Study of Religion

Sixteenth-century Europe witnessed extensive religious wars over the correct nature of worship. Tens of thousands of people were killed and many churches and works of art were destroyed. As the bloody conflict over idolatry was beginning to wind down in Europe, colonialism was ramping up, thus carrying the religious battle to distant shores. It is important to understand that it was precisely at this time that the comparative study of religions came into being.[47] The historian of early modern Europe Jonathan Sheehan points out that in the seventeenth century the discourses about idolatry "were common currency in virtually every area of early modern life . . . virtually every major intellectual and cultural movement of the period took on idolatry, from the missionaries, ethnographers, and geographers."[48] Religious historian Guy Stroumsa concurs. Commenting on seventeenth-century religious scholarship, he writes: "If I were to single out one keyword for the period under discussion, I would choose 'idolatry.' The recognition of the multifaceted presence of idolatry and the study of its origins was a major concern for all students of religion in early modern Europe."[49] The concept of idolatry, then, emerged as the favored interpretive strategy for understanding other religious traditions, particularly those of non-Abrahamic origin.[50] Moreover, it becomes embedded in the very foundation of the comparative study of religion.

Although during the sixteenth century the heightened concern over idolatry was directed primarily at Catholic worship,[51] as European exploration and colonialism expanded in the seventeenth century this concern was extended to forms of worship encountered on other continents. Both Catholics and Protestants were involved in the wider, comparative study of idolatry: Catholics to demonstrate how *dissimilar* pagan rituals were from their religious practices, and Protestants to define true religion by *contrasting* it with erroneous idolatry. Idolatry by definition was considered to be distinct from religion, or at least true religion. Sheehan says of seventeenth-century scholarship, "to understand 'religion' we must understand idolatry; it was only by showing what religion was *not*, that religion could be defined."[52] Consequently, the comparative study of idolatry gave rise to new interest in the history of religion, which was motivated by a search for the origins of paganism, identified principally with the practice of idolatry. This search was connected to the question of historical priority: Which came first, paganism or true religion? Was idolatrous paganism progressively replaced by transcendent monotheism, or was idolatry a later corruption of original monotheism? The comparative study of religion grew out of these concerns over the origin and nature of idolatry, which in the early seventeenth century assumed a sharp boundary between religion and its other, idolatry. Stroumsa maintains that "the search for the roots and nature of idolatry seems to have provided legitimation for the nascent science of religion. . . . What clearly appears from the collection of the evidence is the central role of idolatry, ancient and modern, East and West, in seventeenth-century discourse on religion, its origins, and its historical development."[53]

The world's religious traditions came to be divided in seventeenth-century studies into four types: the three related Abrahamic traditions of Judaism, Christianity, and Islam, and idolatrous paganism.[54] John Spencer, considered by many to be a founding figure in the field of comparative religion, is representative of a change that began to take place in the seventeenth century. In his works, idolatry was transformed from the enemy of religion to a species of religion. Spencer employed the term "religion" in a much more general fashion, using it to refer to a universal anthropological phenomenon rather than as a synonym for Christianity. Sharp distinctions nonetheless remained; as forms of worship labeled idolatry came to be accepted as "religion," the conversation shifted to emphasize the dissimilarity between common religion (connected with embodied ritual) and true religion (associated with interior faith).[55] In many of the seventeenth-century studies of religion, moreover, "vulgar idolatry" was associated with nature, whereas true religion was associated with revelatory law.

Parallel developments were occurring in the burgeoning field of ethnography, as ethnographic discourse on religion often grew out of colonial efforts to describe the actual practices of the varieties of idolatry. While the Protestant Reformation was progressing in Europe, related events were happening on the other side of the world: the Spanish, for example, were engaged in the conversion of the "pagans" and the iconoclastic destruction of their "idols" in Mesoamerica and the Andes. Much of this involved the official Spanish program of the "Extirpation of Idolatries" in Mexico and Peru. Mayan religion in the Yucatan, for example, was labeled idolatry, with disastrous consequences for the religion and its practitioners. In the later part of the sixteenth century, thousands of Mayan "idols" were burned and their worshipers severely punished under the leadership of Bishop Fray Diego de Landa.[56]

Stone worship attracted particular attention. The natural stone forms of the *huacas* worshiped in the Peruvian Andes, for example, were included among the targets of the organized attack on idolatry in the Americas by the Spanish. The historian Kenneth Mills observes: "Calling the huacas 'idolos' (idols), and interpreting them largely in terms of Greco-Roman and biblical traditions, did them more than just a passing injustice."[57] In his seventeenth-century text, Father Pablo Joseph de Arriaga, one of the chief administers of the policy of the Extirpation of Idolatries in Peru, says stone worship is exemplary of the "great evil" that is Andean idolatry.[58] Mills underscores the nature of the a priori interpretive issue in this encounter that curtailed any significant understanding:

> The negative preconception, as well as the ubiquitous use of another loaded rubric, "idol" and thus "idolatry," to describe the Indians' alleged object of worship and their religion effectively precluded any possibility for genuine theological comparison. . . . Superficial understanding of another culture's divine forces and religious ideas, and the way they fit into that people's world view, led to the widespread inability of Spanish Christian observers to grant complexity and profundity to the originally non-Christian people, let alone their belief system. Instead of being represented as an alien people's vision of the world and their particular explanation of the human condition in relation to the forces believed present, Andean religion became "idolatry."[59]

Cross-cultural encounters in the Americas, as well as in Africa and Asia, produced a wealth of missionary and traveler accounts of worship practices in non-Christian cultures; what these descriptions all shared was ready "recognition" of various religions as forms of idolatry. The historian Joan-Pau Rubiés maintains that missionaries and travelers "assumed both the *unproblematic applicability* of the concept of idolatry to all kinds of observed religious practice and the demonic presence underlying them."[60] This included the common interpretive approach to Hindu worship. The application of the concept of idolatry to a certain religious practice, then, served simultaneously to identify and censure it. "The various encounters caused by European colonial efforts in Africa, America, and Asia, but also a small number of medieval accounts of journeys to Central Asia, China, and India, generated what we might call 'spontaneous ethnographies,' in which the concept of idolatry invariably served both to describe and to condemn non-biblical cults."[61] Two types of idolatry were identified: that which focused on natural objects of worship and that involving images fashioned by human hands.[62] The first of these was considered the lowest and most immature: "With their worship of stones, mountains, and rivers, the Indians behaved like children, that is, like potentially rational beings not in full command of their reason."[63]

We witness here the (problematic) beginnings of the anthropology of religion. These early ethnographies all assumed an unquestioned application of the concept of idolatry to a wide-ranging variety of forms of worship. Scholarship appearing during this early colonial period was, of course, informed by very particular religious and political agendas, resulting in a comparative study of religion that grew out of an investigation of other religions with the aim of clarifying and promoting the "true religion" (i.e., European Christianity). Most of this scholarship was driven by a concern to "civilize" the colonized by eradicating idolatry among them. Thus the ultimate objective of the study of the different religions of others, routinely defined as idolatries, was to understand them enough to defeat them. In terms of the interpretive approach of Armstrong and others reviewed in Chapter 2, the productive play of cross-cultural interpretation was over before it even began. Scholars "knew" what the religious practices of others were all about without ever asking.

According to these colonial scholars, then, the project of enlightenment required a progressive movement from the visual, physical, and "idolatrous" to the abstract, intellectual, and "rational." Developments in comparative religion and ethnography were also paralleled in other academic fields, as "seventeenth-century debates about idolatry had a powerful influence, not only in theology and religious struggles but in other disciplines as well."[64] This includes what today are called the natural sciences. As Eire asserts: "Though the connections among Renaissance, Reformation, and 'modernity' form a Gordian knot that no pen or sword can easily unravel, it makes sense to say that the scientific and religious revolutions of the sixteenth century share common traits."[65] Perhaps more than any other figure, this is well illustrated by the seventeenth-century scientist Robert Boyle, whose thought is close to other important seventeen-century thinkers such as Francis Bacon and René Descartes. Boyle is remembered today as the "father of modern chemistry," but this label fails to capture the complexity of the man and his multifaceted presence in the seventeenth century. In addition to chemistry, Boyle was involved in articulating the other natural sciences; he also wrote a number of widely read religious tracts, he was a director of East India Trading Company, and he funded translations of the Bible into Indian languages.

Boyle is closely associated with the development of mechanistic science and mechanical philosophy, which he regarded as strong allies of true religion.[66] The very foundations of Boyle's views of science and the natural world were built upon a fundamental religious concern with idolatry; that is, a particular understanding of religion—not secularism—shaped his views on science. Resisting the notion that Boyle's mechanical philosophy was part of the secularization of knowledge, the historian J. E. McGuire insists: "The 'mechanical philosophy' of Boyle and other seventeenth-century thinkers is, in part, a reformulation of a nominalist ontology arising mainly from the reformed theology of the Calvinists."[67] Since the primary threat to both religion and science for Boyle was idolatry, his articulation of the natural sciences had to include an attack on idolatry.[68] This was one of the major concerns that prompted him to write what many regard to be the summation of his views on nature, *A Free Enquiry into the Vulgarly Received Notion of Nature*.

In this lengthy essay Boyle followed the Calvinist criticism of Catholicism. Any sense of divine immanence was to be condemned as the sin of idolatry, for this confounds the great distance between creator and created things and leads to nature worship. He identified the immanent view of nature as "vulgar," and wrote that "the next thing for which I dislike the vulgar notion (or idea) of nature is, that I think it dangerous to religion in general and consequently, to the Christian. For this erroneous conceit defrauds the true God of divers acts of veneration and gratitude that are due to him from men."[69] A scientist strongly influenced by Protestant Christianity, Boyle maintained a sharp distinction between God and the natural world; as a result, there could be no presence, agency, or sentience in nature whatsoever. The main thesis of *A Free Enquiry into the Vulgarly Received Notion of Nature* is that if power is assigned to inner forces in nature, then nature is idolized and God dishonored. Perhaps Boyle's clearest statement on problematic religious views of nature is this:

To manifest therefore the malevolent aspect that the vulgar notion of nature has had, and therefore possibly may have, on religion, I think it fit in a general way to premise what things they are which seem to me to have been fundamental errors that misled the heathen world, as well philosophers as others. For if I mistake not, the looking upon merely corporeal and oftentimes inanimate things as if they were endowed with life, sense and understanding, and the ascribing to nature and other beings (whether real or imaginary) things that belong but to God, have been some (if not the chief) of the grand causes of the polytheism and idolatry of the Gentiles.[70]

Obviously for Boyle, the worship of a Govardhan stone as a divine presence would involve the most vulgar of all notions of nature. We leave the seventeenth century, then, with a predominant sense from many disciplinary perspectives that the greatest of problems is idolatry—regarding any kind of presence in natural entities. Acute concern with the folly of idolatry continued on into the next century.

Eighteenth- and Nineteenth-Century Applications

One of the eighteenth century's most influential thinkers about the human relationship with the non-human from a religious perspective was David Hume, a scholar greatly shaped by Calvinistic Scottish Presbyterianism. For Enlightenment philosophers such as Hume, who understood religion as largely a human construct, idolatrous notions and practices are not problematic because they are a "sin," but rather because they are "primitive" and "childish." Animated views of material objects are absurd follies that must be abandoned in the progressive march into the modern world. In his most influential work, *The Natural History of Religion*, Hume's main agenda is articulating the origin of religion and tracing an evolutionary development toward perfection that assumes a clear notion of progress. He identifies the lowest and most primitive form of religion as "vulgar, polytheistic, idolatry." He writes: "It appears to me that if we consider the improvement of human society, from rude beginnings to a state of perfection, polytheism or idolatry was, and necessarily must have been, the first and most ancient religion of mankind."[71] So confident is Hume that idolatry is the correct interpretive tool for understanding most "primitive" non-European religions that he sees no real need to listen to their practitioners or investigate their worldview: "The savage tribes of America, Africa, and Asia are all idolaters. Not a single exception to this rule. Insomuch, that, were a traveller to transport himself into any unknown region; if he found . . . them ignorant and barbarous, he might *beforehand declare them idolaters*; and there scarcely is a possibility of his being mistaken."[72]

For Hume the central defining feature of ancient idolatrous polytheism is that it regards everything as sacred: "The vulgar polytheist . . . *deifies every part of the universe*, and conceives all the conspicuous productions of nature, to be themselves so many real divinities. The sun, moon, and stars, are all gods according to his system: Fountains are inhabited by nymphs, and trees by hamadryads."[73] Whereas more enlightened religious thinkers are content to allow invisible power to remain abstract, the vulgar masses "rest their attention on sensible, visible objects."[74] And, of course, worshipful interaction with those natural entities which Enlightenment thinkers like Hume regarded as "inanimate matter" is judged the most absurd of all. For Hume, belief in divine presence in material objects is the very pinnacle of ridiculousness: "I believe, indeed, that there is no tenet in all paganism, which would give so fair a scope to ridicule as this of the *real presence*."[75] Here is a clear condemnation that would certainly include something like the Hindu worship of Mount Govardhan.

Hume promoted a two-tiered notion of religion: Besides the "vulgar religion" of the "raw and ignorant multitude," motivated by fear of unknown causes and involving notions of personified idolatrous embodiment, there is the "rational religion" of the educated elite, which is invested in abstract, transcendent notions of divinity. According to Hume, ancient religion springs from nature worship, or rather from the belief that "all nature was full of invisible powers,"[76] whereas the "high religion" of the educated elite is based on a "doctrine of one supreme deity, the author (not expression or manifestation) of nature."[77] God is the "supreme author" of the visible world, but *not* a part of it. The conception of a god of stone from this perspective belongs undoubtedly to the lowest rung of vulgar idolatrous religion.

The ideas of the philosopher Auguste Comte also had a great impact on nineteenth-century views of religion. His primary concern in *The Positive Philosophy* was with "human progression"; accordingly, he set out to "investigate the natural laws by which the advance of the human mind proceeds." What he purports to have discovered is "the great philosophical law of the succession of the three states—the primitive theological, the transient metaphysical, and the final positive state."[78] Here is reference to the "law of three stages" for which Comte is well known. The primitive theological state involves explanation in terms of personified deities; in this phase, people believe all phenomena to be produced by supernatural beings. This is surpassed by the metaphysical stage wherein the gods are replaced by abstract forces. The evolutionary process culminates in the final positive state, where reason and scientific knowledge become the basis of truth.

Importantly, the "primitive theological" state is itself divided into three progressive phases: fetishism, polytheism, and monotheism. The most primitive of all mental states is fetishism, "that tendency of our nature by which Man conceives of all external bodies as animated by a life analogous to his own."[79] Most likely with Hume in mind, Comte explains: "Fetishism has even been usually confounded with polytheism, when the latter has been called Idolatry."[80] In short, fetishism—the most primitive of all states identified with notions of divine embodiment—is a case of extreme idolatry. It makes the mistake of seeing divinity in everything, and is guilty of "deifying every substance."[81] For Comte, this is the core of the most primitive of all stages of human mental life and is indicative of "the intellectual state of the infant human race."[82] Once again, according to the positive philosophy of the modern era, idolatry is not necessarily a sin, but rather an absurd error. Worship of a stone would certainly have been ranked by Comte among the most childish of all idolatrous practices.

The progressive agenda of modernity was continued by practically every major thinker in the nineteenth century. This was certainly true in the field of anthropology. As Sheehan asserts: "When nineteenth-century anthropologists began their investigation of primitive cultures, then, they brought along an entire intellectual armature inherited from the early modern battles over the nature of religion."[83] Perhaps most illustrative among all nineteenth-century anthropologists is Edward B. Tylor, the first professor of anthropology at Oxford University. Considered by many to be the founder of cultural anthropology, he produced the most complete history of religions to date. Tylor's reflections included consideration of human conceptions of and behavior toward the non-human world. His ideas are representative of a very common nineteenth-century theory of cultural evolution with its concomitant understanding of various hierarchical stages of human development, assumptions about the direction of progress, and notions about the place and role of the worship of natural entities or non-human life forms in this advancement.

Tylor lays out his agenda explicitly in the opening pages of *The Origins of Culture*, the first volume of *Primitive Culture* published in 1871. It is clear that he is primarily interested in tracing the development of what he calls the progressive stages of cultures, asserting, "The main tendency of culture from primaeval up to modern times has been from savagery towards civilization."[84] Modern, educated Westerners establish the norm for the "civilized" state. Concurring with the colonial thinking of his time, Tylor asserts that the primitive stage of culture is still seen among "modern savages." "The educated world of Europe and America practically settles a standard by simply placing its own notions at one end of the social series and savage tribes at the other, arranging the rest of mankind between these limits according as they correspond more closely to savage or to cultured life."[85] For Tylor, progress is the movement from the earlier conditions of mankind to the higher culture of modern Christian Europe; he calls this the "progressive-theory of civilization."[86] Just what, we might ask, are the earlier, primitive conditions of humankind? Tylor provides an answer in *Religion in Primitive Culture*, the second volume of *Primitive Culture*. Here Tylor deploys an analysis of different types of religion to determine where to place a particular society on the hierarchical scale ranging from primitive to civilized.

The chief subject of *Religion in Primitive Culture* is animism, defined by Tylor most simply as "the belief in Spiritual Beings."[87] Although it could be argued that animism is the root of all religion for Tylor, it is primarily the indicator of "the primitive religion of the savage." A fundamental difference between the "civilized" and "savage" mind is that whereas a civilized person believes that only human beings have spirit, primitive people believe that it is pervasive throughout the visible world. For the latter, everything in the world is potentially animate—thus the slippage into idolatry. According to Tylor, the savage, who is deeply invested in animistic thinking, is unable to distinguish between the imaginative and the real.[88] A key element in Tylor's progressive agenda becomes clear: the move toward a rational, scientific way of thinking which is able to correctly discern the absence of spirit in non-human entities. This civilized ability, he insists, is most lacking in "the lower races." This judgment allows Tylor to establish a hierarchically progressive typology of religions.

Tylor posits degrees to the childish mistake of animism, with the belief that all things have spirit at the very bottom of his hierarchical scale of primitive animism. Speaking pejoratively about the primitive past, Tylor writes: "There was a period of human thought when the whole universe seemed actuated by spiritual life." The wider the circle of sacrality, the more primitive the religion. The very lowest form of primitive, animistic religion for Tylor, therefore, includes recognition of sentience in inanimate objects, such as stones. This recognition is found in that "primitive stage of thought in which personality and life are ascribed not to man and beast only, but to things. It has been shown how what we call inanimate objects—rivers, *stones*, trees, and so forth—are treated as living intelligent beings."[89] The path of progress, then, follows lockstep with the movement away from the belief that spirit is present in the great multiplicity of natural entities. The narrower a culture's conception of sacrality, the more civilized it is. The most extreme cases of lower animism involve the recognition of sacrality in "inanimate objects." "The souls of animals are recognized by a natural extension from the theory of human souls; the souls of trees and plants follow in some vague partial way; and the souls of inanimate objects expand the general category to its extremest boundary."[90] Consequently, Tylor uses the worship of "inanimate objects" to illustrate the lowest and most absurd form of primitive religion. Stones and stone worshipers are at the very bottom of the heap.

And how does Tylor categorize this lowest form of religion? Not surprisingly, he considers stone worship in his discussion of idolatry and fetishism in *Religion in Primitive Culture*.[91] Tylor references Comte's work on fetishism, but uses the term as a subcategory of idolatrous animism that involves religious interaction with material objects. He writes that fetishism "has obtained great currency by Comte's use of it to denote a general theory of primitive religion, in which external objects are regarded as animated by a life analogous to man's. It seems to me, however, more convenient to use the word Animism for the doctrine of spirits in general, and to confine the word Fetishism to that subordinate department which it properly belongs to, namely, the doctrine of spirits embodied in, or attached to, or conveying influence through, certain material objects. Fetishism will be taken as including the worship of 'stocks and stones.' "[92] For Tylor, a "fetish" is a material object that "is treated as having personal consciousness and power, is talked with, and worshipped."[93] Tylor's interpretive approach would certainly regard the non-dual conception and worship of stones associated with Mount Govardhan as embodied forms of Krishna as idolatrous "fetishism."

Beyond discerning whether a stone is merely functioning as a sacred space or altar, or if "worship is actually addressed to them," one of the key issues in determining whether a stone is a fetish or not has much to do with the notion of *embodiment*. "Then arises the difficult question, are the stones set up as mere ideal representations of deities, or are these deities considered as physically connected with them, embodied in them? . . . In other words, are they only symbols, or have they passed in the minds of their votaries into real fetishes?"[94] Tylor illustrates the latter with an example drawn from early ethnography on the Dakota Sioux: "Among the lower races of America, the Dacotas would pick up a round boulder, paint it, and then, addressing it as grandfather, make offerings to it and pray to it to deliver them from danger." He also considers the practice of stone worship among the Hindus of India, which he attributes to the "lower" elements in Hindu culture. "This stone-worship among the Hindus seems a survival of a rite belonging originally to a low civilization, probably a rite of the rude indigenes of the land, whose religion, largely incorporated into the religion of the Aryan invaders, has contributed so much to form the Hinduism of to-day."[95] For Tylor, the phenomenon of a sacred stone is "a rude object" and "a relic of early barbarism," and as such exemplifies the most primitive form of religion. He therefore proclaims that contemporary Hindus "are among the greatest idolaters of the world."[96]

Tylor asserts that embodiment is "the doctrine of the lower races" and "is the key to strict fetishism, and in no small measure to idolatry."[97] He makes an important distinction between symbolic representation and embodiment. For Tylor, higher forms of idolatry have to do with the iconic representation of some deity. Idolatry becomes lowly fetishism to the degree that the deity is identified with the material object. "But it is only so far as the image approximates to the nature of the material body provided for a spirit, that Idolatry comes properly into connexion with Fetishism."[98] He claims that this is rooted in "the tendency to identify the symbol and the symbolized—a tendency so strong in children and the ignorant everywhere—led to the idol being treated as a living powerful being, and thence even to explicit doctrines as to the manner of its energy or animation."[99] Like others before him, Tylor reads notions of divine embodiment—which he explicitly associates with Hindu worship—as symbolic representation gone awry, wherein an embodied form (the symbol or signifier) is confused with the transcendent deity (the symbolized or signified).[100] Here is a close interpretive link between the ideas of embodiment, symbolic representation, and idolatry. "Now these idols are not to be taken as mere symbols or portraits of deities, but the worshippers mostly imagine that the deity dwells in the image or, so to speak, is embodied in it, whereby the idol becomes a real god capable of giving health and prosperity to man."[101] Tylor opposes the superior symbolic representation of the "modern educated" to the real presence of "barbaric thought." He concludes that progress leads inevitably to the truly modern disenchanted world. "No indwelling deity now regulates the life of the burning sun, no guardian angels drive the stars across the arching firmament, the divine Ganges is water flowing down into the sea to evaporate into cloud and descend again in rain."[102]

The issue of embodiment is pertinent to another important nineteenth-century figure, W. Robertson Smith. In his influential book *The Religion of the Semites: The Fundamental Institution*, Smith demarcates two types of religion: (1) the "positive religions" of Judaism, Christianity, and Islam that are the result of great religious innovators, who were the organs of "divine revelation," and who "deliberately departed from the traditions of the past"; and (2) "ancient heathenism," the unconscious, natural religious traditions of the past.[103] Hinduism, of course, is included in the latter category. The central feature of ancient heathenism for Smith is the idolatrous notion of embodiment: "All acts of ancient worship have a material embodiment."[104] Smith further maintained that ancient heathenism was based on the understanding of pervasive relationship, and this is in part what makes it idolatrous. "Primitive thought," he writes, "treats all nature as a kindred unity. . . . The worshipped and the worshippers are parts of one physical unity of life."[105] For this reason, ancient peoples erroneously related to natural things, such as stones, as they would to persons. But again, it is the notion of idolatrous embodiment that most significantly signals for Smith the presence of ancient heathenism: "In ritual the sacred object (such as a stone) was spoken of and treated as the god himself; it was not merely his symbol but his embodiment, the permanent centre of his activity in the same sense in which the human body is the permanent centre of man's activity. In short, the whole conception belongs in its origin to a stage of thought in which there was no more difficulty in ascribing living powers and personality to a *stone*, tree or animal, than to a being of human or superhuman build."[106] Moreover, the god was not "wholly outside nature, but was himself linked to the physical world by a series of affinities connecting him not merely with man but with beasts, trees and *inanimate things*."[107] For all these reasons, Smith too regards stone worship as representative of the very lowest type of erroneous religion. [108]

Smith finds references to ancient stone worship in early biblical literature where the stone is not just an altar, but the "idol" itself. Here is a situation where "the deity were conceived actually to dwell in the stone, or manifest himself therein to his worshipers. And this is the conception which appears to have been associated with sacred stones everywhere."[109] Primitive stone worshipers believe "that the god comes into the stone, dwells in it or animates it, so that for practical purposes the stone is thenceforth an embodiment of the god, and may be spoken of and dealt with as if it were the god himself."[110] Conceptions of Mount Govardhan and its many stones could surely be exemplary of this view. The distinguishing mark of the primitive for Smith was the belief that the sacred is pervasive throughout nature, whereas civilized people following the positive religions were able to make a distinction between God and nature and understand the sacred as transcendently removed from the world of physical embodiment. In sum, for many nineteenth-century scholars of religion, the issue of embodiment is what distinguished the idolatrous practices of ancient heathenism from the more spiritual perspective of the positive Abrahamic traditions. As a minister in the Church of Scotland very familiar with the teachings of Calvin, Smith conceptualized idolatry as lurking dangerously within the concept of embodiment. Applied as interpretive label, idolatry is always decisive and pejorative.

These inherited notions about idolatry and the religions of others were common currency in the study of religion in the nineteenth century when scholars like Ward and Dubois constructed their widely read representations of Hinduism. The distinction between more benign forms of idolatry (i.e., symbolic representation) and its pernicious forms (embodiment) is also evident in their work. Dubois, for example, maintains that Hindu idolatry is the worst of all its forms, calling it "extravagant and barbarous," and identifies what he believes to be its most disturbing feature: "Let us first observe that Hindu idolatry differs in one essential point from that which prevailed formerly in Athens and Rome. In Greece and Rome it was not the sea that was worshipped, but its monarch, the god Neptune. . . . The idolatry of India, which is of a much grosser kind, has for the object of its worship the material substance itself."[111] Although he does not use this exact vocabulary, Dubois's point is—whether true or not—that whereas the better Greek and Roman idolatry maintained an important distinction between the signifier and signified or the symbol and the symbolized, lowly Hindu idolatry does not. Stone worship for him, as we saw at the beginning of this chapter, is among the worst of the "follies of idolatry." For this reason, it is to be thoroughly condemned.

Hindu Applications

Concepts of idolatry influenced not only nineteenth-century Western scholarly representations of Hindu worship of embodied forms, but also some nineteenth-century developments within Hinduism itself. Although these developments did not have a strong or lasting effect on all contemporary Hindu practices, they did help support nineteenth-century academic representations of Hindu worship as a corrupt and idolatrous form of religion. It must be acknowledged that there are some older schools of Hindu thought that place great emphasis on the formless nature of divinity or ultimate reality. One pertinent example is the eighth-century philosopher Shankaracharya and his school of Advaita Vedanta, which ultimately aimed for the realization of unity with undifferentiated Brahman. Even in this school, however, the devotional worship of a form of God (Ishvara) is not condemned as a terrible mistake; rather, Shankara regards it as a beneficial yet finally penultimate position that is to be superseded by the supreme realization of formless unity. Moreover, the fifteenth-century Hindu Sant poet Kabir ridiculed the temple worship of divine forms, but did not go so far as to regard it as evil.[112] To account for the more vituperative attitude toward the worship of embodied forms of divinity, or *murti-puja,* of nineteenth-century "Hindu Reformers," one has to recognize the strong presence of the British Raj, Christian missionaries, and British Orientalists during this period, especially in the colonial centers of Calcutta and Bombay.

Exemplary nineteenth-century "Hindu Reformers" include Rammohun Roy of the Brahmo Samaj, Dhayananda Saraswati of the Arya Samaj, and Karsandas Mulji of the Prarthana Samaj. Roy explicitly acknowledged that the Protestant Reformation was a major source of his own reformative thinking. He is recorded as saying to perhaps the most influential Presbyterian of the missionaries and educators in nineteenth-century Calcutta, Alexander Duff: "As a youth I acquired some knowledge of the English language. Having read about the rise and progress of Christianity in apostolic times, and its corruption in succeeding ages, and then of the Christian Reformation which shook off these corruptions and restored it to its primitive purity, I began to think that something similar might have taken place in India, and similar results might follow here from a reformation of the popular idolatry."[113] Roy and other nineteenth-century Hindu reformers not only saw Hindu "idol-worship" as a deviation from "original" or "authentic" Hinduism, but as the very source of all moral depravity. Their writings are full of blistering attacks on Hindu "idolatry" as they call for a return to a pristine past represented by early Vedic literature. Roy was clearly familiar with the critique of the ever-present Christian missionaries who condemned Hinduism as an idolatrous and polytheistic religion, but what is the source of his notions about the "pure" past and "authentic" Hinduism?

We turn to the scholarship of British Orientalists or Indologists, whose works were familiar to the Hindu reformers like Roy.[114] Based on their reading of the Vedas, Orientalists such as H. T. Colebrooke, William Jones, and Horace H. Wilson (and later Max Müller) were firmly committed to the notion that deep in the past India had experienced a golden age; importantly, this notion carried with it a concomitant critique of current Hindu practices. Jones, for example, wrote at the close of the eighteenth century: "nor can we reasonably doubt, how degenerate and abased so ever the Hindus now appear, that in some early age they were splendid."[115] The culprit of post-Vedic corruption, of course, had much to do with idolatry. The influential nineteenth-century Orientalist Max Müller stated confidently: "The religion of the Vedas knew no idols. The worship of the idols in India is a secondary formation, a later degradation of the more primitive worship of ideal gods."[116]

Although he recognizes some independent sources to their thinking, Noel Salmond argues that the Hindu reformers such as Rammohun Roy were sensitive to the critiques of Hinduism being articulated by British missionaries and Orientalist scholars. "Rammohun represented a new class of Indians in Bengal (the *bhadralok*) who were educated, wealthy, and financially dependent on interaction with the British. Many in the group wanted a religion which would not embarrass them in the eyes of the Europeans."[117] Accordingly, Roy established the Brahmo Samaj in the colonial center of Calcutta on a foundation that strongly condemned "idol-worship," the most embarrassing element of all.

Dayananda Sarasvati closely follows the thought of Roy. After meeting with Brahmo Samaj leaders in Calcutta in 1872, he emerged "as the foremost opponent of image-worship in Hindu India since Rammohun Roy."[118] Although he was raised in a very traditional Hindu family, Salmond contends that "there is little doubt that Dayananda often borrowed the idiom of Protestantism in his attack on idolatry."[119] In fact, Salmond calls the Reformed Hinduism of the nineteenth century "Protestant Hinduism."[120] Based on his conversations with Dayananda, the Reverend John Robson reported in his *United Presbyterian Record* of 1866 that Dayananda "was an uncompromising iconoclast, and was quite willing to unite with the Christians to move the government to destroy all the idols of India."[121] Not surprisingly, the Arya Samaj that Dayananda Sarasvati officially founded in Bombay grew out of the movement opposing Krishna temple worship started by Karsandas Mulji of the Prarthana Samaj, who gained fame as the defendant in the famous Maharaj Libel Case of 1862.[122] During this trial, Hinduism itself was scrutinized, and based on Orientalist interpretations, temple worship was condemned in favor of an ascetic worship of a formless absolute. In all these instances, we witness the mutual corroboration of Western scholars of religion and the nineteenth-century Hindu reformers. At the heart of the matter was the disparagement of the worship of divine forms, or to use the pejorative language, "idolatry."

Embodied Forms of Divinity Reconsidered

Efforts intended to remove religious practices such as stone worship from the dominant and denigrating interpretive perspective of idolatry began to appear by the mid-twentieth century. Perhaps there is no better illustration of this than the work of the prominent historian of religions Mircea Eliade. Neither vilifying stone worship as an idolatrous sin (Cavinistic approach) nor dismissing it as an absurd childish act (Enlightenment perspective), Eliade attempted to explain it as a valid religious practice. Nonetheless, his efforts were limited by the very structure he aimed to resist. In his widely read book, *The Sacred and the Profane*, Eliade states that "the sacred can be manifested in stones or trees, for example. But as we shall soon see, what is involved is not a veneration of the stone itself. The sacred tree, the sacred stone are not adored as stone or tree; they are worshipped precisely because they are *hierophanies*, because they show something that is no longer stone or tree but the sacred, the *ganz andere*."[123] By conceptualizing the sacred as *ganz andere*, "wholly other," Eliade continues the dualistic tradition of the German theologian and comparative religionist Rudolf Otto, wherein the sacred is radically removed from the natural world.[124] "The numinous presents itself as something 'wholly other' (*ganz andere*), something basically and totally different. It is like nothing human or cosmic. . . . The sacred always manifests itself as a reality of a wholly different order from 'natural' realities."[125] The other-worldliness of the sacred is certainly true for some religious traditions, but is it fitting to employ this notion for interpreting all religious traditions?

We saw in Chapter 3 that the divinity of Mount Govardhan is both the immanent mountain (*adhibhuta* form) and a transcendent reality (*adhyatma* form), which in its most supreme and relatable form (*adhidaiva svarupa*) remains, importantly, linked to material form. As a man from Jatipura insisted: "God is not *in* Giriraj, Giriraj himself *is* God." Relatedly, Vallabhacharya insists in his *Siddhantamuktavali* that the Goddess of the Ganges River is different from, but not unrelated to the water itself, and extends his analogy to characterize the relationship between the Supreme Personality of Krishna and the physical world.[126] There is a long history within Vaishnava Hinduism of seeing the physical world as an aspect of divinity.[127] The material and the spiritual are both aspects of divinity in the non-dual Vedantic Braj Vaishnavism that informs much of the worship of Mount Govardhan. Vaishnava views of Mount Govardhan seem to suggest a case of "both-and," wherein the physical stone as well as something beyond it are simultaneously worshiped.[128]

According to Eliade, however, the sacred is manifest *in* the stone, but not *as* the stone; he insists that there is "no continuity" between "some ordinary object" like a stone and the sacred. He argues that it is not the stone itself that is venerated; rather the veneration is directed to something completely other (*ganz andere*) than the stone.[129] This is classic expression of symbolic representation. The stone symbolizes something other, which is not to be confused with the stone itself. In other words, this is not embodied "idolatry." Something has been gained in this interpretive move, but something has also been lost. In his efforts to rescue practices such as stone worship from the interpretive clutches of "idolatry," Eliade has nonetheless reinscribed its interpretive limitations, for once again the very notion of divine embodiment gets dismissed.

The point I stress here is that the concept of symbolic representation is still linked to the "idolatry tradition," which makes an important distinction between the visible object and the divine or sacred (as in the example of a wooden cross and Christ). For Eliade, the stone reveals or manifests the sacred, but as material object it is not sacred. We might wonder, however, if it is possible to move beyond the dualistic conceptual world established by the idolatry tradition of Western interpretation. What interpretive approaches are called for to better understand non-dual religious traditions such as Braj Vaishnavism? Are we able to ponder a case of "both-and" rather than "either-or?" Can the sacred in some contexts indeed be identified with the material? Might the "natural" and "supernatural" be more related than Eliade allows?

In other words, might there be other ways of understanding and interpreting something like stone worship that are not dependent on the distinction between symbolized and symbol (or between creator and created thing)?

In the last couple of decades a number of art historians have taken up reconsideration of the concept of idolatry and have inched cautiously toward recognition of some kind of (non-demonic) presence in material objects. One of the earliest and most influential of these was David Freedberg in his book *The Power of Images*.[130] This is a study of the relationship between people and sculptural or pictorial images, with particular concern for the power these images have for humans. His examination of Western Christian art provides a fruitful counterpoint to Hindu images. Freedberg argues that in the West the attraction humans feel for images has led to a great deal of anxiety, for often images are feared to be seductively corrupting. This produced a great deal of resistance to images, particularly those considered "idols." In a chapter titled "Idolatry and Iconoclasm," Freedberg confirms that extreme anxiety regarding artistic images erupted in heightened intensity in Europe in the sixteenth century. Theological assumptions about the unseen nature of God makes sight particularly suspicious, for the eyes are most susceptible to seduction and the sense of sight leads one into realms of the seen and thus depravity. Hindu theism, of course, rests on a different set of assumptions wherein the materiality of God is not problematic, and therefore, is not limited to the unseen (*avyakta*); in fact, the seen (*vyakta*) is often regarded as the avenue through which connection or relationship with the divine is most easily established. Thus *darshan* ("seeing") is notably a central feature of Hindu worship.

But sight alone is not the only problem for many concerned with the nature of art in the West. Freedberg shows that the most dangerous development in the adoration of images has been understood to be when "the body in the image loses its status as representation; image is the body itself."[131] Within the non-dual context of much theistic Hinduism, this is precisely how the *murti* is regarded. In the case of Mount Govardhan, the mountain with its many stones is considered to be an important "body" of God. Nonetheless, Freedberg establishes that images have a tremendous power over humans, who experience within them some kind of captivating presence—though Freedberg keeps this well within the realm of psychology, avoiding the perhaps more promising—and challenging—notion of embodiment. Depending on one's outlook on the visible world, religious images or material objects are either the source of much anxiety or the locus of divine connection.

In a book with the provocative title *What Do Pictures Want?*, W. J. T. Mitchell continues the investigation of the relationship between people and images from an art historical perspective.[132]

> What do pictures want? I'm aware that this is a bizarre, perhaps even objectionable, question. I'm aware that it involves a subjectivizing of images, a dubious personification of inanimate objects; that it flirts with a regressive, superstitious attitude toward images, one that if taken seriously would return us to practices like totemism, fetishism, idolatry, and animism. These are practices that most modern, enlightened people regard with suspicion as primitive, psychotic, or childish in their traditional forms (the worship of material objects).[133]

And yet, to a large degree, this is the perspective into which the reader of this book is invited. Mitchell too gives serious consideration to the concept of idolatry, and recognizes that there are challenging issues that need be addressed in the modernist approach. He suggests ways of regarding images in a manner that overcomes the past few centuries of conditioning: "We might even have to entertain what I would call a 'critical idolatry' or 'secular divination' as an antidote to the reflexive critical iconoclasm that governs intellectual discourse today. Critical idolatry involves an approach to images that does not dream of destroying them."[134] Going even further, Mitchell proposes an examination of people's experience with material objects that may lead us to reconsider our interpretive categories. Objects labeled as idols and fetishes "are uncanny things that we should be able to dismiss as naïve, superstitious objects of primitive subjectivities, but which at the same time *awaken a certain suspicion or doubt about the reliability of our own categories.*"[135] What possibilities ensue in the wake of the doubter's doubt? Mitchell recognizes that "[t]he idea that images have a kind of social or psychological power of their own is, in fact, the reigning cliché of contemporary visual culture."[136] Although Mitchell does not stray far from thinking of presence sociologically or psychologically, he invites deep and novel thought on ways of regarding the presence in/of material objects. A truly open and "playful" ethnographic study of the worship of Mount Govardhan stimulates us to think of presence in terms beyond the social and psychological.[137] Dare we think of it ontologically? How far might we go in affirming the viability of such different ways of being in the world? Just how tight is the lingering grip of the fear of "idolatry"?

Mitchell identifies concepts that have been used to designate three kinds of "bad objects": totemism, fetishism, and idolatry. The foundation for all views of these material objects, however, is idolatry, the most "despised object of the Other."[138] Among the three conceptualized objects, Mitchell explains that the "fetish" is often regarded as the crudest form of idolatry. "A contrast is sometimes made between the idol, which is a relatively refined iconic symbol of a deity, and the fetish, regarded *not as symbolic* but as the place of the real presence of the animating spirit; hence fetishism has often been equated with crude materialism, in contrast with the relative refinement and sophistication of idolatry."[139] Once again, the worst kind of idolatry is a case in which symbolic representation becomes skewed: the object is understood not as a "symbol" of the deity, but rather the "body" of the deity. Max Müller is a classic example. Although he never visited India, as the greatest authority on Hinduism in nineteenth-century Europe he confidently labeled the Hindu worship of sacred stones "idolatrous fetishism."

Importantly, Mitchell emphasizes the point that these concepts tell us much more about the people who apply them than the objects themselves.

> It is crucial to remind ourselves at this point of what is probably ob-
> vious: these objects—totems, fetishes, and idols—are anything but objec-
> tive. They are really objectivist projections of a kind of collective imperial
> subject, fantasies about other people, specifically other people's beliefs
> about certain kinds of objects. Totemism, fetishism, and idolatry are thus
> "secondary beliefs," *beliefs about the beliefs of other people*, and thus insepa-
> rable from (in fact, constitutive of) systems of racial or collective prejudice.
> They involve quite general notions about the operations of the "savage"
> or "primitive" mentality—that the natives are invariably gullible and su-
> perstitious; that they live in a world of fear and ignorance where these
> objects compensate for their weakness; that they lack the ability to make
> distinctions between animate and inanimate objects. These objects are,
> moreover, firmly held collective and official imperial belief systems, axioms
> within scientific discourses of ethnography and comparative religion, not
> just private opinions.[140]

Mitchell and Freedberg agree that the power images have over human beings is not something limited to the past, but rather is an ever-present feature of human experience. The challenge for them, then, is to reconsider the ways in which we think about the power of certain material objects. Since "pre-modern attitudes" toward objects remain for even the so-called moderns, our task is not to eliminate such attitudes, but to better understand them.[141]

The social anthropologist Alfred Gell has attempted this interpretive task. He acknowledges that people often treat material objects as living persons, especially in religious contexts wherein "image-worship has a central place, since nowhere are images more obviously treated as human persons than in the context of worship and ceremonies."[142] Gell recognizes that the central problem in considering human interaction with personified material objects is related to the interpretive concept of idolatry. Although he feels the need to declare that he is not a "religious person," Gell sets out to present a theory of idolatry that is fair to the worshiper. He claims that "idolatry has had a bad press since the rise to world domination of Christianity and Islam, which have both inherited the anti-imagistic strain of biblical Judaism," and that it "is enormously difficult for Westerners and non-believers to empathize with idol-worshippers because of the bombardment with anti-idolatrous propa-ganda which we have experienced from the moment we became conscious of such things."[143] Rather than accepting the pejorative connotation of the term and avoiding its usage, he opts to "call the practice of worshipping images by its true name, deeming it better to explain idolatry, rather than rechristen it—by showing that it emanates, not from stupidity or superstition, but from the same fund of sympathy which allows us to understand the human, non-artefactual, 'other' as a copresent being, endowed with awareness, intentions, and passions akin to our own."[144]

Accordingly, Gell proceeds in an attempt to explain idol worship, in-cluding the worship of stones: "One need not imagine that worshippers of stones would 'prefer' to worship more realistic portrayals of their gods, but have to make do with unshaped stones for lack of any local stone-carvers of the necessary ability. . . . The stone is a 'representative' of the god, like an ambassador, rather than a visual icon."[145] But what kind of "representation" is this? For Gell, the ambassador is a "detached fragment" of his nation; in that sense he is not a representation of something absent, but rather a pre-sent and visible part of a larger whole. Thus, "the idol-form is the visual form of the god made present in the idol. . . . Idols, in other words, are not depictions, not portraits, but *bodies*."[146] Among other things, this means that idols are not symbols. "We can only distinguish between idolatrous and non-idolatrous use of religious images because idolatry is in an important sense not 'symbolic' at all, whereas the use of images as aids to piety, rather than physical vehicles of divinity, is symbolic."[147]

Gell argues that the particularity of the object is not as important as the perspectival lens through which it is seen. Therefore, "anything can, under some interpretation, be regarded as 'depicting' anything you like. Consequently an uncarved stone can be an iconic representation of a god just as well as a minutely carved stone idol which looks much more 'realistic' to us."[148] Gell readily dismisses the common criticism that belittles the idolater for worshiping dead matter. "The criticism of idolatry on the grounds that idols are not 'alive' as human beings are (biologically) alive, or that idols are not realistic automata, but only statues, misses the point on both counts. The idol is worshipped because it is neither a person, nor a miraculous machine, but a *god*."[149] Gell understands that Hindu "idolatry" stands in a long tradition of sophisticated philosophical thinking. "We certainly do not have to postulate a particular 'mentality' (primitive, uncritical, gullible, etc.) to account for idolatry; the worship of images is compatible with an extreme degree of philosophical and critical acumen, as the example of textual Hinduism amply demonstrates."[150] In the end, Gell presents idols as "physical channels of access to the divinity" that allow the establishment and nurturing of relationships. "The essence of idolatry is that it permits *real physical interactions* to take place between persons and divinities."[151] Gell's interpretation of idolatry as a comparative religious practice is quite different from the demonized version birthed in the sixteenth century and carried into present times. Under his pen, idols are not "symbols," but "indexes of divine presence"; they are embodied forms of divinity that give physical access to intimate interactions with the divinity fully present in, but not fully contained by the material object, whether that be an uncarved stone or a fully sculpted figure.

Gell marshals one of the most sympathetic defenses of idolatry, using the term in a descriptive and neutral manner rather than the usual pejorative one. It may be worthwhile to add that many Hindu Indians today use the term "idol" to refer to a *murti*, or embodied form of divinity, when speaking or writing in English. Might it be time for reclamation of the term "idolatry," such as has already begun to occur for the previously pejorative terms "paganism," and "animism"? I know of only one published academic piece that explicitly proposes to do this. In a short article titled "Idolatry, Paganism, and Trust in Nature," religious studies scholar Bron Taylor writes: "I would also like to speak emphatically, and even explicitly for idolatry. But I should first be clear about the kind of idolatry I have in mind."[152] And just what kind of idolatry is this? It is a deep embrace of and trusting connection with nature. "I propose emphatically, then, that trusting and relying on the sources of existence, in natural systems and processes, is not an idolatry to be suppressed but *embraced*. When we embrace this sort of idolatry, we will, with Thoreau, stand up for the wild natural processes, to which we, and all life, owe our existence, our vitality, and therefore, our fidelity."[153] Taylor notes that this kind of "idolatrous paganism," which regards presence in the natural non-human world, is on the rise in the United States.[154]

What these developments share is willingness for more serious consideration of presence in material objects and divine embodiment. Many have called this a "new materialism," which is to be distinguished from the old materialism that depends upon a split between spirit and matter. In the former, this gap is bridged and suffused with interpretive possibilities in which spirit is not disassociated from matter. Perhaps it could be called "inspirited matter." In addition to art history and anthropology, developments in this area can also be observed in the academic field of religious studies.

Although he does not use the term "idolatry," Robert Orsi's studies of contemporary American Catholicism are conducted with an awareness that this interpretive concept is central to religious conflicts, as Catholic "idolatry" was the primary target of the Protestant revolution, and informs much of the Enlightenment agenda of modernity that puts constant pressure on Catholics to "mature" from "an infantile faith focused on bodies and things to a rational faith."[155] I am particularly drawn to his contention that the greatest problem for modernity is the notion of "sacred presence—the literal presence of the holy in things and places."[156] Orsi argues that since absence has been strongly privileged in modern Western societies, the notion of presence in material entities is that which is least tolerated. "Of all aspects of religion, the one that has proven least tolerable to modern societies—has been the radical presence of the gods to practitioners."[157] In an article titled "Abundant History," Orsi cites a statement by Hume that places the denial of presence at the very center of the modernist project,[158] and calls instead for a type of religious scholarship that strives to disentangle itself from modernist assumptions about presence. As one who does not want simply to replicate the modernist agenda in his scholarship, he accordingly calls for serious engagement with cultural realities of presence, particularly in things, bodies, and places—or to call it by a different name, "idolatry."

In his recent book *More Than Belief: A Materialist Theory of Religion*, Manuel Vasquez observes that the Protestant "excarnation" that rejects material expressions of religion still shapes much of the contemporary academic study of religion. In light of this, he asserts that a non-reductive materialist approach to the study of religion must be grounded firmly within an immanent frame: "immanence for me is a way to restore the full materiality of our being-in-the-world, and particularly of religion as a dimension of that being. By adopting an immanent frame, we can fully reintroduce embodiment, emplacement, and practice to the discipline of religion, which has been, at best, highly ambivalent about these existential realities."[159] A new journal titled *Material Religion* appeared in 2005 as one of the major voices of this new approach to the study of religious objects. The journal aims to neither privilege nor denigrate human interaction with material objects in the study of religion, but simply to better understand it. The editorial statement published in the inaugural issue states that "*Material Religion* sets out to consider religion through the lens of its material forms and their use in religious practice. . . . Religion is what people do with material things and places, and how these structure and color experience and one's sense of oneself and others."[160] Perhaps more than with any other tradition, scholars of Hinduism have played a key role in a reconsideration of divine embodiment within religious studies.

Divine Forms and Embodiment within Hinduism

Hindu worship of embodied forms of divinity offers a productive environment for exploring different human conceptions of and interaction with material objects. Whereas many early scholars of religion take for granted that the only legitimate way to approach consideration of religious objects is through the notion of symbolic representation, where patrolling the boundary between the symbolized transcendent divinity and the symbolic material itself must remain ever vigilant and any confusion between the two is regarded as an idolatrous error, here we see something other. The material form (*murti, rupa*, or *svarupa*) is considered a tangible and accessible embodiment of complex divinity, although by no means does any particular form exhaust or completely account for divinity, which by definition is understood to be infinite. In the case of the worship of Mount Govardhan, for example, we encounter a religious worldview in which there is no hard boundary between the transcendent and immanent, or between the infinite and the finite. From this perspective, cordoning off the finite from the realm of God that typically takes place in traditions that emphasize extreme transcendence would result in a loss of any reliable use of the senses in an approach to God. It would also eliminate any physically approachable form of God. One of the claims to be found in the context of a so-called idolatrous tradition as that associated with the worship of Mount Govardhan is that worship of the finite is not ultimately all that different from worship of the infinite. The big question becomes: Does the infinite contain the finite? If it does, then this all makes sense. If it doesn't, then one has to ask what kind of infinite it is that somehow does not include everything, especially the finite.

Some have called this way of looking at a religious object "metonymic representation," defined as a part representing the whole. This is a case of "both-and." The embodied form is like a handle on a cup. The handle on a cup is not the same as the entire cup, but on the other hand it is not *not* the cup either. The finite handle is that part of the cup that allows one to get a grip on the cup—which, in this case, is infinite. The physical form, then, while not the totality, gives one available access to God. From this perspective, any religious outlook that disassociates divinity from materiality ends up limiting the infinite nature of God. Acknowledging the impossibility of any complete knowledge of ultimate reality, we cannot say which position is correct, the radically transcendent one or the one that includes concrete forms. But employing one to judge the other is a judgmental setup from the onset. The interpretive lens of the idolatry tradition simply does not fit the case of Hindu worship, for this is a religious tradition that asserts an all-encompassing nature of divinity—one which includes a multitude of forms as well as the unmanifest formless (*Brihadaranyaka Upanishad* 2.3).

For many branches of devotional Hinduism this is all a matter of grace. In an act of supreme kindness, the infinite divine takes finite form to be accessible for interaction with worshipers in pursuit of intimate relationship. The thirteenth-century Shri Vaishnava theologian Pillai Lokacharya is often quoted to demonstrate this view: "This is the greatest grace of the Lord, that being free He becomes bound, being independent He becomes dependent for all His service on His devotee . . . the Infinite has become finite, that the child soul may grasp, understand and love Him."[161] It is the finite embodied form that allows for the development of the close relationship between the worshiper and God and that makes possible the beneficial use of powerful emotions in the embodied worship. This view was expressed frequently in my conversations. A woman who worships a Govardhan stone in her home said, "Because of the Lord's immense grace (*kripa*), he has come to live with us in this form."

It is not unusual to still find Hindu embodied forms of divinity (*murtis*) represented as "symbols" in secondary literature.[162] But currently scholars of Hinduism are increasingly resisting the interpretation of Hindu *murtis* in terms of symbolism, a discourse that, as we have seen, is still tied to the concept of idolatry. In her groundbreaking 1981 book *Darśan: Seeing the Divine Image in India*, Diana Eck stressed that "the *murti* is more than a likeness; it is the deity itself taken 'form.'"[163] Among a newer generation of scholars of Hinduism, this book signaled a major revolt against ignoring or discrediting the centrality of the worship of embodied forms of divinity within Hinduism and to labeling those forms "symbols." The distancing of interpretation from the notion of the *murti* as a symbol continued with more forceful expression in the 1985 publication of *Gods of Flesh, Gods of Stone*.[164] In the introduction to this volume, Joanne Waghorne employs the language of "embodiment" and "presence" to explain the worshipful interaction with divine forms. She attributes much of the misguided past representations of Hinduism to the survival of the modernist project. "In the march of progress, the identification of divine powers with the physical world was seen as an anachronism. It was simply impossible to suppose that religion did *not* move from a vague sense of matter-made-divine toward a separation of such misplaced concreteness. . . . The twentieth century discovered the 'symbol' and knew for certain that the dilemma of god's seeming concrete reality was simply a false metaphysical issue."[165]

Yet Waghorne and other scholars included in this volume hoped to reverse this very impossibility. "The problem with this twentieth-century two-step around concrete divinity is that it denied the possibility that devoted Hindus, themselves, ever actually thought that god had an embodied reality."[166] Accordingly, many of the volume's authors resist the language of symbol and symbolic representation. James Preston, for example, states that "the image *is* the deity, *not* merely a symbol of it."[167] Vasudha Narayanan explains: "This image (*arca*) is an actual and real manifestation of the deity, neither lesser than nor a symbol of other forms. It is wholly and completely God, though it does not exhaust his essence."[168] She includes in her considerations of *arcas* the sacred *salagrama* stones, which she presents as a concrete and approachable form of Vishnu. Norman Cutler asserts that although "the image does not exhaust God's nature . . . God and God's embodiment are indistinguishable."[169] Waghorne summarizes the aim of the entire volume: "The single conviction behind all of these essays remains the certainty that the process of embodiment of god in India is not a mere popular phenomenon nor is it a relic of a by-gone age. These essays seek to present the embodiment of divinity as the central feature of Hinduism and as a central feature in the study of religion."[170]

Exemplary of more recent examinations of Hindu notions of embodiment or *murtis* is Richard Davis's book *The Lives of Indian Images*. Davis presents the worship of embodied forms of divinity within theistic Hinduism "as the central program through which most humans could best accomplish both their spiritual and worldly aims."[171] He too insists that for most Hindus the *murti* is not a symbol, but is God. Davis maintains, importantly, "The Vaishnavas see no contradiction between transcendence and immanence."[172] He quotes a Vaishnava text in which the question is asked: How can one worship the Highest God Vishnu, who is unlimited? The answer given is: "He can be worshiped in embodied form only. There is no worship of one without manifest form."[173] For comparative purposes, Davis examines medieval Christian attitudes toward images. "Medieval Christian images, then, are instrumental and representational. Aquinas and Bonaventure locate them within a semiotic aesthetics, where the image is seen as conveying a message separate from the image itself."[174] In contrast: "Vaishnava and Shaiva theologians locate their holy icons within an aesthetics of presence. As an instantiation of the godhead, the image is ultimately the message."[175]

Along similar lines, I argue that a theology of presence and embodiment is fundamental to Hindu interaction with sacred objects such as Mount Govardhan and its many stones. In many ways, these ideas are very different from those labeled "modern." Nonetheless, these ideas need to be taken seriously in order to move beyond the limitations created by modernist boundaries that have for the most part remained unexamined in much of the interpretive work of comparative religion since its inception in the seventeenth century. In fact, rendering the worship of Mount Govardhan at all sensible depends on such a move. None of the people I spoke with near Mount Govardhan explained a stone from the mountain as a "symbol"; instead, they described it as a "body" (*murti, rupa, svarupa,* or *sarir*). Rather than relying on a single interpretive approach to the comparative study of religious practices, it seems that it would be better to at least have a minimal typology of two: the worship of embodied forms of divinity (associated here with Mount Govardhan) and worship of the spiritual transcendent (associated with Mount Sinai).

Divine embodiment, many Hindus assert, is an act of grace by which divinity makes itself accessible for intimate interaction. The worshipful interaction with Mount Govardhan, then, involves not only the worship of a readily available embodied form of divinity; it also involves the pursuit of close relationships through specific ritual techniques that are entirely dependent on that form.

6

Drawing Personality Out of a Stone

Techniques of Intimacy

When there is a face on a Giriraj *shila* it makes the *svarupa* more apparent, and it makes it easier for us to recognize Krishna in the stone. This makes our connection with Giriraj stronger.

When you put eyes on a Giriraj *shila* you can communicate with it.
Since my stone has had eyes he talks to me;
And because of this I have become very close to him.

When you put eyes and face on a Giriraj shila you feel it is a person.
It is easier to see the stone as a person with the face and clothing added.[1]

It should be clear by now that Braj Vaishnavism is a religious tradition that aims for an intimate relationship (*sambandha*) with Krishna through interaction with embodied forms, and that Mount Govardhan is regarded as a very approachable and loving form of Krishna. But what kind of form is most conducive to relational *bhakti*, and how is one to establish, maintain, and celebrate an intimate relationship with something as large as a mountain? By world standards Mount Govardhan is a small mountain; nonetheless, it is still difficult to have intimate interaction with the entire seven-mile long rocky ridge. As we saw in Chapter 4, devotees can and do have worshipful engagements with the mountain as a whole through *parikrama* and in some public *puja*s; however, much more intimate connections are achieved with individual stones from Mount Govardhan (Figure 6.1). The love affair with the mountainous form of Krishna, then, is typically expressed and experienced with a particular stone of a size that can be easily handled.

Loving Stones. David L. Haberman, Oxford University Press (2020) © Oxford University Press.
DOI: 10.1093/oso/9780190086718.001.0001

Figure 6.1. Individual Govardhan stone worshiped in small shrine in Jatipura.

Individual Stones

I was initially puzzled as to why people who live near the mountain would have a home shrine accommodating a Govardhan stone when they could simply worship the mountain directly. I asked a number of people about the advantages of worshiping an individual stone in their homes. One benefit is convenience, especially for women who are often confined to the home throughout the day with household chores and activities. A temple worker I met in the Dan Ghati Mukharvind temple in the town of Govardhan reported, "There is a Giriraj *shila* in each and every house around Mount Govardhan. This is so those who might not be able to come out of the house every day can have daily *darshan*." But it's more than convenience, he said, "We also develop a closer relationship (*sambandha*) with the mountain through the particular *svarupa* in our homes." A man who frequents the famous Jatipura Mukharvind stone told me why he has a smaller Govardhan stone in his home shrine.

It's for my wife. For me too, but mainly for her. Sometimes she comes out here, but our Giriraj *shila* at home allows her to have *darshan* of Giriraj-ji in our own house every day. This also allows us to have more intimate interaction with Shri Giriraj-ji than we can have here at this site that is maintained by hired priests. At home we perform all the worship with our own hands and because of this become much closer to him.

A stone in the home provides rich opportunity for the loving hands-on activities that generate and nurture a close relationship with the mountain through this particular stone. A common notion is that the highest worship of a Govardhan stone is that which is performed with one's own body and personal wealth (*tanu-vitta-ja*).

In addition to personal convenience, there are other devotional advantages of worshiping a single stone. Just as a part is easier to grasp than the whole, a single stone provides an accessible devotional handle on the entire mountain. One man explained it this way: "Water is always everywhere in the air, but when it becomes condensed on a cold bottle you can easily see it (*darshan*) and touch it (*sparshan*) in the form of small drops. So too the mountain is vast, but individual stones are much more accessible for the acts of worship." Intimate interaction is more possible through a particular manageable form, and a Govardhan stone is much more wieldy and human-scaled than the entire mountain. Another devotee of Mount Govardhan spoke of this advantage of worshiping a particular stone. He used the example of a famous Pushti Margiya embodied form (*svarupa*) of Krishna named Mathuradhish that was once housed in the temple complex in which I lived in Jatipura.

Mathuradhish manifest from the bank of the Yamuna River in a gigantic form in the presence of Shri Vallabhacharya for his disciple Padmanabhdas. But the form was so huge that Padmanabhdas could not interact with it or perform its *seva*. So Shri Vallabhacharya requested that the *svarupa* reduce its size in order that it would be small enough to sit on his lap, reaching up only to his chin. This is what happened, and afterwards Padmanabhdas was able to engage with it in the loving acts of *seva*. In a similar manner, a worshipful Giriraj *shila* is the right size for *seva*. It can be held and placed on one's lap. But how can one do this with the whole mountain?[2]

A woman I met who has a Govardhan stone shrine in her home in Jatipura added an intimate touch by telling me that it is best if the stone one worships is about "the size of one's heart."

Worshipers of Mount Govardhan insist there is no difference between the worship of a particular stone and worship of the entire mountain. As any part is non-different from the whole, the whole can be approached through any part. Echoing many others, Brajesh Joshi explained: "Each and every stone from Mount Govardhan is Krishna; a particular stone is non-different from the whole mountain." Here is apt illustration of metonymic representation, where a part stands for the whole. A man who frequents the Mukharvind site in Jatipura clarified this point graphically. He pointed a long needle used for stringing flowers into garlands at me and asked: "If I prick your hand with this needle would you say I am pricking you?" A bit alarmed, I affirmed that I would indeed. "And if I prick your foot, or your side, or your head, or anywhere else on your body, wouldn't you think that I am still pricking you?" I nodded warily, hoping his demonstration would not turn physical. Sensing my discomfort, he shifted to a less threatening example. "Or if I applied an honorific *tilak* mark on any part of your body, I would be honoring your whole body with the *tilak*. Right? It's like this with Govardhan. It doesn't matter where you worship Him, or through which particular stone you worship, you still are worshiping the whole body of the mountain. You can make an offering to Giriraj anywhere on the mountain and it will be received by the whole mountain wherever it is offered." The entire mountainous form of Krishna, therefore, accepts an act of love offered to any particular stone from Mount Govardhan.

The gracious accessibility, tangibility, and manageability of the mountain god in the form of a particular stone lead to greater and more intimate devotional interaction, which in turn leads to deeper connections and closer relationships. A woman who worships a Giriraj *shila* in a home shrine that takes up a large portion of her small house near the edge of the mountain informed me: "Worship of a single *shila* is equivalent to worship of the entire mountain. There are many, many *shila*s here at Govardhan. One can worship any one of them. They are all *svarupa*s of Krishna." Why does she worship a single stone instead of the whole mountain?

Because I can do *seva* to this one stone much more easily than the whole mountain. I can bathe it with milk and water, I can massage its body with scented oils, I can dress it with fine clothes, I can feed it tasty sweets, and

I can even put it to bed at night. I can't do that to the whole mountain. And it is by doing these acts of *seva* to a single stone rather than worshiping the entire mountain that I experience a stronger connection (*mazbut sambandha*) with Giriraj as a whole. For these reasons we worship an individual Giriraj *shila*.

Human nature is such that our most intense emotional bonds are with particular individuals. Universal love that includes all people is a noble notion, but the love that seems to seize us and most powerfully rivet our attention is the passionate love for a specific person. Likewise, love of the entire mountain is venerable, but intimate connection with Giriraj occurs by means of personal interaction with one of its distinctive stones. An individual stone is an expedient venue to the entire mountain. Both Vallabhacharya and Chaitanya serve as models for intimate interaction with the mountain through an individual stone. The most personal worship of Mount Govardhan by Vallabhacharya recorded in Pushti Margiya literature was performed to a single stone called Sundar Shila, identified by some as Dandavat Shila and by others as the Jatipura Mukharvind Shila.[3] Gaudiya Vaishnava literature records that Chaitanya revered the entire mountain, but his deep connection and emotional experience with it came from hugging a single stone: "Upon seeing Mount Govardhan, Chaitanya bowed low; after embracing a single stone he became ecstatic."[4]

People develop relationships with a very particular stone that is felt to have a distinctive personality, determined largely by the emotional disposition of the individual devotee. This connective relationship also involves a sense of ownership, or perhaps more accurately, "myness." One devotee of Giriraj explained: "I have a special relationship with this Giriraj *shila*. There are many *shila*s here (waving his hand in the direction of the nearby mountain), but this is the one I worship." A man who worships a particular individual stone every day in his home stressed personal ownership even more: "There are many Giriraj *shila*s on this mountain, but *this one is mine*. This is the one I have a close relationship (*sambandha*) with. For me it is very special." A woman who maintains a Giriraj shrine in her home near Jatipura confirmed this viewpoint: "There are many men in the world who are husbands, but the one who lives in this house is *my* husband. Likewise, there are many Giriraj *shila*s, but this one (gesturing to the Giriraj *shila* in her home shrine) is *mine*."

Although it has decidedly negative connotations in most Hindu ascetic traditions in which it is deemed to be a problematic emotion that obstructs spiritual progress, here the concept of "myness" (*mamata*) takes a positive turn. An attitude of ownership in the interaction with an individual stone is productive, for a sense of possession nurtures feelings of intimacy. The Hindi word for intimate is *atmiya*. When one acquires an individual Giriraj stone and interacts with it in loving service (*seva*), it becomes *atmiya* in two senses: it becomes "intimate" as well as "one's own."[5] One of the meanings of *svarupa*—the term used frequently to refer to a particular Giriraj stone— is "one's *own* form (of divinity)." A Pushti Margiya leader explained the dynamic involved with these words:

> A deep worshipful connection with Govardhan depends on a personal rela-
> tionship with an individual *shila* that is one's own. There has to be *mamata*,
> a sense of "myness." *Mamata* or myness is an essential element for the
> loving acts (*seva*) that lead to deep connection. The *svarupa* is "one's own
> form," just as the child or paramour we love most is considered to be our
> own, as in "this is *my* beloved."

The sense of myness, then, is an important ingredient in the close relationship that approaches the whole through a particular.[6]

Home Shrines

The most intimate interaction with Govardhan stones occurs in the privacy of the home shrine. Home shrines for a Giriraj *shila* are a regular feature of virtually every household in the five towns around Mount Govardhan; they are also found in many homes throughout the Braj region, and are not uncommon in homes in other parts of India, especially in those of Pushti Margiya and Gaudiya Vaishnavas. I even met a few Pushti Margiya and Gaudiya Vaishnavas around the mountain that have Giriraj *shila*s in their home shrines in the United Kingdom and the United States. Home shrines are the primary stage on which people engage in the worship and loving acts of service (*seva*) with their own hands and interact in intimate ways with their Giriraj *shila*s, thereby developing personal connections with God in this concrete form. It is here that the relationship is pursued, expressed, and experienced in a privacy that allows for greater emotional freedom and depth. One of the priests in a large temple in Jatipura told me that although he connects with forms of Krishna in his official worship, it is in the intimate context of his home shrine that he experiences his strongest connection.

Home shrines can be as simple as a shelf built into a wall or as elaborate as a separate room dedicated to the worship of a particular divinity. A small wooden, metal, or sandstone freestanding temple located in the corner of a regularly used room is also a common option. The stone is seated on some kind of cushioned throne, and decorative cloth and pictures are often hung on the walls in or around the shrine. Storage units for items used to bathe, dress, and adorn the Giriraj *shila* are either part of the shrine or situated nearby. The shrine is usually close to the kitchen, making it easier to serve regular food offerings. Whether the shrine is in the center of the home or not, it often conceptually functions in this way. Many consider their home to belong to Krishna in the form of Giriraj, so that all domestic work becomes sacralized, as it is regarded as *seva* for the guru, friend, lover, or any other relational form in which the deity of the stone is conceived.

Home-shrine practice parallels in a more simplified fashion the *seva* and ornamentation the priests perform at well-known sites such as the Jatipura Mukharvind stone.[7] One of the primary differences, however, is that in home shrines, devotees perform the acts of *seva* and ornamentation with their own hands. This creates a mental engagement and physical intimacy that is lacking when just watching another perform the worship. Observing a parent dress and feed an infant may have some affectual results, but a much greater connection with the child is achieved by the parent who is actually dressing and feeding the child. Physical touch, or haptic contact, is a very important form of non-verbal interaction for building intimacy in interpersonal relationships.[8] Worship in a home shrine allows the devotee to touch (*sparshan*) the Giriraj *shila* in a much more engaging manner. A great deal of emotion is expressed and experienced through touch, with sensual connections developed through such acts as massaging scented oils on the surfaces of a Giriraj *shila*. The intimacy of the home shrine also allows opportunity for personal conversations with a Govardhan stone. A woman in Jatipura told my wife and me that she made a habit of going before the Giriraj *shila* in her home shrine every evening to review her day and to talk about her emotional challenges. In a very poignant moment, she revealed how her conversations with Giriraj comforted her on the occasion of her brother's unexpected death.

The home shrine of Jatipura resident Lakshmi (Figure 6.2) is exemplary of a common style of home shrines. She has placed her Govardhan stone on recessed shelves where a cloth curtain is drawn to create privacy. Although she has enhanced her shrine with a number of pictures and figures, Lakshmi considers her Giriraj *shila* to be her primary *svarupa*. She makes her food offerings to God in this form on a wooden table before the shrine.

The shrine in the home of a priest living in Jatipura is a bit more intricate. Constructed out of sheets of cut sandstone that were painted white, it houses two particular forms of Krishna: the cowherd in the mountain-lifting posture and a stone of the mountain that was lifted. A nearby recessed shelf serves as a storage space for various items used in worship, and here too food offerings are generally placed on a small wooden table in front of the shrine. Brightly colored fabric provides the background and a cloth curtain is dropped to provide privacy.

A Pushti Margiya woman living alone in Jatipura has an entire room dedicated for her *seva*. A sizable wooden temple stands in the center of this bright room, and in the heart of this temple the woman's Giriraj *shila* sits on an elaborate wooden throne. A wooden table is brought in for food offerings, and a set of stairs is placed before the throne to allow Krishna access to an area

Figure 6.2. Home shrine of Lakshmi, a resident of Jatipura.

below the shrine that is arranged for his entertainment. Owners of home shrines located away from Mount Govardhan have told me that they try to create the environment of Braj in their shrine rooms, or sometimes more specifically the Govardhan *tareti*.

Intentional Anthropomorphism

Perhaps the most important ingredient in the connective relationship with a Giriraj *shila* is what I choose to call *intentional anthropomorphism*.[9] Standing one day on the roof of the temple complex where I resided in Jatipura, I watched an adolescent boy and girl set up a softball-sized Giriraj stone near the pathway that leads to the Shri Nath-ji temple situated atop Mount Govardhan. Through binoculars I saw them add eyes, a red crystal *tilak*, and a peacock-feather crown. They wrapped the stone in an ornate red cloth, and strung a red-and-white *gunja* bead necklace around its neck. They completed the ornamentation by draping a long orange scarf around its shoulders. I was moved by the reverence of these actions, but what interested me most was the manner in which people climbing up the hill treated this stone, stopping to touch the "feet" of the decorated stone with their right hand, and bringing this hand to their forehead in a gesture of veneration. The surface of the mountain is covered with individual stones, but when one is augmented with eyes, a peacock-feather crown, and ornate clothing, dramatic changes occur. The stone's presence is accentuated and attracts the attention of those passing by it. The adornment seems to function as a ritual frame that demarcates a particular stone for special consideration and interaction.

But what form is most conducive to deep connection? During a conversation in his Vrindaban ashram, Shrivatsa Goswami said, "Our situation is that we are in human form, so for us the most familiar form is human, and that's what we connect with most intimately." Accordingly, the formless must be given welcoming form and assume familiar personality, or perhaps in other words, the aniconic becomes transformed into an anthropomorphic icon. Relationships with the sacred mountain differ according to the disposition of the devotee and are established through a stone with a particular personality. Some Giriraj stones are selected for worship because their natural features suggest a humanlike face (Figure 6.3), but ritual augmentation is typically employed to aid in the development of a deep connection or intimate relationship with the Krishna stone.

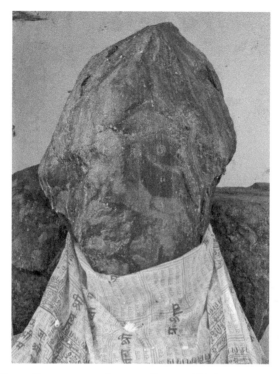

Figure 6.3. Govardhan stone with natural humanlike features on *parikrama* pathway.

Although there are distinctive styles to each worshiper's approach, the ritual techniques for relational enhancement are largely culturally patterned. Eyes are the most essential element; they are the first feature added and can be found alone when nothing else is attached (Figure 6.4). The anthropologist Gell maintains that the addition of eyes to an object opens up and gives access to interiority.[10] Indeed, eyes are sold in the markets around the mountain for this purpose (Figure 6.5). Additionally, humanlike facial features, jewelry, various ornamentations, and clothing are appended to the stones (Figure 6.6).

What is gained by adding these anthropomorphic features to a stone? Worshipers of Giriraj s*hilas* articulate a variety of benefits. Ornamentation (*sringar*) is a way of adorning and honoring a deity. It makes the stone beautiful and more attractive. One of the priests attending the Manasi Ganga Mukharvind stone explained: "When a Giriraj *shila* is decorated with a face and clothing, love comes. It's just like when you see a person in

Figure 6.4. Eyes added to a Govardhan stone in Radhakund.

Figure 6.5 Eyes for sale in the Jatipura market.

Figure 6.6. Fully ornamented Govardhan stone.

beautiful clothing; you feel more attraction for that person. The eyes especially attract us." A woman who maintains a home shrine for her Giriraj *shila*
added: "Putting eyes and other things on a Giriraj *shila* makes him more
beautiful. This is all done out of love (*bhava*), but it also increases the love we
feel for God in this form." In addition to being an act of devotion for the stone
itself, then, the adornment has a powerful effect on the worshiper; it both
expresses love as well as enhances it. A Giriraj *shila* is regarded as a naturally
embodied form of God with or without the eyes and other ornamentation,
but the adornment elicits deeper emotional feelings. A Govardhan worshiper from the Braj town of Gokul said: "Adding eyes and other decorations
to a Giriraj *shila* is not absolutely necessary because each and every Giriraj
shila is naturally Krishna, but when you add the eyes and ornamentation
(*sringar*) it makes him look more beautiful. It is done as a way of honoring
him, but it also increases our love (*bhava*) so that we develop a stronger relationship (*sambandha*) with him." This two-way flow of love is the glue that
binds worshipers in a close relationship with Krishna in this stone form.

Figure 6.7. Adorned Govardhan stone under tree in Jatipura.

In addition to enhanced love from their hearts, worshipers allege the adornment "draws out" *personality* from the stone (Figure 6.7). The formless is given a welcoming form and assumes a familiar personality. "*The devotional tendency is to draw out form and personality from the formless*" is a catchphrase I have come to rely on while thinking about the worshipful interaction with Giriraj stones. This phrase was articulated by Shrivatsa Goswami in one of several productive conversations we had about the common practice of embellishing stones from Mount Govardhan with faces and clothing. In a combination of Hindi and English, he elaborated:

> This is the key to achieving an intimate connection with any form of God. You have to understand the way of personal adoration of the Lord within Vaishnava Hinduism. People worship in their own way, through their own relationship. They turn the aniconic into an iconic form (he used these English terms) of Krishna, they give form (*rupa*) to the formless (*arupa*). Devotees need something tangible. They need *saguna* ["with qualities"]

and *sakara* ["with shape"]. Giriraj is not fully *saguna* or *sakara*, so the devotees complete the process by making the *saguna* and *sakara* aspects more fully manifest. They add eyes, ornaments, clothing, and sometimes even arms to the Giriraj stones. They bring out qualities and form more fully through this technique and draw out the full personality. This makes it easier to see the stone as Krishna and Krishna as the stone. Personal form is the source and foundation of the relationship (*sambandha*) with God. As the *Bhagavad Gita* says, it is not really possible to have a relationship with the formless.

Giving form to the formless with the aid of anthropomorphic features— or rendering the aniconic iconic—draws out the personality of a Govardhan stone, and this in turn is the key to establishing significant relationship. As the scholarly priest said: "Personal form is the source and foundation of the relationship." What this means in actual practice is that it is commonplace to augment a Giriraj *shila* with the addition of human-like facial features and ornate clothing, particularly in the context of home shrines. The common scholarly term for such practices is anthropomorphism.

I asked Shrivatsa-ji what Sanskrit or Hindi term he had in mind for "personality." He thought for a moment and replied "*svarupa*," a word he said that indicates "full presence in every way: physical, mental, and emotional." That is, the adornment of a Giriraj *shila* amplifies the divine presence of the stone; "it is always there, but the ornamentation—especially the eyes—makes it more fully manifest and perceptible, and this is the key to a close relationship with God in this form."

There are two allied claims operative here: first, the anthropomorphized additions bring out the *svarupa*—the "true nature," "essential form," or "personality" of the stone; and second, the anthropomorphized additions make the stone more relatable. There is a difference between these two: the first regards the technique as a method of making evident what is always there; the second suggests that the enhancements are for the sake of human relatability. The first concerns the true nature of the divine, whereas the second the benefit of the worshiper. But the two come together when we understand that the personality of a Giriraj *shila* is by nature infinitely variable, as the particular form that the *svarupa* takes is largely determined by the emotional temperament of the individual devotee. The essential form that is revealed, then, is the form most relatable for the worshiper.

The *svarupa*'s specific form, Shrivatsa maintained, is a form that is non-different from the infinite formless, but nonetheless is a form. He offered a Sanskrit compound term for this: *arupa-rupa-rupa*, "a form that is simultaneously form and formless." "The emotional state of the seeker establishes the specific personality of the stone. The intangible infinite formless becomes tangible in a specific form determined by the seeker." He gave two examples. One featured the embodied form of Krishna in his own temple, the Shri Radharaman Mandir. The founding saint of the Radharaman temple, Gopal Bhatt Gosvamin, used to worship an aniconic *shaligram* stone as Krishna.[11] His love for Krishna, the Beloved of the Cowherd women, was so intense that over time it drew out of this large *shaligram* stone the exquisite anthropomorphic form of Radharaman, Krishna as the Lover of Radha, still worshiped in festive fashion in the Radharaman temple today.

Whereas Gopal Bhatt Gosvamin's emotional state was passionate love, Shrivatsa's other example demonstrates that different forms can be drawn out of stone through other emotions, including fear. He told the story of the terrifying form of Narasinha, drawn out of a stone pillar. The demon Hiranyakashipu received a boon that he could not be killed by man nor beast, which resulted in quasi-immortality with tyrannical consequences. He then forbade the worship of the supreme lord Vishnu, only to learn that his own son Prahlad had become an ardent devotee of Vishnu. Angrily confronting his son with the intension of killing him, Hiranyakashipu shouted: "Where is this Lord of the Universe? If he is present everywhere why is he not present in this stone pillar?" Prahlad assured him that he was. Hiranyakashipu struck the stone pillar with his fist, and out emerged the Man-Lion Narasinha—precisely the hybrid form he feared most—who proceeded to disembowel him. Shrivatsa's point was that Hiranyakashipu's emotional state of fear determined the specific form of Vishnu that was drawn out of the pillar. For Gopal Bhatt Gosvamin and Hiranyakashipu, the particular form and personality assumed by God was established by the disposition of the worshiper.[12]

During my research period, my friend Mohan and I often visited a Govardhan stone located in a secluded shrine sheltered by a tree in the forest north of Jatipura. This particular stone is augmented with eyes and mouth, and is regularly draped with ornate cloth (see Figure 4.9 in Chapter 4). On one of our visits, Mohan commented, "When people decorate a Giriraj *shila* and worship it, the personality comes out. Look, there are many Giriraj *shilas* here, but the *svarupa* is really showing itself in this one (*svarupa nikal deta hai*) because people have added eyes and decorations, and have worshiped it."

One Pushti Margiya teacher explained to me: "There are two understandings of Giriraj: Haridasavarya ("Best Devotee of Krishna") and Purushottama (Krishna himself as the "Supreme Personality"), and it is through the Purushottama identity that one develops an intimate relationship with Giriraj. The whole mountain in its natural state is generally thought of as Haridasavarya, but when one selects or is given a particular stone for one's own (*mamata*) and adds eyes, a peacock feather, and other ornamentations, a general stone becomes your own personal *svarupa*. Then it is experienced as *purna* Purushottama—the full divine personality of Giriraj." Devakipran Baba expressed a similar notion:

> When you put eyes and a face on a Giriraj *shila* you feel it is a person. It is easier to see the stone as a person with the face and clothing added. We are *purusha*s (persons), but Giriraj is the Adipurusha (Original Person). We are persons, but he is the unlimited, the Infinite Person. Dressing a Giriraj *shila* with eyes, face, jewelry, and clothing makes the presence of the Adipurusha, the Divine Personality, more evident. When you decorate the *shila* then you feel that you are honoring and serving him, but it is also a way to feel the presence of the person of Giriraj. If a stone with no decoration is next to a fully decorated *shila* your eyes will immediately go to the decorated *shila*. Putting eyes and other ornamentations on a *shila* makes its personality more perceptible. This makes relationship (*sambandha*) with the *svarupa* more possible. It's like when I don't know a man I walk right by him, but if I know his face I'll stop because then I have a relationship with him. If I interact with him, maybe feed him or something like that, I will develop an even stronger relationship with him.

Many others supported the claim that the eyes and ornamentation made the divine presence or personhood (*svarupa* or *vyaktitva*) of the stone more evident. Some simply affirmed that the appendages made it easier to see the stone as Krishna. As a man from Jatipura who serves a Giriraj *shila* in his home shrine said, "Giriraj is Purna Purushottama (The Complete Ultimate/ Supreme Person). Giriraj is a *svayam svarupa* (a self-manifest form) of Bhagavan Shri Krishna. The eyes, face, and ornamentation help people see this, to see the stone as Krishna." Like Shrivatsa Goswami, many used the term *svarupa* to express the presence or personality. "Putting eyes, a face and clothing on a Giriraj *shila* brings out the *svarupa*. It is there always and in all Giriraj *shila*s, but adding the eyes and clothing brings it out so that it is easier to see it." A woman who is very devoted to the Govardhan stone residing in her home expressed the presence of personality in a more sensorial way: "When you put eyes on a Giriraj *shila* you can communicate with it. Since he has had eyes my stone talks to me; and because of this I have become very close to him." Another woman who worships a Giriraj *shila* at home insisted: "A bare Giriraj *shila* is Krishna to be sure, but when you put eyes and a face and ornamentations on a stone it speaks to you and you can speak to it. Then you can interact with it like a close relative." Establishing a deep connection or relationship (*sambandha*) with some form of Krishna is the goal of the Vaishnava religious culture associated with the worship of Mount Govardhan, and worshipers assert that anthropomorphic form effectively aids in establishing and nurturing this relationship.

These are ideas expressed in central Vaishnava scriptures, perhaps most notably in the eleventh chapter of that foundational text for Krishna *bhakti*, the *Bhagavad Gita*. As we saw in Chapter 3, here in the text Arjuna has just realized that Krishna cannot be fully accounted for in the particular form of his friend the chariot driver. He therefore requests Krishna to reveal his unlimited, imperishable, unmanifest, majestic form (*aishvara rupa*). Krishna responds with a revelation of his universal form that consists of the infinity of all forms. Human perception, however, is such that it is not designed to take in the vast totality of all reality, identified in the *Bhagavad Gita* as the formless, all-pervasive dimension of divinity. This is acknowledged as a valid perspective, but not one that lends itself to intimate connectivity. Arjuna gains important insight from this revelation of the all-encompassing non-dual nature of Krishna, but as time passes he discovers that he is disoriented and finds no peace, no approach, and no intimacy or loving connection with his former friend. The all-pervasive universal form is too much, too immense and amorphous; its endless and directionless infinity is also terrifyingly unattractive (*ugra*).

Consequently, Arjuna requests Krishna to return to that particular form that is recognizable to him, and was the basis of their personal relationship. Specifically, Arjuna asks Krishna to return to an approachable form that makes affectionate connection possible, "like a Father to a son, a Friend to a friend, or a Beloved to a lover." This attractive form will, of course, vary from devotee to devotee, according to personal predilection. Importantly, the form that produces the most intimate relationship is identified in the *Bhagavad Gita* as a "familiar human form," the *saumya manusha rupa*. This special form that fosters close relationship is also called in this text Krishna's "own form," *svayam rupa*. Krishna resumes the particular human form familiar to Arjuna, and the intimacy of their prior friendship is restored, though now enriched with knowledge of the infinite nature of finite form. These ideas are developed further in the *Bhagavata Purana*, which explains, for example: "Assuming a human body (*manusha deha*) for the beneficial assistance of people, Krishna engages in various playful activities so that people become attracted to him" (10.33.37). Krishna's assumption of human form is portrayed as an act of divine grace (*anugraha*) intended to enhance relational connectivity with human beings.

Reflecting on the dynamics of the worship of embodied forms of divinity, the Pushti Margiya writer Pratik Shah maintains:

> We consider God to be *sakara-vyapak* [pervasive in all forms]. He is omnipresent; He can be seen in everything, from objects which are abstract, which don't have any shape, like wind, objects which have an un-definable shape, like water, and to objects which have a definite shape, like stones, trees, human beings, and countless more. However, since *shastra-gocara vidhi* [scriptural rules for worshiping perceivable objects] as well as puja mantras are not possible for a shapeless entity, we cannot worship any formless object as God. So, it asks us to decide upon any object, which has a shape to be worshipped as God. Psychologically, it has been proven that a human being can relate itself more comfortably with the shape of a human being rather than any other shape. It can concentrate more on and *create relationship* with only a human form.[13]

These words reinforce the devotional contention that anthropomorphism enhances connectedness. In sum, the adornment of a Govardhan stone is not only a way of honoring the entity as a divine person and drawing out its personality; stone worshipers report that the addition of the face and ornamentation make stronger and more intimate relationship or connection possible with this non-human entity.[14] In practice, the mountain is approached through a particular Govardhan *shila* and is personified in an attractive and familiar human (*manusha*) form. Since regarding a non-human entity or God with human features is typically referred to as "anthropomorphism," it could be said that worshipers of Mount Govardhan are asserting that "anthropomorphic form" (*manusha rupa*) is instrumental in establishing and nurturing a close relationship with mountain.

Anthropomorphism Scorned

Anthropomorphism is commonly defined as the attribution of human characteristics or form to non-human entities. As a widespread feature of much human activity, the concept of anthropomorphism has drawn scholarly attention for a long time, but until recently the majority of this attention has been unreservedly negative. It has been much maligned in biological disciplines, particularly within ethology, the study of non-human animals; demeaned as a childish, primitive practice by colonial anthropologists and scholars of religion; criticized as an egregious sin or at least wrong-mindedness by some theologians; and regarded with much suspicion by certain environmentalists who tend to conflate it with anthropocentrism, the notion that human beings are superior to and separate from all other entities. As anthropomorphism is being reconsidered in a number of academic disciplines, this denigration has recently begun to change.

Although applied to a variety of attributions, the negative consideration of anthropomorphism first arose in a religious context, and in significant ways certain religious presuppositions still underlie many of its unfavorable judgments in other contexts as well—particularly regarding issues of boundary maintenance between human and other entities. The origin of anthropomorphism as a negative concept is typically traced back to the fifth-century-BCE Greek philosopher and religious critic Xenophanes. His major complaint was that the gods were too human in terms of their characteristics, behavior, and form. The true God, he insisted, is not at all like humans in body or in mind. He concludes that the gods of the people were mere projections that had their origins in self-centered understandings. Xenophanes was also one of the first to establish a bifurcation that was often repeated in subsequent views of religions: he developed a two-tiered taxonomy that separated "vulgar" popular religion from "true" philosophic religion. The former worships anthropomorphic gods, whereas the latter postulates a transcendent conception of divinity. In a frequently quoted statement, Xenophanes quipped: "If horses, oxen and lions had hands or could draw with hands and create works of art like those made by men, horses would draw pictures of gods like horses, and oxen of gods like oxen, and they would make the bodies of their gods in accordance with the form that each species itself possesses."[15]

While Xenophanes is credited with instigating the critique of anthropomorphism, the negative assessment did not stop with him. Although much transpired between Xenophanes and the sixteenth century, one could argue that the disparaging attitudes toward anthropomorphism in scientific and cultural studies were intensified following the religious transformations that occurred during this reformational period. Significantly, the attitudes coming out of the sixteenth century were the most relevant for the emerging comparative study of religions. The concomitant shift to more denigrating attitudes toward anthropomorphism had much to do with the contentious disputes about idolatry discussed in the previous chapter. As Carlos Eire and others have established, this was a period that witnessed a sharpening of boundaries—in both religion and science—between God and the world, and between the human and the non-human. The seventeenth century was a particularly active time for furthering the critique and broadening the rejection of anthropomorphism, which was not confined to matters of religion, but also extended into developments that defined the physical sciences.

The environmental historian Neil Evernden provides an account of the emergence of the scientific concept of the "purification of nature" by contrasting the modern Western worldview with that of the previous medieval one; the former he understands as largely the product of the humanistic revolution of the Renaissance that strongly influenced modern scientific ways of knowing. He maintains that the medieval world was characterized by an empathetic approach to knowing nature, "which is of course only possible if the subject and the object, the knower and the known, are of the same nature; they must be members and parts of one and the same vital complex."[16] But this is precisely what gets rejected in the humanistic revolution of the reformational times in which the human becomes the measure of all things and is set apart from the natural world. In this context, Evernden demonstrates, the perception of nature must be cleansed of all human projections. "The expulsion of qualities from nature, although radical in the extreme, was justified through the assertion that only when the distorting effects of human projection are removed can we achieve an understanding of the 'primary' or real properties of nature."[17] Evernden explains that the resulting picture of nature that emerged from these European developments created a world lacking any kind of vitality or sentience. Nature by definition becomes what is non-human: "Indeed, that is what Nature is: a world devoid of properties we associate with humans—in short, devoid of subjectivity."[18] In such a world, meaningful communication and significant relationships between humans and non-human entities become highly suspect, if not impossible, as so few characteristics are assumed to be shared.

A lasting effect of this has been that "in our understanding, in our 'system' called Nature, human characteristics are out of place and constitute a serious contamination."[19] With this development, a thorough separation between human and nature was accomplished; the resulting dualism caused a de-animation of the non-human world. Any notion of personhood or any other human quality in the non-human realm was thus dismissed as misguided "projectionism" by many after the Renaissance; consequently, personhood came to be identified solely with the human. Hence, the modern period was initiated with a view of nature that is devoid of any human qualities or even sentience and subject to indifferent exploitation. Importantly, this perspective heightens the negative understanding of anthropomorphism, for "the sin we commit in attempting to attribute such [human] properties to Nature is 'anthropomorphism.'"[20] Seventeenth-century Renaissance scientists who would exemplify this position would include Francis Bacon, Robert Boyle, and Rene Descartes, all of whom attacked the very concept of anthropomorphism and fought hard to maintain a firm boundary between the human and non-human. Although Evernden does an admirable job of accounting for the scientific revolution that helped shape the viewpoints of modernity, his portrayal of these developments accounts for little of its connection with the religious revolution that took place in Europe during the sixteenth century.

Lorraine Daston, a historian of early modern European science, does a better job of identifying the religious contributions to these changes while asking: "How did the natural come to be so other than human? More pointedly, how and why did anthropomorphism—the conceptual habit of seeing the non-human in human terms—come to be suspect in science?"[21] She begins by looking at crucial developments in the seventeenth century.

Despite the several upheavals in the historiography of the Scientific Revolution since the early nineteenth century, one part of the story has survived more or less intact. It was sometime in the middle decades of the seventeenth century, we are told, that natural philosophers began explicitly and emphatically to abandon anthropomorphic modes of description as applied to nature . . . there is surprising unanimity not only that seventeenth-century natural philosophy banned anthropomorphism, but also that this anthropomorphism taboo is partly constitutive of what is modern about "modern science."[22]

Unlike Evernden, Daston stresses the important links between the development of modern science and specific religious trends prominent in the seventeenth century. "Anthropomorphism means to describe the nonhuman in human terms, and it was a cardinal religious sin long before it became a cardinal scientific sin."[23] Daston wonders why anthropomorphism was considered to be not just an error, but a morally and dangerously wrong error called a "sin." "What were the preconditions for this first emergence of the anthropomorphism taboo in the study of nature, and how did it transform not only the category of the natural, but also that of the human and the divine?"[24] Addressing this question, she contends that "the seventeenth-century ban on anthropomorphism represents a vigorous imposition of Judeo-Christian theology upon natural philosophy, rather than a step towards secularization."[25] I would only add that the particular form of the theology in question was in tune with the anti-idolatrous Protestant Reformation under the influence of theologians such as John Calvin that resulted in a religion of extreme transcendence and a "disenchantment" of the natural world.

Others have affirmed that a specific theological agenda shaped the development of the modern scientific view of nature.[26] The scientific revolution of the seventeenth century that promoted a mechanical philosophy adopted "a barren conception of matter."[27] The cultural transformation that brought about a radically new view of nature "was deeply rooted in a new religious attitude, the main result of which was the Protestant Reformation of the sixteenth century."[28] One of the major results of this development was a complete rejection of personification or what is often called anthropomorphism. The important seventeenth-century religious scientist Robert Boyle exemplifies this attack on anthropomorphism. The development of mechanistic science and mechanical philosophy articulated in his influential work *A Free Enquiry into the Vulgarly Received Notion of Nature* was shaped not only by his understanding of idolatry, but also the related idea of anthropomorphism. For him, the "vulgar" concept of nature, which tended to personify nature, was dangerous to the "true religion" of Christianity.[29] As Daston points out, Boyle "was adamant on a priori, and largely theological grounds that anthropomorphism paid nature too great a compliment, bordering on idolatry."[30] For Boyle this violated the view of the Protestant Christian God prevalent in his time: "For ours is a God . . . both incorporeal and too excellent to be so united to matter as to animate it like the heathen's mundane soul."[31] Based on his religious commitments, Boyle condemned the recognition of any subjectivity outside the human as "a dangerous thing."[32] Thus, the human was set completely apart from all other entities in the world, and a serious attack on anthropomorphism in both science and religion became well established in the seventeenth century.

One of the early and most influential modern writers on the subject of anthropomorphism in the comparative study of religion was David Hume, the eighteenth-century Scottish Enlightenment thinker examined in the previous chapter, whose thinking was largely shaped by Calvinistic Presbyterianism and influenced by Boyle and other mechanical philosophers. Alongside his condemnation of "primitive idolatry," Hume identified with lasting authority a negative tendency to which humans are prone: "There is an universal tendency among mankind to conceive all beings like themselves, and to transfer to every object, those qualities with which they are familiarly acquainted, and of which they are intimately conscious . . . trees, *mountains* and streams are *personified*, and the inanimate parts of nature acquire sentiment and passion."[33] For Hume, anthropomorphism is a cognitive strategy for coping with the insecurity of living in a world of unknown causes; it is an application of what is familiar to what is unfamiliar. He associates anthropomorphism in his writings particularly with the popular or "vulgar religion" of the "ignorant multitude."[34] Although Hume is not without sympathy for those who utilize anthropomorphic strategies, ultimately for him their approach is a mistake that is to be replaced with objective science. He presses his criticism of anthropomorphism further by sarcastically proposing: "And why not become a perfect anthropomorphite? Why not assert the deity or deities to be corporeal, and to have eyes, a nose, mouth, etc?"[35] Many Hindu worshipers of the stones from Mount Govardhan as well as other embodied forms of divinity might well reply: Why not? For these features help us connect with a particular form of God.

Nineteenth-century anthropologists continued the disparagement of anthropomorphism. Maintenance of proper boundaries that sharply divide the human from all other entities is one of the most important marks of the "civilized," according to many of the colonial anthropologists. As we saw in the last chapter, E. B. Tylor, for example, paired the concepts of idolatry and anthropomorphism by associating the most primitive of all religions with the belief that sentience and personality are present in non-human life forms, with the lowest category being such presence in inanimate objects. The perspective that pursues personhood in a stone would thus represent the most confused and primitive thought for Tylor.[36] In a similar fashion, Sir James Frazer writes:

When man began seriously to reflect on the nature of things, it was almost inevitable that he should explain them on the analogy of what he knew best, that is, by his own thoughts, feelings, and emotions. Accordingly he tended to attribute to everything, not only to animals, but to plants and inanimate objects, a principle of life like that of which he was himself conscious, and which, for want of a better name, we accustomed to call a soul. This primitive philosophy is commonly known as animism. It is a childlike interpretation of the universe in terms of man.[37]

Although much of the nineteenth-century evolutionary theory about religion and culture is no longer accepted, many of these ideas are yet assumed in "civilized" Western cultures, with many today finding themselves in agreement with the sentiments expressed in these judgments of anthropomorphism. The notion that a stone might be a "person" with whom one can nurture a meaningful relationship through anthropomorphic tactics is quite alien and absurd to most people in the West.

Anti-anthropomorphism has persisted into the twentieth century and shows little sign of fading in many circles in the twenty-first century. In his book *The Science of Culture*, for example, the anthropologist Leslie White identifies the "philosophy of anthropomorphism" as a viewpoint in which "man unconsciously projects himself into the external world, describing and interpreting it terms of his own psychic processes. . . . Thus man creates the world in his own image."[38] He cites as a representative illustration a 1910 publication about the American Omaha people: "To the Omaha nothing is without life: the rock lives, so does the cloud, the tree, the animal. He projects his own consciousness upon all things, and ascribes to them experiences with which he is familiar; there is to him something in common between all creatures and all natural forms . . . this something he conceives of as akin to his own conscious being."[39] Without questioning whether consciousness is truly restricted to humans, he also characterizes anthropomorphism as "the projection of the human ego into the external world." Championing "objective" modern science, he concludes in strong judgmental terms that an anthropomorphic philosophy is a primitive mode of thought that is "worse than worthless, for false knowledge is often worse than none at all."[40]

One of the strongest criticisms of anthropomorphism to appear lately in the field of ethology, the study of non-human animals, is John Kennedy's *The New Anthropomorphism*. Acknowledging the persistence of anthropomorphism in the study of animals today, he writes: "People have always been very ready to believe that animals are like us in having feelings and purposes and acting upon them. Yet there has never been any direct evidence for this ancient anthropomorphic belief, and some three centuries ago Rene Descartes broke with tradition by arguing that animals were, in principle, machines. . . . If the study of animal behaviour is to mature as a science, the process of liberation from the delusions of anthropomorphism must go on."[41] Kennedy deems anthropomorphism as "a throw-back to primitive animism."[42] Attitudes that are sympathetic toward anthropomorphism clearly have no place in the study of animals or in any reasonable human thought for scientists like Kennedy.

The concept of anthropomorphism has not faired much better in environmental studies. As one environmental writer reports: "Ecologists and environmentalists have attacked anthropomorphism in recent years as a token of humanity's inability to understand and respect other creatures on their own terms."[43] Most expressly, though, anthropomorphism has been rejected by conflating it with anthropocentrism, the viewpont that humans are completely separate from and superior to all other entities. In its extreme form, anthropocentrism has it that the rest of the world is nothing but a stage for the human drama. Luke Strongman, for example, argues that anthropocentrism and anthropomorphism are similar and closely related concepts. More specifically, he writes: "Anthropomorphism denotes specific instances and useages of the anthopocentric concept."[44] It is not uncommon for some environmental activists to resist anthropomorphic tendencies as a form of projectionism and domineering anthropocentrism.[45]

But are anthromorphism and anthropocentrism really the same thing? Daston's historical work provides a good entry point for considering the relationship between anthropomorphism and anthropocentrism. She maintains that the major thinkers of the scientific revolution of the seventeenth century "were antianthropomorphism because they were *pro*anthropocentrism." On the other hand, she points out, we today tend to be "antianthropomorphism because we are antianthropocentrism."[46] The current dominant position on anthropomorphism, however, begs questioning since as Daston asserts, "the anthropocentrism of exploitation entailed the antianthropomorphism of the mechanical philosophy."[47] That is, the promotion of anthropocentrism required the denigration of anthropomorphism.

There are important distinctions between anthropomorphism and anthropocentrism. Anthropomorphism perceives things as human-like and therefore promotes a sense of relatedness, whereas anthropocentrism retains all that is special for humans alone and therefore promotes a sense of non-relatedness. Anthropomorphism tends generously toward sharing too much, while anthropocentrism tends stingily toward sharing too little. Anthropomorphism challenges human supremacy, whereas anthropocentrism supports human supremacy or exceptionalism. Anthropomorphism acknowledges that humans are part of a greater whole and cultivates affinities and kinship, while anthropocentrism assumes that humans are on top or outside of all others and fosters separation and distance. In sum, anthropomorphism is a boundary crosser, whereas anthropocentrism is a boundary maintainer; anthropomorphism cultivates relationality; anthropocentrism truncates it.

Anthropomorphism Reconsidered

Divisive boundaries are now beginning to crumble. The perspective constructed during the last few centuries that insists on firm boundaries between the human and other entities is starting to change as we enter a postmodern period increasingly influenced by such disciplines as paleontology, quantum physics, ecology, and especially evolutionary biology that teach the interconnectedness of all life—in a manner that even questions the animate-inanimate boundary. The philosopher Hans Jonas, for example, recognizes that Charles Darwin's widely accepted theory of evolution strongly contends that humans and nature are inseparable. "Thus . . . the case against anthropomorphism in its extreme becomes problematical and is on principle reopened."[48] It turns out that humans are closely related to more of the non-human world than has been acknowledged in "modern thought." This had led to some recognition of the affinities between human and non-human entities, and to a re-examination of anthropomorphism. Evernden, for example, highlights one consequence of this development: "Once we accept, through the study of Nature, that all life is organically related, organically the same through the linkage of evolution, then humanity is literally part of Nature." He accordingly raises the significant question: "if humanity is 'just' a part of nature, then what sense does it make to suppose that nature may not have properties similar to our own? What is the justification for the ban on anthropomorphism?"[49]

In recent years the field of ethology has been an active arena for serious questioning of the "ban" on anthropomorphism, much of this led by Jane

Goodall and her associates, including Marc Bekoff.[50] With views such as Kennedy's in mind, science writers Jeffrey Masson and Susan McCarthy relate: "Science considers anthropomorphism towards animals a grave mistake, even a sin. It is common in science to speak of 'committing' anthropomorphism."[51] In the introduction to *When Elephants Weep*, Masson explains that this book was written in part to expose the "sin" of anthropomorphism as a false accusation: "Many scientists have avoided thinking about the feelings of animals because they have been frightened—and realistically so—of being accused of anthropomorphism. That is why I have looked carefully at the issue of anthropomorphism. If it can be disposed of as a false criticism, then the study of animal emotions can proceed on a scientific basis, freed from a bogus fear."[52] The remainder of his book is an investigation of the mental and emotional life of animals in which humanlike characteristics are noted and taken seriously.

More relevant to the anthropomorphic techniques employed in the worship of Mount Govardhan, however, is research being conducted on anthropomorphism in the various fields of social psychology and cognitive sciences. Much of it seems to corroborate the notion expressed by many worshipers of Mount Govardhan, that anthropomorphism is a means of *establishing connections* with a non-human entity. Among the varieties of anthropomorphic ornamentation added to a Mount Govardhan stone, a humanlike face is the most important—especially the eyes. A consensus has now emerged in the fields of cognitive, evolutionary, and developmental psychology, as well as cognitive neuroscience concerning the special nature of face recognition in human beings,[53] and much of the current reconsideration of anthropomorphism rests on this assertion. Neuroscientists Olivier Pascalis and David Kelly, for example, demonstrate that face processing holds a unique status within the human brain, and that there is evidence of an innate tendency to pay attention to and connect with faces from birth.[54] Brain researchers assert that face processing played an important role in human development, and that it has been a crucial factor for the continuation of a species that depends heavily on establishing strong relationships for survival. We are evolutionarily conditioned to bond with human faces, and the perception of faces is key to establishing strong connections and relationships for human beings. In short, we are programmed at birth for establishing relationships through face recognition; and of course, the face we connect with most intimately is the human face, with the eyes of utmost importance.[55] Pascalis and Kelly maintain that the face newborn humans connect with most closely is a human face with a frontal view in which both eyes are wide open in a direct gaze. This is exactly the kind of face added to Govardhan stones. Whether present at birth or learned, human beings establish and maintain connections with and through faces. Indeed, worshipers of Govardhan stones report that the face helps them recognize and connect with the divine presence of the stone. A typical statement goes: "A face on a Giriraj *shila* makes its personality more apparent, and this makes our connection (*sambandha*) with Giriraj-ji more firm." From this perspective, the addition of a face on a Govardhan stone might best be regarded as an intentional and effective cultural strategy to connect with a non-human entity.

Beneficial attraction and bonding via face recognition has at least four important functional arenas: the infant's connection with the mother, the mother's bonding to the infant, sexual partner selection, and ongoing social interaction that is dependent on facial cues and non-verbal communication. Relatedly, all of this seems to be important for many other non-human mammalian species, such as sheep, dogs, and monkeys. Recent research demonstrates that face recognition is not just a human trait, but is also found in other social species, as "faces appear to play an important role for individual social and sexual attraction in other species besides humans."[56] And similar to humans, eyes are confirmed to be the most significant feature of face recognition among non-human animals.[57] Eyes are the first, and sometimes only, piece of adornment added to Govardhan stones. What, we might ask, do these researchers say is gained by face recognition among social mammalian species? Once again, the answer has to do with connectivity: "The ability to recognize faces and their emotional content is a key feature underlying successful social interaction and *bonding*."[58]

So, in a way, it turns out that Xenophanes was right. His famous quip makes complete sense from an evolutionary biological perspective, since in addition to humans, other social mammalian species connect most closely with the faces of their own kind. If horses, oxen, and lions could fashion highly significant "gods," then horses would indeed fashion them to look like horses, oxen would fashion them like oxen, and lions would fashion them like lions. Anthropocentrism would have it that the human face is the highest form, but this is true only for humans. Face recognition of one's own species is a general feature of our mammalian biological, neurological development. Researchers have demonstrated that monkeys are facially attracted to monkeys, sheep are facially attracted to sheep, and dogs are facially attracted to dogs. We are all social animals hardwired for establishing and maintaining important relationships through face recognition, with a special focus on the eyes. Face recognition is all about *connection*, and for human beings the most significant face is a human one.

The theme of connective bonding through anthropomorphism has been taken up lately by social psychologists, many of whom corroborate the notion that anthropomorphism is frequently a means of establishing connection with non-human entities. Recognizing that human well-being is heavily dependent upon connectivity, a team of University of Chicago social psychologists investigating anthropomorphism of domestic pets and other entities suggests, "this need is so strong that people sometimes create humans out of nonhumans through a process of anthropomorphism," or in other words, anthropomorphism is a way of achieving "social connection."[59] These same researchers affirm in a subsequent research article that anthropomorphism creates "an empathetic *connection* with nonhuman agents."[60] Anthropomorphizing non-human entities has been shown to "serve as a source of social connection, and the link between connection to those nonhuman agents and one's health and well-being is well documented."[61] Anthropomorphic connectivity, moreover, not only is a source of well-being for the human who anthropomorphizes, but also has positive consequences for the non-human entity being anthropomorphized. "Anthropomorphizing at least some nonhuman agents creates an agent that deserves concern for its own well-being. Such agents are not just represented as humanlike, but are also more likely to be treated as humanlike."[62] An example they evoke is the environmentalists' reference to the physical planet as "Mother Earth."

This last claim has been taken up by a group of Hong Kong–based social psychology researchers who have published a study on the effects of the anthropomorphization of natural entities. They too begin by recognizing that the quest for significant connection is a major factor motivating anthropomorphism, and then hypothesize that "people experience stronger connectedness to nature when they anthropomorphize it. Because anthropomorphism of nature highlights the similarity between nature and humans, this hypothesis is also consistent with the notion that similarity breeds affiliation."[63] Their experimental research also shows that anthropomorphizing enhances connectedness to natural entities: "Anthropomorphism of nature was associated with *connectedness* to nature, which in turn led to conservation behavior."[64] The ethnographic work that Sarah Pike has done with North American radical eco-activists confirms the veracity of this claim. Her book *For the Wild* is filled with the accounts of eco-activists who personify non-human entities as they develop protective kinship relationships with them. In a nutshell she concludes: "Activists shamelessly anthropomorphize."[65] Here is additional affirmation that people experience stronger caring connectedness to some natural entity when they anthropomorphize it, and corroboration of the claim made by the worshipers of Govardhan stones that giving human form (*manusha-rupa*) to some non-human entity creates and nurtures a connection with it. The specific concern in this case, of course, is the enhancement of the devotee's intimate relationship (*sambandha*) with a Giriraj *shila* as an embodied form of Krishna. We can see that anthropomorphism is an unconscious or conscious way of connecting with some non-human entity, whether that be a domestic pet like a dog, or a natural entity like a tree, or an inanimate object like a car.[66] In the case of a religious tradition that identifies God with some non-human entity—as in the Braj Vaishnavism associated with the worship of Mount Govardhan—it becomes an intentional strategy to connect with God. The anthropomorphization of a Govardhan stone enables worshipers to better perceive its divine presence and thereby establish a close relationship with Krishna. Seen in this light, then, "intentional anthropomorphism" is a culturally developed method for connecting with some non-human entity—like a stone—by augmenting it with a human face, characteristics, and form.

Anthropomorphism as a Pathway to Relationality

Anxiety about anthropomorphism seems primarily to be a Western and dualistic concern, since the dualistic (monotheistic) traditions are more eager to maintain boundaries between human, world, and God. The non-dual Vedantic traditions that inform the Vaishnava Hinduism associated with the worship of Mount Govardhan for the most part do not share this concern, and are therefore much more comfortable with anthropomorphism. Here is a worldview in which God/Brahman/Krishna is the totality of all reality. While discussing with my friend Mohan the nature of stones from Mount Govardhan, he remarked: "*Atma* (divine presence or soul) is not just there in Giriraj *shila*s, but in all stones. Really in all beings, in all things. It's in everything!" Worshipers of Mount Govardhan also dwell within a cultural atmosphere of *murti-puja* that promotes "physical anthropomorphism" in which God is present bodily in anthropomorphic form.

Many of the religious and scientific developments that have roots in the early modern period reject any notion of high value in the natural world. This undermines the possibility of any special relationship with a natural entity like a mountain. Many see anthropomorphism as an antidote to this blockage. In her work on anthropomorphism and anthropocentrism, Daston suggests that the promotion of anthropomorphism might function as a form of resistance to the matter-numbing anthropocentrism of the modernist mechanical philosophy.[67] The political theorist Jane Bennett concurs in her recent book *Vibrant Matter*:

> We need to cultivate a bit of anthropomorphism—the idea that human agency has some echoes in nonhuman nature—to counter the narcissism of humans in charge of the world. . . . If a green materialism requires of us a more refined sensitivity to the outside-that-is-inside-too, then maybe a bit of anthropomorphizing will prove valuable. Maybe it is worth running the risk associated with anthropomorphizing (superstition, the divinization of nature, romanticism) because it, oddly enough, works against anthropocentrism. . . . I believe it is wrong to deny vitality to nonhuman bodies, forces, and forms, and that a careful course of anthropomorphization can help reveal that vitality, even though it resists full translation and exceeds my comprehensive grasp.[68]

Although there are important differences between the Hindu devotional concept of *svarupa* and Bennett's concept of vitality, both refer to a special kind of wondrous presence that includes non-human entities. Bennett finally asks: "Are there more everyday tactics for cultivating an ability to discern the vitality of matter?"[69] Perhaps the intentional ritualized anthropomorphic techniques of the worship of Govardhan stones within devotional Hinduism has something very concrete to offer the quest for wondrous vitality that Bennet places before us, an offering that has much to do with establishing and nurturing relationality through anthropomorphic strategies.

Certain environmental philosophers agree that relationality is a key factor in, and positive consequence of, anthropomorphism.[70] Leesa Fawcett has argued: "To be anthropomorphic does not necessarily mean one is anthropocentric. . . . The definition of anthropomorphism one works from depends on one's focal point. Do you see humans as the centre point, and then you magnanimously ascribe human characteristics to animals? Or do you see humans in *relationship* with (historically and bodily), and continuous with nature?" [71] She concludes that "[a]nthropomorphism is a way for life (humans) to know life (non-humans)."[72] Anthropomorphism in Fawcett's view, then, is a productive method for coming to better approach and relate to non-human entities.[73] Environmental philosopher Freya Mathews adds support from a panpsychism perspective for understanding anthropomorphism as a pathway to relationality. "To personify natural phenomenon may be the only way of representing the subjectivity of the world in humanly accessible terms. . . . From a panpsychist viewpoint, the aim is not to theorize the world, but to *relate* to it, and to rejoice in that *relationship*. For this we need practices of invocation and response—ritual practices, for instance, recovered and adapted from the great treasure houses of traditional religious forms."[74] The anthropomorphic techniques employed to establish a close relationship with Mount Govardhan may just be one of those resourceful treasure houses.

What might the pursuit of relationships with tangible embodied forms of divinity such as Giriraj *shila*s suggest about the nature of religion itself? Among other things, it implies that religion has a great deal to do with profound relationships. This notion finds confirmation in Robert Orsi's understanding of religion as "the *relationships* that form between humans and holy figures."[75] Although he makes this claim in the context of Catholicism, he maintains that "thinking of religion as relationships" is relevant for other cultures, too. I must agree, for we have certainly seen how the notion of relationship or *sambandha* is at the very heart of the Braj Vaishnava worldview and religious practices. Here is a case of the quest for sacred relationships pursued through concrete forms of divinity. In thinking about religion as relationships, Orsi is eager to raise the issue of presence, highlighting "the deep antipathy between modern ('anti-idolatrous') cultures all over the world and the practice and experience of sacred presence. Of all aspects of religion, the one that has proven least tolerable to modern societies—has been the radical presence of the gods to practitioners. The modern world has assiduously and systematically disciplined the senses not to experience sacred presence; the imaginations of moderns are trained toward sacred absence."[76] The issue of presence in the worship of Mount Govardhan becomes decisive, for if there is no presence present in a Giriraj *shila*, then relational connection is either meaningless or impossible. This brings us back to a crucial question: Is it even possible for those raised in the modern cultures to which Orsi refers to acknowledge the assertion of divine presence in a stone?

7

Non-Duality, Play, and an Invitation

In the beginning this world was only one, without a second.
And it thought to itself: "Let me become many."[1]

And he worshiped himself by means of himself.[2]

The function of translation is precisely to cross borders, to indicate
that it is possible to speak of the world in other terms, other rhythms,
other accents, with nuances of sound and colour.[3]

Speaking with God: The Problem of Presence

An enormous amount of anxiety and energy has been spent during the
modern period trying to divorce relationships with inanimate entities from
the realm of human rationality. That there could be anything like a divine
presence or personality in a stone was readily dismissed as absurdly impossible. Lurking beneath the surface of such "modern" assertions, though, is
a sense that something vital has been lost. In her collection of essays titled
Teaching a Stone to Talk, Annie Dillard ponders how the modern diminish-
ment of divine presence has greatly reduced our world and left us alone in
search of more extensive communion. She laments the advent of modernity in which God has become silent and absent: "God used to rage at the
Israelites for frequenting sacred groves. I wish I could find one. . . . The very
holy mountains are keeping mum. . . . What have we been doing all these centuries but trying to call God back to the mountain?"[4] In a similar vein, the
environmental philosopher Freya Mathews asks: "How can we sing back to
life a world that has been so brutally silenced?"[5] The word "we" in both these
questions, however, implores further consideration since cultures remain on
the planet today—even among those deeply engaged in the latest information technology—in which mountains and stones still speak.

Loving Stones. David L. Haberman, Oxford University Press (2020) © Oxford University Press.
DOI: 10.1093/oso/9780190086718.001.0001

While Dillard and Mathews bemoan the silence of modern stones, the experience of Mount Govardhan worshipers is quite different. Many of them assert that "the divine presence shows itself" in a Govardhan stone, especially when enriched with facial ornamentation and interacted with in worshipful ways. Those who worship Govardhan stones in their home shrines report a powerful divine presence in Giriraj *shilas* with whom they develop intimate relationships. One woman recounted, "when you put eyes and a face and ornamentations on a stone it speaks to you and you can speak to it. Then you can interact with it like a close relative. I have had many wonderful conversations with mine." Whereas the addition of eyes makes visual communion (*darshan*) possible, hearing the stone speak greatly boosts the affirmation of presence so necessary for relational intimacy. Another woman disclosed her habit of sitting before her adorned Govardhan stone every evening to review her day and seek counsel for any emotional challenges she may have encountered. For these women, God has never left the mountain and stones are not mute. The lament of modernity's disenchantment and its attendant desire for re-enchantment disappears in a cultural context in which enchantment has never vanished. Could it be possible that the non-human world is not so silent after all, and that we are not so alone?

Is there a divine presence in the world of matter? Human beings have produced a variety of answers to this question, which cannot be answered with certainty. But rather than unreflectively resorting to cultural modes of interpretation that automatically render this impossible, the playful interpretive approach discussed in this book remains open to such a possibility. Just what has been lost in the moves of modernity? What kind of stones might be useful for paving the road to a return to vibrant enchantment? More specifically, what does the worship of Mount Govardhan—a context in which matter matters—have to offer considerations of this possibility? The premise that matter doesn't matter rests on an inherited worldview that makes a sharp distinction between the creator and creation, spirit and matter, mind and body, human and all other entities, and so forth. The boundaries between these divisions were reinforced in the modified worldview that emerged in sixteenth-century Europe.

Robert Orsi has recently claimed that developments during this period produced a bipolarity of presence or absence within Christianity, with Catholics being identified with the former and Protestants with the latter.[6] Orsi demonstrates that the dominant intellectual climate of modernity that gave birth to the academic study of religion, which hinged on the concept of idolatry, favored absence. "Modernity exists under the sign of absence. The reimagining of the relationship between God and human that commenced in the early sixteenth century introduced an ontological fault line that would run through all of modernity. . . . The absence of the gods became a sign of mental health, whereas their real presence, in the 'old' Catholic sense, was a symptom of mental illness."[7] To be a mature modern person meant to be free of the infantile and superstitious belief in physical presence, most surely within inanimate things or material objects such as stones.

Pertinent to our considerations, the sharp contrast between presence and absence, initially instigated in the conflict between Catholics (presence) and Protestants (absence), largely determined the way in which other religious traditions were regarded. As Orsi maintains, it "became the metric for mapping the religious worlds of the planet."[8] This was certainly the case for assessing the worship of stones in India. That is, the gauge of Protestant absence was used by Europeans to establish who and what is modern, and to interpret and evaluate the religions of the peoples of Asia, Africa, and the Americas, for whom the gods were often present in physical forms.[9] The chief task of the scholar of religion became the assessment of the veracity of a given religious tradition while removing the mask of presence from some religious phenomenon and exposing its real meaning. This was typically accomplished with functional explanations or the apparatus of symbolic representation, which led to very probable distortions in the understanding of certain religious traditions. Jonathan Z. Smith asserts that the fundamental issue that divides the academic study of religion "is the debate between an understanding of religion based on *presence*, and one based on *representation*."[10] One wonders, however, whether this inherited polarity need be continued.

Might it be more productive to claim presence is the best approach for comprehending some religions, and representation (or absence) is the best for others, particularly in the context of extensive human interaction with a variety of religious objects? The playful interpretive approach, which remains open to difference, has no need to resolve the incongruity of these two options, though it would not shy away from giving serious consideration to the implications of their differences. Understanding Hindu regard for a Giriraj *shila*, for example, requires a different interpretive approach than understanding Protestant regard for the wooden cross mounted on the unadorned wall of a Reformed church, for these are informed by very different worldviews. The employment of a more flexible interpretive approach that recognizes difference, therefore, seems more prudent than aiming for a universal theory that fits all cases. The worldview of modernity that shaped many of the West's academic disciplines—including the comparative study of religions—is rooted in an assumption of dualistic absence. But what does the worldview that informs the pursuit of an awareness of and intimate relationship with divine presence in a Govardhan stone look like? If we take this culture to be as valid as our own, as I think we must, then we need to give serious consideration to its assertion that some kind of presence may be encountered in a sacred stone. How far are we willing to go? Where and why are the limits? In many ways, the particular philosophical foundation of Vaishnava Vedanta that informs much of the interaction with Mount Govardhan dissolves the problem of presence.

Non-Duality: It's All One . . .

One of the major tenets of Vedantic religious philosophy is non-duality (*advaita*). Foundational Vedantic texts recount that in the beginning the One Ultimate Reality (*Brahman*) was lonely and bored, as there is not much joy in playing with one's self alone. The One desired others, and so divided itself. Through this creative means the unmanifest One produced out of itself the manifold world of all entities, both animate and inanimate, and proceeded to interact with itself in a multitude of forms. Accordingly everything in the world is simultaneously different and non-different, many and one. Although difference is recognized, sharp ontological divides do not exist. Everything is *Brahman*. In stark contrast to Calvin's view, there are no impenetrable boundaries between the supreme reality (*Brahman* or God) and the visible world. Everything in the world is a part of the ultimate Whole, and as such is sacred. Divine presence pervades everything. Consequently, anything can potentially be disclosed at any moment as an embodied form of divinity.

In a book on the philosophical system of Vallabhacharya that underlies the Braj Vaishnava Vedantic school of Pushti Marg, Raghunath Sharma identifies a pair of popular Upanishadic verses central to Pushti Margiya philosophical thinking. Both are from the *Chandogya Upanishad*: "In the beginning there was only one Real Entity, only one without a second" (6.2.1); and "That one Real Entity wished: Let me become many, let me multiply myself" (6.2.3).[11] Importantly, he observes, Vallabhacharya emphasizes both of these aspects of reality—singularity and multiplicity. "Ultimate reality

[Brahman/Krishna], though One, is nevertheless capable of becoming infinitely Many."[12] Gaudiya Vaishnavas express a similar position with the compound Sanskrit term *bheda-abheda*, difference in non-difference. The prominent place of such ideas in Braj Vaishnavism confirms that from this Vedantic viewpoint, the unified infinite is therefore non-different from the interminably multiple finite. To cordon God off from the realm of manifest forms limits the divine.

Such is the complex non-dual (*advaita*) perspective that informs the Vaishnava Vedantic viewpoint underlying the worship of Mount Govardhan. The simultaneously unified and diversified reality is identified in the Pushti Margiya Vaishnava tradition as *viruddha-dharma-ashraya*, the "coexistence of contradictory opposites," and in the Gaudiya Vaishnava tradition as *achintya-bheda-abheda*, or "the inconceivable simultaneity of difference and non-difference." Vedantic texts characterize this multifaceted nature of reality by employing pairs of seemingly oppositional terms such as form (*murta*) and formless (*amurta*), manifest (*vyakta*) and unmanifest (*avyakta*), changing (*kshara*) and unchanging (*akshara*), many (*bahu*) and one (*eka*), with qualities (*saguna*) and without qualities (*nirguna*), and particular (*svarupa*) and universal (*vishvarupa*). It is important to remember, however, that these are not two different realities, but two different dimensions of the very same non-dual reality. While acknowledging distinctiveness, Vedantic texts insist that all reality is in the end indivisible.[13] Therefore, while there is acknowledgment of a transcendent dimension of ultimate reality, there is also vital recognition of an immanent one. This means that although a vast and infinite aspect of divinity surpasses the tangible world, the world of finite visible forms is also fully divine. In other words, divine presence is here and now, in and as concrete entities, which are often considered to be the most accessible forms of divinity. From this perspective, recognition of divine presence in something like a stone is far from problematic.

Shrivatsa Goswami explained it to me this way: "The world is the body of God, and all nature is divinized. Whereas for many Europeans nature worship is regarded as primitive, the nature worship exemplified in the worship of Mount Govardhan is the highest form of worship; it is the highest form of religion. The *Bhagavata Purana* reveals that Krishna was the first to perform the worship of Mount Govardhan, and in so doing teaches the key to how to celebrate life and survive, as life is always lived in the theater of nature." He concluded, "The problem of presence is really more of a problem for the dualistic Abrahamic traditions; whereas from a Vedantic perspective *Brahman* encompasses everything, so any particular thing is a part of the all-pervasive whole. Therefore divine presence permeates everything."

What does serious reflection on the worship of a stone have to offer a reconsideration of presence in the physical world, particularly for those European cultures shaped by the anti-idolatrous ideology that prompted much of the modernist worldview? One important contribution may be its avowal of radical inclusivity. Keep in mind that stone has been regarded as occupying the very bottom of the hierarchical heap of religious objects, and stone worshipers have been deemed the most primitive of humanity. Thus, recognizing the possibility of divine presence in a stone implies by extension the all-inclusive acknowledgment of presence in potentially anything and a holistic acceptance of the difference represented by stone worshipers. As we have seen, the foundational anthropologist Tylor is exemplary of the modernist perspective in early anthropology that led to the widespread assumption that any sense of presence in physical matter is completely absurd and a clear sign of misguided primitive thought. Fashioned not so long ago, the modernist "progressive" assessment of human civilization ranked societies in a hierarchical order that was contingent on a rejection of any recognition of presence within the non-human. Certainly any sense that rocks have personality marked the very lowest of human understanding. The wider the circle of presence or personhood, the more primitive the religion. Modern progress implies a silencing of the world outside of the human, most certainly that of a mountain. Giving serious consideration to the claims of the millions of people who worship Mount Govardhan instigates the reassessment of this assumption, perhaps even breaking down hierarchical judgment. If one can acknowledge the possibility of presence in stone, then it can be acknowledged effectively in everything.

In stark contrast to the modernist perspective, a major goal of Braj Vaishnavism is *sarvatma-bhava*, the "realization of *Brahman*/God in everything and everything as *Brahman*/God." Shrivatsa Goswami and other learned worshipers of Mount Govardhan claim that the worship of this mountain is "the highest form of religion." The Braj Vaishnava traditions associated with the worship of Mount Govardhan insist that the greatest realization involves understanding that conscious worship is itself the supreme reward of worship. The experience of wondrous reverence toward and in the natural world is the reward of that reverence. It's all It playing with Itself. Recognizing the possibility of presence in a stone upsets and challenges the modernist paradigm, turning it topsy-turvy, at least for those willing to

concede the historically constructed nature of this paradigm, thereby becoming playfully open to serious consideration of alternative constructions.

Playing with Itself

Non-duality leads to an understanding of the infinite in the finite, but so
does play, as play is one of the consequences of non-dualism. Play is non-
teleological; it is action in which there is nothing to be accomplished.[14] From
the non-dual Vedantic perspective that underlies Braj Vaishnavism everything is already complete (*purnam*), thus nothing remains to be achieved.
A famous Upanishadic verse states this well: "That is full (or complete,
purnam), this is full. Fullness proceeds from fullness. When fullness is taken
from fullness, only fullness remains."[15] When full presence is everywhere
here and now, joyful play becomes the only option. Infinite Krishna's play
(*lila*) includes his capacity to manifest himself in multiple finite forms within
the world. If it's all One, then all players are radically interconnected as they
are established in the same source. Much of this assertion rests on that central
insight of Vedantic ontology expressed in various accounts of creation: out of
the primordial state of static joyless singularity, the original One separated
itself into multiplicity for the purpose of experiencing joyful interactive play.
God and Goddess, God and the world, and God and devotee are simultaneously the same and different, all playing with itself. This is one of many conceptual applications of the "simultaneity of difference and non-difference"
(*bheda-abheda*) philosophical position of the Braj Vaishnava traditions. The
only real motive for any activity then is *prema-vilasa*, the joyful play of love,
a state of being in which difference in unity is vital and has no objective other
than its own enjoyment.

The anthropologist Don Handelman recognizes that the concept of play
(*lila*) is given elevated significance within Hinduism, arguing that in Hindu
cosmology "an idea of play seems to be embedded at a high level of abstrac-
tion."[16] He contends that this high level of playful engagement has cosmic
implications. "The boundaries throughout such a cosmos are more mal-
leable, and the entire cosmos may approximate more closely a system of
self-transformation."[17] He has in mind the accounts of creation referenced
earlier in which all of creation is understood to be expressions of the playful
interactions of the One, or manifestations of the One playing with itself.
"Cosmos continually transformed itself continuously, reproducing itself

as phenomenal form. . . . One may argue that a paradox of self-reference is embedded in that initial moment of differentiation when the cosmic Self became to itself simultaneously one thing and another, Self and Other."[18] This kind of playful paradox implies a unity of being, and the mystery of the part and the whole is a particularly ludic way of seeing things. Importantly, Handelman insists: "Prominent among these puzzles is the paradox of the infinite god who is 'embedded' in finite form." We see, then, that the notions of radical non-dual interconnectivity and play are intimately linked. "Embedded at a high level of cosmic organization, the idea of play influences the fluidity and permeability of boundaries."[19]

The concept of play pervades the stories and worship of Mount Govardhan, and the mountain itself serves as an excellent illustration of the coexistence of seemingly contradictory opposites within the playful, all-inclusive, and shape-shifting god Krishna. The paradigmatic episode of the worship of Mount Govardhan provides a productive illustration of the One playing with itself. Krishna is said to have lifted the mountain in play (*lilaya*), and the "great secret" (*guhya*) in the worship of Mount Govardhan is that Krishna is playing with himself. He is both the lifter of the mountain as well as the mountain being lifted (*giridharana*); by means of one form of himself (the cowherd worshiper) he worships another form of himself (the mountain being worshiped), which in turn (as Haridasavarya) worships the worshiper. Playful non-duality, then, underlies the twofold nature of Govardhan: the mountain is the highest object of devotion as a direct and full form of Krishna (*sakshat* Purna-Purushottama), as well as the highest devotee of Krishna as Haridasavarya. Furthermore, from a philosophical perspective, every devotee of Mount Govardhan is also considered to be an aspect of Krishna. How could it be otherwise if Krishna is everything, the totality of all reality? Again, it is the One playing with itself. This is called *prema-vilasa*, the ongoing play of love that instigated the opening differentiation in the first place, for love itself is dependent upon difference—yet importantly, a difference that assumes non-difference.

Handelman maintains that the location of play within a culture greatly determines its influence. He points out that in Hindu cosmology play is a "top-down idea," as it is embedded at a high and wide-ranging level and is integral to all cosmic operations. Thus, to be in play is to be "attuned to cosmic processes." In contrast to this, other cultures exist in which play erupts from the bottom. "By bottom-up play I mean that play often is phrased in opposition to, or as a negation of, the order of things."[20] In such cultures, play is less prominent and usually is regarded as subversive. Handelman identifies cultures holding this latter view with the transcendent monotheistic cosmologies in which absolute differences abound and hardened boundaries exist between God and the world. The cultural location of play, then, is closely related to the question of presence. Top-down cultures imbue play with cosmic significance and embrace non-dual thinking in which divinity can be present in material forms, whereas bottom-up cultures devalue play and enforce rigid boundaries that hold the divine at a transcendent distance. An understanding of Hindu worship of Mount Govardhan by those situated in Western monotheistic traditions may be impossible, for it seems that the capacity to which individuals from differing cultures are receptive to significant relationships with a natural entity such as a stone is dependent upon perceptions of reality shaped by culturally constructed concepts of play in human and divine matters. How, then, is the scholar to render the impossible feasible for someone whose inherited worldview does not immediately accommodate the requisite conception of play? Or, more simply, how is one to make sense of the worshipful interactions with a playful divinity that willingly takes the form of a stone mountain? Perhaps the answer itself is to be found in a form of play. Play is not only a central characteristic of ultimate reality within Braj Vaishnavism; some scholars claim that it is also relevant for the academic study of religion.

Invitation into a Playful Adventure

The flexibility and malleability of play lead to greater openness to and appreciation of difference. But how might play be incorporated into the very study of religion? What is the value of play seen from the perspective of religious studies, and what might it promise for the study of different religions? Handelman contends that play "is to simultaneously do one thing and its contrary, *to do the impossible.*"[21] The religious studies scholar Sam Gill corroborates this definition, beginning an essay on the study of different religions with these words: "Play, among its many and varied meanings, may denote a type of structural dynamics, a being at once of two minds or a holding at once of mutually exclusive positions. . . . I believe play is often experienced as enjoyable because it celebrates the distinctive human capacity to simultaneously do one thing and its opposite and to be aware of the process by which it is *possible to do the impossible.*"[22]

We return to the playful nip of Bateson's monkey, wherein play occupies the anomalous in-between that somehow encompasses polar opposites: the playful nip is simultaneously a bite and not a bite. Importantly, play requires vulnerability toward the other. The position of one pole with regard to one's relationship with reality would be to sit unquestioningly and "securely" within the religious reality into which one was socialized; the opposite pole would involve switching to another religious reality and decisively occupying it as the singular judgmental home. The playful approach is to surrender such certainty and embrace the incongruous position of holding mutually exclusive positions. The goal here is not conversion, but rather understanding and appreciation—to expand minds and perspectives.[23] Complete conversion may be extremely difficult anyway. The influential sociologist Alfred Schutz pointed out that the world internalized in primary socialization is much more firmly entrenched in consciousness than worlds internalized in secondary socialization or conversion.[24] But it may be possible to inhabit one's primary social reality while simultaneously being open to others as equally valid. This openness would have a considerable effect on one's sense of reality. Specifically, the path to understanding would not mean necessarily or unquestioningly adapting the view that regards rocks as a form of divinity as the singular truth, but not rejecting it either. Play opens up an alternative approach to certainty: occupation of the space in-between two different views where both become possible. Non-dual play embraces a position of difference without exclusive hierarchy. From the perspective of a Pushti Margiya understanding of divine play, this is the holistic abode of *viruddha-dharma-ashraya*—the simultaneous coexistence of contradictory positions.

Gill further elaborates the playful interpretive stance: "It is the perspective from which we can simultaneously embrace two or more opposing positions without declaring ourselves mad."[25] Play itself is the key to resisting madness, for the playful nip of the monkey results in nothing but expansive enjoyment. For Gill this is the most creative stance one can take. "To take a stance, in this complex multi-cultural world, without recognizing its absurdity is either religious, narrow-minded, or naïve. To refuse to take any stance at all is either to indulge infinite regress, a favorite of many post-modernists, or silence. The alternative, which is at least more interesting, is the perspective of play: seriously taking a stance while acknowledging its absurdity."[26] Gill's playful absurdity differs notably from the modernist's absurdity in that he embraces an uncertainty that leaves difference intact, whereas the modernist view of the absurd is rooted in an assertion of judgmental certainty that aims to eliminate difference. The playful adventure of religious studies promises edifying expansion, not definite dogma or positive proclamations. It aims not to provide a single answer, but rather a rich variety of food for thought.

But why embark on the playful adventure of religious studies? What does this type of play have to offer a human life? What is to be gained from living with a sensitive awareness of multiple possibilities? Specifically, what are some of the social, personal, and environmental benefits?

Honoring Stones and Expanding Horizons

Xenophobia is a common response to the insecurity of changing times. We are witnessing an increase in violence motivated by religious domination and hegemonic designs. Much of this stems from the firm convictions of certainty and a desire to stamp out difference, even within a given religious tradition. War on difference is nothing new; people were put to death in Mexico and Peru in the sixteenth century, for example, for worshiping stones. Honoring the difference represented by Mayan and Andean religious worship had no place in the official Spanish policy of the Extirpation of Idolatries. Nineteenth-century British colonial scholars ridiculed Hindu stone worship as an absurd religious practice that demonstrated the lowest of human mentality and, for some, a most egregious form of sinful idolatry. This was to be left behind in the new "civilized" India that was the objective of British imperialism.

A paradigm for many aggressive approaches to difference was the slaughter of the three thousand Israelites who dared continue the customary practice of worshiping an embodied form of divinity.[27] One difference today is that our weapons have become more destructive. The exponential growth of the human population with increasing contact, moreover, leads to even more conflicts. Consequently, there is a great need for humans to learn not just to tolerate difference, but to come to truly appreciate it. Acceptance of the validity of different conceptions of reality is an essential feature of a considerate attitude toward the other that nurtures productive understanding and that might lead to an honoring of difference, such as sacred stones and their worshipers, instead of the violent slinging of stones.

In his book *The Comparative Study of Religions*, Joachim Wach promoted what he called the "irenic characteristic" of comparative religion.[28] Although I believe that Wach's approach to religious difference can be greatly improved,

I agree that the study of religious otherness has much to offer the appreciation of cultural difference—if conducted in a "playful" mode. Sincere and humble openness to difference not only engenders a better sense of why people in other cultures act the way they do; cases of radical difference present the opportunity to stretch us the most. Acceptance of such religious difference as that represented by the worship of stones from Mount Govardhan has the potential to yield a social flexibility and compassionate inclusivity beneficial to others. This contributes to constructive cross-cultural understanding between countries, as well as a method for addressing otherness in the increasingly complex and pluralistic societies within many countries today.

But what benefits does the open attitude toward difference extend to the individual experiencing this attitude? The answer, in short, is an expansion of a sense of human possibilities—a widening of both what it means to be human and our comprehension of the world we inhabit. The vulnerability of a playful approach to the study of religions entails openness to change. I suggested in the Introduction that what I call "conscious living" involves moving beyond the narrow boundaries of primary socialization and exposing oneself to wider realms of novel possibilities. This leads not only to greater freedom through acquaintance with viable choices, but also to existential enrichment through the broadening of one's understanding of what is possible for a lived human life. During these times when we witness the transformation of institutions of higher education into centers for vocational training, it is important to remind ourselves that higher education should be not only for a job, but also for a life. Exploring other ways of being human and coming to accept their validity broaden one's horizons, expanding one's perception of and experience in the world. The playful practice of religious studies has much to offer such enrichment.

As a lifelong student of religious studies, I believe that I have gained much from stepping out of the limited room defined by my own primary socialization into realms available through sincere consideration of radical difference, accepting worldviews other than my own as equally plausible. My world of meaning has been expanded particularly by my intimate exposure to the world of Braj religious culture, especially as it relates to natural entities. Among other things, this has allowed me to acquire a greater appreciation of human relationships with non-human entities—including animals, trees, rivers, and mountains—within many cultures worldwide. It has enabled me to have an expansive glimpse of what is possible for me as a human being, and has deeply enriched my life by enlarging my understanding and experience of the world and extending my potential relationships with others, both human and more-than-human. I cannot now imagine life without this adventurous augmentation. Every life journey will take a different form, but this is the general adventure I affirm.

As Gill suggests in the preceding, after vulnerably exposing oneself to a variety of expansive differences, there does come a time to take a stance. What about the claims of worshipers of Mount Govardhan? This book began with the proposition that God not only can appear as a stone mountain, but did so in a marvelous way, according to many Hindus, in the form of Mount Govardhan. As I passed time living "playfully" among many worshipers of this mountain—many of whom became good friends—opening to otherness and allowing my inherited worldview to slip, the notion that there is a remarkable presence in a stone became a perspective that makes sense. My initial assessment of this notion as "silly" shifted over time, and the impossible became possible. This is a "difference" I have come to take seriously, especially in the context of thinking about the relationship between the human and other-than-human. The profound meanings expressed by worshipers of Mount Govardhan regarding the concreteness of Krishna's divinity, moreover, pose valuable environmental implications and make promising contributions to considerations of relationality and conservational concerns.

Navneet's Shovel: Environmental Considerations

This book has championed openness to the real presence of divine embodiment encountered through anthropomorphic relationality as a plausible possibility, rather than its immediate dismissal through either assertions of anthropocentric mechanical philosophy or transcendent accusations of idolatry or faulty symbolic representation. Among other things, this implies an openness to the sacredness of the physical world. An open and playful approach to the study of Hindu conceptions and interactions with Mount Govardhan renders possible a reconsideration of certain environmental issues in terms of our perception of and behavior toward non-human entities. The modernist perspective of the sixteenth century gave shape to an attitude toward the non-human world that has contributed significantly to behaviors that have now culminated in a life-threatening environmental crisis. The environmental historian Evernden contends that this calls for "the re-creation of *the things themselves.*"[29] This involves a deep reassessment of how we conceive other-than-human entities. Such "re-creation" relates to a re-evaluation of presence and absence, for in a mechanistic and disenchanted world characterized by absence, all that is left is inert matter vulnerable to human manipulation and exploitation.[30] In the world of presence associated with Mount Govardhan, something else becomes possible. As an environmental philosopher, Mathews maintains that alternative views (including those of premodern Europe) toward natural entities such as mountains and stones "might be philosophically retrieved in an intellectual climate that is now prepared to reconsider the mindset of modernity."[31] She sees great potential for this reassessment in "*any* view that reunites mentality with materiality, and thereby dismantles the foundational dualism of Western thought."[32] Natural entities such as stones hold a solid place in Mathew's reconsiderations. The environmental psychologist Ralph Metzner has asserted that giving serious consideration to non-dual worldviews and religious practices of non-Western traditions "is probably the best antidote to the West's fixation in the life-destroying dissociation between spirit and nature."[33] Indeed, the conceptions of and behavior toward Mount Govardhan present a productive challenge to some of the problematic features of Western thought to which Mathews and Metzner refer. The following incident provides exemplary illustration of the non-dual worldview of Braj Vaishnavism and concomitant conduct in the context of Mount Govardhan.

On a trip from his home in Varanasi to Delhi, my friend Navneet visited me in Jatipura. He has a small tree nursery on his property and brought with him a few trees to plant on the slopes of Mount Govardhan, a long-held desire. We set out one morning in search of a shovel with which to plant the young trees. But once they understood what he had planned, most of the villagers living next to the mountain refused to loan Navneet a shovel. When he finally obtained one and started up the mountain, a large number of villagers quickly assembled and shouted at him to stop. "Don't use a shovel! It will harm Giriraj-ji! You must use only your hands for planting trees on the mountain!" Eventually, Navneet surrendered the shovel and found a place where pockets of soft dirt could be removed by hand.

The villagers were greatly worried that a shovel would strike the mountain's stone surface, thereby causing pain. This reveals a strong assumption of presence in the stone of Mount Govardhan, and demonstrates a tender concern and protective attitude for the mountain. Here, in the case of Navneet's shovel, an ethical position of reverence and care toward rocks was asserted. What might be the implications of the notion of pervasive presence in the physical world for environmental ethics, and more specifically, what might the worship of Mount Govardhan contribute to such considerations?

In a follow-up article to his seminal statement on the relationship between religion and environmental attitudes and behavior, Lynn White wrote:

"Do people have ethical obligations toward rocks?" . . . If the time comes when to any considerable group of us such a question is no longer ridiculous, we may be on the verge of a change of value structure that will make possible measures to cope with the growing ecological crisis.[34]

Although he makes no mention of Hinduism in this article, Navneet's incident on Mount Govardhan makes clear Braj Vaishnavism's contribution to the expansion of environmental ethics that White promotes. Devotees of Mount Govardhan typically exhibit great love for the mountain and all its stones through a great variety of worshipful activities. Moreover, shoes are never to be worn on the mountain, and any harm to it is to be assiduously avoided. Although some careless pilgrims do throw trash around Mount Govardhan's circumambulatory pathway, there are devotees of the mountain who engage in picking up this garbage as a form of loving service (*seva*). All this has to do with the belief that the mountain is an embodied form of divinity to which people have ethical obligations.

To be clear, the environmental ethic associated with Mount Govardhan is not an explicit or elaborate ethic, but rather an implicit and emerging one. Poul Pedersen has warned that since the environmental crisis we are experiencing today is a new one for humanity, no full-blown environmental ethic can be found in the scriptures or practices of any existing Asian religious traditions.[35] More recently Emma Tomalin has argued for a distinction between what she calls bio-divinity and environmental concerns. Bio-divinity refers to the notion that nature is infused with divinity, an idea prevalent in India for centuries. Tomalin insists that "there is an immense difference between the priorities and concerns of the modern environmentalist and the world-views of much earlier Hindu sages, poets, and philosophers."[36] Acknowledging that an explicit environmental ethic may not be found within established Hinduism, however, does not mean that aspects of Hinduism cannot be interpreted in a manner that supports contemporary environmental thinking, as religious traditions are always changing in the face of the historical challenges of their day. This, in fact, is what is happening in a variety of ways within Hinduism today, including Braj Vaishnavism. In face of new problematic conditions in the landscape, devotional behavior toward rivers, trees, and mountains is now beginning to take a form that many would label environmental activism.[37]

But can the worship of a particular mountain, or even more so a particular stone, lead to a more universal ethic of wider environmental care? Although some worshipers of Mount Govardhan limit their concern to this singular mountain, the following testimony suggests it might. A man living in the town of Govardhan who had been worshiping a Giriraj *shila* for over thirty years told me that on several occasions he has had an experience where the presence (*svarupa*) of his particular *shila* expanded in a vision to include the entire Govardhan mountain. The vision of this particular stone, however, did not stop there; it expanded successively to include all of Braj, then all of India, and finally the whole world. He informed me that this led him to see not just a Govardhan stone, but all mountains, and eventually everything in the world, as part of Krishna. (Here is an apt illustration of the realization of the philosophical proposal that "God is everything and everything is God" [*sarvatma-bhava*] through worshipful interaction with a particular form.) This, he said, was one of the great benefits of worshiping Mount Govardhan. This motivated the man to become more involved in caring for the physical environment as an aspect of Krishna.[38] The finite opened and broadened to reveal itself as non-different from the all-inclusive universal. Here is an environmental application of the fundamentally operative notion of non-dual play (*lila*) that underlies the theology and worship of Mount Govardhan in which there is a simultaneity of the finite particular with the all-inclusive infinite (i.e., *viruddha-dharma-ashraya*).[39]

Shrivatsa Goswami offered what he thought was a model for the extension of an implicit environmental ethic from a particular to a more general one:

The immediate effect of worshiping Mount Govardhan is a respect for the world. Generating respect and sensitivity toward nature is the direct effect of Govardhan *puja*. When Chaitanya saw Mount Govardhan he treated it with great respect. After this, wherever he saw a mountain he would treat it as Mount Govardhan and respect it. Here is a model for extending the care of Govardhan to other mountains. But this, of course, is rare. Ordinary devotees will most likely not act in this way, but *something* will happen. There will be some kind of effect. Many people will not even climb the mountain; they treat it in a very special way through *puja* and *parikrama*.

Then even if they are a thousand miles away from Mount Govardhan, they will have more general respect for mountains and trees.

He went on to express some environmental issues that arise for him while thinking about the worship of Mount Govardhan, as he understands the worship of Mount Govardhan to be an "environmental ritual."

Everything comes from nature; nature is divinized as the very source of all life. The central point of the Govardhan story is the realization of divine presence in all of nature. This world is the body of God, and God comes out of the physical heart of Mount Govardhan. The worship of Mount Govardhan is nature worship, the highest form of religion. It is an environmental ritual. Krishna only worships nature in the *Bhagavata Purana*, and he was the first to perform the exemplary worship of Mount Govardhan. He replaced the annual tax demanded by Indra with the loving service of the mountain, and by extension, all of nature. He demonstrated that worship of the gods like Indra is nonsense; worship of nature is the highest form of worship. Krishna lovingly serves his beloved (*priya*), who is Nature (*prakriti*). He thereby gives the key to how to celebrate and survive.

The *prasad* (graceful gift) of Govardhan is a vision of the unity of all being and the divinity of the world. Ecology's number one enemy is exploitation. Its opposite is treating nature with love, as a friend or a beloved. Deep exploitation is there in religion too. Thus Krishna had to push aside demanding ruler gods like Indra and worship nature directly. He made a temple out of the 14-mile boundary around Mount Govardhan that was open and accessible to all with no mediating priests. Krishna broke the hegemony of the vested interests and initiated direct worship. Everybody has direct access to worship Mount Govardhan with their own hands. Sharing resources fairly with all beings is important to our survival.[40]

Shrivatsa Goswami claims that the gift available in the worship of Mount Govardhan is an understanding of the divinity of the world, and that a central point of the mountain's story is the realization of divine presence in all nature. Major lessons in the worship of Mount Govardhan, then, include the assertion of divine presence throughout the material world, the realization of the sacrality of the natural world, and the benefits of a worshipful attitude toward the physical world. All this opens up the possibility of a different relationship with the world, particularly with the other-than-human. As

Shrivasta Goswami has said to me on many occasions: "Loving relationship (*sambandha*) is the key to ecological sustainability!"

All of this speaks to a general ethic derived from the worship of Mount Govardhan. But what might examples of specific environmental action conducted by devotees of Mount Govardhan look like on the ground? In an earlier work I wrote about a man named Madhava Das who had a special devotional attachment to Mount Govardhan and was dedicated to protecting the land of Braj as an embodied form of Krishna. The government of India had plans to build a railway line across Mount Govardhan in the late 1960s. He worried that this would cause painful damage to the mountain. A road had already been built over the mountain during the British period through a passageway just south of the Manasi Ganga pond, but first the stone had to be covered with a thick layer of dirt so as to pad the mountain and not injure it or the sensibilities of its worshipers.[41] Motivated by his view of Mount Govardhan as a living being, Madhav Das was instrumental in stopping plans for the railway line. His love for Govardhan, however, did not stop at this single mountain, but rather extended to include other sacred hills. In 1973 he succeeded in getting the government to pass legislation to protect eleven such hills that were slated to be sold and crushed for road-building materials. His devotion to the physical land of Braj inspired him to work to save not only sacred hills, but also their wildlife, ponds, and trees—all of which he considered as vital parts of the sacred hills. Because he regarded it as a very special embodied form of Krishna, this was particularly true of Mount Govardhan. I had the opportunity to interview him as he lay on his deathbed and asked him what he thought was the most important thing he did in his life. He replied, "I planted trees at the foot of Mount Govardhan."[42]

Environmental devotional efforts to plant trees in the *tareti* of Mount Govardhan and to save the sacred hills of Braj continue. The organization Seva Sansthan, located in the town of Govardhan under the leadership of a man named Bansi Bat Baba, is dedicated to restoring the forest surrounding Mount Govardhan. After obtaining permission from the Forest Department (Vana Vibhag) in charge of the land in the *tareti*, this organization established four tree nurseries and employed around 150 workers to plant and care for trees. Once planted, the young trees are caged to protect them from cows, monkeys, humans, and nilgai, then are watered and fertilized with compost made from shredded leaves and cow manure. In the spring of 2014 the general manager of these operations told me they had planted more than 200,000 trees since beginning in 2004, and that all this work is being done as *seva* ("loving service") to Giriraj-ji. He showed me a statement in one of the organization's brochures declaring that while many devotees of the mountain place an honorific flower garland (*phul mala*) around a single Govardhan stone, the aim of this *seva* is to provide a permanent natural garland (*prakriti mala*) around the entire mountain in the form of green trees and flowering bushes. "This," he concluded "is our great *seva* to Mount Govardhan."

Ramesh Baba, who lives in Braj near Radha's hometown of Barsana, is a man well known for his dedication to saving the natural features of Braj. He too is an ardent devotee of Mount Govardhan. Although he has organized demonstrations to draw awareness to the alarming plight of the polluted Yamuna River, his major passion has been the protection of the sacred hills in Braj threatened with mining for roadbed and building construction. In 2009 he led a protest against commercial mining of the sacred hills of Braj and was eventually successful in saving many of them through legal action. This environmental activism is motivated by his close relationship with Mount Govardhan. He told me that if any company were ever foolish enough to attempt to mine Mount Govardhan, he would personally lead an army of protestors from Braj to stop them. "We will never let any harm come to Giriraj-ji. Never!" he exclaimed, "He is our Great Lord!"

The worldview associated with the worship of Mount Govardhan avows that divine presence pervades the entire physical world, but is particularly present in special forms such as Mount Govardhan. Worshipers of Mount Govardhan report an important link between establishing a loving relationship with the mountain, often through anthropomorphic ritual techniques, and an ethics of care.[43] The research team of social psychologists headed by Kim-Pong Tam at the University of Hong Kong referenced in the previous chapter have corroborated this, claiming that anthropomorphism not only enhances close connection to some anthropomorphized natural entity, but also leads to greater care and involvement with conservation. In fact, this is their main interest in considering the place of anthropomorphism within environmentalism. Their research concludes: "This finding suggests that anthropomorphism can generate a sense of *connectedness* to the anthropomorphized entity, which in turn motivates *protective behavior*."[44] Although the Hong Kong researchers do not use this terminology, the worshipers of Mount Govardhan associate these anthropomorphic results with the acquisition of a greater sense of divine personality or presence; they routinely report that although divine presence is pervasive, the anthropomorphic ornamentation of a stone is a means to draw out and amplify its *svarupa*—that presence of the playful shape-shifting god Krishna who displays endless circularity in his paradoxical loving actions.

Krishna is the loving cowherd worshiping the mountain, and the loving mountain worshiping the cowherd. Or we might say that he is the cowherd worshiping the cowherd as a mountain, and the mountain worshiping the mountain as a cowherd. In this non-teleological circular play of love, we glimpse another claim made by many worshipers of Mount Govardhan, and perhaps this is the most "impossible" aspect made possible in the worship of Mount Govardhan. At the highest level, loving worship itself is not only a means but also the supreme reward. It is a way of consciously participating (*bhakti*) in the marvelous play of the Ultimate. The experience of a joyful love toward the world around us is itself the reward of that special love.

The issue of presence is linked in important ways to other issues raised in this book: the potential shortcomings inherent in the routine interpretive application of the concept of idolatry, reconsiderations of the value of "materiality," reflections on the significance of a theology of immanence, a renewed assessment of anthropomorphism, and deliberations on possibilities involved in regarding the unified infinite in and as a multitude of finite forms. Consideration of these issues jointly facilitates the opening of new possibilities in the human relationship with the more-than-human world. Whether it be with a mountain (Govardhan), a river (Yamuna), a forest (Vrindaban), or the land itself (Braj), all loving interaction is an opportunity to experience the sacred blissful quality of life from which egoistic exploitation—as Shrivatsa Goswami declares—cuts one off. It's all One playing with Itself, and the point is to participate reverently in that play with sensitive care and appreciative joy. To feel a loving presence in a stone, how wonderful would that be.

Translations

"Forty Verses in Praise of the King of Mountains" (*Giriraj Chalisa*)[1]

Glory be to Giriraj, the Great King of the region of Braj, who is honored by the whole world. (1)

You are an embodied form of Vishnu, and the whole world offers its all to your grandeur. (2)

Brilliant splendor graces your golden peak, and all the gods and sages come to see you. (3)

You have peaceful heavenly caves, in which ardent meditators remain in contemplation. (4)

You are the crown prince of Mount Drona who makes successful all the activities of your devotees. (5)

You won the heart of the sage Pulastya, who showed you the great favor of taking you away with him. (6)

When all the best of the sages gathered together in Braj, you saw this and came to dwell in the land of Braj. (7)

The land of Braj is Vishnu's charming paradise that features the Yamuna River, Govardhan Mountain, and Vrindaban Forest. (8)

Upon seeing it, the gods desired in their hearts to live here, and so turned themselves into many different forms. (9)

Some assumed the form of monkeys, while others became deer; some took the form of trees, and others creepers. (10)

This heavenly abode is extremely blissful, and became known as the land for supreme spiritual practice. (11)

At the end of the third of the four ages Krishna, the very source of bliss and enemy of the demon Mura, manifest here. (12)

Your magnificence is praised as Krishna, and all hearts became intent on worshipping you. (13)

All the residents of Braj were called to gatherer everything necessary to worship Mount Govardhan. (14)

The announcement for this worship was made, and all the residents of Braj brought what was needed from their homes. (15)

While the cowherds assembled and performed your worship, you assumed a thousand-armed form. (16)

During the worship, Krishna revealed himself (to be the mountain) and received all the food for which he asked. (17)

The hearts of all the men and women filled with delight upon witnessing this, and they sang glorious praises to Giriraj, Best of Mountains. (18)

Indra, king of the gods, became very angry with this and sent stormy rain clouds to destroy Braj. (19)

Lifting the mountain with his hand and using it as a huge umbrella, Krishna saved Braj; not a single drop of water fell beneath it. (20)

The heavy rains lasted for seven days, until the stream of water flowing from the clouds was spent. (21)

Cowherd Krishna held you upon his finger; all glory be to the Savior of Braj. (22)

After the arrogance of Indra was exhausted, he begged for forgiveness again and again as he acknowledged his offense. (23)

"Save me! I take your refuge! Please forgive my mistake, O Lord!" (24)

After bowing humbly again and again, Indra performed the fourteen-mile circum-ambulation of Mount Govardhan. (25)

He joined his palms together and sang a song of praise, accompanied by his cow Surabhi and his elephant Airavat. (26)

Astonished by having received the gift of fearlessness, Indra bowed in gratitude and returned to his own abode. (27)

Anyone who listens to this story intently, goes to the abode of Indra, king of the gods, upon death. (28)

Devotees who recite your name, O Govardhan, achieve salvation. (29)

All sorrows are eliminated for the person who has sight (*darshan*) of you. (30)

This human life will be very blessed for a person who sips water (*achaman*) from one of the ponds (situated at the base of Govardhan). (31)

The person who bathes in the Manasi Ganga pond will go directly to heaven. (32)

No trouble or sickness will come near the person who pours milk on and offers food to (Mount Govardhan). (33)

All the heart's desires will certainly be fulfilled by offering water, flowers, and *tulsi* leaves (to Mount Govardhan). (34)

The treasure house of a person who offers a continual stream of milk around the mountain will be filled with abundance. (35)

A person who stays awake all night worshiping (Mount Govardhan) will never experience the sorrows of poverty. (36)

You are the savior who has taken the form of a dark stone that gives to his devotees complete liberation and devotion. (37)

A person without a son who meditates on you will surely obtain a son. (38)

Those who circumambulate you prostrating continuously (*dandavati parikrama*) will easily cross over the ocean of worldly troubles. (39)

No other god in this decadent age (*kali yug*) is equal to you; therefore, all the gods, sages and people worship you. (40)

"Eight Verses in Praise of the Holder of Shri Giriraj" (*Shri Girirajadhari Ashtakam*)[2]

He acts according to the desires of his devotees; he spreads his fame by means of such acts as stealing milk; and he gives immense joy to the young cowherd women. This is my Lord, the one holding the Blessed King of Mountains. (1)

He forever sports with the many women of Vraja; he drives away all darkness with the brilliance of his limbs; and he overwhelms all ignorance with the ecstasy of his love play. This is my Lord, the one holding the Blessed King of Mountains. (2)

He provides great joy to the peacocks with the sweet sound of his flute; he spreads his infinite nectar with his dancing feet; and as mere play he killed the demon that assumed the form of a calf.
This is my Lord, the one holding the Blessed King of Mountains. (3)

He slayed the demon Shambara for the benefit of the forest-dwelling women; he showers kindness on the Goddess of Abundance (Lakshmi); and he enjoys the fruits and roots found on Mount Govardhan.
This is my Lord, the one holding the Blessed King of Mountains. (4)

He steals the clothes of the women on the bank of the Yamuna; he satisfies the desires of the young women with his arts of love; and he grazes his herd of cows in the forest of Vrindavana.
This is my Lord, the one holding the Blessed King of Mountains. (5)

He brings great happiness to Nanda, chief of Vraja; he quells the arrogance of Indra, king of the gods; and he relishes fruits and roots in the forest of Vrindavana.
This is my Lord, the one holding the Blessed King of Mountains. (6)

He eradicates the darkness that obscures the brilliant moon of the heart/mind; he calls young women to him with the sound of his flute; and he revels in an ocean of delight while dancing enthusiastically in the celebratory love dance.
This is my Lord, the one holding the Blessed King of Mountains. (7)

He moves like a lusty, intoxicated elephant; he wears a long garland of beautiful
flowers that sways as he walks; and he expands its immense joy by letting it mingle
with the delightful place of Lakshmi upon touching his chest.
This is my Lord, the one holding the Blessed King of Mountains. (8)

Selection of Well-known Poems about Mount Govardhan

Braj poem of praise by Paramananda[3]

Worship Govardhan and sing the praises of Govardhan.
All the worshipers of Govardhan always
   bow their heads to Govardhan. (1)
Govardhan is mother, father, and guru.
All the gods meditate continuously on Govardhan.
Govardhan is the cow of plenty and the wishing tree.
Whatever one requests from Govardhan is granted. (2)
Govardhan features narrow valleys to shelter cows and deep caves.
He provides protection in the home, the forest, or wherever.
Govardhan is the Beloved of Paramananda,
   and we too ever love Govardhan. (3)

Three Braj poems identifying the two identities of Krishna by Surdas[4]

Nanda experienced great joy watching the offering being consumed
   after Krishna manifested himself as the deity (Mount Govardhan). (1)
Observing the mountain consume the food offering,
   the residents of Braj considered their lives to be successful. (2)
Lalita informed Radha: "The one eating is Krishna, who is the same as the boy
   holding Nanda's hand. (3)
I recognize Krishna's cleverness; he himself (as the mountain)
   is devouring Indra's sacrifice. (4)
Over there he is eating and here he is beginning to speak,
   saying to the feasting mountain: (5)
   'What I said has come to be!'
Assuming a form with a thousand arms
   he gobbled up the food offering. (6)
Other gods take his refuge, for here he is talking and
   over there he is eating." (7)
Such is the divine play (*lila*) of Surdas's lord, the darling of Nanda and
   the handsome dandy of Braj. (8)

The Best of Mountains is the same as Krishna (Shyam). He (as the mountain)
   stretched out his thousand arms and was able to eat the entire food offering. (1)[5]
He (as the cowherd boy) held the hand of Nanda, and also stood in the form of the
   mountain. Radha's girlfriend Lalita said to her: "Look at this divine form
   (*svarupa*). (2)
"There are the earrings, and there is the yellow shawl. The splendor of the beauty of
   Dark Krishna is identical to the beauty of the Dark Mountain." (3)
The woman Badarola, who lives in Brishabhanu's house as Radha's attendant, made
   a food offering to the mountain, and he stretched out his arms and took it. (4)
Radha was mesmerized while gazing at the Dark One and observing his divine
   beauty. Sur's Lord charmed his Beloved Radha with a passionate sidelong
   glance. (5)

Seeing the divine beauty (of the mountain), Radha was awestruck. Blossoming into
   understanding, she said to her girlfriends: (1)[6]
"He himself is the (mountain) god, and he is the one conducting the worship. He
   himself is eating the mound of food." (2)
Hastily he eats his fill. One of Radha's companions came with her from
   Barsana. (3)
Her name is Badarola, and she made a food offering to the mountain, who reached
   out his arms to receive it.
Over there the mountain ate up and relished the entire offering of Badarola. (4)
Surdas's Lord (Krishna) is the one who is eating. How could he possibly take the
   form of a mountain? (5)

Braj poem about Govardhan puja by Meha[7]

Please listen to my view Father:
You should worship Govardhan.
All the offerings you gathered for Indra
   should be given to Govardhan.
This Treasure of Abundance
   provides us with roots and fruits.
Whatever we ask for Govardhan grants us.
Every day I graze my cows
   on this mountain without fear.
Fill pots with vast amounts of milk,
   yogurt, relishes,and ambrosia to offer him;
And trays heaped with honeyed fruits, cooked foods, and sweets.

The elders sat and decided to do what Krishna had said.
We should prepare a mound of various foods
   and offer it to the mountain.

This mountain assumes a variety of forms.
He is the protector of the people of Braj,
   the Supreme God of the gods, and my Beloved.
Krishna, the son of Nanda, assumed the form of the mountain
   and ate the food.
Meha says: The Beloved who assumes the form of the mountain
   asked for more and more of the offering and consumed it all.

Braj poem about Govardhan puja *by Surdas*[8]

Krishna, son of Nanda, explained the method of worshiping Giriraj, King of
   Mountains. Groups of cowherd women gathered together and sang auspicious
   songs. (1)
They bathe Giriraj with Ganges water and then honor him with large quantities of
   milk. They dress him with an assortment of clothing and apply sandal paste to his
   body. (2)
They burn incense and wave the honorific *arati* flame before him, then offer him a
   heap of food. They apply a tilak to his forehead, give him a spiced betel-leaf treat,
   and drape a flower garland around his neck. (3)
They then go to the cow pen and feed the cows and their calves. Afterwards
   Krishna, Holder of the Mountain, eats and Sur becomes blissful. (4)

Braj poem about Govardhan puja *by Chaturbhujadas*[9]

Krishna, Holder of the Mountain, comes chattering effusively before Shri
   Govardhan to perform the mountain's worship.
Krishna bathed the mountain with water from the Mansi Ganga pond, and then
   honored him by pouring milk over him. (1)
Krishna rinsed the mountain clean, massaged him with perfumed oil, venerated
   him with incense and an honorific flame, then offered him a large quantity
   of food. The Holder of the Mountain then gave the mountain a spiced betel-leaf
   treat and waved the honorific *arati* lamp before him as the women of Braj
   gathered and sang auspicious songs. (2)
The cowherds shouted jubilant praises and feasted the mountain. They set him up
   on a seat and fastened a turban to his head. Caturbhujadas' Lord, Holder
   of the Mountain,[10] is loved as the King of Braj now and in age after age. (3)

Braj poem about Govardhan puja *by Paramanandadas*[11]

Again and again Hari (Krishna) taught the people with his sweet words. "Listen, I
give you the single most important instruction of all four goals of life. (1)
Please quickly do what I say: Gather together milk and rice, and satisfy
Govardhan by worshiping him (with it)." (2)
Here the celebrated words of Krishna, the Son of Nanda, are honored.
Paramananda's Supreme Lord broke the anger of Indra, who performed the
misdeed with rain. (3)

Braj poem about the Govardhan tareti *by Hairiray*[12]

Reside at the base (*tareti*) of Blessed Govardhan.
Fix your mind constantly on the lotus-feet of the
Enchanting Cowherd Lad.
Your body will become ecstatic rolling in the dust of Braj
and bathing in the Govinda Pond.
Reveal the highest love in your heart to the
Sensitive Beloved, who assumes the form
of the Blessed Mountain.

Braj poem about the Govardhan tareti *by Rasikadas*[13]

The blessed land (*tareti*) around Shri Giriraj is a treasure of joy.
One should sip from and bathe in the water of its ponds, thereby taking refuge in
Braj again and again. (1)
There one should offer barley flatbread topped with *tenti* berries. (2)
Says Rasikadas, the supreme feet of the Divine Beloved destroy all sorrows. (3)

Govardhan Aratis

Shri Giriraj-ji ki Arati[14]

I continually perform *arati* to the Best of the Mountains (Girivar).
He is a form of Hari dressed in a peacock-crown and holding a flute.
He is the most beloved of the Daughter of Shri Brishabhanu (Radha).
He is the son of Drona and protector of the devotees.
He is the remover of all suffering, poverty, fear, and destruction.
He gives wonderful pleasure with his vegetation and medicinal herbs.
The sage Pulasta brought this mountain here through his ascetic powers.
Seeing Braj, the King of Mountains became very heavy.

The best of the sages could not budge him.

Because of this the King of Mountains received a curse to diminish in size.

He accepted the command to shrink the amount of a sesame seed every day.

The King of Mountains brings great success and abundance.

He is the compassionate Lord who removes all troubles.

So says Ramdas, who has taken refuge with this Lord.

Shri Giriraj Arati[15]

Om, the highest of all glories to Giriraj!

The highest of all glories to Lord Giriraj!

You protect the honor of your devotees in difficult situations.

All the gods headed by Indra remain in meditation on you.

The seers, sages, and people sing your glories,

thereby crossing over the ocean of troublous existence.

Om, the highest of all glories to Giriraj!

You have a beautiful form that consists of dark shiny stone.

The devotees' hearts become enchanted while looking at your groves and forests.

Om, the highest of all glories to Giriraj!

In your middle is Manasi Ganga, a pond that removes the filth of this decadent age.

One can cross over the river of death by lighting lamps around its shores.

Om, the highest of all glories to Giriraj!

Navala and Apsara Ponds adorn your right side, creating great joy.

Radha and Krishna Ponds are on your left side, removing great misfortunes.

Om, the highest of all glories to Giriraj!

You are the granter of liberation and the Supreme Lord for this decadent age.

You are the protector of the humble, and the Lord who is the Inner Controller.

Om, the highest of all glories to Giriraj!

We take refuge in you, O Giridhari, Best of Mountains.

O Son of Devaki, you who are the cause of the well-being of your devotees,

shower us with your brilliant grace.

Om, the highest of all glories to Giriraj!

A person who circumambulates you, performs your worship, and sings your *arati*
regularly does not take conditioned birth again.

Om, the highest of all glories to Giriraj!

Shri Giriraj-ji ki Arati[16]

Om, glory be to Krishna in the form of Giriraj (King of Mountains)!
All glory be to Lord Giriraj!

You fulfill the wishes of those who take your refuge.

You appeared in a body of stone,
as the Lord who is compassionate toward devotees.

You fulfill their wishes, since you are their inner spirit.

You have a beautiful dark blue body, and speak sweet words.

You look upon us full of love, and see the splendor of our lives.

You have a peacock-feather crown on your head,
and a sandalwood *tilak* on your forehead.

You wear a Vaijanti garland around your neck,
which cuts through the bondage of conditioned existence.

You sport an attractive lower garment, with a yellow scarf above.

You play the flute with your lips while you frolic in the form of a human.

When Indra became very angry with the residents of Braj,
you subdued his pride for the benefit of the good.

You led the residents of Braj in the worship of the Best of the Mountains,
and worshiped yourself (in the form of the mountain), Oh Lord,
in a display of your creative power (*maya*).

When Brahma stole the cowherds and their cows and you took on their form,
Brahma became greatly confused, but you instantly took away his troubles.

When as the Charming Flute Player you placed the flute to your lower lip,
You enchanted the Braj gopis and fulfilled their desires.

One who sings this *arati* with love to the Lord of Braj,
receives *bhakti* along with the liberation offered in Kashi.

Om, glory be to Krishna in the form of Giriraj!
All glory be to Lord Giriraj!

You flood with compassion those who take your shelter.

Notes

Introduction

1. From a conversation with a devotee of Mount Govardhan in the town of Govardhan, located in the western portion of the Indian state of Uttar Pradesh. I spent the academic year of 2013–14 living on the edge of Mount Govardhan in the small pilgrimage town of Jatipura while studying conceptions of and worshipful interaction with this sacred mountain. In addition, I had two follow-up periods of a few months in the spring of 2015 and the fall of 2016, plus a couple weeks in 2017 and 2018. During this time I compiled several notebooks of interviews, conversations, and observations of devotees of Mount Govardhan.
2. *People Trees: The Worship of Trees in Northern India* (New York: Oxford University Press, 2013).
3. Clifford Geertz, *The Interpretations of Cultures* (New York: Basic Books, 1973), p. 22.
4. Ibid., p. 21.
5. Clifford Geertz, *Local Knowledge* (New York: Basic Books, 1983), p. 69.

Chapter 1

1. Resident of Jatipura.
2. Brajesh Joshi, *Shri Giriraj Kripa Phal* (Jatipura: Shri Giriraj Yamuna Bharati Sahitya Sansthan, 2013), p. 23.
3. Resident of the town of Govardhan.
4. This account of the creation of Mount Govardhan is drawn from the "Girirajakhanda" of the *Garga Samhita* 5.9.25–43. The edition of this Sanskrit text I draw from is *Garga Samhita*, part 1, edited by Vibhutibhushan Bhattacharya (Varanasi: Sampurnananda Sanskrit University, 1996), pp. 337–39. I cite and translate from this Sanskrit text throughout this book. An English translation of this text is available in multiple volumes. This story is described in a volume titled *Giriraja: King of Mountains* (3.9.25–43 in this version) translated by Danavir Goswami (Kanas City, MO: Rupanuga Vedic College, 2010), pp. 264–77.
5. The *Garga Samhita* is of enormous importance for understanding conceptions of Mount Govardhan. It is a text known and extolled by many Braj pandits. One explained, "One comes to understand much about Govardhan from reading the *Bhagavata Purana*, but the *Garga Samhita* is most important." Unfortunately, Western scholars have largely disregarded this text. Moreover, Alan Entwistle claims the *Garga Samhita* to be a Pushti Margiya text (*Braj: Centre of Krishna Pilgrimage*

[Groningen: Egbert Forsten, 1987], p. 47). I'm not convinced of this, and have found in my own research that all Braj Vaishnava groups refer to it as authoritative. See, for example, the collection of articles published in *Giriraj Govardhan*, ed. Madhur Bhagra (Vrindaban: Shri Hari Nikunj Ashram, 1989).

6. I have taken this account from Narad Baba Mohan Das, *Sampurna Braj Darshanam* (Vrindaban: Shri Radha Mohan Satsang Mandal, 1987), p. 52; and from Narayana Bhatta, *Vraja Bhakti Vilasa*, ed. Krishnadas Baba (Kusum Sarovar: Krishnadas Baba, 1951), 5.1. In his telling of this story, Devakinandan Kumheriya states that Krishna will worship Govardhan with his own hands and will establish him as God of gods (*devo ke deva*)—an extra bonus for missing the opportunity to serve Rama (*Govardhan Mahatmya* [Govardhan: Giriraj Pushtak Bhandar, 2007], pp. 17–20).

7. I owe great thanks to Professor Abhijit Basu of the Department of Geological Science at Indiana University–Bloomington for much of this information.

8. *Garga Samhita* 5.9.39.

9. Shyammanohar Goswami, *Giriyaga* (Varanasi: Giridhar Prakashan, 2011), p. 301. This Pushti Margiya leader is head of the sixth house in Varanasi. He is different from the well-known Pushti Margiya scholar by the same name who lives in Mumbai.

10. Rupa Gosvamin, *Hansaduta*, verse 22. See Sanskrit text with Bengali translation and commentary by Vibhas Prakash Gangopadhyaya (Calcutta: Shri Amritalal Dutt, 1923), p. 28.

11. More information about the culture and landscape of Braj can be found in my book *Journey through the Twelve Forests: An Encounter with Krishna* (New York: Oxford University Press, 1994).

12. Alan Entwistle, *Braj: Centre of Krishna Pilgrimage*, pp. 279, 286.

13. Kumheriya, *Govardhan Mahatmya*, p. 10.

14. Diana L. Eck, *Darśan: Seeing the Divine Image in India* (New York: Columbia University Press, [1981] 1998), p. 48.

15. Charlotte Vaudeville writes: "If the cowherd god comes from the banks of the Yamuna, if he is the 'child of Mathura in the north,' it is in Southern India neverthe-less that he prospered and that his legend, highly charged with its primitive origins, was progressively refined by and assimilated in Vaishnava *bhakti*. This process comes to an end, in the South, towards the end of the tenth century, with the compilation of the *Bhagavata Purana*, a real Krishnaite bible, which becomes the starting point for medieval and modern Vaishnavism throughout India" ("The Cowherd God in Ancient India," in *Pastoralists and Nomads in South Asia*, ed. L. S. Leshnik and G. D. Sontheimer [Wiesbaden: Otto Harrassowitz, 1975], p. 116). See also Friedhelm E. Hardy, *Viraha Bhakti: The Early History of Krishna Devotion in South India* (Oxford: Oxford University Press, 1983).

16. This date is given by Entwistle in his work on Braj, but he questions its accuracy by suggesting that the date was more likely around the beginning of the second decade of the sixteenth century. See Entwistle, *Braj*, pp. 141–42.

17. This was accomplished in a sixteenth-century Sanskrit text titled the *Bhaktirasamritasindhu*. See my translation of this text: *The Bhaktirasamritasindhu of*

Rupa Gosvamin (New Delhi: Indira Gandhi National Centre for the Arts in association with Motilal Banarsidass, 2003).

18. K. M. Jhaveri, *Imperial Farmans (A.D. 1577 to A.D. 1805) granted to the Ancestors of His Holiness the Tikayat Maharaj* (Bombay, 1928), Farman No IV-A.

19. For a good account of this, see Cynthia Packert, *The Art of Loving Krishna: Ornamentation and Devotion* (Bloomington: Indiana University Press, 2010), pp. 132–44.

20. K. Natwar-Singh, *Maharaj Suraj Mal* (New Delhi: Vikas, 1983), p. 2.

21. Lord Lake's failed siege of Bharatpur took place in 1805.

22. *Bhagavata Purana* 10.24–25. The *Bhagavata Purana* is the authoritative text par excellence for the Vaishnava culture of Braj.

23. One of the earliest and finest surviving sculptural depictions of Krishna holding Mount Govardhan is a fourth-century one housed in the Bharat Kala Bhavan art museum on the Banaras Hindu University campus in Varanasi. The mountain appears as a composite of stones, a feature that appears to be consistent through the ages.

24. "*shailo (a)smi,*" *Bhagavata Purana* 10.24.35.

25. "*namo cakre . . . atmana atmane,*" *Bhagavata Purana* 10.24.36. This is referred to as the "great secret" in later Vaishnava writings.

26. *Tarahati Shri Govardhana ki rahiyai. Nitya prati Madana Gopala Lala ke carana kamala cita laiyai. Tana pulakita Braja-raja me lotata, Govinda kunda me nhaiyai. "Rasika Pritama" hita cita ki bate, Shri Giridhari-ji so kahiyai.* This poem, composed by Hariraya (a great-great-grandson of Vallabhachaya), is very well known around Mount Govardhan and throughout Braj. The version I have cited here is in *Hariraya-ji ka Pada Sahitya*, compiled and edited by Prabhudayal Mital (Mathura: Sahitya Sansthan, 1962), p. 218. Another similar poem follows the translation of this one in the Appendix.

27. R. S. McGregor, *Hindi-English Dictionary* (Delhi: Oxford University Press, 1993), p. 443.

28. *Garga Samhita* 5.10.14.

29. *Bhaktirasamritasindhu* 1.1.12. See Haberman, *The Bhaktirasamritasindhu of Rupa Gosvamin*, pp. 4–5. The citation is from the *Narada Pancharatra*.

30. Vallabhacharya, *Nirodhalakshana*, verses 7 and 12. See Redington, pp. 178–79, and Shyamdas, pp. 100–101. Vallabhacharya's text *Sannyasanirnaya*, verse 11, is also relevant here. Both of these short texts form part of the "Sixteen Books" of Vallabhacharya.

31. Paul M. Toomey, *Food From the Mouth of Krishna: Feasts and Festivities in a North Indian Pilgrimage Centre* (Delhi: Hindustan, 1994), p. 43.

32. See, for example, Omprakash Yadav, *Haridasvarya: Shri Giriraj Govardhan* (Baravani, M. P.: Antarrashtiya Pushti-Margiya Vaisnava Parishad, 2011), p. 16.

33. One wonders if this might have some connection to the *saptapadi*, the "seven steps" taken by a couple around a sacred fire to consummate their wedding.

34. A story is told in the *Do Sau Bavan Vaishnavan ki Varta* about a devotee of Govardhan named Ramdas who achieved a high level of devotional ability and a direct vision of Shri Govardhan Natha-ji by reciting mantras at the Dandavati *shila*. See Gokulnath, *Do Sau Bavan Vaishnavan ki Varta*, ed. Vrajbhushanlal Maharaj and Dvarakadas Parikh, vol. 2, varta #95, (Indor: Vaishnava Mitra Mandal, 2000), pp. 52–58. For

an English translation of this story, see *252 Vaishnavas*, trans. Shyamdas (Gokul, India: Pratham Peeth Publications, 2003), vol. 2, pp. 37–40.

35. Joshi, *Shri Giriraj Kripa Phal*, p. 86.

36. Yadav, *Haridasvarya*, p. 16.

37. This story was told to me at the pond by a resident of Jatipura; it is also recorded in ibid., p. 17.

38. According to Pushti Margiya literature, each of the eight famous poets known as the Ashta Chap are associated with eight doorways into Govardhan, through which it is said they entered the mountain. These are listed in the life story (*varta*) of Surdas: Bilachukund is identified as the doorway of the poet Krishnadas. Additionally, Surdas's doorway is above Govindakund in front of Chandrasarovar in Parasoli, Chita Swami's doorway is just above Apsarakund, Paramananda's doorway is above Surabhikund, Govinda Swami's doorway is near Kadamkhandi, Chaturbhujadas's doorway is near Rudrakund, Nandadas's doorway is near Manasi Ganga, and Kumbhandas's doorway is in front of Anyor in the village of Yamunavati. See Gokulnath, *Chaurasi Vaishnavan ki Varta*, ed. Jayaben Shukla (Indor: Vaishnava Mitra Mandal, 2011), pp. 466–67. For an English translation of this account, see Shyamdas and Vallabhadas, *Krishna's Inner Circle: The Ashta Chap Poets* (Gokul, India: Pratham Preeth Publications, 2009), p. 57.

39. This particular account is taken from Krishnadas Baba, *Braj Mandal Darshan* (Kusum Sarovar, Govardhan: Krishnadas Baba, 1958), p. 43. Some versions name the threatening demon as the bull Arishta.

40. *Varaha Purana* 162 15–17. For Sanskrit text and English translation, see *The Varaha Purana*, ed. Anand Swarup Gupta (Varanasi: All-India Kashiraj Trust, 1981), pp. 704–705.

41. An account of Vallabha's circumambulation of Mount Govardhan is found in the seventeenth-century text written by Gokulnath, *Chaurasi Baithak Charitra*, ed. Niranjandev Sharma (Mathura: Shri Govardhan Granthamala Karyalaya, 1967), pp. 21–31. This text is translated by Shyamdas, *Chaurasi Baithak: Eighty Four Seats of Shri Vallabhacharya* (Baroda: Shri Vallbha Publications, 1985. The account of Chaitanya's circumambulation of Govardhan after a bath in Manasi Ganga is recorded in the *Chaitanya Charitamrita*, Madhya Lila, Chapter 18. For the Bengali text, see Krishnadas Kaviraj, *Shri Chaitanya Charitamrita*, with commentaries by Sacchidananda Bhaktivinod Thakur and Barshobhanabidayita Das (Calcutta: Gaudiya Math, 1958), p. 681. A very good English translation of this text is the *Chaitanya Charitamrita of Krishnadasa Kaviraja*, trans. Edward C. Dimock, ed. Tony K. Stewart (Cambridge, MA: Harvard University Press, 1999), p. 598.

42. Rupa Gosvamin, *Mathura Mahatmya*, verse 420. For an English translation with Sanskrit text, see *Mathura Mahatmya: The Glories of the Mathura-mandala*, ed. Pundarika Vidyanidhi, trans. Bhumipati Dasa (Vrindaban: Rasbihari Lal & Sons, n.d.), p. 139.

43. The first two incidents are referred to in Vijay, *Braj Bhumi Mohini* (Vrindaban: Shri Prem Hari Press, 1985), p. 117. The latter incident is recorded in Gokulnath, *Chaurasi Baithak Charitra*, pp. 22–23.

44. Kumheriya, *Govardhan Mahatmya*, p. 46.
45. Based on a reading of Shrisvarupadas Maharaj, *Shri Govardhan Parikrama* (Radhakund: Pulak and Samir Devanath, 2011), pp. 46–47
46. This declaration is sometimes supported by the assertion in the *Chaitanya Charitamrita* that "the sweetness of the pond is the same as the sweetness of Radha, and the greatness of the pond is the same as the greatness of Radha" (*Chaitanya Charitamrita*, Madhya-lila 18.11).
47. I use the term "Braj Vaishnavism" to refer to those religious traditions that originated during the Krishnaite cultural renaissance that flourished in the region of Braj in the sixteenth century and still regard Braj as their main focus yet today. These primarily include the Pushti Margiya and Gaudiya Vaishnava traditions, but also other smaller *sampradayas* and non-denominational groups that all share a similar theological perspective, such as the Radhavallabhis, Nimbarkis, and followers of Swami Haridas.
48. Rupa Goswamin's *Upadeshamrita*. For a complete translation, see my *Journey Through the Twelve Forests*, p. 100.
49. Based on account found in Kumheriya, *Govardhan Mahatmya*, p. 37.
50. This story is also found in the *Bhagavata Purana* 10.27.
51. Legend has it that Shri Nath-ji will return to Braj and reside on the Govardhan Hill near Punchari. See *Giriyaga*, p. 301.
52. Shrisvarupadas, *Shri Govardhan Parikrama*, p. 39.
53. Some people regard Lautha as a form of Hanuman. See Padmalochan Das, *Madhurya Dhama* (Mayapur: Bhaktivedanta Book Trust, 1992), p. 92.
54. This account is based primarily on Charlotte Vaudeville's translation of this text found in "The Govardhan Myth in Northern India," *Indo-Iranian Journal*, vol. 22, no. 1 (1980): 15–45.
55. See ibid., pp. 37–38.
56. Friedhelm Hardy, "Madhavendra Puri: A Link between Bengal Vaishnavism and South Indian Bhakti," *Journal of the Royal Asiatic Society*, no. 1 (1974): 23–41.
57. *Chaitanya Charitamrita*, Madya-lila 4.21–109.
58. For a Pushti Margi account of this dispute, see the short biography (*varta*) of Krishnadas translated in Richard Barz, *The Bhakti Sect of Vallabhacharya* (Faridabad: Thomas Press, 1976), pp. 216–22.
59. The original form of Mathuradhish is now housed in a temple in Kota, Rajasthan. The form described here was taken out from a back room in the sixteenth-century temple in Jatipura and placed on the throne where the original Mathuradhish was worshiped.

Chapter 2

1. Sam D. Gill, "Play," in *Guide to the Study of Religion*, ed. Willi Braun and Russell T. McCutcheon (London and New York: Cassell, 2000), pp. 451–52.
2. The Rolling Stones, "Steel Wheels" (1989).

3. See Monier Monier-Williams, *A Sanskrit-English Dictionary* (Delhi: Motilal Banarsidass, 1981 [Oxford University Press, 1899]), pp. 586–87.

4. See R. S. McGregor, *The Oxford Hindi-English Dictionary*, p. 601.

5. I still think that the best book written on this subject is *The Social Construction of Reality: A Treatise in the Sociology of Knowledge* by Peter L. Berger and Thomas Luckmann (New York: Doubleday, 1966). This book was ranked the fifth most important book of the twentieth century by the International Sociological Association (http://www.isa-sociology.org/books/books10.htm). Berger and Luckmann further developed the work on multiple realities by Alfred Schutz, who himself was deeply influenced on this subject by William James's *Principles of Psychology*. See, for example, Alfred Schuetz, "On Multiple Realities," *Philosophy and Phenomenological Research*, vol. 5, no. 4 (June 1945): 533–76.

6. The anthropological implications of "world-openness" were first developed by the German biologist and philosopher Arnold Gehlen. See Peter L. Berger and Hansfried Kellner, "Arnold Gehlen and the Theory of Institutions," *Social Research*, vol. 32, no. 1 (Spring 1965): 110–115 (specifically referred to on p. 111).

7. Michael Taussig, *Mimesis and Alterity* (New York: Routledge, 1993), p. xv.

8. "We act and have to act as if mischief were not afoot in the kingdom of the real and that all around the ground lay firm" (ibid., p. xvii).

9. Quoted by Clifford Geertz, "Anti Anti-Relativism," *American Anthropologist*, new series, vol. 86, no. 2 (June 1984): 264–65.

10. *Histories*, 3.38; see Herodotus, *The Histories*, trans. Aubrey de Selincourt (London: Penguin Classics, 1996).

11. This man also explained that even within Hinduism there are people who do not accept this view. I spoke with another man who concurred: "People believe different things. Some believe God takes the form of a mountain or stone, others do not. If you regard (*manta*) the stone as God then you see God in it. If not, then you won't. Like the Arya Samajis. They do not worship any forms of God. For them God is formless. There are two ways of understanding God: with form (*sakar*) and without form (*nirakar*). Both are okay, but Bhagavan reveals himself to us in this mountain and we regard every stone on it as God."

12. Bronislaw Malinowski, *Argonauts of the Western Pacific* (Abingdon, UK: Routledge & Kegan, 1922), p. 25.

13. Edward W. Said, *Orientalism* (New York: Pantheon Books, 1978).

14. James Clifford and George E. Marcus, eds. *Writing Culture: The Poetics and Politics of Ethnography* (Berkeley: University of California Press, 1986).

15. Orin Starn, eds. "Introduction," in *Writing Culture and the Life of Anthropology* (Durham, NC: Duke University Press, 2015), p. 1.

16. Maurice Godelier, "In Today's World, Anthropology Is More Important than Ever," *Paideuma*, Bd. 56 (2010): 205.

17. This is a point made by Emmanuel Levinas. See *Totality and Infinity: An Essay on Exteriority* (Pittsburgh: Duquesne University Press, 1991).

18. R. Heber Newton, "Religion and Religions," *The North American Review*, vol. 178, no. 569 (1904): 546.

19. Ibid., pp. 553–54.

20. George Marcus and Michael Fischer argue that the Western intellectual atmos-phere has tended to promote the idea of a universal essence by downplaying differ-ence: "Consider, for instance, the humanist assertions of Mircea Eliade and others that, despite differences, all religions are ultimately the same, answering the same existential questions, and are capable of being placed in a common evolutionary sequence" (George E. Marcus and Michael M. J. Fischer, *Anthropology as Cultural Critique: An Experimental Moment in the Human Sciences* [Chicago: University of Chicago Press, 1999], p. 38).

21. Edward Said, *Orientalism*, p. 3.

22. See Edward B. Tylor, *The Origins of Culture* (New York: Harper and Brothers, [1871] 1958), p. 26.

23. Edward B. Tylor, *Religion in Primitive Culture* (New York: Harper and Brothers, [1871] 1958), p. 61. Emphasis added.

24. Ibid., pp. 250–51 and 254.

25. See my "On Trial: The Love of the Sixteen Thousand Gopees," *History of Religions*, vol. 33, no. 1 (1993): 44–70.

26. Abbe J. A. Dubois, *Hindu Manners, Customs and Ceremonies* (New Delhi: Book Faith India, [1897] 1999), p. 655.

27. Hans H. Penner, "Interpretation," in *Guide to the Study of Religion*, ed. Willi Braun and Russell T. McCutcheon (London: Cassell, 2000), p. 62.

28. Ibid., p. 68.

29. Many trace this phrase back to the second-century BCE Roman playwright Terence (Publius Terentius Afer), who wrote in one of his plays: "I am human, and nothing of that which is human is alien to me" (*Heauton Timorumenos*).

30. Slavenka Drakulic, *The Balkan Express: Fragments from the Other Side of the War* (New York: W.W. Norton, 1993), p. 144.

31. Rene Girard explores the demonizing and scapegoating of the other. See *The Scapegoat* (Baltimore, MD: John Hopkins University Press, 1989).

32. James Clifford and George E. Marcus, ed., *Writing Culture: The Poetics and Politics of Ethnography*, p. 7.

33. "Though we discern immediately the distinctive accent of Margaret Mead, Raymond Firth, or Paul Radin, we still cannot refer to the Samoans as 'Meadian' or call Tikopia a 'Firthian' culture as freely as we speak of Dickensian or Flaubertian worlds" (ibid., p. 13).

34. Ibid., pp. 23–24.

35. David Zeitlyn, "Understanding Anthropological Understanding: For a Merological Anthropology," *Anthropological Theory* 9 (2009): 211.

36. Ibid., p. 219.

37. The major source for this is *Bhagavata Purana* 10.25.19. The term *lilaya* also appears in this incident in *Vishnu Purana* 5.11.16. See Sanskrit text with English translation by H. H. Wilson (Delhi: Nag, [1864] 1980), vol. 2, p. 727, and *Garga Samhita* 5.3.15 (Bhattacharya edition, p. 311). For a study of the important concept of *lila* in Hindu

culture, I direct readers to William S. Sax, ed., *The Gods at Play: Lila in South Asia* (New York: Oxford University Press, 1995).

38. Gregory Bateson, *Steps to an Ecology of Mind* (Northvale, NJ: Jason Aronson, [1972] 1987), pp. 185–86.

39. Gregory Bateson, *Mind and Nature* (New York: Dutton, 1979), p. 139

40. Paul B. Armstrong, "Play and Cultural Differences," *The Kenyon Review*, new series, vol. 13, no. 1 (Winter, 1991): 157.

41. Ibid., p. 164.

42. Ibid., p. 162.

43. Godelier, "In Today's World, Anthropology Is More Important than Ever," p. 212.

44. Diana L. Eck, *Darśan: Seeing the Divine Image in India* (New York: Columbia University Press, [1981] 1998); Joanne Waghorne and Norman Cutler, eds., *Gods of Flesh, Gods of Stone: The Embodiment of Divinity in India* (New York: Columbia University Press [1985] 1996).

45. The *Bhaktirasamritasindhu*, a Sanskrit text composed in Vrindaban in the sixteenth century. I later published a translation of this text as *The Bhaktirasamritasindhu of Rupa Gosvamin*.

46. After my initial year of residence in this temple in Vrindaban, I lived within the Radharaman temple compound for three more years during subsequent research projects, have returned to this temple virtually every year since my first visit, and have spent time in hundreds of Hindu temples all over India, striving constantly to understand the kind of behavior taking place within them.

47. Armstrong, "Play and Cultural Difference," p. 163.

48. Godelier, "In Today's World, Anthropology Is More Important than Ever," p. 211.

49. Ibid., p. 212.

50. Armstrong, "Play and Cultural Difference," p. 162.

51. Ibid., p. 163.

52. Emmanuel Levinas, *Otherwise than Being or Beyond Essence*, trans. Alphonso Lingis (Pittsburg: Duquesne University Press, 1998).

53. Vincent Crapanzano, "The End—the Ends—of Anthropology," *Paideuma* (Frobenius Institute) Bd. 56 (2010): 186.

54. Alexis Nouss, "Translation and métissage," in *In Translation—Reflections, Refractions, Transformations*, ed. Paul St-Pierre and Prafulla C. Kar (Amsterdam: John Benjamins, 2007): 247.

55. Marcus and Fischer, *Anthropology as Cultural Critique*, p. 1.

56. Margaret Mead, *Coming of Age in Samoa: A Psychological Study of Primitive Youth for Western Civilization* (New York: William Morrow, [1928] 1966).

57. Crapanzano, "The End—the Ends—of Anthropology," p. 173.

58. Nouss is particularly interested in the "subjectivity of the translator and the nature of the translation act." He draws attention to the "sub-*versive* function of translation that destabilizes set cultural values as it introduces foreign values" ("Translation and métissage," p. 246). Nouss also marks the political value of translation, which by its existence undermines efforts to deny the artifactual nature of social institutions. "Totalitarian regimes and fundamental factions attempt to eliminate translators.

This is so because the move to eliminate translators is tantamount to the elimination of other valid ways of being, thereby obscuring the artifactual nature of the given socio-political world" (ibid., p. 252).

59. Neil Evernden, *The Social Creation of Nature* (Baltimore, MD: John Hopkins University Press, 1992) p. 123.

60. Ralph Metzner, *Green Psychology: Transforming Our Relationship to the Earth* (Rochester, VT: Park Street Press, 1999), p. 97.

61. I have in mind mountain-top removal coal mining. For a critical view of this practice, see "I Love Mountains" (ilovemountains.org).

62. "The General Animacy Scale is based on a literal sense of the concept of animacy—i.e. an assumed cognitive distinction between animate and inanimate, and analogically, between human and nonhuman. It has been maintained that its distinction is not merely a matter of dichotomy, but that it exhibits a certain kind of hierarchic nature. However, it must be pointed out that such a hierarchical scale of animate and inanimate beings is a product of anthropocentric human cognition" (Mutsumi Yamamoto, *Animacy and Reference: A Cognitive Approach to Corpus Linguistics* [Amsterdam: John Benjamins, 1999], p. 9).

63. See, for example, the works of Marc Bekoff, *Minding Animals: Awareness, Emotions, and Heart* (New York: Oxford University Press, 2002); and *Emotional Lives of Animals* (Novato, CA: New World Library, 2007).

64. See, for example, the works of Matthew Hall, "Plant Autonomy and Human-Plant Ethics," *Environmental Ethics*, vol. 31 (2009): 169–81; and *Plants as Persons: A Philosophical Botany* (Albany: State University of New York Press, 2011).

65. Ithamar Gruenwald, "God the 'Stone/Rock': Myth, Idolatry, and Cultic Fetishism in Ancient Israel," *The Journal of Religion*, vol. 76, no. 3 (1996): 429.

66. Ibid., p. 430.

67. Ibid., p. 431.

68. Ibid., pp. 442 and 444.

69. Ibid., p. 435.

70. See Lynn Margulis and Dorian Sagan, *What Is Life?* (New York: Simon & Schuster, 1995).

71. Cited by Cynthia A. Freeland, "Nourishing Speculation: A Feminist Reading of Aristotelian Science," in *Engendering Origins: Critical Feminist Readings in Plato and Aristotle*, ed. Bat-Ami Bar On (Albany: State University of New York, 1994), p. 163.

72. Cited in Stewart Guthrie, *Faces in the Clouds: A New Theory of Religion* (New York: Oxford University Press, 1993), p. 53.

73. While camping in the desert of Death Valley, California, on the occasion of John Muir's birthday in April 1984, Arne Naess and George Sessions articulated eight principles that they thought best summarized fifteen years of thinking about deep ecology. These have been reprinted in Alan Drengson and Yuichi Inoue, eds., *The Deep Ecology Movement: An Introductory Anthology* (Berkeley, CA: North Atlantic Books, 1995), pp. 49–53.

74. Ibid., p. 50.

75. John Seed et al., *Thinking Like a Mountain: Towards a Council of All Beings* (Gabriola Island, BC: New Society, 1988), p. 36.
76. David Skrbina, *Panpsychism in the West* (Cambridge, MA: MIT Press, 2005), p. 3.
77. Ibid., p. 4.
78. Ibid., p. 17.
79. Roderick Nash, "Do Rocks Have Rights?" *Center Magazine*, vol. 10 (1977): 2–12.
80. Skrbina, *Panpsychism*, p. 228.
81. Lynn White, Jr., "Continuing the Conversation," in *Western Man and Environmental Ethics*, ed. Ian Barbour (Boston: Addison-Wesley, 1973), p. 63.
82. Sallie McFague, *The Body of God: An Ecological Theology* (Minneapolis: Fortress Press, 1993), especially p. 38.
83. Graham Harvey, *Animism: Respecting the Living World* (London: Hurst, 2005), p. 17.
84. Ibid., p. 18.
85. Ibid., p. 37.
86. John Fire Lame Deer and Richard Erdoes, *Lame Deer: Seeker of Visions* (New York: Simon & Schuster, 1976), pp. 174–76.
87. Ibid., pp. 101–103.
88. J. Baird Callicott, "Traditional American Indian and Western European Attitudes toward Nature: An Overview," *Environmental Ethics*, vol. 4, no. 4 (1982): 301. Emphasis added.
89. Luis Alberto Urrea, *The Hummingbird's Daughter* (New York: Little, Brown, 2005), pp. 94–95.

Chapter 3

1. "*Govardhan parvat hi sakshat Shri Krishna hai.*" Joshi, *Shri Giriraj Kripa Phal*, p. 7.
2. "*Govardhan parvat ke har ek shila Shri Krishna ka svarupa hai.*" Man from Jhansi performing Govardhan *parikrama*.
3. Edwin Bernbaum, *Sacred Mountains of the World* (San Francisco: Sierra Club Books, 1992), pp. xxii–xxiii.
4. Ibid., p. xiii.
5. Ibid., p. 208.
6. Mircea Eliade, *The Sacred and the Profane: The Nature of Religion*, trans. Willard Trask (New York: Harcourt, Brace & World, 1959), p. 37.
7. Diana L. Eck, "Mountains," in *The Encyclopedia of Religion*, ed. Lindsay Jones (New York: Macmillan, 2005), vol. 9, p. 6212.
8. Eliade, *The Sacred and the Profane*, p. 39.
9. Mircea Eliade, *Patterns in Comparative Religion*, trans. Rosemary Sheed (New York: Meridian Books, 1963), p. 216.
10. Bernbaum, *Sacred Mountains of the World*, p. 209.
11. Sacred mountains in Japanese Shinto, for example, are considered *shin-tai-zan*, the mountain as the "body of a god (*kami*)." The divinity of sacred mountains is celebrated in early Japanese poetry, most notably in a collection called the *Manyoshu*. The

scholar of Japanese religions Joseph Kitagawa wrote: "To many *Manyo* poets, therefore, mountains were not only the *kami*'s dwelling places; mountains were the *kami* themselves." Examples cited by Kitagawa include Mount Tachi, which is called in an eighth-century poem "a *kami* standing." But Mount Fuji is perhaps the best-known example; in another poem from this era, Mount Fuji is called a "mysterious god (*kami*)." Kitagawa emphasizes that in this case the sacred mountain is not a symbol of god, but rather the body of the god. "The epistemological basis of the nonsymbolic understanding of the early Japanese was their aesthetic, magico-religious apprehension of the primeval totality as well as everything within it not as representations of *kami* but as *kami*." See Joseph M. Kitagawa, *On Understanding Japanese Religion* (Princeton, NJ: Princeton University Press, 1987), pp. 46–47.

12. The Sanskrit word *linga* literally means an "indication" or "characteristic" of that which is beyond all indication or characterizing. The major source for this story is found in the "Arunachala Mahatmya" section of the Maheshvara Khanda of the *Skanda Purana*. For the Sanskrit text, see *Skanda Mahapuranam*, ed. Nag Sharan Singh (Delhi: Nag, 1984), vol. 1, pp. 142–70. For an English translation of this text, see *The Skanda Purana*, trans. G. V. Tagare (Delhi: Motilal Banarasidass, 1993), part 3 (vol. 51).

13. *Shiva Purana*, Vidyeshvara Samhita 9.15. For an English translation of the appearance of the firey Shiva *linga*, see chapters 6–9 in *The Shiva Purana*, edited by J. L. Shastri and translated by a board of scholars (Delhi: Motilal Banarasidass, 1970), pp. 52–63.

14. Iswari Kamalabaskaran, *The Light of Arunachaleswar* (Chennai: Alpha Land Books, 2012), p. 163.

15. Ramana Maharishi, *Notes from Ramana's Arunachala: Ocean of Divine Grace* (Tiruvannamalai: Sri Ramanasramam, 2012), p. 17.

16. Ibid., p. 29.

17. *Skanda Purana* 1.3.5.67–68. Singh, p. 146; Tagare, pp. 30–31.

18. K. Swaminathan, "Sri Bhagavan's Love for Arunachala," *The Mountain Path* 25, no. 3 (1988): 130.

19. Authur Osborne, "Physical Supports of Grace," in *Notes from Ramana's Arunachala: Ocean of Grace Divine* (Tiruvannamalai: Sri Ramanasrama, 2012), p. 509.

20. From the subtitles to a two-minute video available at http://www.survivalinternational. org/tribes/dongria (accessed October 12, 2013). See also Debabrata Mohanty, "12th Gram Sabha Votes against Vedanta Mining: Dongaria Kondhs in Rayagada District Say 'The Entire Hill Region Is Our God,'" in *The India Express* (New Delhi, August 20, 2013).

21. "Indian Supreme Court Rules to Protect Sacred Hills against UK Mine Operation Vedanta Resources," in *Independent*, April 18, 2013.

22. Ram Lakhan Sharma, "Shri Giriraj Govardhan ka Mahatmya," in *Giriraj Govardhan*, ed. Bhagra Kishorilal (Vrindaban: Shri Hari Nikunj Ashram, 1989), p. 40.

23. Joshi, *Shri Giriraj Kripa Phal*, p. 7.

24. This perspective is also commonly found in printed texts published in the area of Braj. For example, Vasant Yamadagni asserts that "Shri Giriraj is a form of Krishna himself

(*svayam Krishna-rupa*)." See his *Dagar Chali Shri Govardhan ki Or* (Barsana, UP: Shri Manmandir Seva Sansthan, 1994), p. 5.

25. Umashankar Sharma, "Shri Giriraj hi Sakshat Shri Krishna," in *Rishi Jivan*, ed. Shyamsundar Patodiya (Vrindaban: Shri Bhagavan Bhajan Asram, 1988), p. 82.

26. "*namo . . . cakre atmana (a)tmane*," *Bhagavata Purana* 10.24.36. See the fuller version of this story in Chapter 1.

27. Joshi, *Shri Giriraj Kripa Phal*, p. 59.

28. *Bhagavata Purana* 10.24.35 reads: *shailo (a)smi*, whereas in his Hindi account Joshi has Krishna saying: "*mai Giriraj hu*" (*Shri Giriraj Kripa Phal*, p. 27).

29. Monier Monier-Williams, *Sanskrit English Dictionary*, pp. 510, 515, and 519.

30. Joshi, *Shri Giriraj Kripa Phal*, p. 23.

31. Surdas poem included in *Pushti Margiya Kirtan Sangraha*, ed. Bacchubhai Javeri (Mumbai: Krishnarpan Trust and Indore: Vaishnava Mitra Mandal, 1995), vol. 2, poem #27, p. 30. It is difficult to discern the authenticity of the attributed authorship of such poems, but nonetheless this famous poem gives expression to the dual identity of Krishna as both cowherd boy and mountain. I thank Vallabhdas for his help in translating this difficult poem. This poem is included in the Appendix, followed by another related poem also involving Lalita.

32. *Eka rupa se pujata hai; duja rahyo pujaya. Sahasra bhuja phailaya ke, manga-manga kai khaya.*

33. *Garga Samhita* 5.7.33–34 in Sanskrit text. This text is quoted near the beginning of the *Shri Nathji ki Prakaya Varta*. (In Braj text edited by Ramnath Shastri, p. 2.)

34. See the Appendix for a translation of this entire poem.

35. The official estimate was 8 million, but other estimates put the figure closer to 10 million. See "More than Ten Million Footfall in Govardhan during Guru Purnima," *Vrindavan Today*, August 1, 2015 (http://news.vrindavantoday.org/2015/08/ten-million-footfall-govardhan-guru-purnima).

36. Kumheriya, *Govardhan Mahatmya*, p. 5. For the identification of Braj with the body of Krishna, see my *Journey through the Twelve Forests*, pp. 125–27.

37. Joshi, *Shri Giriraj Kripa Phal*, p. 7.

38. Ibid., p. 9. *Sakshat darshan* of God is often thought to be impossible in the decant age of *kali yug*, but through the grace of Govardhan the impossible becomes possible.

39. This incident is told in the latter half of *Bhagavata Purana* 11.30. Devotees of Giriraj say that the present age of *kali-yug* will end followed by the universal dissolution (*pralaya*) when Mount Govardhan is completely gone; that is, when the mountain becomes totally concealed (*tirobhut*).

40. Navanitpriya Shastri, "Pushti-margiya Sadhana-pranali me Svarupa-seva aur Murti-puja," in *Sadhana-pranali*, ed. Goswami Sharad (Mandavi Gujarat: Shri Vallabhacharya Trust, 2003), p. 10.

41. This incident is told in the *Bhagavata Purana* 10.46–47.

42. Yogeshbhai Shastri, *Pushti Swadhyay*, trans. from Gurarati into English by Niranjan G. Bateriwala (Baroda: Antar Rashtriya Pushti Margiya Vaishnava Parishad, 2005), p. 83.

43. Joshi, *Shri Giriraj Kripa Phal*, p. 8. The English statement "One for all, all for One" is written in English using the Devanagari script in Joshi's Hindi book on Govardhan.

44. Ibid., p. 23. For Joshi's comments on Mount Govardhan's availability to all castes, see p. 9.

45. Pushti Margiya *varta* literature is full of references to the sacredness of Mount Govardhan. Two well-informed Pushti Margiya women living at Chandra Sarovar told me: "All Pushti Margis are worshipers of Giriraj-ji. There are three treasures in Pushti Marg: Shri Yamuna-ji, Shri Giriraj-ji, and Shri Mahaprabhu-ji. But all Pushti Margis are devoted worshipers of Giriraj-ji."

46. Omprakash Yadav, *Haridasavarya: Shri Giriraj Govardhan*, introduction.

47. Pushti Margiya biographical accounts report that at a young age Vallabhacharya engaged in a debate with other scholars gathered at Jagannathpuri. Among the questions put to them was: Which is the best of all scriptures? Vallabhacharya answered: "*ekam shastram devakiputragitam*" (The best of scriptures is the Gita of Devakiputra [Krishna], i.e., the *Bhagavad Gita*).

48. See in particular *Bhagavad Gita* 15.18.

49. This is one of the "Sixteen Books" of Vallabhacharya. The Sanskrit version I use is Vallabhacharya's *Shorashagrantha*, edited with Braj Bhasha commentary by Narasinhalal (Gwalior: Kailash Narayan Khandelal, n.d.). A good English translation of this text is included in *The Teachings of Shri Vallabhacharya*, trans. Shyamdas (Kota: Pratham Peeth, 2003), pp. 38–44. It also appears in James D. Redington's translations with commentary, *The Grace of Lord Krishna: The Sixteen Verse-Treatises of Vallabhacharya* (Delhi: Sri Satguru, 2000), pp. 26–42.

50. See *varta* 54 in the *84 Vaishnavan ki Varta*, a text written in Braj Bhasha by Vallabhacharya's grandson Gokulnath. This narrative briefly portrays the life of Achyutadas Sanoriya, a devotee of Mount Govardhan (Gokulnath, *Chaurasi Vaishnavan ki Varta*, pp. 314–16).

51. See my *River of Love in an Age of Pollution: The Yamuna River of Northern India* (Berkeley: University of California Press, 2006), especially pp. 105 and 188–89.

52. Yadav, *Haridasavarya*, p. 10. Here we see the adjectival forms of the three nouns *adhibhuta, adhyatma*, and *adhidaiva*.

53. Goswami Shyammanohar, *Giriyaga* (Varanasi: Giridhar Prakashan, 2011). This Goswami Shyammanohar should not be confused with the well-known Pushti Margiya philosopher with the same name who lives in Mumbai.

54. Ibid., p. 267.

55. Ibid., p. 268.

56. The acceptance of the changing dimension of reality as divine is one of the things that distinguishes Vaishnava Vedanta from Shankara's Vedanta. This goes along with the Vaishnava teaching that as an aspect of Krishna the world (*jagat*) is real (*sat*).

57. Yadav, *Haridasavarya*, pp. 10–11.

58. Barbara G. Myerhoff, *The Peyote Hunt: The Sacred Journey of the Huichol Indians* (Ithaca, NY: Cornell University Press, 1974).

59. Yadav, *Haridasavarya*, p. 10.

60. The following quotations and discussion of the *adhyatmik svarupa* are found in Shyammanohar's *Giriyaga*, pp. 268–69.
61. Purushottama is defined most concisely in *Bhagavad Gita*, 15.18.
62. Shrivasta Goswami introduced me to this complex term.
63. The term *saumya* is more literally translated as "gentle," but I translate it as "familiar" since it is the personal form that allows intimate relationship.
64. Shyammanohar, *Giriyaga*, p. 269.
65. Yadav, *Haridasavarya*, p. 10.
66. Shyammanohar, *Giriyaga*, p. xvii.
67. Ibid., p. 273.
68. Ibid., p. 269. Here, as well as many other places in his text, Shyammanohar identifies Giriraj as "*sakshat Bhagavan Parabrahma Purna Purushottam.*" The identification of Mount Govardhan as *hridaya-svarupa* and *ghani-bhuta-rasa* is found on p. 275.
69. See Shyammanohar, *Giriyaga*, pp. 298–99.
70. The second verse of Raghunathdas Gosvamin's poem of ten verses, *Govardhana-vasa-prarthana-dashakam*, celebrates a desire for the sight of the amorous love play of Radha and Krishna in Mount Govardhan's many caves: "O Govardhan, allow me to live near you so that I may see the passionate *lilas* of the divine young couple taking place in your many caves."
71. The eight are listed in the Pushti Margiya *varta* of Surdas. See the *Chaurasi Vaishnavan ki Varta*, pp. 466–67.
72. "Beloved Radha and Krishna have spent the night in a cave on the Govardhan Hill. Awakening this morning, the Son of Nanda and the Darling of Brishabhana are drenched in the mood of love" (Shyamdas and Vallabhadas, *Krishna's Inner Circle: The Ashta Chap Poets*, p. 337).
73. The Gaudiya Vaishnava teacher Narayana Maharaja makes this point in his commentary on the Venu Gita. See Bhaktivedanta Narayana Maharaja, *Venu Gita* (Mathura: Gaudiya Vedanta, 1999), p. 137.
74. For further discussion of this issue, see the section entitled "Shri Giriraj-ji ki Bhavatmak Svarup" in *Mahakavi Vallabhdas-ji ka Varta Sahitya* (Gwalior: Vallabhdas Smarak-Mandala, n.d.), pp. 70–80.
75. *Hariray-ji ka Pada-Sahitya*, ed. Prabhudayal Mital (Mathura: Sahitya Samsthan, 1962), p. 219.
76. Gour Govinda, *Giriraja Govardhana, Hari-Dasa-Varya: The Chief Devotee of Lord Hari* (Nambour, Australia: Tattva Vicara, 2012), pp. 3 and 12.
77. Those wishing to know more about the rasa aesthetic theory of Rupa Gosvamin can consult my translation, *The Bhaktirasamritasindhu of Rupa Gosvamin* (New Delhi: Indira Gandhi National Centre for the Arts, 2003).
78. Blissful love is composed of a special divine form of pure luminosity (*shuddha-sattva-vishesatma*), according to Rupa Gosvamin (*Bhaktirasamritasindhu* 1.3.1).
79. Technically the term is *sthayi-bhava*, or "foundational emotion." The more common Hindi word used today in Braj discourse about *bhakti* is *bhav*, which is short for *sthayi-bhava*, the very basis of the *rasa* Krishna-*prem*, supreme love.

80. Pushti Margiya ways of thinking about the relationship between Krishna and the devotee share much with Gaudiya viewpoints. After establishing in his Hindi commentary on Vallabhacharya's short Sanskrit text titled *Chatur-shloki* that Vallabhacharya taught the oneness of the devotee with the Supreme Krishna, the Pushti Margiya philosopher Goswami Shyammanohar emphasizes the desirable twoness of the devotee and Krishna for the purpose or benefit of the love play (*lila-artha*). See his *Dharma, Artha, Kama, Moksha ki Pushtimargiya Vivechana* (Kishnagar, Rajasthan: Pushti Prakashan, 1984), p. 23.
81. Shyammanohar, *Giriyaga*, p. 283.
82. Ibid., p. 273.
83. *Garga Samhita* 5.9.33 (Sanskrit text, p. 338; verse 3.9.33, p. 270 in English translation).
84. Shyammanohar, *Giriyaga*, p. 275.
85. Here Govardhan is characterized as "*ratna-dhatu-maya.*" *Garga Samhita* 5.9.34.
86. Shyammanohar quotes a poem by Surdas in which the blind poet says that the *gopis* consist of *ratna*. Shyammanohar, *Giriyaga*, p. 277.
87. Ibid., p. 279.
88. Ibid., pp. 273–74.
89. Ibid., p. 276.
90. Ibid., p. 283.
91. Since I do not have a written reference for these poetic lines, I supply them here as they were written down for me by Devakipran Baba: *Kuch makhan ka bal milo. Kuch gopin kari sadhaya. Shri Radha ki kripa se taine dhariyo giri Govardhan.*

Chapter 4

1. A worshiper of Mount Govardhan living in Jatipura.
2. Joshi, *Shri Giriraj Kripa Phal*, p. 9.
3. *Bhagavata Purana* 10.24.31–34. This incident is also told in the *Vishnu Purana* 5.10 and *Garga Samhita* 5.2.19. The Sanskrit term used for the clockwise circumambulation in all three texts is *pradakshina*.
4. Joshi, *Shri Giriraj Kripa Phal*, p. 80.
5. See footnote #41 in Chapter 1 for textual references to the *parikrama* of Govardhan by Vallabhacharya and Chaitanya.
6. Guru Purnima is the full-moon day on which devotees travel to the home of their guru and honor him. Since many consider Govardhan to be their guru, they come to the mountain to honor it with a reverent *parikrama*. The name Muriya means "shaved head." It refers to the tradition that the great Gaudiya saint and devotee of Govardhan, Sanatana Gosvamin, died on Guru Purnima, and his distraught followers shaved their heads and performed the Govardhan *parikrama* with his body. Since the great sage and author of many Hindu scriptures, Vyas, is regarded by many to be one of the greatest gurus, this day is also named after him. The day is also considered the birthday of Vyas. A grand day by all accounts! For the mid-1980s reports, see the newspaper articles copied in Ashok Chaitanya, "Govardhan ki Parikrama

Dai Lai, Terau Purnajanma Nahi Hoya," in *Giriraj Govardhan*, ed. Madhur Bhagra (Vrindaban: Shri Bhagavan Bhajan Asram, 1988), pp. 182–83.

7. See footnote #35 in Chapter 3.

8. The Chandra Sarovar pond is identified as an important site where Krishna danced the *rasa-lila* with the *gopis*; it is also known as the place where the great poet-saint Surdas breathed his last breath.

9. Bhakti is defined, for example, in the *Bhaktirasamritasindhu* of Rupa Gosvamin as worship with the senses to the Lord of the Senses (1.1.12). *Smarana*, or complete absorption of the heart/mind in Krishna, is understood to be the goal of Vaishnava practice according to major Gaudiya Vaishnava theoreticians. See my *Acting as a Way of Salvation: A Study of Raganuga Bhakti Sadhana* (New York: Oxford University Press, 1988), especially pp. 124–28.

10. Kumheriya, *Govardhan Mahatmya*, p. 7.

11. Some make exceptions for those who are physically unable to walk the *parikrama* path barefoot. See Shrisvarupa Das, *Shri Govardhan Parikrama* (Radhakund, India: Pulak and Samir Devanath, 2011), p. 20.

12. Joshi, *Shri Giriraj Kripa Phal*, p. 23.

13. Ibid., p. 115.

14. Described in Chapter 1, pp. 38–40.

15. Joshi, *Shri Giriraj Kripa Phal*, p. 34.

16. These observations were recorded on the morning of November 25, 2013.

17. Joshi, *Shri Giriraj Kripa Phal*, p. 34.

18. Ibid., p. 9.

19. Gokulnath, *Do Sau Bavan Vaishnavan ki Varta*, #28, pp. 269–71.

20. These observations were recorded on the evening of December 8, 2013.

21. *namaste girirajaya shri govardhana-namine. ashesa-klesha-nashaya paramananda-dayine.*

22. For more on this, see my *River of Love in the Age of Pollution: The Yamuna River of Northern India*, p. 102.

23. Nirmalchandra Goswami, *Shri Radhadamodar Dainik Stuti*, (Vindaban: Shri Radhadamodar Mandir, n.d.), pp. 5–6.

24. See the Appendix for a translation of this hymn. The refrain is: "This is my Lord, the one holding (or assuming the form of) the Blessed King of Mountains."

25. Joshi, *Shri Giriraj Kripa Phal*, p. 9.

26. See *Garga Samhita* 5.10.1–14, pp. 341–42 in Sanskrit edition; and 3.10.1–14, pp. 281–92 in English translation. This popular story is retold in numerous written texts, from scholarly texts including Mukunda Hariji, "Shri Giriraj Mahima," in *Giriraj Govardhan*, ed. Madhur Bhagra (Vrindaban: Shri Hari Nikunj Ashram, 1989), pp. 13–14, and Kumheriya, *Govardhan Mahatmya*, pp. 15–17.

27. Kumheriya, *Govardhan Mahatmya*, pp. 16–17.

28. Keshavdas Sharma, "Chamatkari Sarvadev Shri Giriraj," in *Giriraj Govardhan*, pp. 49–75. The story of the handicapped woman appears on p. 50; the story of the man who was blessed with a child appears on pp. 57–58, and the story of the barber appears on pp. 55–56.

29. Ibid., p. 58.

30. Joshi, *Shri Giriraj Kripa Phal*, p. 25.

31. Yadav, *Haridasavarya*, p. 1.

32. See my "The Accidental Ritualist" in *Essays in South Asia Rituals in Honor of Fredrick Clothey*, ed. Linda Powers and Tracy Pintchman (Columbia: University of South Carolina Press, 2014).

33. *Bhagavata Purana* 6.2.14–19.

34. *pritama prita hi te peyi*. This is from a poem by the famous Braj poet Chaturbhujadas.

35. Kumheriya, *Govardhan Mahatmya*, p. 6.

36. The Hindi vocabulary I cite here was used by a Pushti Margiya preacher during a talk he gave to a group of Pushti Margiya pilgrims doing a Ban Yatra pilgrimage. (Satish Sharma, camp at Surbhi Kund, September 13, 2013.)

37. Goswami, *Giriyaga*, p. xxi.

38. Cited by Ram Lakhan Sharma in "Shri Giriraj Govardhan-ji ka Mahatmya," p. 44.

Chapter 5

1. David Morgan, *The Sacred Gaze: Religious Visual Culture in Theory and Practice* (Berkeley: University of California Press, 2005), p. 115.

2. Devotee of Mount Govardhan, Jatipura, November 14, 2013.

3. William Ward, 4 vols., *History, Literature, and Mythology of the Hindoos* (Delhi: Low Price, [1820] 1990), vol. 3, p. ciii.

4. Cited in Timothy Beal, *Religion and Monsters* (New York: Routledge, 2001), p. 109.

5. Ward, 4 vols., *History, Literature, and Mythology of the Hindoos*; Abbe J. A. Dubois, *Hindu Manners, Customs and Ceremonies* (New Delhi: Book Faith India, [1897] 1999). Brian Pennington maintains that Ward's book "became a centerpiece in the British construction of Hinduism"; and that Dubois's book "served as an important source of knowledge about Hinduism for many years" (*Was Hinduism Invented? Britons, Indians, and the Colonial Construction of Religion* [New York: Oxford University Press, 2005], pp. 85 and 70, respectively).

6. Dubois, *Hindu Manners, Customs and Ceremonies*, p. 655.

7. W. Crooke, *An Introduction to the Popular Religion and Folklore of Northern India* (Allahabad: Government Press, North-Western Provinces and Oudh, 1894). See his discussion of stone fetishes, pp. 289–304.

8. F. Max Müller, *Origin and Growth of Religion as Illustrated by the Religions of India* (London: Longmans, Green, 1880), pp. 63–64.

9. I am most interested in the lingering tendencies of the employment of idolatry as an interpretive strategy in the academic study of religion, but it might be worth mentioning that the concept also remains strong in much popular Christianity today. In a sermon titled "The Sin of Idolatry and Its Judgments" on the *Bible Hub* website, R. Tuck writes: "A spiritual and invisible God asks from his creatures a spiritual and invisible worship, with a material expression held within careful limitations. . . . All idolatrous systems are more or less immoral, and give license to the bodily lusts

and passions." In another sermon titled "The Worship of Stones," he makes the point that stone worship is an early and "coarse" form of idolatry deserving harsh condemnation. http://biblehub.com/sermons/auth/tuck/the_sin_of_idolatry_and_its_judgments.htm and http://biblehub.com/sermons/auth/tuck/the_worship_of_stones.htm (accessed August 2016).

10. The English word idolatry is derived from the Greek compound *eidololatria*, which is comprised of the two words: *eidolon* ("image") and *latria* ("worship"). See Josh Ellenbogen and Aaron Tugendhaft, ed., *Idol Anxiety* (Stanford, CA: Stanford University Press, 2011), p. 3.

11. Jan Assmann, "What's Wrong with Images?" *in Idol Anxiety*, p. 20.

12. There is evidence, however, of the worship of stones in ancient Israel. See Gruenwald, "God the 'Stone/Rock': Myth, Idolatry, and Cultic Fetishism in Ancient Israel." Archeological records also suggest that Mount Sinai itself was most likely worshiped as a sacred mountain.

13. See, for example, Jeremiah 10:1–16, Isaiah 44:9–20, and Psalms 115.

14. Assmann, "What's Wrong with Images?," p. 20.

15. Ibid., p. 28.

16. Assmann, "Introduction," in *Representation in Religion*, ed. Jan Assmann and Albert I. Baumgarten (Leiden: Brill, 2001), p. xvi.

17. Ibid..

18. Assmann, "What's Wrong with Images?," p. 28.

19. This question gets expressed in Hindu Vedantic philosophy as: Is the world (*jagat*) real (*sat*) or unreal (*asat*)? *Sat*, or "existence," is considered to be an important aspect of divinity. The Vaishnava Vedantic traditions associated with Braj Vaishnavism hold that the world is real (*sat*), thus divine.

20. Exodus 32.

21. Assmann, "What's Wrong with Images?," pp. 21–22.

22. W. J. T. Mitchell, "Idolatry: Nietzsche, Blake, and Poussin," in *Idol Anxiety*, p. 57.

23. Moshe Halbertal and Avishai Margalit, *Idolatry*, trans. Naomi Goldblum (Cambridge, MA: Harvard University Press, 1992), p. 3.

24. Mitchell, "Idolatry: Nietzsche, Blake, and Poussin," p. 58.

25. Halbertal and Margalit, *Idolatry*, pp. 5 and 8.

26. Ibid., p. 39.

27. Ibid., p. 42.

28. Ibid., p. 52.

29. Guy Stroumsa writes: "surprisingly enough, the great intellectual figure of the seventeenth century is none other than the twelfth-century Jewish thinker Maimonides (1136–1204) . . . the major reason for the strong attraction to Maimonides on the part of Christian intellectuals: more than any other ancient or medieval thinker, Greek, Christian, or even Muslim, Maimonides had offered a powerful reflection about the phenomenon of idolatry, reaching dramatic conclusions on its origin and nature" ("John Spencer and the Roots of Idolatry," *History of Religions*, vol. 41, no. 1 [August 2001]: 14).

30. From Maimonides' *Laws of Idolatry*; cited by Halbertal and Margalit, p. 43.

31. Halbertal and Margalit, *Idolatry*, p. 44.

32. Ibid., p. 110.

33. Ibid., p. 111.

34. Ibid., p. 186.

35. I acknowledge that historical debates regarding idolatry did occur within Eastern Christian Orthodoxy, as well as within Islamic policy, but since the comparative study of religion as we know it in the Western academy was for the most part a Western European (colonial) enterprise, I focus exclusively on the contentious discussions of idolatry there.

36. Clement of Alexandria, for example, writes: "In our view the image of God is not a sensible object, made of matter perceived by the senses, but a mental object . . . let no one deify the universe; rather let him seek after the creator" (cited by Joan-Pau Rubiés, "Theology, Ethnography, and the Historicization of Idolatry," *Journal of the History of Ideas*, vol. 67, no. 4 (October 2006): 577).

37. Augustine's Confessions are shot through with such claims. Addressing God, he says, "I did not find you among physical things" (*Saint Augustine Confessions*, trans. Henry Chadwick [New York: Oxford University Press, 2009], p. 200).

38. It might be worth noting that the historian Thomas Berry thought that the deadly Black Plague that ravished Europe in the fourteenth century contributed to a growing distrust and desacralization of nature, which over time became replaced with a desire to control it. See his book, *The Dream of the Earth* (San Francisco: Sierra Club Books, 1988), pp. 125–27.

39. Carlos Eire, *War against the Idols: The Reformation of Worship from Erasmus to Calvin* (Cambridge: Cambridge University Press, 1989), p. 1.

40. Ibid., p. 2.

41. Ibid., p. 3.

42. Cited by Eire, ibid., p. 34.

43. Employing dualistic Platonic notions of spirit and matter in his commentary on the Song of Songs, the third-century Church Father Origen advises one to "despise visible and corporeal things" and "renounce the whole world" as a prison for the soul. See *Origen*, trans. Rowan A. Greer (New York: Paulist Press, 1979), especially p. 234.

44. Jonathan Sheehan, "Sacred and Profane: Idolatry, Antiquarianism and the Polemics of Distinction in the Seventeenth Century," *Past & Present*, no. 192 (2006): 47.

45. The following quotations are drawn from Chapter 11 of John Calvin's major work, *Institutes of the Christian Religion,* trans. Henry Beveridge (Woodstock, Ontario: Devoted, 2016), pp. 47–53.

46. On Karlstadt's justification of iconoclastic violence, see Eire, *War against the Idols*, pp. 56–65.

47. I am aware that this statement contradicts a common understanding that the nineteenth-century scholar Max Müller was the "father of comparative religion." Joachim Wach, for example, wrote: "There can be little doubt that the modern comparative study of religions began with Max Müller" (*The Comparative Study of Religions* [New York: Columbia University Press, 1958], p. 3.).

48. Jonathan Sheehan, "Thinking about Idols in Early Modern Europe," *Journal of the History of Ideas*, vol. 67, no. 4 (October 2006): 564.

49. Stroumsa, "John Spencer and the Roots of Idolatry," p. 2.

50. The religions of the world during this period were divided into the three Abrahmanic traditions and all other religions. The latter was singularly labeled "paganism," which was defined principally in terms of idolatry.

51. A seventeenth-century link between the identification of Hindu idolatry and Catholic practice can be observed in the works of Henry More. "More defines idolatry as the proper fruit of animal life, a pathological immersion in sensuality and materiality, and immersion reflected not only in the worship of the sun and moon in the East Indies, but also in Catholic cult" (Stroumsa, p. 13). The connection between Hindu and Catholic "idolatry" remained robust in nineteenth- and early twentieth-century scholarship on religion.

52. Sheehan, "Sacred and Profane: Idolatry, Antiquarianism and the Polemics of Distinction in the Seventeenth Century," pp. 52–53.

53. Stroumsa, "John Spencer and the Roots of Idolatry," pp. 3 and 13.

54. Good examples of the early study of religions around the world would be Samuel Purchas, *Purchas his Pilgrimage, or Relations of the World and the Religions Observed in All Ages and Places Discovered, from the Creation Unto This Present* (London: Kessinger, [1613] 2010), and Edward Brerewood, *Enquiries Touching the Diversity of Languages and Religions, Through the Chief Parts of the World* (London: Kessinger, [1641] 2008). This fourfold division had lasting effects. Writing in the late nineteenth century, for example, W. Robertson Smith categorizes religion into the fourfold distinction of the "positive religions" of Judaism, Christianity, and Islam, and the "ancient heathenism" of idolaters (*The Religion of the Semites: The Fundamental Institutions* [New York: Schocken Books, [1889] 1972], p. 1).

55. Sheehan, "Sacred and Profane," p. 63.

56. See John F. Chuchiak, "In Servitio Dei: Fray Diego de Landa, the Franciscan Order, and the Return of the Extirpation of Idolatry in the Colonial Diocese of Yucatan, 1573–1579," *The Americas*, vol. 61, no. 4 (April 2005): 611–46.

57. Kenneth Mills, *Idolatry and Its Enemies: Colonial Andean Religion and Extirpation, 1640–1750* (Princeton, NJ: Princeton University Press, 1997), p. 42.

58. Father Pablo Joseph de Arriaga, *The Extirpation of Idolatry in Peru*, trans. L. Clark Keating (Lexington: University of Kentucky Press, [1621] 1968).

59. Mills, *Idolatry and Its Enemies*, pp. 196–97.

60. Joan-Pau Rubiés, "Theology, Ethnography, and the Historicization of Idolatry," *Journal of the History of Ideas*, vol. 67, no. 4 (October 2006): 587. Emphasis added.

61. Ibid., p. 585–86.

62. These correspond to what is called in contemporary Hindi-speaking worlds *prakriti-rupa* and *murti-rupa*. For a discussion of this, see my *People Trees*, pp. 145–46.

63. Rubiés, "Theology, Ethnography, and the Historicization of Idolatry," p. 590.

64. Martin Mulsow, "Idolatry and Science: Against Nature Worship from Boyle to Rudiger, 1680–1720," *Journal of the History of Ideas* vol. 67, no. 4 (2006): 697.

65. Eire, *War against the Idols*, p. 311.

66. "Indeed for Boyle, one of the most attractive features of the mechanical philosophy was the extent to which it removed mediating influences between God and the world, thereby preserving God's sovereignty more clearly than the 'vulgar' notion of nature which, in Boyle's opinion, elevated nature to the status of a semi-deity" (Introduction in Robert Boyle, *A Free Enquiry into the Vulgarly Received Notion of Nature*, ed. Edward B. Davis and Michael Hunter [Cambridge: Cambridge University Press, [1686] 1996], p. xv.).

67. J. E. McGuire, "Boyle's Conception of Nature," *Journal of the History of Ideas*, vol. 33, no. 4 (1972): 525. J. R. Jacob agrees: "In any case in writing the *Enquiry* Boyle employed his natural philosophy to defeat the threats posed to true religion by the virtual idolatry in the scholastic natural religion of the Catholics and the flagrant idolatry of the atheists. Both would debase Christianity into one form or another of pagan naturalism, if not stopped by a correct understanding of the relationship between God and nature, creator and creation, which Boyle's philosophy alone could supply" ("Boyle's Atomism and the Restoration Assault on Pagan Naturalism," *Social Studies of Science*, vol. 8, no. 2 [1978]: 220–21).

68. "Robert Boyle was worried about the whole complex of implicit and iconological idolatry. He understood himself as a truly Christian scientist whose program of anti-idolatrous science had to rest on the principle of denying Nature any attribution of activity" (Mulsow, "Idolatry and Science," p. 699).

69. Boyle, *A Free Enquiry into the Vulgarly Received Notion of Nature*, p. 62.

70. Ibid., p. 41.

71. David Hume, *The Natural History of Religion* (New York: Macmillan, [1757] 1992), p. 4. Emphasis added. Hume tends to use the terms "idolatry" and "polytheism" interchangeably.

72. Ibid., p. 5. Emphasis added.

73. Ibid. p. 25.

74. Ibid. p. 25.

75. Ibid., p. 48.

76. Ibid., p. 16.

77. Ibid., p. 29. Parenthetic information added.

78. Auguste Comte, *The Positive Philosophy*, trans. Harriet Martineau (New York: AMS Press, [1855] 1974), p. 522.

79. Ibid., p. 545.

80. Ibid., p. 546.

81. Ibid., p. 547.

82. Ibid., p. 548.

83. Sheehan, "Sacred and Profane," p. 64.

84. Tylor, *The Origins of Culture* (New York: Harper and Brothers, [1871] 1958), p. 21.

85. Ibid., p. 26.

86. Ibid., p. 35.

87. Edward Burnett Tylor, *Religion in Primitive Culture* (New York: Harper and Brothers, [1871] 1958), pp. 8–9.

88. Ibid., p. 29.

89. Ibid., p. 61. Emphasis added.

90. Ibid., p. 84.

91. Ibid. The section on fetishism, pp. 229–47; the section on stone worship, pp. 247–53; the section on idolatry, pp. 254–66.

92. Ibid., p. 230.

93. Ibid., p. 231.

94. Ibid., p. 247.

95. Ibid., p. 250.

96. Ibid., p. 253.

97. Ibid., pp. 246 and 209.

98. Ibid., 255.

99. Ibid., p. 255. For Tylor, Hinduism is a prime exemplar of idolatry; see pp. 254 and 256.

100. Ibid., p. 264. Following Hume, Tylor makes a distinction between the symbolic religion of the "intelligent Hindu" and the "fetish-theory" of the "popular religion of his country."

101. Ibid., p. 263. Writing around the same time as Tylor, Max Müller claims (reviewing Charles de Brosses's notion of the origins of religion in fetishism in a manner that follows Comte): "De Brosses did not keep what he calls fetish-worship distinct even from idolatry, though there is a very important distinction between the two. A fetish, properly so called, is itself regarded as something supernatural; the idol, on the contrary, was originally meant as an image only, a similitude or a symbol of something else" (F. Max Müller, *Lectures on the Origin and Growth of Religion as Illustrated by the Religions of India* [London: Longs, Green, 1880], pp. 63–64).

102. Tylor, *Religion in Primitive Culture*, p. 269.

103. W. Robertson Smith, *The Religion of the Semites*, p. 1.

104. Ibid., p. 84.

105. Ibid. pp. 85 and 89.

106. Ibid. p. 87. Emphasis added.

107. Ibid., pp. 90–91.

108. "The worship of sacred stones is often spoken of as if it belonged to a distinctly lower type of religion than the worship of images" (ibid., p. 209). Following Comte, Smith identifies this lowest form of idolatry as fetishism.

109. Ibid., p. 205. Also: "But for most rituals it is not sufficient that the worshipper should present his service on holy ground: it is necessary that he should come into contact with the god himself, and this he believes himself to do when he directs his homage to a natural object . . . which is believed to be the actual seat of the god or embodiment of a divine life, or when he draws near to an artificial mark of the immediate presence of the deity. In the oldest forms of Semitic religion this mark is a sacred stone" (p. 213).

110. Ibid., p. 206.

111. Dubois, *Hindu Manners, Customs and Ceremonies*, p. 555.

112. For a discussion of the dating and character of Kabir, see John S. Hawley, "Can There Be a Vaishnava Kabir?," *Studies in History*, vol. 32, no. 2 (2016): 147–61.

113. Cited in Noel A. Salmond, *Hindu Iconoclasts: Rammohaun Roy, Dayananda Sarasvati, and Nineteenth-Century Polemics against Idolatry* (Waterloo, ON: Wilfrid Laurier University Press, 2004), p. 104.

114. Salmond demonstrates that the work of the Orientalists "was known to the two nineteenth-century reformers: Wilson was a personal acquaintance of Rammohun, and later, Dayananda would come to know the work of Müller" (ibid., p. 15). Interestingly, Dayananda received his first copy of the Vedas from a Christian missionary (see ibid., p. 115). Karsandas Mulji of the Prarthana Samaj was deeply influenced by the well-known Bombay-based nineteenth-century Indologist and Scottish Presbyterian missionary John Wilson. Regarding current Hindu worship, Wilson declared: "It is an historical fact, that the more modern religions are less moral and less pure" (see my "On Trial: The Love of the Sixteen Thousand Gopees," p. 57).

115. William Jones, "On the Hindus," in *Asiatik Researches*, vol. 1 (1798): 421.

116. Cited by Jitendra Nath Banerjea, *Development of Hindu Iconography* (Calcutta: University of Calcutta Press, 1956), p. 43.

117. Salmond, *Hindu Iconoclasts*, p. 61.

118. Ibid., p. 64.

119. Ibid., p. 84.

120. Ibid., p. 62.

121. Cited in ibid., p. 115.

122. For an account of this trial, see my "On Trial: The Love of the Sixteen Thousand Gopees." During this trial, Hinduism itself was scrutinized and temple worship was condemned in favor of an ascetic worship of a formless absolute. Dayananda Sarasvati was invited to Bombay in 1874 by a group of merchants who had directly supported Karsandas Mulji in the Maharaj Libel Case. See J. T. F. Jordens, *Dayananda Sarasvati: His Life and Ideas* (Delhi: Oxford University Press, 1978), p. 142; and Christine Dobbins, *Urban Leadership in Western India: Politics and Communities in Bombay City 1840–1885* (London: Oxford University Press, 1972), pp. 254–55.

123. Mircea Eliade, *The Sacred and the Profane: The Nature of Religion*, trans. Willard Trask (New York: Harcourt Brace & World, 1959), pp. 11–12.

124. Eliade begins his book with direct reference to Rudolf Otto's idea of the sacred as laid out in *Das Heilige*, published in 1917. This book is available in English as *The Idea of the Holy*, trans. John Harvey (London: Oxford University Press, 1923).

125. Ibid., pp. 9–10.

126. Vallabhacharya, *Siddhantamuktavali*, Verse 7.

127. Examples would include the *Bhagavad Gita*'s description of the material nature (*apara prakriti*) of Krishna as made up of the five physical elements (7.4), and the *Bhagavata Purana*'s inclusion of the natural entities of the world, such as mountains, rivers, and trees, as parts of the physical body (*sthula rupa*) of Vishnu (2.1.32–33).

128. The theological position that embraces both the immanent as well as the transcendent is often referred to as "panentheism." For more on this, see *Panentheism across the World's Traditions*, ed. Lorilai Biernacki and Philip Clayton

(New York: Oxford University Press, 2013), wherein panentheism is presented as "an animistic force in rocks and trees" that implies that God is both in the world, immanent, as well as beyond matter, transcendent.

129. Eliade, *The Sacred and the Profane*, p. 11.
130. David Freedberg, *The Power of Images* (Chicago: University of Chicago Press, 1989).
131. Ibid., p. 406.
132. W. J. T. Mitchell, *What Do Pictures Want? The Lives and Loves of Images* (Chicago: University of Chicago Press, 2005).
133. Ibid., pp. 28–29. Parentheses in original.
134. Ibid., p. 26.
135. Ibid., p. 159. Emphasis added.
136. Ibid., p. 32.
137. In his book *Provincializing Europe*, Dipesh Chakrabarty has argued for the need to move away from the "assumption running through modern European political thought and the social sciences that the human is ontologically singular, that gods and spirits are in the end 'social facts,' that the social somehow exists prior to them" (*Provincializing Europe: Postcolonial Thought and Historical Difference* [Princeton, NJ: Princeton University Press, 2000], p. 16).
138. Mitchell, *What Do Pictures Want?*, pp. 97–99.
139. Ibid., p. 161. Emphasis added.
140. Ibid., p. 162. Emphasis added.
141. See Bruno Latour, *We Have Never Been Modern* (Cambridge, MA: Harvard University Press, 1993).
142. Alfred Gell, *Art and Agency: An Anthropological Theory* (Oxford: Clarendon Press, 1998), p. 96.
143. Ibid., pp. 96 and 116.
144. Ibid., p. 96.
145. Ibid., p. 98.
146. Ibid., p. 98.
147. Ibid., p. 135.
148. Ibid., p. 131.
149. Ibid., p. 125. Emphasis added.
150. Ibid., p. 123.
151. Ibid., p. 135.
152. Bron Taylor, "Idolatry, Paganism, and Trust in Nature," *The Pomegranate*, vol. 12, no. 1 (2010): 103.
153. Ibid., p. 105. Emphasis added.
154. Bron Taylor, *Dark Green Religion: Nature Spirituality and the Planetary Future* (Berkeley: University of California Press, 2009).
155. Robert A. Orsi, *Between Heaven and Earth* (Princeton, NJ: Princeton University Press, 2005), p. 9.
156. Ibid., p. 10.
157. Ibid., p. 12.

158. Robert A. Orsi, "Abundant History: Marian Apparitions as Alternative Modernity," *Historically Speaking,* vol. 9, no. 7 (2008): 12. The quotation of Hume: "I believe, indeed, that there is no tenet in all paganism, which would give so fair a scope to ridicule as this of the *real presence*" (*The Natural History of Religion*, p. 48).

159. Manuel Vasquez, *More Than Belief: A Materialist Theory of Religion* (New York: Oxford University Press, 2011), p. 323.

160. http://www.tandfonline.com/doi/abs/10.2752/174322005778054474 (accessed October 8, 2018).

161. Cited by Eck, *Darśan: Seeing the Divine Image*, p. 46.

162. A standard textbook on world religions when I was in college was John B. Noss, *Man's Religion*, 4th ed. (London: Macmillan, 1972). An exemplary passage reads: "A priest or someone in the family conducts the simple domestic rites on behalf of the family before an image or symbol of the household god" (217).

163. Eck, *Darśan*, p. 38.

164. Joanne Waghorne and Norman Cutler, eds., *Gods of Flesh, Gods of Stone: The Embodiment of Divinity in India* (New York: Columbia University Press, [1985] 1996).

165. Ibid., pp. 3 and 5. Waghorne attributes the "discovery of the symbolic" to Ernst Cassirer, but as we have seen, the interpretive move that relies on symbolic representation predates the nineteenth century.

166. Ibid., p. 5.

167. James Preston, "Creation of the Sacred Image," *Gods of Flesh*, p. 9.

168. Vasudha Narayanan, "Arcavatara: On Earth as He Is in Heaven," *Gods of Flesh*, p. 54.

169. Norman Cutler, "Conclusion," *Gods of Flesh*, pp. 164 and 168.

170. Waghorne, "Introduction," *Gods of Flesh*, p. 7.

171. Richard Davis, *The Lives of Indian Images* (Princeton, NJ: Princeton University Press, 1997), p. 27.

172. Ibid., p. 29.

173. Ibid., p. 30.

174. Ibid., p. 32. Commenting on Bonaventure's theory of the image and highlighting the Christian origins of the notion of symbolic representation, the art historian Freedberg writes: "Here too are the real origins of a general theory of signs" (*The Power of Images: Studies in the History and Theory of Response*, p. 166).

175. Davis, *The Lives of Indian Images*, p. 33.

Chapter 6

1. All three statements were made by worshipers of Mount Govardhan who live in one of the five villages within its surrounding plain.

2. This story can also be found in the fourth story of Gokulnath's *Chaurasi Vaishnavan ki Varta*, pp. 40–53.

3. For a brief account of Vallabhacharya's first *puja* to Mount Govardhan at the Sundar Shila, see Gokulnath, *Chaurasi Baithak Charitra*, p. 30.

4. The translation is from Krishnadas Kaviraj's *Shri Chaitanya Charitamrita*, Madhya Lila, chapter 18, verse 16, p. 680.

5. These are two dictionary meanings for *atmiya*. See McGregor, *The Oxford Hindi-English Dictionary*, p. 84.

6. In his *Bhaktirasamritasindhu*, Rupa Gosvamin identifies *mamata* as an essential constituent of more intimate relationships with Krishna. Compare verses 2.5.18 and 22. See Haberman, *The Bhaktirasamritasindhu of Rupa Gosvamin*, pp. 358–59.

7. For a description of the ornamentation and worship at the Jatipura Mukharvind site, see Chapter 4, pp. 120–27.

8. For a psychological perspective on this, see Phyllis J. Davis, *The Power of Touch: The Basis for Survival, Health, Intimacy, and Emotional Well-Being* (Carlsbad, CA: Hay House, 1999).

9. In contrast to the unintentional or unconscious anthropomorphism of Stewart Guthrie, whose account of anthropomorphism holds that "anthropomorphism stems from a practice that is largely unconscious" (*Faces in the Clouds*, p. 187).

10. Gell, *Art and Agency*, p. 96.

11. A *shaligram* is a fossilized stone from a sacred river in Nepal that is considered to be a naturally embodied form of Vishnu.

12. The classic example of this, of course, is the episode in the *Bhagavata Purana* (10.43.17) when Krishna enters the arena in Mathura with the intent of killing the demonic king Kansa. As he enters the arena, the yogis see as him as ultimate reality, the elders see him as a vulnerable child, the cowherds see him as a relative, his male friends see him as their heroic buddy, the young women see him as their paramour, wrestlers see him as a frightening opponent, and Kansa sees him as death incarnate. This is used frequently to make the point that Krishna takes multitude of forms simultaneously, determined by the emotional disposition of the observer.

13. Pratik Shah, "Ahanta-Mamata: I-ness and My-ness and Pushti Bhakti" in *Sadhanapranali*, ed. Goswami Sharad (Mandavi, Gujarat: Shri Vallabhacharya Trust, 2003), p. 408. Emphasis added.

14. It might be fruitful to compare the conception and treatment of Govardhan stones and stones from the southern Indian sacred mountain Mount Arunachala, which are not ritually anthropomorphized. Arunachala stones are also conceived of as natural embodied forms divinity—specifically Shiva—but are regarded quite differently than Govardhan stones—embodied forms of Krishna. One worshiper of Arunachala with whom I spoke told me that "Arunachala is my true Self (*atman*). That is how I see it." Here is a kind of relationship—one of identity—but not one in which the personality of the stones is of particular importance, nor is the relationship nearly as intimate as that achieved with anthropomorphized Govardhan stones.

Presence is assumed in Arunachala stones, too, but affectual relationality is not emphasized. Thus we see a much weaker from of anthropomorphism at play here. The religion associated with Mount Arunachala tends to strive for *moksha* or "liberation," understood as either complete identification with Shiva or the achievement of a similar form; the religion associated with Mount Govardhan aims for a loving and joyful *relationship* with Krishna. It is not surprising, then, that although the aniconic Mount

Arunachala stones are anthropomorphized to a certain degree, there is no practice of adding a face or clothing to them, nor interacting with them in the intimate ways commonly found at Mount Govardhan, where loving relationality is strongly emphasized.

15. Xenophanes, trans. Kathleen Freeman, *Ancilla to the Pre-Socratic Philosophers* (Cambridge, MA: Harvard University Press, [1948] 1996), p. 22.

16. Neil Evernden, *The Social Creation of Nature* (Baltimore, MD: Johns Hopkins University Press, 1992), p. 41.

17. Ibid., p. 49.

18. Ibid., p. 49.

19. Ibid., p. 57.

20. Ibid., p. 53.

21. Lorraine Daston, "How Nature Became the Other: Anthropomorphism and Anthropocentrism in Early Modern Natural Philosophy," in *Biology as Society, Society as Biology: Metaphors*, ed. Sabine Maasen, Everett Mendelsohn, and Peter Weingart (Dordrecht: Kluwer Academic, 1995), p. 37.

22. Ibid., pp. 37–38.

23. Ibid., p. 38.

24. Ibid. pp. 39–40.

25. Ibid., p. 40.

26. See, for example, Charles Webster, "Puritanism, Separatism, and Science," in *God and Nature: Historical Essays on the Encounter between Christianity and Science*, ed. David Lindberg and Ronald Numbers (Berkeley: University of California Press, 1986), 192–217. Webster maintains that "any truly historical account of the Scientific Revolution must pay due attention to the deep interpenetration of scientific and religious ideas" (213).

27. The phrase is drawn from Keith Hutchison, "Supernaturalism and the Mechanical Philosophy," *History of Science*, vol. 21 (1983): 297–333.

28. Jacques Roger, "The Mechanistic Conception of Life," in *God and Nature: Historical Essays on the Encounter between Christianity and Science*, ed. David Lindberg and Ronald Numbers (Berkeley: University of California Press, 1986), 279 (chapter: 277–95).

29. This point is also made by Edward B. Davis, "Robert Boyle's Religious Life, Attitudes, and Vocation" *Science & Christian Belief*, vol. 19, no. 2 (2007):133.

30. Daston, "How Nature Became the Other," pp. 48–49.

31. Boyle, *A Free Enquiry into the Vulgarly Received Notion of Nature*, p. 158.

32. "It is a dangerous thing to believe other creatures than angels and men to be intelligent" (ibid., p. 57).

33. Hume, *The Natural History of Religion*, p. 12. Emphasis added.

34. Ibid.

35. David Hume, *Dialogues Concerning Natural Religion*, ed. H. D. Aiken (New York: Hafner, 1948), p. 40.

36. Tylor, *Religion in Primitive Culture*, p. 61.

37. James George Frazer, *The Worship of Nature* (New York: Macmillan, 1926), p. 6.

38. Leslie A. White, *The Science of Culture: A Study of Man and Civilization* (New York: Grove Press, 1949), pp. 64–65. The notion of "projectionism" has strong roots in the thought of the nineteenth-century figure Ludwig Feuerbach. See his *The Essence of Christianity*, trans. George Eliot (New York: Dover, [1854] 2008).

39. White, *The Science of Culture*, pp. 66.

40. Ibid., pp. 399–400.

41. John Kennedy, *The New Anthropomorphism* (Cambridge: Cambridge University Press, 1992), pp. 1 and 5.

42. Ibid., p. 9.

43. David Peterson del Mar, *Environmentalism* (London: Routledge, 2006), p. 52.

44. Luke Strongman, *Modern Nature: Essays in Environmental Communication* (Boca Raton, FL: Universal, 2012), p. 62.

45. While on lecture tour giving presentations related to my book *People Trees*, audience members would sometimes question whether the addition of faces to neem trees was not really a way for humans to avoid encountering the radical otherness of trees.

46. Daston, "How Nature Became the Other," p. 39.

47. Ibid., p. 48.

48. Hans Jonas, *The Phenomenon of Life: Toward a Philosophical Biology* (Chicago: University of Chicago Press, 1982), p. 37.

49. Evernden, *The Social Creation of Nature*, p. 93.

50. Marc Bekoff is one of a number of ethologists who want to reclaim a positive attitude toward anthropomorphism. Among his many books, one might see *Minding Animals: Awareness, Emotions, and Heart* (New York: Oxford University Press, 2002) and *The Cognitive Animal* (Cambridge, MA: MIT Press, 2002).

51. Jeffrey Moussaieff Masson and Susan McCarthy, *When Elephants Weep: The Emotional Lives of Animals* (New York: Delacorte Press, 1995), p. 32.

52. Ibid., p. xxiii.

53. Charles A. Nelson, "The Development and Neural Bases of Face Recognition," *Infant and Child Development*, vol. 10 (2001): 3–18.

54. Olivier Pascalis and David Kelly, "The Origins of Face Processing in Humans: Phylogeny and Ontogeny," *Perspectives on Psychological Science*, vol. 4, no. 2 (2009): 200–209. Others concur: "The evidence presented here suggests that the infant enters the world with a detailed representation of the human face" (Paul Quinn and Alan Slater, "Face Perception at Birth and Beyond," in *The Development of Face Processing in Infancy and Early Childhood: Current Perspectives*, ed. Oliver Pascalis and Alan Slater [New York: Nova Science, 2003], p. 9). This entire volume is an excellent sourcebook for state-of-the-art research in this area.

55. Two Canadian psychologists have found: "For newborns, a pair of eyes may have privileged status; they track schematic eyes as far as a complete schematic face. Two-month-olds presented with photographs of faces exhibit visual fixation patterns similar to those of adults, in that they focus more on the eyes than on any other facial feature." See Laura Smith and Darwin Muir, "Infant Perception of Dynamic Faces: Emotion, Inversion and Eye Direction Effects," in ibid., p. 126.

56. Andrew J. Tate, Hanno Fischer, Andrea E. Leigh, and Keith M. Kenrick, "Behavioural and Neurophysiological Evidence for Face Recognition and Face Emotion Processing in Animals," *Philosophical Transactions: Biological Sciences*, vol. 361, no. 1476 (2006): 2168. These researchers report: "Behavioural studies in our laboratory using choice mazes and operant discrimination tasks have revealed quite remarkable face-recognition abilities in sheep, similar to those found in humans" (2156).

57. "The eyes appeared to play the most important single feature in recognition similar to humans" (ibid., p. 2156).

58. Ibid., p. 2168; emphasis added.

59. Nicholas Epley, Adam Waytz, Scott Akalis, and John T. Cacioppo, "When We Need a Human: Motivational Determinants of Anthropomorphism," *Social Cognition*, vol. 26, no. 2 (2008): 144. These authors argue that people who are dispositionally lonely are more likely to anthropomorphize non-human entities, but they also recognize that some cultures are more prone to anthropomorphizing that others. "Seeing humanlike attributes in nonhuman agents is therefore likely to be determined by the relative accessibility and applicability of anthropomorphic representations compared to nonanthropomorphic representations" (146). I do not think that one could make the case that the large number of people who dress up Govardhan stones in an anthropomorphic fashion are motivated by loneliness; rather, this is a case in which Hindu temple practices such as *murti-puja* provide ready cultural access to personifying theories and anthropomorphized forms of divinity.

60. Adam Waytz, John Cacioppo, and Nicholas Epley, "Who Sees Human? The Stability and Importance of Individual Differences in Anthropomorphism," *Perspectives on Psychological Science*, vol. 5, no. 3 (2010): 220.

61. Epley et al., "When We Need a Human," p. 152.

62. Ibid.

63. Kim-Pong Tam, Sau-Lai Lee, and Melody Manchi Chao, "Saving Mr. Nature: Anthropomorphism Enhances Connectedness to and Protectiveness Toward Nature," *Journal of Experimental Social Psychology*, vol. 49, no. 3 (2013): 515.

64. Ibid., p. 518. Emphasis added.

65. Sarah M. Pike, *For the Wild: Ritual and Commitment in Radical Eco-Activism* (Berkeley: University of California Press, 2017), p. 89. Another illustration that could be cited is Julia Butterfly Hill's reports of her anthropomorphic interaction with the redwood tree she refers to as Luna and calls her "best friend." See *The Legacy of Luna* (San Francisco: Harper Collins, 2000).

66. A great example of this is the anthropomorphized volleyball "Wilson" in the 2000 film Cast Away, in which the character Chuck Nolan (played by Tom Hanks) paints a face on a volleyball with his own blood. Wilson is the only social companion Nolan has to help him survive during the four years he is stuck alone on a deserted island.

67. Daston, "How Nature Became the Other."

68. Jane Bennett, *Vibrant Matter: A Political Ecology of Things* (Durham, NC: Duke University Press, 2010), pp. xvi, 120, and 122.

69. Ibid., p. 122.

70. Several conclude that anthropomorphism is a natural feature of our being. Luke Strongman maintains: "Thus anthropomorphism shares more conceptual ground (than anthropocentrism) with evolutionary biology: it is an inescapable quality of our being" (Strongman, *Modern Nature: Essays in Environmental Communication*, p. 66).

71. Leesa Fawcett, "Anthropomorphism: In the Web of Culture," *UnderCurrents: Journal of Critical Environmental Studies*, vol. 1, no. 1 (1989): 14–15.

72. Ibid., p. 19.

73. This seems to be one of the important points made in Wendy Doniger, "Zoomorphism in Ancient India," in *Thinking with Animals: New Perspectives on Anthropomorphism*, ed. Lorraine Daston and Gregg Mitman (New York: Columbia University Press, 2005), pp. 17–36.

74. Freya Mathews, *For Love of Matter: A Contemporary Panpsychism* (Albany: State University of New York Press, 2003), pp. 79 and 88. Emphasis added.

75. Orsi, *Between Heaven and Earth*, p. 2. Emphasis added.

76. Ibid., p. 12. Parenthetical material added.

Chapter 7

1. Cha*ndogya Upanishad* 6.4.2. See Olivelle, p., 149.

2. "*namo . . . cakre atmana (a)tmane,*" *Bhagavata Purana* 10.24.36.

3. Alexis Nouss, "Translation and Métissage," p. 252.

4. Annie Dillard, *Teaching a Stone to Talk* (New York: HarperCollins Publishers, 1982), pp. 87–89.

5. Mathews, *For Love of Matter*, p. 8.

6. One does have to acknowledge, however, the Catholic persecution of those with religious commitments to divine presence in physical forms, such as the Spanish Extirpation of Idolatries in colonial Mexico and Peru. Even though a figure like the seventeen-century Jesuit Roberto de Nobili assumed some of the traditional Hindu garb while in India and came to respect Sanskrit texts, he still condemned *murti-puja*, the Hindu worship of embodied forms of divinity.

7. Robert A. Orsi, *History and Presence* (Cambridge, MA: Harvard University Press, 2016), pp. 38 and 40.

8. Ibid., p. 249.

9. In an article titled "Is God Touchable? On the Materiality of Akan Spirituality," the historian of religions Jan Platvoet argues that the modern Western Christian cosmology that is dependent on the conceptual opposition between the material and the spiritual has "been guiding virtually all of Western academic research of religions, Christian and other" (2). He contends that this cosmology is alien to the cosmologies of the traditional religions of Africa such as the Akan of Ghana, and has therefore greatly constrained and misguided research of the religions indigenous to Africa, which assume the "materiality of the spiritual." (http://jangplatvoet.nl/wp-content/uploads/2017/03/IsGodTouchable.pdf). Accessed March 17, 2018.

10. Jonathan Z. Smith, "A Twice-Told Tale: The History of the History of Religions' History," *Numen*, vol. 48, no. 2 (2001): 132.

11. Raghunath Sharma, *The System of Shuddhavaita Vedanta of Shri Vallabhacharya* (Bombay: Raghunath Goswami, 1992), p. 35. These verses are translated in Olivelle, *Upanishads*, p. 149.

12. Sharma, *System of Shuddhavaita Vedanta*, p. 69.

13. For example, "All this is Brahman" (*sarvam khalvidam brahma* [*Chandogya Upanishad* 3.14.1]), and "Krishna is all this" (*Vasudevah sarvam* [*Bhagavad Gita* 7.19]).

14. See Bhagavad-gita 3.22.

15. See *Brihadaranyaka Upanishad* 5.1.1.

16. Don Handelman, "Passages to Play: Paradox and Process," *Play and Culture*, vol. 5 (1992): 2.

17. Ibid., p. 7.

18. Ibid.

19. Ibid., p. 9.

20. Ibid., p. 12.

21. Ibid., p. 4. Emphasis added.

22. Sam D. Gill, "Play," pp. 451 and 454.

23. Jonathan Z. Smith, "Playful Acts of Imagination," *Liberal Education*, vol. 73, no. 5 (1978): 14–20.

24. See Alfred Schutz, *Collected Papers I: The Problem of Social Reality*, ed. Maurice Natanson (The Hague: Martins Nijhoff, 1973).

25. Sam Gill, "No Place to Stand: Jonathan Z. Smith as *Homo Ludens*, The Academic Study of Religion as *Sub Specie Ludi*," *Journal of the American Academy of Religion*, vol. 66, no. 2 (1998): 307.

26. Ibid., p. 306.

27. Exodus 32.25–29.

28. Joachim Wach, *The Comparative Study of Religions* (New York: Columbia University Press, 1958).

29. Evernden, *The Social Creation of Nature*, p. 123.

30. The contemporary practice of mountaintop-removal coal mining in the American Appalachian Mountains, which has already obliterated over 500 named mountains, is an apt expression of this attitude.

31. Mathews, *For Love of Matter*, p. 1.

32. Ibid., p. 4.

33. Ralph Metzner, *Green Psychology: Transforming Our Relationship to the Earth*, p. 97.

34. See footnote 81 in Chapter 2.

35. Poul Pedersen, "Nature, Religion and Cultural Identity: The Religious Environmental Paradigm," in *Asian Perspectives of Nature*, ed. Ole Bruun and Arne Kallard (Richmond, UK: Cruzon Press, 1995).

36. Emma Tomalin, "Bio-Divinity and Biodiversity: Perspectives on Religion and Environmental Conservation in India," *Numen*, vol. 51, no. 3 (2004): 267. Tomalin

has also written a book expanding on this subject: *Biodivinity and Biodiversity: The Limits to Religious Environmentalism* (Aldershot, UK: Ashgate, 2009).

37. I document this transformation in my book *River of Love in an Age of Pollution*. The environmental effects of neoliberal global capitalism in India are now becoming quite alarming. The real estate boom in the region of Braj has been extensive and now threatens to transform the area around Mount Govardhan.

38. I record a similar development with regard to trees in *People Trees*, pp. 196–98.

39. Raghunath Sharma identifies the philosophical system of Vallabhacharya's philosophical system as *viruddha-dharma-ashraya-vada* and translates this as the "Doctrine of Mutually Conflicting Qualities residing in One and the Same Substance" (*The System of Shuddhavaita Vedanta*, p. 84). The concept of *bhedha-abheda* is also applicable here.

40. Shrivatsa Goswami, Jai Singh Ghera, Vrindaban, November 5, 2016.

41. See Frederick S. Growse, *Mathura, A District Memoir* (New Delhi: Asian Educational Services, 1882), p. 301.

42. Haberman, *Journey through the Twelve Forests*, pp. 128–29.

43. In giving consideration to environmental concerns, I want to acknowledge a valid critique of some of the ornamentation of natural entities within Hindu India, especially when it becomes excessive. Jack Hawley expressed this negative reaction to the excessive ornamentation of stones from Mount Govardhan. After reading an early draft of this book, he wrote in the notes he sent to me: "To me, let me say it, it can also be a form of litter. John Muir's effort to keep mountains pristine is something I deeply admire. And I know you do too. Does play have its limits? Some things (like mountains) are sacred!"

44. Tam et al., "Saving Mr. Nature: Anthropomorphism Enhances Connectedness to and Protectiveness Toward Nature," p. 519. Emphasis added.

Appendix

1. This is a translation from Braj Bhasha of Devakinandan Kumheriya's *Shri Giriraj Chalisa* (Govardhan: Giriraj Pushtak Bhandar, n.d.), pp. 3–13.

2. A translation of the sixteenth-century Sanskrit *Shri Girirajadhari Ashtakam* by Vallabhacharya. The text is available in scores of publications. The Sanskrit word *dhari* can mean either "holding" or "assuming the form of." Although I translate the term as "holding," the second meaning is always implied. Since this is a Sanskrit text, I have left "Braj" in the Sanskrit form of "Vraja."

3. I translate this well-known Braj Bhasha poem by the well-known Ashtachap poet Paramananda Das from *Laghu Kirtan Kusumakar*, ed. Niranjandev Sharma (Mathura: Shri Govardhan Granthmala Karyalaya, 1990), p. 170.

4. This first Braj Bhasha poem attributed to the famous blind poet Surdas is found in *Pushti Margiya Kirtan Sangraha*, ed. Bacchubhai Javeri (Mumbai: Krishnarpan Trust and Indore: Vaishnava Mitra Mandal, 1995), vol. 2, poem #27, p. 30.

5. Omprakash Yadav, *Haridasvarya: Shri Giriraj Govardhan* (Baravani, MP: Antarrashtiya Pushti-Margiya Vaisnava Parishad, 2011), poem #13, p. 75.

6. *Pushti Margiya Kirtan Sangraha*, vol. 2, poem #28, p. 31.

7. I translate this Braj Bhasha poem from the *varta* of Meha, which appears as #136 of Gokulnath's *Do Sau Bavan Vaishnavan ki Varta*, Vol. 2, p. 153.

8. *Kirtan Maniratna Mala*, ed. Ghanashyamdas (Indore: Vaishnava Mitra Mandal,1999), p. 125.

9. Ibid., p. 126. I inserted the name "Krishna" and the word "mountain" where I thought it was necessary to clarify the action being described.

10. The name could also be translated as the One Who Assumed the Form of the Mountain.

11. *Kirtan Prakash Punj*, ed. Sharadvallabha Betiji (Varanasi: Chowkhambha, 1995), p. 139. See also ibid., p. 125.

12. *Tarahati Shri Govardhana ki rahiyai. Nitya prati Madana Gopala Lala ke carana kamala cita laiyai. Tana pulakita Braja-raja me lotata, Govinda kunda me nhaiyai. 'Rasika Pritama' hita cita ki bate, Shri Giridhari-ji so kahiyai.* This Braj Bhasha poem, composed by the Pushti Margiya leader and poet Hariray, is very well known around Mount Govardhan and throughout Braj. The version I have cited here is in *Hariray-ji ka Pada Sahitya*, compiled and edited by Prabhudayal Mital (Mathura: Sahitya Sansthan, 1962), p. 218.

13. Yadav, *Haridasvarya: Shri Giriraj Govardhan*, poem #13, p. 50.

14. This *arati* in Braj Bhasha is printed in Siyaram Das, *Shri Giriraj Utpati Katha* (Govardhan: Sarvajanik Seva Sansthan, 2013), p. 14.

15. Kumheriya, *Shri Giriraj Chalisa*, pp. 13–15.

16. This is a translation of the *arati* posted in Braj Bhasha above one of the entrances to the Mukut Mukharvinda Mandir at Manasi Ganga. People commonly stand at this entrance and sing this *arati* as part of their worship of the stones from Mount Govardhan housed in the temple.

Glossary

abhishek	Honorific ritual bath
adhibhuta (adj., *adhibhautika*)	The physical dimension of reality comprising the bodies of all animate and inanimate entities
adhidaiva (adj., *adhidaivika*)	The divine dimension of reality in which personhood is encountered
adhyatma (adj., *adhyatmika*)	The spiritual, undifferentiated, and unmanifest dimension of reality
akar(a)	Form
anurag(a)	Loving passion
Anyor	A town located on the southeastern edge of Mount Govardhan
arati	A form of worship in which an honorific lamp is waved clockwise in circles before a divinity, person, or sacred object
baba	"Father"; common name for a respected male religious figure
baithak	A "seat"; usually refers to a place where a holy figure sat to give a notable teaching. The most important *baitak*s in the Pushti Marg are those of Vallabhacharya and his son Vitthalnath
Balaram	The elder brother of Krishna
bandhi	A side-tied shirt worn in the region of Braj
Bhagavan	A proper noun that refers to the more personal form of God
Bhagavata Purana	The most important scripture for Braj Vaishnavism; it narrates many of the important stories about Krishna, including the one that links him to Mount Govardhan
bhakta	A devotee; one who lovingly participates in the ultimate reality
bhakti	Literally, "participation"; loving devotion
bhav(a)	Emotion, specifically love

bhavatmak	A perspective based on an affectually insightful realization of the true nature of reality
bhukti	Worldly enjoyment; synonymous with *bhoga*
Brahman	Complex non-dual Ultimate Reality
Braj	A cultural region associated with Krishna that is located about ninety miles south of Delhi on the Yamuna River. Mount Govardhan is located in the center of this region
Braj Vaishnavism	The form of Vedantic Vaishnavism that grew out of the religious renaissance that took place in Braj at the beginning of the sixteenth century. Braj Vaishnavism focuses on the worship of various forms of Krishna, and most popularly includes the Pushti Marg, founded by Vallabhacharya, and Gaudiya Vaishnavism, founded by Chaitanya
Chaitanya	The sixteenth-century inspirational founding saint of Gaudiya Vaishnavism
dandavat	Literally, "like a stick"; it comes to mean a prostration
dandavat parikrama	A way of circumambulating Mount Govardhan by which one moves around the mountain by means of full-bodied prostrations
darshan	Literally, "seeing," but better translated as "visual communion" with some divine form
dhoti	An unsewn long cloth that is wrapped around the waist and worn as lower garment by men
Drona	A mythological character, but more importantly a Himalayan mountain that is considered to be the father of Mount Govardhan
Garga Samhita	A sixteenth-century Sanskrit text that narrates the features of Braj. Stories told in this text provide the basis of much of the sophisticated theology constructed about Mount Govardhan
Gaudiya Vaishnava	One who follows the inspirational saint Chaitanya and the religious tradition of Gaudiya Vaishnavism
Gaudiya Vaishnavism	The religious tradition inspired by Chaitanya and elaborated by the teachings of the six Vrindaban Gosvamins, such as Rupa Gosvamin
ghat	Stone stairway leading down into a river or pond
Giriraj	An affectionate name for Mount Govardhan (often followed by the honorific suffix "-ji") meaning "King of Mountains"
gopi	A cowherdess lover of Krishna and exemplary devotional figure

Govardhan	Name of a sacred mountain and a town in the middle of the mountain
guna	A quality, property or characteristic
guru	A religious teacher
jagat	The physical world
Jatipura	A town located on the southwestern edge of Mount Govardhan
Krishna	One of the major Hindu conceptions of Ultimate Reality or God
kos	A distance of about two miles
kumkum	A powder made from turmeric mixed with quicklime in a manner that turns the yellow turmeric a bright red. It is used in India for social or religious markings, often as a way of honoring a person
kund	A pond
Lalita	An exemplary gopi who is a favorite girlfriend of Radha
lila	Play, usually "divine play"
linga	Literally, an "indication" of that beyond all indication; it is the most common form worshiped as an embodiment of Shiva
Madhavendra Puri	An important sixteenth-century figure involved in the initial worship of Shri Govardhan-Natha-ji on Mount Govardhan
Manasi Ganga	A sacred pond located in the middle of Mount Govardhan
marg	Path, pathway
Mukharvind	The "lotus mouth" (or face) of Mount Govardhan. Three of the most important Mukharvinds are located at Jatipura, Dan Ghati, and Manasi Ganga
mukti	Liberation (from conditioned existence); synonymous with *moksha*
murti	Embodied form of divinity
murti-puja	Worship of an embodied form of divinity
Nanda	Krishna's father
Nathdwara	The temple town in Rajasthan built up around the famous Govardhan-Natha-ji temple. The original Govardhan-Natha-ji temple was located atop Mount Govardhna in Braj
nilgai	"Blue cow"; a kind of antelope found around and on Mount Govardhan
nirakar(a)	Without form, formless

nirgun(a)	Without qualities or characteristics
parikrama	Clockwise circumambulation of some sacred entity; synonymous with *pradakshina*
prasad	Literally, "grace," but commonly refers to food that has been offered to a deity and then is received back as "grace in edible form"
prem(a)	Supreme love
puja	Worship; usually refers to devotional interaction with embodied forms of divinity
Pulastya	The powerful sage who transported Mount Govardhan from the high Himalayas to the plains of Braj
Punchari	The "tail" of Mount Govadhan. This name also refers to a town located near the southern tip of the mountain
Purushottama	The "Highest Person"; refers to that dimension of divinity that both encompasses and transcends form and formlessness
Pushti Marg	The religious tradition inspired by the life and teachings of the saint Vallabhacharaya
Pushti Margi	A Vaishnava who follows the inspirational saint Vallabhacharya and the religious tradition of the Pushti Marg
Pushti Margiya	Related to the Pushti Marg
Radha	The chief lover of Krishna. She is often regarded as an essential aspect of Krishna in Braj Vaishnava theology
Radhakund	A pond and town located on the northern tip of Mount Govardhan
rasa	Aesthetic emotion, often equated with supreme love
rupa	Form or body
Rupa Gosvamin	One of the major seminal teachers of Gaudiya Vaishnaism in the early sixteenth century
sadhu	A religious figure who has renounced ordinary domestic life for the pursuit of higher spiritual goals
sagun(a)	With qualities or characteristics
sakar(a)	With form
sakshat	Direct and visible
sampradaya	A religious "tradition" that follows a particular saint or teaching
sannyasi	A religious figure who has renounced ordinary domestic life for the pursuit of higher spiritual goals

sari	A long wrapped garment worn by women in India
Shaiva/Shaivism	A Shaiva is one who follows Shaivism, a type of Hinduism that conceives of the Ultimate Reality as Shiva
shakti	Divine "energy" or "power"
shaligram	A fossilized stone from a sacred river in Nepal that is considered to be a naturally embodied form of Vishnu
shila	A stone; this term tends to be the preferred name for a Govardhan stone as it is more intimate than the term *pathar*, which typically refers to a common stone
Shiva	One of the major Hindu conceptions of Ultimate Reality or God
Shri Nath-ji	A shortened form of Govardhan-Nath-ji, the famous embodied form of Krishna that emerged from Mount Govardhan. Shri Nath-ji is now housed in a temple in the Rajasthani town of Nathdwara
sindur	Vermilion powder or paste
sparshan	"Touch"; a more intimate way of interacting with Giriraj shila
Svamini	The Beloved of Krishna; typically refers to Radha
svarupa	Literally, "own form"; intrinsic form of a divinity. The notion of "own form" has a double meaning: it is an essential form of God, and also the devotee's own form of God that he or she is drawn to for developing a personal relationship with God. The term also has a general usage as simply a dimension or form of divinity
tareti	The flat plain surrounding a mountain (also *tarahati* and *talahati*)
tilak	Honorific mark applied to the forehead of both an embodied deity and a devotee
tulsi	A sacred plant considered to be the physical form of a goddess. Leaves from a *tulsi* plant are offered in Vaishnava worship, and strings of small beads made from the plant are worn as a necklace and larger ones are used to make rosaries for meditation
Vaishnava	A worshiper of Krishna or Vishnu
Vaishnavism	A religious tradition that involves the worship of Krishna or Vishnu as the Ultimate Reality
Vallabhacharya	The sixteenth-century founding saint of the Pushti Marg

Vedanta/Vedantic	A major school of Hindu philosophy based on the non-dual teaching of such texts as the Upanishads, Brahma Sutras, and *Bhagavad Gita*
Vishnu	One of the major Hindu conceptions of Ultimate Reality or God that is often identified with Krishna
Vitthalnath	Son of Vallabhacharya, who is remembered by Pushti Margis as a great teacher and the one who developed the elaborate form of Pushti Margiya worship
Yashoda	Krishna's mother

Bibliography

Armstrong, Paul B. "Play and Cultural Differences." *The Kenyon Review*, new series, vol. 13, no. 1 (1991): 157–71.

Assmann, Jan. "What's Wrong with Images?" In *Idol Anxiety*. Edited by Josh Ellenbogen and Aaron Tugendhaft. Stanford, CA: Stanford University Press, 2011: 19–31.

Assmann, Jan, and Baumgarten, Albert I, eds. *Representation in Religion*. Leiden: Brill, 2001.

Augustine. *Saint Augustine Confessions*. Translated by Henry Chadwick. New York: Oxford University Press, 2009.

Banerjea, Jitendra Nath. *Development of Hindu Iconography*. Calcutta: University of Calcutta Press, 1956.

Barz, Richard. *The Bhakti Sect of Vallabhacharya*. Faridabad: Thomas Press, 1976.

Bateson, Gregory. *Mind and Nature*. New York: Dutton, 1979.

Bateson, Gregory. *Steps to an Ecology of Mind*. Northvale, NJ: Jason Aronson, [1972] 1987.

Beal, Timothy. *Religion and Monsters*. New York: Routledge, 2001.

Bekoff, Marc. *The Cognitive Animal*. Cambridge, MA: MIT Press, 2002.

Bekoff, Marc. *Emotional Lives of Animals*. Novato, CA: New World Library, 2007.

Bekoff, Marc. *Minding Animals: Awareness, Emotions, and Heart*. New York: Oxford University Press, 2002.

Bennett, Jane. *Vibrant Matter: A Political Ecology of Things*. Durham, NC: Duke University Press, 2010.

Berger, Peter L., and Kellner, Hansfried. "Arnold Gehlen and the Theory of Institutions." *Social Research*, vol. 32, no. 1 (1965): 110–15.

Berger, Peter L., and Luckmann, Thomas. *The Social Construction of Reality: A Treatise in the Sociology of Knowledge*. New York: Doubleday, 1966.

Bernbaum, Edwin. *Sacred Mountains of the World*. San Francisco: Sierra Club Books, 1992.

Berry, Thomas. *The Dream of the Earth*. San Francisco: Sierra Club Books, 1988.

Bhagavata Purana. 2 vols. Sanskrit text with English translation by C. L. Goswami. Gorkhapur: Gita Press, 1982.

Bhagra, Madhur, ed. *Giriraj Govardhan*. Vrindaban: Shri Hari Nikunj Ashram, 1989.

Bhatta, Narayana. *Vraja Bhakti Vilasa*. Edited by Krishnadas Baba. Kusum Sarovar: Krishnadas Baba, 1951.

Biernacki, Lorilai, and Philip Clayton, eds. *Panentheism across the World's Traditions*. New York: Oxford University Press, 2013.

Boyle, Robert. *A Free Enquiry into the Vulgarly Received Notion of Nature*. Edited by Edward B. Davis and Michael Hunter. Cambridge: Cambridge University Press, [1686] 1996.

Brerewood, Edward. *Enquiries Touching the Diversity of Languages and Religions, Through the Chief Parts of the World*. London: Kessinger, [1641] 2008.

Callicott, J. Baird. "Traditional American Indian and Western European Attitudes toward Nature: An Overview." *Environmental Ethics*, vol. 4, no. 4 (1982): 293–318.

Calvin, John. *Institutes of the Christian Religion.* Translated by Henry Beveridge. Woodstock, Ontario: Devoted, 2016.

Chaitanya, Ashok. "Govardhan ki Parikrama Dai Lai, Terau Purnajanma Nahi Hoya." In *Giriraj Govardhan.* Edited by Madhur Bhagra. Vrindaban: Shri Bhagavan Bhajan Asram, 1988: 181–94.

Chakrabarty, Dipesh. *Provincializing Europe: Postcolonial Thought and Historical Difference.* Princeton, NJ: Princeton University Press, 2000.

Chuchiak, John F. "In Servitio Dei: Fray Diego de Landa, the Franciscan Order, and the Return of the Extirpation of Idolatry in the Colonial Diocese of Yucatan, 1573–1579." *The Americas*, vol. 61, no. 4 (2005): 611–46.

Clifford, James, and Marcus, George E., eds. *Writing Culture: The Poetics and Politics of Ethnography.* Berkeley: University of California Press, 1986.

Comte, Auguste. *The Positive Philosophy.* Translated by Harriet Martineau. New York: AMS Press, [1855] 1974.

Crapanzano, Vincent. "The End—the Ends—of Anthropology." *Paideuma* (Frobenius Institute), Bd. 56 (2010): 165–88.

Crooke, W. *An Introduction to the Popular Religion and Folklore of Northern India.* Allahabad: Government Press, North-Western Provinces and Oudh, 1894.

Das, Shrisvarupa. *Shri Govardhan Parikrama.* Radhakund, India: Pulak and Samir Devanath, 2011.

Das, Siyaram. *Shri Giriraj Utpati Katha.* Govardhan: Sarvajanik Seva Sansthan, 2013.

Daston, Lorraine. "How Nature Became the Other: Anthropomorphism and Anthropocentrism in Early Modern Natural Philosophy." In *Biology as Society, Society as Biology: Metaphors.* Edited by Sabine Maasen, Everett Mendelsohn, and Peter Weingart. Dordrecht: Kluwer Academic, 1995: 37–56.

Davis, Edward B. "Robert Boyle's Religious Life, Attitudes, and Vocation." *Science & Christian Belief*, vol. 19, no. 2 (2007): 117–38.

Davis, Phyllis J. *The Power of Touch: The Basis for Survival, Health, Intimacy, and Emotional Well-Being.* Carlsbad, CA: Hay House, 1999.

Davis, Richard. *The Lives of Indian Images.* Princeton, NJ: Princeton University Press, 1997.

De Arriaga, Pablo Joseph. *The Extirpation of Idolatry in Peru.* Translated by L. Clark Keating. Lexington: University of Kentucky Press, [1621] 1968.

Del Mar, David Peterson. *Environmentalism.* London: Routledge, 2006.

Dillard, Annie. *Teaching a Stone to Talk.* New York: HarperCollins, 1982.

Dobbins, Christine. *Urban Leadership in Western India: Politics and Communities in Bombay City 1840–1885.* London: Oxford University Press, 1972.

Doniger, Wendy. "Zoomorphism in Ancient India." In *Thinking with Animals: New Perspectives on Anthropomorphism.* Edited by Lorraine Daston and Gregg Mitman. New York: Columbia University Press, 2005: 17–36.

Drakulic, Slavenka. *The Balkan Express: Fragments from the Other Side of the War.* New York: W.W. Norton, 1993.

Drengson, Alan, and Inoue, Yuichi, eds. *The Deep Ecology Movement: An Introductory Anthology.* Berkeley: North Atlantic Books, 1995.

Dubois, Abbe J. A. *Hindu Manners, Customs and Ceremonies.* New Delhi: Book Faith India, [1897] 1999.

Eck, Diana L. *Darśan: Seeing the Divine Image in India.* New York: Columbia University Press, [1981] 1998.

Eck, Diana L. "Mountains." In *The Encyclopedia of Religion*. Edited by Lindsay Jones. New York: Macmillan, 2005, vol. 9: 6212–15.

Eire, Carlos. *War against the Idols: The Reformation of Worship from Erasmus to Calvin*. Cambridge: Cambridge University Press, 1989.

Eliade, Mircea. *Patterns in Comparative Religion*. Translated by Rosemary Sheed. New York: Meridian Books, 1963.

Eliade, Mircea. *The Sacred and the Profane: The Nature of Religion*. Translated by Willard Trask. New York: Harcourt, Brace & World, 1959.

Ellenbogen, Josh, and Tugendhaft, Aaron, eds. *Idol Anxiety*. Stanford, CA: Stanford University Press, 2011.

Entwistle, Alan. *Braj: Centre of Krishna Pilgrimage*. Groningen: Egbert Forsten, 1987.

Epley, Nicholas, Waytz, Adam, Akalis, Scott, and Cacioppo, John T. "When We Need a Human: Motivational Determinants of Anthropomorphism." *Social Cognition*, vol. 26, no. 2 (2008): 143–55.

Evernden, Neil. *The Social Creation of Nature*. Baltimore, MD: Johns Hopkins University Press, 1992.

Fawcett, Leesa. "Anthropomorphism: In the Web of Culture." *UnderCurrents: Journal of Critical Environmental Studies*, vol. 1, no. 1 (1989): 14–20.

Feuerbach, Ludwig. *The Essence of Christianity*. Translated by George Eliot. New York: Dover, [1854] 2008.

Frazer, James George. *The Worship of Nature*. New York: Macmillan, 1926.

Freedberg, David. *The Power of Images*. Chicago: University of Chicago Press, 1989.

Freeland, Cynthia A. "Nourishing Speculation: A Feminist Reading of Aristotelian Science." In *Engendering Origins: Critical Feminist Readings in Plato and Aristotle*. Edited by Bat-Ami Bar On. Albany: State University of New York, 1994: 145–87.

Freeman, Kathleen. *Ancilla to the Pre-Socratic Philosophers*. Cambridge, MA: Harvard University Press, 1948/1996.

Garga Samhita. Edited by Vibhutibhushan Bhattacharya. Varanasi: Sampurnananda Sanskrit University, 1996. English translation of relevant sections in *Giriraja: King of Mountains*. Translated by Danavir Goswami. Kanas City, MO: Rupanuga Vedic College, 2010.

Geertz, Clifford. "Anti Anti-Relativism." *American Anthropologist*, new series, vol. 86, no. 2 (1984): 263–78.

Geertz, Clifford. *The Interpretations of Cultures*. New York: Basic Books, 1973.

Geertz, Clifford. *Local Knowledge*. New York: Basic Books, 1983.

Gell, Alfred. *Art and Agency: An Anthropological Theory*. Oxford: Clarendon Press, 1998.

Ghanashyamdas. Ed. *Kirtan Maniratna Mala*. Indore: Vaishnava Mitra Mandal, 1999.

Gill, Sam D. "No Place to Stand: Jonathan Z. Smith as *Homo Ludens*, The Academic Study of Religion as *Sub Specie Ludi*." *Journal of the American Academy of Religion*, vol. 66, no. 2 (1998): 283–312.

Gill, Sam D. "Play." In *Guide to the Study of Religion*. Edited by Willi Braun and Russell T. McCutcheon. London and New York: Cassell, 2000: 451–62.

Girard, Rene. *The Scapegoat*. Baltimore, MD: John Hopkins University Press, 1989.

Godelier, Maurice. "In Today's World, Anthropology Is More Important than Ever." *Paideuma*, Bd. 56 (2010): 205–20.

Gokulnath. *Chaurasi Baithak Charitra*. Edited by Niranjandev Sharma. Mathura: Shri Govardhan Granthamala Karyalaya, 1967.

Gokulnath.. *Chaurasi Vaishnavan ki Varta*. Edited by Jayaben Shukla. Indor: Vaishnava Mitra Mandal, 2011.

Gokulnath.. *Do Sau Bavan Vaishnavan ki Varta*. Edited by Vrajbhushanlal Maharaj and Dvarakadas Parikh. 3 volumes. Indor: Vaishnava Mitra Mandal, 2000. English translation by Shyamdas: *252 Vaishnavas*. 3 volumes. Gokul, India: Pratham Peeth, 2003.

Gosvamin, Rupa. *Hansaduta*. Sanskrit text with Bengali translation and commentary by Vibhas Prakash Gangopadhyaya. Calcutta: Shri Amritalal Dutt, 1923.

Gosvamin, Rupa. *Mathura Mahatmya: The Glories of the Mathura-mandala*. Sanskrit text with English translation. Edited by Pundarika Vidyanidhi and translated by Bhumipati Dasa. Vrindaban: Rasbihari Lal & Sons, n.d.

Goswami, Nirmalchandra. *Shri Radhadamodar Dainik Stuti*. Vrindaban: Shri Radhadamodar Mandir, n.d.

Goswami, Shyammanohar. *Dharma, Artha, Kama, Moksha ki Pushtimargiya Vivechana*. Kishnagar, Rajasthan: Pushti Prakashan, 1984.

Goswami, Shyammanohar. *Giriyaga*. Varanasi: Giridhar Prakashan, 2011.

Govinda, Gour. *Giriraja Govardhana, Hari-Dasa-Varya: The Chief Devotee of Lord Hari*. Nambour, Australia: Tattva Vicara, 2012.

Growse, Frederick S. *Mathura, A District Memoir*. New Delhi: Asian Educational Services, 1882.

Gruenwald, Ithamar. "God the 'Stone/Rock': Myth, Idolatry, and Cultic Fetishism in Ancient Israel." *The Journal of Religion*, vol. 76, no. 3 (1996): 428–49.

Guthrie, Stewart. *Faces in the Clouds: A New Theory of Religion*. New York: Oxford University Press, 1993.

Haberman, David L. "The Accidental Ritualist." In *Essays in South Asia Rituals in Honor of Fredrick Clothey*. Edited by Linda Powers and Tracy Pintchman. Columbia: University of South Carolina Press, 2014.

Haberman, David L. *Acting as a Way of Salvation: A Study of Raganuga Bhakti Sadhana*. New York: Oxford University Press, 1988.

Haberman, David L. *The Bhaktirasamritasindhu of Rupa Gosvamin*. New Delhi: Indira Gandhi National Centre for the Arts, 2003.

Haberman, David L. *Journey through the Twelve Forests: An Encounter with Krishna*. New York: Oxford University Press, 1994.

Haberman, David L. "On Trial: The Love of the Sixteen Thousand Gopees." *History of Religions* 33, no. 1 (1993): 44–70.

Haberman, David L. *People Trees: The Worship of Trees in Northern India*. New York: Oxford University Press, 2013.

Haberman, David L. *River of Love in an Age of Pollution: The Yamuna River of Northern India*. Berkeley: University of California Press, 2006.

Halbertal, Moshe and Margalit, Avishai. *Idolatry*. Translated by Naomi Goldblum. Cambridge, MA: Harvard University Press, 1992.

Hall, Matthew. "Plant Autonomy and Human-Plant Ethics." *Environmental Ethics*, vol. 31 (2009): 169–81.

Hall, Matthew. *Plants as Persons: A Philosophical Botany*. Albany: State University of New York Press, 2011.

Handelman, Don. "Passages to Play: Paradox and Process." *Play and Culture*, vol. 5 (1992): 1–9.

Hardy, Friedhelm E. "Madhavendra Puri: A Link between Bengal Vaishnavism and South Indian Bhakti." *Journal of the Royal Asiatic Society*, no. 1 (1974): 23–41.

Hardy, Friedhelm E. *Viraha Bhakti: The Early History of Krishna Devotion in South India.* Oxford: Oxford University Press, 1983.

Hariji, Mukunda. "Shri Giriraj Mahima." In *Giriraj Govardhan.* Edited by Madhur Bhagra. Vrindaban: Shri Hari Nikunj Ashram, 1989: 8–18.

Hariraya-ji ka Pada Sahitya. Compiled and edited by Prabhudayal Mital. Mathura: Sahitya Sansthan, 1962.

Harvey, Graham. *Animism: Respecting the Living World.* London: Hurst, 2005.

Hawley, John S. "Can There Be a Vaishnava Kabir?" *Studies in History,* vol. 32, no. 2 (2016): 147–61.

Herodotus. *The Histories.* Translated by Aubrey de Selincourt. London: Penguin Classics, 1996.

Hill, Julia Butterfly. *The Legacy of Luna.* San Francisco: Harper Collins, 2000.

Hume, David. *Dialogues Concerning Natural Religion.* Edited by H. D. Aiken. New York: Hafner, 1948.

Hume, David. *The Natural History of Religion.* New York: Macmillan, [1757] 1992.

Hutchison, Keith. "Supernaturalism and the Mechanical Philosophy." *History of Science,* vol. 21 (1983): 297–333.

Jacob, J. R. "Boyle's Atomism and the Restoration Assault on Pagan Naturalism." *Social Studies of Science,* vol. 8, no. 2 (1978): 211–33.

Javeri, Bacchubhai, ed. *Pushti Margiya Kirtan Sangraha.* Mumbai: Krishnarpan Trust and Indore: Vaishnava Mitra Mandal, 1995.

Jonas, Hans. *The Phenomenon of Life: Toward a Philosophical Biology.* Chicago: University of Chicago Press, 1982.

Jones, William. "On the Hindus." *Asiatik Researches,* vol. 1 (1798): 415–31.

Jordens, J. T. F. *Dayananda Sarasvati: His Life and Ideas.* Delhi: Oxford University Press, 1978.

Joshi, Brajesh. *Shri Giriraj Kripa Phal.* Jatipura: Shri Giriraj Yamuna Bharati Sahitya Sansthan, 2013.

Kamalabaskaran, Iswari. *The Light of Arunachaleswar.* Chennai: Alpha Land Books, 2012.

Kennedy, John. *The New Anthropomorphism.* Cambridge: Cambridge University Press, 1992.

Kishorilal, Bhagra, ed. *Giriraj Govardhan.* Vrindaban: Shri Hari Nikunj Ashram, 1989.

Kitagawa, Joseph M. *On Understanding Japanese Religion.* Princeton, NJ: Princeton University Press, 1987.

Krishnadas Baba. *Braj Mandal Darshan.* Kusum Sarovar, Govardhan: Krishnadas Baba, 1958.

Krishnadas Kaviraj. *Shri Chaitanya Charitamrita.* Bengali text with commentaries by Sacchidananda Bhaktivinod Thakur and Barshobhanabidayita Das. Calcutta: Gaudiya Math, 1958. A very good English translation of this text is the *Chaitanya Charitamrita of Krishnadasa Kaviraja.* Translated by Edward C. Dimock and edited by Tony K. Stewart. Cambridge, MA: Harvard University Press, 1999.

Kumheriya, Devakinandan. *Govardhan Mahatmya.* Govardhan: Giriraj Pushtak Bhandar, 2007.

Kumheriya, Devakinandan. *Shri Giriraj Chalisa.* Govardhan: Giriraj Pushtak Bhandar, n.d.

Lame Deer, John Fire, and Erdoes, Richard. *Lame Deer: Seeker of Visions.* New York: Simon & Schuster, 1976.

Latour, Bruno. *We Have Never Been Modern.* Cambridge, MA: Harvard University Press, 1993.

Levinas, Emmanuel. *Totality and Infinity: An Essay on Exteriority.* Translated by Alphonso Lingis. Pittsburgh: Duquesne University Press, 1991.

Maharaj, Shrisvarupadas. *Shri Govardhan Parikrama.* Radhakund: Pulak and Samir Devanath, 2011.

Maharishi, Ramana. *Notes from Ramana's Arunachala: Ocean of Divine Grace.* Tiruvannamalai: Sri Ramanasramam, 2012.

Malinowski, Bronislaw. *Argonauts of the Western Pacific.* Abingdon, UK: Routledge & Kegan, 1922.

Marcus, George E., and Fischer, Michael M. J. *Anthropology as Cultural Critique: An Experimental Moment in the Human Sciences.* Chicago: University of Chicago Press, 1999.

Margulis, Lynn, and Sagan, Dorian. *What Is Life?* New York: Simon & Schuster, 1995.

Masson, Jeffrey Moussaieff, and McCarthy, Susan. *When Elephants Weep: The Emotional Lives of Animals.* New York: Delacorte Press, 1995.

Mathews, Freya. *For Love of Matter: A Contemporary Panpsychism.* Albany: State University of New York Press, 2003.

McFague, Sallie. *The Body of God: An Ecological Theology.* Minneapolis: Fortress Press, 1993.

McGregor, R. S. *Hindi-English Dictionary.* Delhi: Oxford University Press, 1993.

McGuire, J. E. "Boyle's Conception of Nature." *Journal of the History of Ideas,* vol. 33, no. 4 (1972): 523–42.

Mead, Margaret. *Coming of Age in Samoa: A Psychological Study of Primitive Youth for Western Civilization.* New York: William Morrow, [1928] 1966.

Mills, Kenneth. *Idolatry and Its Enemies: Colonial Andean Religion and Extirpation, 1640– 1750.* Princeton, NJ: Princeton University Press, 1997.

Mital, Prabhudayal, ed. *Hariray-ji ka Pada-Sahitya.* Mathura: Sahitya Samsthan, 1962.

Mitchell, W. J. T. "Idolatry: Nietzsche, Blake, and Poussin." In *Idol Anxiety.* Edited by Josh Ellenbogen and Aaron Tugendhaft. Stanford, CA: Stanford University Press, 2011: 56–73.

Mitchell, W. J. T. *What Do Pictures Want? The Lives and Loves of Images.* Chicago: University of Chicago Press, 2005.

Mohan Das, Narad Baba. *Sampurna Braj Darshanam.* Vrindaban: Shri Radha Mohan Satsang Mandal, 1987.

Mohanty, Debabrata. "12th Gram Sabha Votes against Vedanta Mining: Dongaria Kondhs in Rayagada District Say 'The Entire Hill Region Is Our God.'" *The India Express.* New Delhi, August 20, 2013.

Monier-Williams, Monier. *A Sanskrit-English Dictionary.* Delhi: Motilal Banarsidass, 1981 (Oxford University Press, 1899).

Morgan, David. *The Sacred Gaze: Religious Visual Culture in Theory and Practice.* Berkeley: University of California Press, 2005.

Müller, F. Max. *Origin and Growth of Religion as Illustrated by the Religions of India.* London: Longmans, Green, 1880.

Mulsow, Martin. "Idolatry and Science: Against Nature Worship from Boyle to Rudiger, 1680–1720." *Journal of the History of Ideas,* vol. 67, no. 4 (2006): 697–712.

Myerhoff, Barbara G. *The Peyote Hunt: The Sacred Journey of the Huichol Indians.* Ithaca, NY: Cornell University Press, 1974.

Narayana Maharaja. *Venu Gita*. Mathura: Gaudiya Vedanta, 1999.

Nash, Roderick. "Do Rocks Have Rights?" *Center Magazine*, vol. 10 (1977): 2–12.

Natwar-Singh, K. *Maharaj Suraj Mal*. New Delhi: Vikas, 1983.

Nelson, Charles A. "The Development and Neural Bases of Face Recognition." *Infant and Child Development*, vol. 10 (2001): 3–18.

Newton, R. Heber. "Religion and Religions." *The North American Review*, vol. 178, no. 569 (1904): 543–57.

Noss, John B. *Man's Religion*. Fourth edition. London: Macmillan, 1972.

Nouss, Alexis. "Translation and métissage." In *In Translation—Reflections, Refractions, Transformations*. Edited by Paul St-Pierre and Prafulla C. Kar. Amsterdam: John Benjamins, 2007: 245–52.

Origen. *Origen*. Translated by Rowan A. Greer. New York: Paulist Press, 1979.

Orsi, Robert A. "Abundant History: Marian Apparitions as Alternative Modernity." *Historically Speaking*, vol. 9, no. 7 (2008): 12–16.

Orsi, Robert A. *Between Heaven and Earth*. Princeton, NJ: Princeton University Press, 2005.

Orsi, Robert A. *History and Presence*. Cambridge, MA: Harvard University Press, 2016.

Osborne, Authur. "Physical Supports of Grace." In *Notes from Ramana's Arunachala: Ocean of Grace Divine*. Edited by Shri Bhagavan's Devotees. Tiruvannamalai: Sri Ramanasrama, 2012: 507–10.

Otto, Rudolf. *The Idea of the Holy*. Translated by John Harvey. London: Oxford University Press, 1923.

Packert, Cynthia. *The Art of Loving Krishna: Ornamentation and Devotion*. Bloomington: Indiana University Press, 2010.

Padmalochan Das. *Madhurya Dhama*. Mayapur: Bhaktivedanta Book Trust, 1992.

Pascalis, Olivier, and Kelly, David. "The Origins of Face Processing in Humans: Phylogeny and Ontogeny." *Perspectives on Psychological Science*, vol. 4, no. 2 (2009): 200–209.

Pedersen, Poul. "Nature, Religion and Cultural Identity: The Religious Environmental Paradigm." In *Asian Perspectives of Nature*. Edited by Ole Bruun and Arne Kallard. Richmond, UK: Cruzon Press, 1995.

Penner, Hans H. "Interpretation." In *Guide to the Study of Religion*. Edited by Willi Braun and Russell T. McCutcheon. London: Cassell, 2000: 57–72.

Pennington, Brian. *Was Hinduism Invented? Britons, Indians, and the Colonial Construction of Religion*. New York: Oxford University Press, 2005.

Pike, Sarah M. *For the Wild: Ritual and Commitment in Radical Eco-Activism*. Berkeley: University of California Press, 2017.

Platvoet, Jan G. "Is God Touchable? On the Materiality of Akan Spirituality." http://jangplatvoet.nl/wp-content/uploads/2017/03/IsGodTouchable.pdf

Purchas, Samuel. *Purchas his Pilgrimage, or Relations of the World and the Religions Observed in All Ages and Places Discovered, from the Creation Unto This Present*. London: Kessinger, [1613] 2010.

Quinn, Paul, and Slater, Alan. "Face Perception at Birth and Beyond." In *The Development of Face Processing in Infancy and Early Childhood: Current Perspectives*. Edited by Oliver Pascalis and Alan Slater. New York: Nova Science, 2003: 3–11.

Redington, James D. *The Grace of Lord Krishna: The Sixteen Verse-Treatises of Vallabhacharya*. Delhi: Sri Satguru, 2000.

Roger, Jacques. "The Mechanistic Conception of Life." In *God and Nature: Historical Essays on the Encounter between Christianity and Science*. Edited by David Lindberg and Ronald Numbers. Berkeley: University of California Press, 1986: 277–95.

Rubiés, Joan-Pau. "Theology, Ethnography, and the Historicization of Idolatry." *Journal of the History of Ideas*, vol. 67, no. 4 (October 2006): 571–96.

Rupa Gosvamin. *Mathura Mahatmya*. Sanskrit text with English translation by Pundarika Vidyanidhi and Bhumipati Dasa. *Mathura Mahatmya: The Glories of the Mathura-mandala*. Vrindaban: Rasbihari Lal & Sons, n.d.

Said, Edward W. *Orientalism*. New York: Pantheon Books, 1978.

Salmond, Noel A. *Hindu Iconoclasts: Rammohaun Roy, Dayananda Sarasvati, and Nineteenth-Century Polemics against Idolatry*. Waterloo, ON: Wilfrid Laurier University Press, 2004.

Sax, William S. Ed. *The Gods at Play: Lila in South Asia*. New York: Oxford University Press, 1995.

Schutz, Alfred. *Collected Papers I: The Problem of Social Reality*. Edited by Maurice Natanson. The Hague: Martins Nijhoff, 1973.

Schutz, Alfred. "On Multiple Realities." *Philosophy and Phenomenological Research*, vol. 5, no. 4 (1945): 533–76.

Seed, John, et al. *Thinking Like a Mountain: Towards a Council of All Beings*. Gabriola Island, BC: New Society, 1988.

Shah, Pratik. "Ahanta-Mamata: I-ness and My-ness and Pushti Bhakti." In *Sadhanapranali*. Edited by Goswami Sharad. Mandavi, Gujurat: Shri Vallabhacharya Trust, 2003: 403–11.

Sharadvallabha Betiji. Ed. *Kirtan Prakash Punj*. Varanasi: Chowkhambha, 1995.

Sharma, Keshavdas. "Chamatkari Sarvadev Shri Giriraj." In *Giriraj Govardhan*. Edited by Madhur Bhagra. Vrindaban: Shri Hari Nikunj Ashram, 1989: 49–75.

Sharma, Niranjandev, ed. *Laghu Kirtan Kusumakar*. Mathura: Shri Govardhan Granthmala Karyalaya, 1990.

Sharma, Raghunath. *The System of Shuddhavaita Vedanta of Shri Vallabhacharya*. Bombay: Raghunath Goswami, 1992.

Sharma, Ram Lakhan. "Shri Giriraj Govardhan ka Mahatmya." In *Giriraj Govardhan*. Edited by Madhur Bhagra. Vrindaban: Shri Hari Nikunj Ashram, 1989: 40–48.

Sharma, Umashankar. "Shri Giriraj hi Sakshat Shri Krishna." In *Rishi Jivan*. Edited by Shyamsundar Patodiya. Vrindaban: Shri Bhagavan Bhajan Asram, 1988: 82–85.

Shastri, Navanitpriya. "Pushti-margiya Sadhana-pranali me Svarupa-seva aur Murti-puja." In *Sadhana-pranali*. Edited by Goswami Sharad. Mandavi Gujarat: Shri Vallabhacharya Trust, 2003: 8–36.

Sheehan, Jonathan. "Sacred and Profane: Idolatry, Antiquarianism and the Polemics of Distinction in the Seventeenth Century." *Past & Present*, no. 192 (2006): 35–66.

Sheehan, Jonathan. "Thinking about Idols in Early Modern Europe." *Journal of the History of Ideas*, vol. 67, no. 4 (2006): 561–70.

Shiva Purana. Edited by J. L. Shastri and translated by a board of scholars. Delhi: Motilal Banarasidass, 1970.

Shyamdas. Trans. *The Teachings of Shri Vallabhacharya*. Kota, India: Pratham Peeth, 2003.

Shyamdas and Vallabhadas. *Krishna's Inner Circle: The Ashta Chap Poets*. Gokul, India: Pratham Preeth, 2009.

Shyam Manohar, Goswami. *Dharma, Artha, Kama, Moksha ki Pushtimargiya Vivechana*. Kishnagar, Rajasthan: Pushti Prakashan, 1984.

Skanda Mahapuranam. Edited by Nag Sharan Singh. Delhi: Nag, 1984.

The Skanda Purana. Part 3, vol. 51. Translated by G. V. Tagare. Delhi: Motilal Banarasidass, 1993.

Skrbina, David. *Panpsychism in the West.* Cambridge, MA: MIT Press, 2005.

Smith, Jonathan Z. "A Twice-Told Tale: The History of the History of Religions' History." *Numen*, vol. 48, no. 2 (2001): 131–46.

Smith, Jonathan Z. "Playful Acts of Imagination." *Liberal Education*, vol. 73, no. 5 (1978): 14–20.

Smith, Laura, and Muir, Darwin. "Infant Perception of Dynamic Faces: Emotion, Inversion and Eye Direction Effects." In *The Development of Face Processing in Infancy and Early Childhood: Current Perspectives.* Edited by Oliver Pascalis and Alan Slater. New York: Nova Science, 2003: 119–30.

Smith, W. Robertson. *The Religion of the Semites: The Fundamental Institutions.* New York: Schocken Books, [1889] 1972.

Starn, Orin, ed. *Writing Culture and the Life of Anthropology.* Durham, NC: Duke University Press, 2015.

Strongman, Luke. *Modern Nature: Essays in Environmental Communication.* Boca Raton, FL: Universal, 2012.

Stroumsa, Guy G. "John Spencer and the Roots of Idolatry." *History of Religions*, vol. 41, no. 1 (2001): 1–23.

Swaminathan, K. "Sri Bhagavan's Love for Arunachala." *The Mountain Path*, vol. 25, no. 3 (1988): 130–32.

Tam, Kim-Pong, Lee, Sau-Lai and Chao, Melody Manchi. "Saving Mr. Nature: Anthropomorphism Enhances Connectedness to and Protectiveness toward Nature." *Journal of Experimental Social Psychology*, vol. 49, no. 3 (2013): 514–21.

Tate, Andrew J., Fischer, Hanno, Leigh, Andrea E. and Kenrick, Keith M. "Behavioural and Neurophysiological Evidence for Face Recognition and Face Emotion Processing in Animals." *Philosophical Transactions: Biological Sciences*, vol. 361, no. 1476 (2006): 2155–72.

Taussig, Michael. *Mimesis and Alterity.* New York: Routledge, 1993.

Taylor, Bron. *Dark Green Religion: Nature Spirituality and the Planetary Future.* Berkeley: University of California Press, 2009.

Taylor, Bron. "Idolatry, Paganism, and Trust in Nature." *The Pomegranate*, vol. 12, issue 1 (2010): 103–106.

Tomalin, Emma. "Bio-Divinity and Biodiversity: Perspectives on Religion and Environmental Conservation in India." *Numen*, vol. 51, no. 3 (2004): 265–95.

Tomalin, Emma. *Biodivinity and Biodiversity: The Limits to Religious Environmentalism.* Aldershot, UK: Ashgate, 2009.

Toomey, Paul M. *Food from the Mouth of Krishna: Feasts and Festivities in a North Indian Pilgrimage Centre.* Delhi: Hindustan, 1994.

Tylor, Edward B. *The Origins of Culture.* New York: Harper and Brothers, [1871] 1958.

Tylor, Edward B. *Religion in Primitive Culture.* New York: Harper and Brothers, [1871] 1958.

Urrea, Luis Alberto. *The Hummingbird's Daughter.* New York: Little, Brown, 2005.

Vallabhacharya. *Shorashagrantha.* Edited with Braj Bhasha, commentary by Narasinhalal. Gwalior: Kailash Narayan Khandelal, n.d..

Vallabhadas. "Shri Giriraj-ji ki Bhavatmak Svarup." In *Mahakavi Vallabhdas-ji ka Varta Sahitya.* Gwalior: Vallabhdas Smarak-Mandala, n.d.

Varaha Purana. Sanskrit text with English translation. Edited by Anand Swarup Gupta and translated by Ahibhushan Bhattacharya. Varanasi: All-India Kashiraj Trust, 1981.

Vasquez, Manuel. *More than Belief: A Materialist Theory of Religion.* New York: Oxford University Press, 2011.

Vaudeville, Charlotte. "The Cowherd God in Ancient India." In *Pastoralists and Nomads in South Asia.* Edited by L.S. Leshnik and G. D. Sontheimer. Wiesbaden: Otto Harrassowitz, 1975.

Vaudeville, Charlotte. "The Govardhan Myth in Northern India." *Indo-Iranian Journal,* vol. 22, no. 1 (1980): 1–45.

Vijay. *Braj Bhumi Mohini.* Vrindaban: Shri Prem Hari Press, 1985.

Vishnu Purana. Sanskrit text with English translation by H. H. Wilson. Delhi: Nag, [1864] 1980.

Wach, Joachim. *The Comparative Study of Religions.* New York: Columbia University Press, 1958.

Waghorne, Joanne and Cutler, Norman, eds. *Gods of Flesh, Gods of Stone: The Embodiment of Divinity in India.* New York: Columbia University Press, [1985] 1996.

Ward, William. *History, Literature, and Mythology of the Hindoos.* 4 volumes. Delhi: Low Price Publications, [1820] 1990.

Waytz, Adam, Cacioppo, John and Epley, Nicholas. "Who Sees Human? The Stability and Importance of Individual Differences in Anthropomorphism." *Perspectives on Psychological Science,* vol. 5, no. 3 (2010): 219–32.

White, Leslie A. *The Science of Culture: A Study of Man and Civilization.* New York: Grove Press, 1949.

White, Lynn. "The Historical Roots of Our Ecologic Crisis." *Science,* vol. 155, no. 3767 (1967): 1205–1206.

White, Lynn. "Continuing the Conversation." In *Western Man and Environmental Ethics.* Edited by Ian Barbour. Boston: Addison-Wesley, 1973.

Yadav, Omprakash. *Haridasvarya: Shri Giriraj Govardhan.* Baravani, MP: Antarrashtiya Pushti-Margiya Vaisnava Parishad, 2011.

Yamadagni, Vasant. *Dagar Chali Shri Govardhan ki Or.* Barsana, UP: Shri Manmandir Seva Sansthan, 1994.

Yamamoto, Mutsumi. *Animacy and Reference: A Cognitive Approach to Corpus Linguistics.* Amsterdam: John Benjamins, 1999.

Zeitlyn, David. "Understanding Anthropological Understanding: For a Merological Anthropology." *Anthropological Theory,* vol. 9 (2009): 209–31.

Index